Safeguarding Financial Data in the Digital Age

Farah Naz
Department of Accounting and Finance, Kinnaird College for Women, Pakistan

Sitara Karim
Department of Economics and Finance, Sunway University, Malaysia

A volume in the Advances in Finance, Accounting, and Economics (AFAE) Book Series

Published in the United States of America by
IGI Global
Business Science Reference (an imprint of IGI Global)
701 E. Chocolate Avenue
Hershey PA, USA 17033
Tel: 717-533-8845
Fax: 717-533-8661
E-mail: cust@igi-global.com
Web site: http://www.igi-global.com

Copyright © 2024 by IGI Global. All rights reserved. No part of this publication may be reproduced, stored or distributed in any form or by any means, electronic or mechanical, including photocopying, without written permission from the publisher.
Product or company names used in this set are for identification purposes only. Inclusion of the names of the products or companies does not indicate a claim of ownership by IGI Global of the trademark or registered trademark.

Library of Congress Cataloging-in-Publication Data

CIP Data in progress

British Cataloguing in Publication Data
A Cataloguing in Publication record for this book is available from the British Library.

All work contributed to this book is new, previously-unpublished material.
The views expressed in this book are those of the authors, but not necessarily of the publisher.

For electronic access to this publication, please contact: eresources@igi-global.com.

Advances in Finance, Accounting, and Economics (AFAE) Book Series

Ahmed Driouchi
Al Akhawayn University, Morocco

ISSN:2327-5677
EISSN:2327-5685

MISSION

In our changing economic and business environment, it is important to consider the financial changes occurring internationally as well as within individual organizations and business environments. Understanding these changes as well as the factors that influence them is crucial in preparing for our financial future and ensuring economic sustainability and growth.

The **Advances in Finance, Accounting, and Economics (AFAE)** book series aims to publish comprehensive and informative titles in all areas of economics and economic theory, finance, and accounting to assist in advancing the available knowledge and providing for further research development in these dynamic fields.

Coverage

- Stock Market
- Statistical Analysis
- Wages and Employment
- Economics of Natural and Environmental Resources
- Theoretical Issues in Economics, Finance, and Accounting
- Field Research
- E-Finance
- Microeconomics
- Bankruptcy
- Auditing

IGI Global is currently accepting manuscripts for publication within this series. To submit a proposal for a volume in this series, please contact our Acquisition Editors at Acquisitions@igi-global.com or visit: http://www.igi-global.com/publish/.

The (ISSN) is published by IGI Global, 701 E. Chocolate Avenue, Hershey, PA 17033-1240, USA, www.igi-global.com. This series is composed of titles available for purchase individually; each title is edited to be contextually exclusive from any other title within the series. For pricing and ordering information please visit http://www.igi-global.com/book-series/advances-finance-accounting-economics/73685. Postmaster: Send all address changes to above address. Copyright © IGI Global. All rights, including translation in other languages reserved by the publisher. No part of this series may be reproduced or used in any form or by any means – graphics, electronic, or mechanical, including photocopying, recording, taping, or information and retrieval systems – without written permission from the publisher, except for non commercial, educational use, including classroom teaching purposes. The views expressed in this series are those of the authors, but not necessarily of IGI Global.

Titles in this Series

For a list of additional titles in this series, please visit: http://www.igi-global.com/book-series/advances-finance-accounting-economics/73685

Decentralized Finance and Tokenization in FinTech
Luan Vardari (University "Ukshin Hoti" Prizren, Kosovo) and Isuf Qabrati (University "Ukshin Hoti" Prizren, Kosovo)
Business Science Reference • copyright 2024 • 392pp • H/C (ISBN: 9798369333464) • US $275.00 (our price)

Comparative Approach on Development and Socioeconomics of Africa
Baimba Yilla (Marymount University, USA)
Information Science Reference • copyright 2024 • 258pp • H/C (ISBN: 9798369324035) • US $255.00 (our price)

Impact of Renewable Energy on Corporate Finance and Economics
Ali Ahmadi (Higher Institute of Business Administration of Gafsa, Tunisia)
Business Science Reference • copyright 2024 • 288pp • H/C (ISBN: 9798369339329) • US $295.00 (our price)

Emerging Perspectives on Financial Well-Being
Dharmendra Singh (Modern College of Business and Science, Oman) Rohit Bansal (Rajiv Gandhi Institute of Petroleum Technology, India) Swati Gupta (K.R. Mangalam University, India) and Yasmeen Ansari (Saudi Electronic University, Saudi Arabia)
Business Science Reference • copyright 2024 • 339pp • H/C (ISBN: 9798369317501) • US $290.00 (our price)

Transforming the Financial Landscape With ICTs
Dharmendra Singh (Modern College of Business and Science, Oman) Garima Malik (Birla Institute of Technology Management, Greater Noida, India) and Shalini Aggarwal (Chandigarh University, India)
Business Science Reference • copyright 2024 • 345pp • H/C (ISBN: 9798369315033) • US $285.00 (our price)

701 East Chocolate Avenue, Hershey, PA 17033, USA
Tel: 717-533-8845 x100 • Fax: 717-533-8661
E-Mail: cust@igi-global.com • www.igi-global.com

Table of Contents

Preface... xv

Chapter 1
Financial Inclusion, Financial Crime, and Fraud Detection 1
    Peterson K. K. Ozili, Central Bank of Nigeria, Nigeria

Chapter 2
Automated Wealth Management: Exploring the Evolution and Impact of
Robo-Advisors in Finance.. 14
    *Mani Tyagi, Manav Rachna International Institute of Research and
        Studies, India*
    *Kirti Khanna, Manav Rachna International Institute of Research and
        Studies, India*

Chapter 3
An Empirical Study on Awareness of Ponzi Schemes in India 24
    *Jagruti Patni, School of Behavioural Sciences and Forensic
        Investigations, Rashtriya Raksha University, India*
    *Naveen Kumar Singh, School of Behavioural Sciences and Forensic
        Investigations, Rashtriya Raksha University, India & INTI
        International University, Malaysia*

Chapter 4
Data Management in the Digital Age: A Financial Institution Case Study 42
    Firdous Mohd Farouk, Taylor's University, Malaysia

Chapter 5
Compliance Challenges and Tech-Driven Solutions in Combating Financial
Crime Within the Fintech Ecosystem 62
    Mushtaq Ahmad Shah, Lovely Professional University, India
    B. Udaya Bhaskara Ganesh, Lovely Professional University, India

Chapter 6
Securing the Future Through AI, Green Finance, and Sustainable
Development in the Digital Age 81
    Numan Khan, Sunway University, Malaysia
    Sitara Karim, Sunway University, Malaysia
    Farah Naz, Kinnaird College for Women, Lahore, Pakistan

Chapter 7
Navigating Fintech Disruptions: Safeguarding Data Security in the Digital
Era 103
    Maizaitulaidawati Md Husin, Universiti Teknologi Malaysia, Malaysia
    Shahab Aziz, King Fahd University of Petroleum and Minerals, Saudi
        Arabia

Chapter 8
Revolutionizing Financial Data Security Through Blockchain and Distributed
Ledger Technology 121
    Misal Ijaz, Kinnaird College for Women, Lahore, Pakistan
    Farah Naz, Kinnaird College for Women, Lahore, Pakistan
    Sitara Karim, Sunway University, Malaysia

Chapter 9
Protecting Investor Sentiment by Detecting Financial Fraud With the Help of
ML and AI Applications 146
    Anumita Chaudhury, Garden City University, India

Chapter 10
Vertical Assimilation of Artificial Intelligence and Machine Learning in
Safeguarding Financial Data 169
    Bhupinder Singh, Sharda University, India
    Christian Kaunert, Dublin City University, Ireland & University of
        South Wales, UK

Chapter 11
Role of Artificial Intelligence and Machine Learning Algorithms in Detecting
Financial Frauds 198
    Bakir Illahi Dar, Baba Ghulam Shah Badshah University, India
    Shweta Jaiswal, CMP Degree College, University of Allahabad,
        Prayagraj, India

Chapter 12
Striking the Balance: Accounting Regulatory Compliance and Standards in Fintech.. 214
    Shir Li Ng, Sunway Business School, Sunway University, Malaysia

Chapter 13
Why Do People Fall Prey to Chit Fund Scams in India? 238
    Vanisha Godara, School of Behavioural Sciences and Forensic
        Investigations, Rashtriya Raksha University, India
    Naveen Kumar Singh, School of Behavioural Sciences and Forensic
        Investigations, Rashtriya Raksha University, India & INTI
        International University, Malaysia

Compilation of References 256

About the Contributors 301

Index 304

Detailed Table of Contents

Preface xv

Chapter 1
Financial Inclusion, Financial Crime, and Fraud Detection 1
    Peterson K. K. Ozili, Central Bank of Nigeria, Nigeria

The objective of this chapter is to discuss the role of financial inclusion in combating financial crime. It was found that financial crime is a challenge in society. Financial crime is any action or omission that leads to unlawful or illegal financial dealings. Many countries are seeking ways to combat financial crime. Many ideas have been considered on how to combat financial crime. Financial inclusion is a possible solution for combating financial crime. Financial inclusion involves granting access to basic formal financial services to all segments of society. The author shows that financial inclusion makes the work of investigators easier by leaving an audit trail whenever financial crime is committed in the formal financial system. It helps investigators to detect fraud or financial crime that has occurred in the formal financial system.

Chapter 2
Automated Wealth Management: Exploring the Evolution and Impact of Robo-Advisors in Finance.. 14
    Mani Tyagi, Manav Rachna International Institute of Research and Studies, India
    Kirti Khanna, Manav Rachna International Institute of Research and Studies, India

This paper presents a comprehensive investigation into the transformative landscape of wealth management through the lens of robo-advisors. The evolution of automated wealth management strategies is examined, tracing the historical trajectory from inception to technological advancements. A comparative analysis of traditional wealth management practices and robo-advisor-driven approaches is conducted, assessing their efficacy, performance, and risk management capabilities. Furthermore, this research explores the market adoption rates, demographic trends, and geographical variances in the utilization of robo-advisors, shedding light on the factors influencing their widespread acceptance. Technological innovations such as artificial intelligence, machine learning algorithms, and predictive analytics are scrutinized for their pivotal This comprehensive exploration provides a foundational understanding of the evolution, impact, and implications of robo-advisors in finance, offering insights that contribute to the ongoing dialogue on the future of wealth management.

Chapter 3
An Empirical Study on Awareness of Ponzi Schemes in India 24
    Jagruti Patni, School of Behavioural Sciences and Forensic
        Investigations, Rashtriya Raksha University, India
    Naveen Kumar Singh, School of Behavioural Sciences and Forensic
        Investigations, Rashtriya Raksha University, India & INTI
        International University, Malaysia

The given point of view on how Indians perceive and relate to Ponzi is taken up for consideration. The rather classic sampling model employed in the study is alarming as it shows that despite the information imbalance between the urban and village areas, there are huge knowledge gaps left in the villages. The survey showcases a scary picture—Indian people are highly attracted to this preposterous rhetoric and speculative investments that underutilize financial rationality. The research points out that celebrity endorsement is a major issue requiring immediate legal action. Scapegoating public figures who had the audacity to lend their dignity to Ponzi schemes means that the public is more trusting of the unknown, the never-heard-of-before enterprises. A highly valuable conclusory statement was developed, which formed the basis for the development of a blueprint for improving public education and financial literacy initiatives. Using this, Indians are allowed to avoid that narrow bridge, which often leads to the drainage of their savings through the wrong investment schemes.

Chapter 4
Data Management in the Digital Age: A Financial Institution Case Study 42
    Firdous Mohd Farouk, Taylor's University, Malaysia

This chapter illustrates the data management in a large financial institution in Malaysia during a major technology implementation phase. The case organisation implemented big data analytics (BDA) as a strategic move towards better decision-making through a better understanding of market needs. The case bank was, at the time of this research being conducted, actively involved in implementing BDA through various planned activities. To begin with, the implementation of BDA was a strategic decision, and it was incorporated as a four-year plan in the bank. While there were many aspects to BDA implementation in the bank, one major aspect was data itself because the way data is used in the financial institution is subject to scrutiny. BDA enables a vast amount of data to be analysed to gain actionable insights, however, the case organisation was heavily regulated. This chapter will revolve around issues in data management and data protection in the case organisation.

Chapter 5
Compliance Challenges and Tech-Driven Solutions in Combating Financial
Crime Within the Fintech Ecosystem 62
    Mushtaq Ahmad Shah, Lovely Professional University, India
    B. Udaya Bhaskara Ganesh, Lovely Professional University, India

The fast-growing Fintech industry has become a battleground for financial crime, posing significant challenges to regulators and business stakeholders. This chapter investigates financial crime threats and regulatory implications in the changing FinTech environment. The study looks into the awareness of financial crimes and examines the major Fintech risks that businesses face. Employing an exploratory research approach, the study examines public awareness of financial crimes through a survey questionnaire sent to the target respondents. Moreover, the recent regulatory actions against FinTech companies are examined, illustrating the growing emphasis on consumer protection and compliance. The chapter concludes by emphasising the importance of an exclusive global legislative framework for combating financial crimes in FinTech. This chapter advances understanding of financial crime risks and regulatory considerations in FinTech, providing significant insights for scholars, regulators, and FinTech enterprises.

Chapter 6
Securing the Future Through AI, Green Finance, and Sustainable
Development in the Digital Age 81
    Numan Khan, Sunway University, Malaysia
    Sitara Karim, Sunway University, Malaysia
    Farah Naz, Kinnaird College for Women, Lahore, Pakistan

Climate change has become one of the pressing challenges in the 21st century. Ensuring and devising strategies to combat climate change is necessary and for this purpose, this study discusses the relationship between artificial intelligence, green finance, and sustainable development. Moreover, this study analyzes the role of green finance, and its connection with AI and sustainable development. Green bonds, stocks, and cryptocurrencies are analyzed with the objective of its support towards sustainable development. The study further discussed that AI has key role in sustainable development through green finance and the interplay of these factors can achieve sustainable development goals. Furthermore, the chapter sheds light on challenges in the data for green finance and sustainable development where AI stands in between which generates data through its different technologies. This chapter offers various insights and implications for policymakers and government officials to help reshape sustainable development in the long run.

Chapter 7
Navigating Fintech Disruptions: Safeguarding Data Security in the Digital Era 103
> *Maizaitulaidawati Md Husin, Universiti Teknologi Malaysia, Malaysia*
> *Shahab Aziz, King Fahd University of Petroleum and Minerals, Saudi Arabia*

The rise of financial technology (fintech) has revolutionized the landscape of financial services, offering innovative solutions that streamline transactions, enhance accessibility, and transform traditional banking processes. However, amidst the rapid expansion of fintech, the issue of data security emerges as a paramount concern. This chapter explores the disruptive impact of fintech on traditional financial systems and the profound implications for data security in the digital age. By analyzing the technological advancements driving fintech innovation and the evolving regulatory landscape, this chapter examines the challenges and opportunities in safeguarding sensitive financial data. This chapter also identifies key vulnerabilities and threats to data security within fintech ecosystems and proposes strategic approaches to mitigate risks and strengthen cybersecurity measures. In sum, this chapter contributes to the ongoing dialogue surrounding the intersection of financial innovation, technology, and cybersecurity in the contemporary digital economy.

Chapter 8
Revolutionizing Financial Data Security Through Blockchain and Distributed Ledger Technology 121
> *Misal Ijaz, Kinnaird College for Women, Lahore, Pakistan*
> *Farah Naz, Kinnaird College for Women, Lahore, Pakistan*
> *Sitara Karim, Sunway University, Malaysia*

In the digital age, safeguarding financial data has become paramount amid increasing cyber threats and data breaches. This chapter explores the transformative role of blockchain and distributed ledger technology (DLT) in enhancing financial data security. Through practical applications and detailed case studies, the chapter illustrates the real-world implementation and efficacy of blockchain and DLT in the financial sector. Security features intrinsic to these technologies, such as decentralization, cryptographic hashing, and consensus mechanisms, are explored in depth, highlighting their contributions to a more secure financial ecosystem. Furthermore, the chapter addresses the regulatory landscape surrounding blockchain and DLT, discussing both the challenges and opportunities posed by these innovations. By presenting a comprehensive analysis of the current state and future potential of blockchain and DLT, this chapter aims to provide valuable insights into how these technologies are reshaping the approach to financial data security and resilience.

Chapter 9
Protecting Investor Sentiment by Detecting Financial Fraud With the Help of
ML and AI Applications 146
    Anumita Chaudhury, Garden City University, India

Investors, in spite of their vigilant moves, often are observed to fall victim to financial fraud. There are several machine learning algorithms both supervised and unsupervised which exists and continue to serve the objective of detecting financial fraud like under supervised machine learning random forest, k-nearest neighbours (KNN), logistic regression and support vector machine (SVM) and unsupervised machine learning includes K-means and SOM (self-organizing map).AI will help in mitigating the impact of volatility in the financial market. There is a necessity to adopt new-age machine learning and Artificial Intelligence which will promptly process millions of data and also identify dubious patterns has become very crucial to evade the losses caused by fraudulent activities.

Chapter 10
Vertical Assimilation of Artificial Intelligence and Machine Learning in
Safeguarding Financial Data 169
    Bhupinder Singh, Sharda University, India
    Christian Kaunert, Dublin City University, Ireland & University of
        South Wales, UK

The rapid evolution of technology has revolutionized the financial industry with digital banking and financial services becoming increasingly prevalent. The prevailing trend in the contemporary financial services sector centers around the transition to digital platforms, particularly mobile and online banking. In an age marked by unparalleled convenience and speed, consumers no longer prefer visiting physical bank branches for their transactions. As banks strive to introduce new features to attract and retain customers, disruptive banking technologies from startups and neo banks are emerging. The integration of artificial intelligence (AI) and machine learning (ML) in the banking sector holds the potential to transform operational processes and enhance services which leads to improved efficiency, productivity and customer experience. This chapter explores the role of AI and ML in addressing information privacy and security concerns in the arena of digital banking and financial services in digital age.

Chapter 11
Role of Artificial Intelligence and Machine Learning Algorithms in Detecting Financial Frauds 198
    Bakir Illahi Dar, Baba Ghulam Shah Badshah University, India
    Shweta Jaiswal, CMP Degree College, University of Allahabad, Prayagraj, India

The integration of artificial intelligence (AI) and machine learning (ML) algorithms to detect fraud in financial transactions has entirely changed the field. Reconfiguration of financial product value chains necessitates the implementation of strong cybersecurity measures and advanced encryption techniques to protect sensitive financial data.. This chapter provides an insight into how AI and ML work as effective tools to deal with financial crimes, describing how they help improve fraud-detection capacities. AI and ML algorithms analyze financial data and make it possible for banks to prevent or mitigate issues such as risks. In addition, the study discusses the difficulties involved in applying AI and ML within the finance industry. Lastly, this study highlights the potential transformation that AI and ML can bring by strengthening the resilience of the financial ecosystem against evolving threats of fraud. According to this study, to effectively detect fraud, the financial and development supervisory agency must leverage more technology, particularly data analytics and AI.

Chapter 12
Striking the Balance: Accounting Regulatory Compliance and Standards in Fintech.. 214
    Shir Li Ng, Sunway Business School, Sunway University, Malaysia

The evolution of fintech significantly impacts the financial industry through technology and regulation. The chapter explores fintech's transformative journey, tracing its historical roots to its present-day importance in reshaping traditional financial processes. Addressing the challenges that emerge when fintech meets accounting regulations, the chapter seeks to highlight how important it is for the regulations to conform themselves with the aim of fostering the required innovation and managing risks. Some of the proposed ways of achieving harmonized compliance focus on international collaboration, adaptability of regulations, stakeholder engagement, and education initiatives. Additionally, the chapter features the importance of fostering a compliance culture, transparency, and investor confidence within the fintech landscape. Proactive measures and technological innovations drive fintech compliance, aiding in regulatory navigation. Overall, the chapter provides insights into the complex relationship between accounting regulatory compliance and standards in the fintech industry.

Chapter 13
Why Do People Fall Prey to Chit Fund Scams in India? 238
> *Vanisha Godara, School of Behavioural Sciences and Forensic Investigations, Rashtriya Raksha University, India*
> *Naveen Kumar Singh, School of Behavioural Sciences and Forensic Investigations, Rashtriya Raksha University, India & INTI International University, Malaysia*

Chit fund schemes have historically been highly popular options for side investing when it comes to savings in Inida. Newspaper headlines about the failure of these funds and the misfortune of gullible investors frequently appear. Since there are thousands of cases of fraud, these media reports have not received much attention up until now. However, several scams involving thousands of crores of rupees have surfaced in recent years. Therefore, it is necessary to understand why people fall victim to these chit-fund scams. A customized questionnaire was used to gather data through convenient sampling to measure public knowledge about financial offense types, illegal chit-fund companies, and financial crime reporting. The findings showed that, compared to older individuals, the majority of investors, who are in the 18–35 age range, had a better understanding of chit-fund schemes. This study may further help to create laws and educate investors aimed at stopping and dealing with these types of scams.

Compilation of References 256

About the Contributors 301

Index 304

Preface

Welcome to *Safeguarding Financial Data in the Digital Age*, a collaborative effort aimed at navigating the intricate terrain of financial data security amidst the rapid advancement of technology and digitization. As editors, it is our privilege to introduce this anthology, which brings together the collective wisdom of scholars, researchers, and experts from diverse disciplines to illuminate the challenges, solutions, and innovations in protecting sensitive financial information.

In today's interconnected world, where financial transactions increasingly occur on digital platforms, the imperative to safeguard financial data has never been more pressing. This book serves as a beacon, guiding readers through the complex landscape of encryption methods, risk management frameworks, regulatory compliance, and emerging technologies that underpin effective financial data protection. Through a multidisciplinary lens encompassing finance, cybersecurity, and technology, we endeavor to offer comprehensive insights that address both current issues and future trends.

The chapters within this volume cover a wide spectrum of topics, ranging from the practical application of encryption methods to the ethical considerations inherent in financial data management. Case studies detailing successful implementations provide invaluable lessons for practitioners and policymakers alike, while discussions on fintech disruptions, machine learning applications, and blockchain technology offer a glimpse into the evolving landscape of financial security.

This book is designed to cater to a diverse audience, including academics, industry professionals, policymakers, and students. Whether you are seeking theoretical frameworks, practical strategies, or ethical insights, this volume endeavors to provide a holistic understanding of financial data security in the digital age. We invite you to delve into its pages, engage with its contents, and join us in shaping the discourse on securing financial data for a sustainable and secure digital future.

Preface

We extend our heartfelt gratitude to all the contributors whose expertise and dedication have made this project possible. It is our hope that this book will serve as a catalyst for collaboration, innovation, and knowledge exchange in the ongoing endeavor to safeguard financial data in our increasingly digitized world.

In *Safeguarding Financial Data in the Digital Age*, each chapter offers a unique perspective on the critical challenges and innovative solutions shaping the modern landscape of financial security. Here's a concise overview of the diverse topics covered in this comprehensive reference book:

In the evolving landscape of financial systems and technologies, understanding the multifaceted nature of financial crimes and innovative financial solutions is imperative. This edited volume brings together insightful research and analyses that delve into various aspects of financial crimes, technological advancements in finance, and their broader implications. Each chapter presents a comprehensive examination of critical issues, offering valuable perspectives for scholars, practitioners, and policymakers. Below is an overview of the key themes and contributions from each chapter.

Chapter 1 explores the significant role of financial inclusion in mitigating financial crime. By ensuring access to formal financial services for all segments of society, financial inclusion creates audit trails that assist investigators in detecting fraud and unlawful financial activities. The discussion highlights the global efforts to combat financial crime and the potential of financial inclusion to enhance transparency and accountability in financial systems.

In chapter 2, the transformative influence of robo-advisors on wealth management is meticulously examined in this chapter. It traces the historical development of automated wealth management strategies, comparing traditional practices with modern robo-advisor approaches. The analysis encompasses market adoption trends, technological innovations such as AI and machine learning, and their implications for the future of wealth management. This chapter provides a foundational understanding of the evolution and efficacy of robo-advisors.

Focusing on the Indian context, this chapter investigates the public perception and susceptibility to Ponzi schemes. It reveals the alarming knowledge gaps between urban and rural areas and the impact of celebrity endorsements on public trust. Chapter 3 underscores the need for improved financial literacy and regulatory measures to prevent fraudulent investments. It offers a blueprint for enhancing public education to protect individuals from falling victim to such schemes.

Chapter 4 details the implementation of big data analytics (BDA) in a major Malaysian financial institution. It discusses the strategic decision to incorporate BDA over a four-year plan to enhance market understanding and decision-making processes. The chapter addresses the challenges of data management and protection

Preface

within the heavily regulated financial sector, highlighting the benefits and complexities of leveraging vast amounts of data for actionable insights.

The rapidly growing FinTech industry presents new challenges for financial crime and regulation. Chapter 5 investigates the awareness of financial crimes within the FinTech sector, examining the major risks faced by businesses and the recent regulatory actions taken to protect consumers. It calls for a global legislative framework to combat financial crimes in FinTech, providing significant insights for stakeholders in the industry.

Addressing the pressing issue of climate change, this chapter explores the intersection of artificial intelligence (AI), green finance, and sustainable development. It examines how AI can support green finance initiatives such as green bonds and cryptocurrencies to achieve sustainable development goals. Chapter 6 also discusses the challenges in data management for green finance and the potential of AI to drive sustainable development.

Chapter 7 delves into the data security concerns arising from the rapid expansion of FinTech. It analyzes the technological advancements driving FinTech innovation and the regulatory landscape's evolution. The discussion identifies key vulnerabilities and proposes strategies to enhance cybersecurity within FinTech ecosystems, contributing to the dialogue on safeguarding sensitive financial data in the digital age.

The potential of blockchain and Distributed Ledger Technology (DLT) to enhance financial data security is the focus of chapter 8. Through practical applications and case studies, the chapter illustrates how these technologies improve security through decentralization, cryptographic hashing, and consensus mechanisms. It also addresses the regulatory challenges and opportunities posed by blockchain and DLT, offering insights into their future potential in the financial sector.

Machine learning and AI have revolutionized financial fraud detection, as explored in chapter 9. It reviews various algorithms used for detecting financial fraud and emphasizes the necessity of adopting advanced technologies to process large datasets and identify dubious patterns. The chapter highlights the transformative potential of AI and ML in enhancing the resilience of financial systems against fraud.

The integration of AI and ML in digital banking is transforming the financial services landscape. Chapter 10 explores how these technologies enhance operational processes, improve efficiency, and address information privacy and security concerns. It discusses the role of AI and ML in driving the transition to digital platforms and the implications for customer experience and service delivery in the banking sector.

Chapter 11 provides an in-depth analysis of how AI and ML algorithms are utilized to detect fraud in financial transactions. It discusses the challenges of data security and privacy and the potential of these technologies to improve fraud detection capacities. The chapter also examines the difficulties in implementing AI and ML in finance and their potential to strengthen the financial ecosystem against evolving fraud threats.

The relationship between FinTech innovations and accounting regulations is critically examined in this chapter. It traces the historical development of FinTech and its impact on traditional financial processes, emphasizing the need for regulatory frameworks that foster innovation while managing risks. Chapter 12 proposes ways to achieve harmonized compliance, highlighting the importance of international collaboration and stakeholder engagement.

Chit fund schemes have long been popular in India, yet they are fraught with risks and fraudulent practices. Chapter 13 investigates why individuals fall victim to chit-fund scams, using survey data to measure public knowledge about these schemes. It provides insights into the demographic factors influencing susceptibility and suggests measures to educate investors and create effective laws to combat such scams.

By bringing together these diverse perspectives, this volume aims to deepen our understanding of financial crimes, technological innovations in finance, and the regulatory challenges in this dynamic field. The insights offered in each chapter contribute to the broader discourse on creating a more secure and inclusive financial ecosystem.

Each chapter in *Safeguarding Financial Data in the Digital Age* contributes valuable insights and solutions to the ongoing discourse on securing financial data in our increasingly digitized world. We hope this book serves as an invaluable resource for scholars, practitioners, policymakers, and students navigating the complex landscape of financial security.

In conclusion, *Safeguarding Financial Data in the Digital Age* represents a collaborative effort to address the critical challenges surrounding financial data security in today's digital era. As editors, we are honored to present this anthology, which encapsulates the collective expertise and insights of scholars, researchers, and practitioners from various disciplines.

The chapters within this volume offer a comprehensive exploration of diverse topics, ranging from encryption methods and compliance challenges to the role of emerging technologies like artificial intelligence and blockchain in financial security. Through empirical studies, case analyses, and theoretical frameworks, each chapter contributes valuable perspectives and solutions to the complex landscape of financial data protection.

We believe that this book serves as a vital resource for academics, industry professionals, policymakers, and students seeking to navigate the intricate terrain of financial security. By fostering collaboration, innovation, and knowledge exchange, we hope to contribute to the ongoing dialogue on securing financial data and shaping a sustainable and secure digital future.

Preface

We extend our sincere gratitude to all the contributors whose dedication and expertise have enriched this project. It is our collective hope that *Safeguarding Financial Data in the Digital Age* will inspire further research, collaboration, and action in safeguarding financial data in our increasingly digitized world.

Farah Naz

Department of Accounting and Finance, Kinnaird College for Women, Pakistan

Sitara Karim

Department of Economics and Finance, Sunway University, Malaysia

Chapter 1
Financial Inclusion, Financial Crime, and Fraud Detection

Peterson K. K. Ozili
https://orcid.org/0000-0001-6292-1161
Central Bank of Nigeria, Nigeria

ABSTRACT

The objective of this chapter is to discuss the role of financial inclusion in combating financial crime. It was found that financial crime is a challenge in society. Financial crime is any action or omission that leads to unlawful or illegal financial dealings. Many countries are seeking ways to combat financial crime. Many ideas have been considered on how to combat financial crime. Financial inclusion is a possible solution for combating financial crime. Financial inclusion involves granting access to basic formal financial services to all segments of society. The author shows that financial inclusion makes the work of investigators easier by leaving an audit trail whenever financial crime is committed in the formal financial system. It helps investigators to detect fraud or financial crime that has occurred in the formal financial system.

1. INTRODUCTION

The aim of this chapter is to discuss the role of financial inclusion in combating financial crime and for fraud detection.

Financial crime is any action or omission that leads to unlawful or illegal financial dealings (Pickett and Pickett, 2002). Financial crime is a challenge in many countries. Financial crime takes many different forms ranging from corporate financial crime, private financial crime, and public sector financial crime (Nerenberg, 2000;

Michel, 2008). Financial crime affects a country – its economy, citizens, government, institutions and social well-being. Some effects of persistent financial crime are that (i) it undermines legitimate and lawful financial dealings, (ii) it undermines the integrity of the financial system; (iii) it gives the impression that existing institutions are weak, (iv) it leads to loss of lives, (v) it leads to market distortion, (vi) it leads to loss of reputation, and (vii) it leads to loss of means of livelihood (Amara and Khlif, 2018; Ozili, 2020b; Ozili, 2015).

Many efforts have been made to combat financial crime in society. These efforts include anti-money laundering efforts, increasing financial disclosures, increasing financial transparency and fraud detection using forensic accounting tools. The literature has examined how these efforts can be used to combat financial crime and to detect fraud (see, for example, Ozili, 2015; Abdallah, Maarof and Zainal, 2016; Pourhabibi et al, 2020; Ozili and Mhlanga, 2024). However, the existing research has not considered the role of financial inclusion in combating financial crime. To date, there are no discussions in the existing literature about the role of financial inclusion in combating financial crime or for fraud detection.

Financial inclusion is very important for society (2023). Financial inclusion helps to improve wellbeing by ensuring that everyone has access to the most basic financial services (Zins and Weill, 2016; Ozili, 2021a). Once access to basic financial services is granted, people will leave an audit trail whenever they make financial transactions using formal channels. The audit trail may be used to track and identify both lawful and unlawful financial dealings in the formal financial system. The audit trail can also be used to detect financial crime. Despite the potential for financial inclusion to contribute to fraud detection and to combat crime, existing studies have not explored how financial inclusion can support efforts to combat financial crime and to assist in fraud detection efforts.

This study adds to the financial crime literature by proposing another strategy that may be used to combat financial crime. Financial inclusion is identified as a potential strategy that can be used by governments to combat financial crime. This chapter also adds to the financial inclusion literature that analyse some consequences of financial inclusion. The present study reveals that financial inclusion may have consequences for financial crime as it can expose financial crime, thereby making it a useful strategy for fraud detection.

The remaining sections of this chapter is categorized in the following way. The related literature is discussed in section 2. The discussion section is presented in section 3. Also, the ways through which financial inclusion can contribute to fraud detection and reduction in financial crime is discussed in section 3.1. The concluding remarks are presented in section 4.

2. LITERATURE REVIEW

Existing research on financial crime has investigated the effect, consequence and mitigation of financial crime. For example, Achim et al. (2021) examined how technology affects financial crime. They analysed 185 countries from 2012 to 2015 and found that there are more financial crimes in low-income countries than in high income countries, and the use of technology reduced financial crime. Abdullah and Said (2019) examined whether having a risk committee in a company mitigates financial crime. They found that having a stand-alone risk committee has an impact on the incidence of financial crime in a company. They conclude that companies need a stand-alone risk committee to enable them combat corporate financial crime. Reid (2018) showed that online financial crime is a challenge to society, it affects the ability of humans to interact with each other online, it affects societal trust, and reduces trust in public institutions. Achim and Borlea (2020) identified some determinants of financial crime which are the need to avoid tax, quality of corporate governance and banking system soundness.

Other studies focused on fraud detection methods. Raj and Portia (2011) emphasized that banks need to adopt efficient fraud detection systems to minimize credit card losses. They suggest some techniques that may be used by banks to minimize fraud which include machine learning, artificial intelligence (AI), data mining, among others. West and Bhattacharya (2016) argue that traditional methods of fraud detection are time consuming, expensive and inaccurate, and there is a need to shift to automated processes using statistical and computational methods particularly data mining methods. In a different study, Bierstaker, Brody and Pacini (2006) showed that system firewalls, protection against virus, password breaches, and periodic review of internal control systems are methods that may be used to combat fraud.

Recent research has also investigated some solutions that financial inclusion offer to society. For instance, Le, Chuc and Taghizadeh-Hesary (2019) investigate the developments in financial inclusion in Asia over the 2004 to 2016 period. They found that financial inclusion is essential for financial sustainability in Asia, implying that financially inclusive societies are financially sustainable.

Ozili et al (2023) undertook a review of the post-2016 literature and found that increase in financial inclusion is associated with increase in economic growth, and the major channel through which this happens is through greater financial intermediation which translates to increase in economic output. Younas, Qureshi and Al-Faryan (2022) examined how financial inclusion impacts economic growth in developing economies and found that high levels of financial inclusion are related to improvements in economic growth. Erlando, Riyanto and Masakazu (2020) analyzed the benefit of financial inclusion for economic growth, poverty alleviation and income inequality. They analyse the case of Eastern Indonesia and found that financial inclusion seems to increase economic growth and increase income inequality. Ahmad et al (2021) examined the likely effect of digital financial inclusion and human capital on China's provincial economic growth. They found that economic growth in the provinces improved after the adoption of digital financial services. Therefore, they recommend that policymakers should consider upgrading their digital financial inclusion efforts to achieve growth outcomes.

Omar and Inaba (2020) examined how financial inclusion affects poverty reduction and income inequality in developing countries from 2004 to 2016. They found that income inequality and poverty is reduced in countries that have greater levels of financial inclusion. Therefore, they conclude that countries should accelerate financial inclusion for the good of poor people. Koomson, Villano and Hadley (2020) examine how financial inclusion affects poverty in Ghana using the Ghana Living Standards Survey in 2016/17. They found that greater financial inclusion reduced the probability of being poor by 27 percent, and it reduced poverty among female-headed households. Tran et al (2022) investigate the effect of financial inclusion on multidimensional poverty in Vietnam and observed that greater financial inclusion reduces multidimensional poverty. In a related study, Nsiah et al (2021) investigate the case of sub-Saharan Africa and found that financial inclusion leads to poverty reduction.

Ozili (2021b) investigated whether high levels of financial inclusion might increase financial risk in the financial sector. It was found that higher account ownership increased financial sector risk by increasing the stock of high nonperforming loan and cost inefficiency in the financial sector of developed and transition economies. The author also found that financial risk was reduced in developed countries when there is greater use of debit and credit cards, and digital finance products. Wang and Luo (2022) examined whether financial inclusion affects bank stability in 36 emerging economies. They found that banks are more stable in financially inclusive countries and the main channels through which this happens are the cost, funding and risk channels.

Ajide (2020) investigated the role of financial inclusion on entrepreneurship in 13 African countries and observed that entrepreneurship improved significantly in financially inclusive African countries. Yang, Huang and Gao (2022) investigate how digital financial inclusion might affect female entrepreneurship and showed that the welfare of women entrepreneurs improved greatly when they used digital financial services for their business activities. Meanwhile, Sakyi-Nyarko, Ahmad and Green (2022) found that financial inclusion increased the financial resilience of households regardless of gender or locality. Niankara and Muqattash (2020) assessed how financial inclusion affects borrowing and saving decisions in the United States and the United Arab Emirates in the year 2014. They found that the US had greater financial inclusion than the UAE, and US consumers were 31.4% more likely to save using formal channels than their UAE counterparts.

Li, Dong and Dong (2022) examined the impact of financial inclusion on the development for renewable energy in China. They analysed the data using system GMM technique and found that high levels of financial inclusion increased the development of renewable energy in China. Wang et al (2022) investigate how financial inclusion might affect green economic efficiency in cities in China from 2011 to 2015. They found that greater financial inclusion increased green economic efficiency. Du et al (2022) examined how financial inclusion and human capital affect environmental quality of emerging nations from 2004 to 2019. They found that financial inclusion significantly improved environmental quality by decreasing CO_2 emission.

Existing research also examined the consequences of financial inclusion. For instance, Le, Le and Taghizadeh-Hesary (2020) investigate the effect of financial inclusion on CO_2 emissions in Asian countries and found that financial inclusion led to greater CO_2 emissions. Ozili (2023) showed that financial inclusion efforts can lead to financial inclusion washing – a situation where promoters of financial inclusion deliberately overstate their support for financial inclusion. Dong et al (2022) investigated the impact of energy efficiency on the financial inclusion-CO_2 nexus in China. They found that greater financial inclusion did not reduce carbon emission in China. Ozili and Adamu (2021) investigate the relationship between financial inclusion and bank non-performing loans and loan loss provisions in 48 countries. They found an inverse relationship between financial inclusion and bank non-performing loans. Zakaria (2023) showed that despite the rapid advancement in digital financial services for financial inclusion, such advancement has led to a rise in digital finance risks and these risks are not mitigated due to presence of poor regulatory frameworks. Sun et al (2023) examined the effect of digital finance on corporate financial fraud. They used panel data of A-share listed corporations in China from 2011 to 2020. They found that widespread usage of digital finance reduces corporate financial fraud. The authors recommend the extensive usage of digital finance in Chinese corporations to curb financial fraud. Barik and Lenka (2023) examined the impact of financial inclusion on corruption control in some upper-middle and lower-middle income countries. They used cross-country annual data from 2004 to 2018 and found that financial inclusion does not reduce corruption in upper-middle income while high levels of financial inclusion reduce corruption in lower-middle-income.

3. DISCUSSION SECTION

3.1. Financial Inclusion for Fraud Detection and Reduction in Financial Crime

Below are some ways in which financial inclusion can help to detect fraud and to reduce financial crime.

3.1.1. Financial Inclusion Leaves Behind an Audit Trail That Is Useful for Fraud Detection

Financial inclusion can help to combat financial crime by leaving behind an audit trail. Banks are the most common agents of financial inclusion (Ozili, 2021a; Hannig and Jansen, 2010). They can use their systems to provide an audit trail of financial transactions that are deemed suspicious and hand it over to investigators when investigators request for such information (Singleton and Singleton, 2007). An audit trail is often presented in the account statements linked to suspicious transactions (Power, 2021; Flowerday and Von Solms, 2005). When there is full financial inclusion in society, financial institutions will be able to provide an audit trail for every transaction that takes place in the financial system. This will make it easier for forensic investigators to investigate and detect fraud. The investigators will be able to use the audit trail to link suspicious transactions to a person or entity and determine whether an actual financial crime has taken place. In contrast, when there is little financial inclusion in a society, financial institutions will not be able to provide an audit trail for every transaction that takes place in the financial ecosystem. As a result, financial institutions will not be able to provide audit trail for most transactions, making it very difficult for forensic investigators to investigate fraud. The investigators will have to find another way to detect fraud.

3.1.2. Financial Inclusion Reduces the Size of the Informal Economy and Reduces Financial Crime

Financial inclusion can help to combat financial crime by reducing or shrinking the size of the informal economy – which is the unregulated, untaxed and unmonitored segment of the economy (Rasanayagam, 2011). Large volume of cash-based transactions take place in the informal economy. Many of such transactions are the proceeds of crime such as extortion, discriminatory lending by loan sharks and financial theft (Maguire, 1993; Tomal and Johnson, 2008; Neef, 2002). One way to curb financial crime in the informal sector is to reduce the size of the informal sector through extensive financial inclusion efforts. This can be done by undertaking an extensive financial inclusion program that bring all individuals and small businesses into the formal financial system. This will reduce the use of informal financial services that expose people to corruption and illegal financial dealings. High levels of financial inclusion can reduce the size of the informal sector and significantly reduce financial crime that occurs in the informal economy. When there are high levels of financial inclusion, individuals and small businesses will reduce their use of cash and increase their use of digital payments or bank transfers. This will reduce the need to patronize informal economy agents such as loan sharks or unlicensed money lenders that dominate the informal economy.

3.1.3. Financial Inclusion Curbs Tax Evasion

Tax evasion generally refers to using illegal means to avoid tax payment (Slemrod, 2007; Ozili, 2020a). Financial inclusion also helps to curb tax evasion in some ways. Taxes can be paid more easily where there is high level of financial inclusion. This is because taxes can be paid electronically or through bank transfers to the tax authorities and such tax payments leave behind an audit trail that can be audited, evaluated and re-evaluated for the purpose of determining whether tax evasion has taken place which constitutes financial crime. The implication is that tax evasion will become less rampant in societies that have high levels of financial inclusion. Meanwhile, in societies where the level of financial inclusion is very low, tax evasion would be more rampant because taxes will be paid in cash, and it create many opportunities for tax evasion. In such societies, the cash payment of taxes does not leave behind an audit trail that can used to justify payment of taxes especially when the tax authorities are in doubt that an entity has made tax payments.

3.1.4. Use Legislation to Enforce Financial Inclusion to Assist in Fraud Detection

Existing studies show that countries can use legislation to enforce financial inclusion in specific activities or sectors (Ozili, 2021c). One way in which financial inclusion can help to combat financial crime is by using legislation to enforce financial inclusion in specific activities or sectors of the economy. For example, in the real estate sector, a country can pass a law that ban individuals, private corporations and government entities from paying property rent in cash and require them to make rent payments through bank transfers. The advantage of this approach is that it will compel people to own a bank account which leads to financial inclusion, and it will ensure that all property rent payments made into bank accounts can be traced to the sender and the recipient. This can assist investigators in dealing with reported cases of property rent fraud. This is one example of how legislation can be used to enforce financial inclusion and support fraud detection efforts. Although the above scenario applies to the case of property rent, such legislation can also be applied to other activities and sectors of the economy such as extraction and mining, education and entertainment. This idea of using legislation to enforce compulsory financial inclusion for people in the specific sectors will help investigators to trace lawful and unlawful financial transactions in the specific sectors so that fraudulent activities in such sectors can be easily traced and detected so that the perpetrators can be found and dealt with.

4. CONCLUSION

The rise in financial crime is a challenge in any society. The first step in combating financial crime is to detect whether financial crime has taken. This chapter assessed the role of financial inclusion in combating financial crime. It was argued that high levels of financial inclusion will ensure that criminals leave behind an audit trail that is useful for fraud detection and for the detection of financial crime. It was also argued that legislation can accelerate financial inclusion in order to assist the authorities in fraud detection activities. It was also argued that high levels of financial inclusion would shrink the size of the informal sector and reduce financial crime. It was also argued that high levels of financial inclusion may curb tax evasion.

The implication is that financial inclusion achieves many purposes. It not only improves individual welfare; it also makes the work of investigators easier by leaving behind an audit trail whenever financial crime is committed in the formal financial system. Therefore, policy makers should intensify their efforts to achieve high levels of financial inclusion to assist investigators in uncovering financial crime in the financial system. Notwithstanding, policymakers seeking to use financial inclusion as a strategy to combat crime should be mindful of the **increasing adoption of digital financial services and the potential vulnerabilities associated with financial inclusion can also be highlighted by the author to enhance the importance of implementing secure and inclusive digital platforms.**

The limitation of the study is that it did not examine the role of big data in financial inclusion and fraud detection. It also did not examine how to uncover fraud in the informal sector. The study also did not consider how artificial intelligence and financial inclusion can assist in fraud detection.

Future research can investigate how to uncover fraud in the informal economy. Future research should also investigate whether big data can assist in detecting financial crime. Future studies can also examine whether demand-side or supply-side financial inclusion play a greater role for detecting financial crime.

REFERENCES

Abdallah, A., Maarof, M. A., & Zainal, A. (2016). Fraud detection system: A survey. *Journal of Network and Computer Applications*, 68, 90–113. 10.1016/j.jnca.2016.04.007

Abdullah, W. N., & Said, R. (2019). Audit and risk committee in financial crime prevention. *Journal of Financial Crime*, 26(1), 223–234. 10.1108/JFC-11-2017-0116

Achim, M. V., & Borlea, S. N. (2020). Economic and Political Determinants of Economic and Financial Crime. In *Economic and Financial Crime* (pp. 73–176). Springer. 10.1007/978-3-030-51780-9_2

Achim, M. V., Borlea, S. N., & Văidean, V. L. (2021). Does technology matter for combating economic and financial crime? A panel data study. *Technological and Economic Development of Economy*, 27(1), 223–261. 10.3846/tede.2021.13977

Ahmad, M., Majeed, A., Khan, M. A., Sohaib, M., & Shehzad, K. (2021). Digital financial inclusion and economic growth: Provincial data analysis of China. *China Economic Journal*, 14(3), 291–310. 10.1080/17538963.2021.1882064

Ajide, F. M. (2020). Financial inclusion in Africa: Does it promote entrepreneurship? *Journal of Financial Economic Policy*, 12(4), 687–706. 10.1108/JFEP-08-2019-0159

Amara, I., & Khlif, H. (2018). Financial crime, corruption and tax evasion: A cross-country investigation. *Journal of Money Laundering Control*, 21(4), 545–554. 10.1108/JMLC-10-2017-0059

Barik, R., & Lenka, S. K. (2023). Does financial inclusion control corruption in upper-middle and lower-middle income countries? *Asia-Pacific Journal of Regional Science*, 7(1), 69–92. 10.1007/s41685-022-00269-0

Bierstaker, J. L., Brody, R. G., & Pacini, C. (2006). Accountants' perceptions regarding fraud detection and prevention methods. *Managerial Auditing Journal*, 21(5), 520–535. 10.1108/02686900610667283

Dong, J., Dou, Y., Jiang, Q., & Zhao, J. (2022). Can financial inclusion facilitate carbon neutrality in China? The role of energy efficiency. *Energy*, 251, 123922. 10.1016/j.energy.2022.123922

Du, Q., Wu, N., Zhang, F., Lei, Y., & Saeed, A. (2022). Impact of financial inclusion and human capital on environmental quality: Evidence from emerging economies. *Environmental Science and Pollution Research International*, 29(22), 33033–33045. 10.1007/s11356-021-17945-x35025039

Erlando, A., Riyanto, F. D., & Masakazu, S. (2020). Financial inclusion, economic growth, and poverty alleviation: Evidence from eastern Indonesia. *Heliyon*, 6(10), e05235. 10.1016/j.heliyon.2020.e0523533088971

Flowerday, S., & Von Solms, R. (2005). Continuous auditing: Verifying information integrity and providing assurances for financial reports. *Computer Fraud & Security*, 2005(7), 12–16. 10.1016/S1361-3723(05)70232-3

Hannig, A., & Jansen, S. (2010). *Financial inclusion and financial stability: Current policy issues*. (ADBI Working Paper No. 259).

Koomson, I., Villano, R. A., & Hadley, D. (2020). Effect of financial inclusion on poverty and vulnerability to poverty: Evidence using a multidimensional measure of financial inclusion. *Social Indicators Research*, 149(2), 613–639. 10.1007/s11205-019-02263-0

Le, T. H., Chuc, A. T., & Taghizadeh-Hesary, F. (2019). Financial inclusion and its impact on financial efficiency and sustainability: Empirical evidence from Asia. *Borsa Istanbul Review*, 19(4), 310–322. 10.1016/j.bir.2019.07.002

Le, T. H., Le, H. C., & Taghizadeh-Hesary, F. (2020). Does financial inclusion impact CO_2 emissions? Evidence from Asia. *Finance Research Letters*, 34, 101451. 10.1016/j.frl.2020.101451

Li, J., Dong, X., & Dong, K. (2022). How much does financial inclusion contribute to renewable energy growth? Ways to realize green finance in China. *Renewable Energy*, 198, 760–771. 10.1016/j.renene.2022.08.097

Maguire, K. (1993). Fraud, extortion and racketeering: The black economy in Northern Ireland. *Crime, Law, and Social Change*, 20(4), 273–292. 10.1007/BF01307715

Michel, P. (2008). Financial crimes: The constant challenge of seeking effective prevention solutions. *Journal of Financial Crime*, 15(4), 383–397. 10.1108/13590790810907227

Neef, R. (2002). Aspects of the informal economy in a transforming country: The case of Romania. *International Journal of Urban and Regional Research*, 26(2), 299–322. 10.1111/1468-2427.00381

Nerenberg, L. (2000). Forgotten victims of financial crime and abuse: Facing the challenge. *Journal of Elder Abuse & Neglect*, 12(2), 49–73. 10.1300/J084v12n02_06

Niankara, I., & Muqattash, R. (2020). The impact of financial inclusion on consumers saving and borrowing behaviours: Retrospective cross-sectional evidence from the UAE and the USA. *International Journal of Economics and Business Research*, 20(2), 217–242. 10.1504/IJEBR.2020.109152

Nsiah, A. Y., Yusif, H., Tweneboah, G., Agyei, K., & Baidoo, S. T. (2021). The effect of financial inclusion on poverty reduction in Sub-Sahara Africa: Does threshold matter? *Cogent Social Sciences*, 7(1), 1903138. 10.1080/23311886.2021.1903138

Omar, M. A., & Inaba, K. (2020). Does financial inclusion reduce poverty and income inequality in developing countries? A panel data analysis. *Journal of Economic Structures*, 9(1), 1–25. 10.1186/s40008-020-00214-4

Ozili, P. K. (2015). Forensic Accounting and Fraud: A Review of Literature and Policy Implications. *International Journal of Accounting and Economics Studies*, 3(1), 63–68. 10.14419/ijaes.v3i1.4541

Ozili, P. K. (2020a). Tax evasion and financial instability. *Journal of Financial Crime*, 27(2), 531–539. 10.1108/JFC-04-2019-0051

Ozili, P. K. (2020b). Advances and issues in fraud research: A commentary. *Journal of Financial Crime*, 27(1), 92–103. 10.1108/JFC-01-2019-0012

Ozili, P. K. (2021a). Financial inclusion research around the world: A review. *The Forum for Social Economics*, 50(4), 457–479. 10.1080/07360932.2020.1715238

Ozili, P. K. (2021b). Has financial inclusion made the financial sector riskier? *Journal of financial regulation and compliance,* 29(3), 237-255.

Ozili, P. K. (2021c). Financial inclusion and legal system quality: Are they correlated? *Journal of Money and Business*, 1(2), 84–101. 10.1108/JMB-10-2021-0041

Ozili, P. K. (2023). Financial inclusion washing. *Journal of Financial Crime*, 30(5), 1140–1149. 10.1108/JFC-07-2022-0159

Ozili, P. K., & Adamu, A. (2021). Does financial inclusion reduce non-performing loans and loan loss provisions? *Journal of Corporate Governance, Insurance, and Risk Management*, 8(2), 10–24. 10.51410/jcgirm.8.2.2

Ozili, P. K., Ademiju, A., & Rachid, S. (2023). Impact of financial inclusion on economic growth: Review of existing literature and directions for future research. *International Journal of Social Economics*, 50(8), 1105–1122. 10.1108/IJSE-05-2022-0339

Ozili, P. K., & Mhlanga, D. (2024). Why is financial inclusion so popular? An analysis of development buzzwords. *Journal of International Development*, 36(1), 231–253. 10.1002/jid.3812

Pickett, K. S., & Pickett, J. M. (2002). *Financial crime investigation and control*. John Wiley & Sons.

Pourhabibi, T., Ong, K. L., Kam, B. H., & Boo, Y. L. (2020). Fraud detection: A systematic literature review of graph-based anomaly detection approaches. *Decision Support Systems*, 133, 113303. 10.1016/j.dss.2020.113303

Power, M. (2021). Modelling the micro-foundations of the audit society: Organizations and the logic of the audit trail. *Academy of Management Review*, 46(1), 6–32. 10.5465/amr.2017.0212

Raj, S. B. E., & Portia, A. A. (2011, March). Analysis on credit card fraud detection methods. In *2011 International Conference on Computer, Communication and Electrical Technology* (ICCCET) (pp. 152-156). IEEE.

Rasanayagam, J. (2011). Informal economy, informal state: The case of Uzbekistan. *The International Journal of Sociology and Social Policy*, 31(11/12), 681–696. 10.1108/01443331111177878

Reid, A. S. (2018). Financial crime in the twenty-first century: the rise of the virtual collar criminal. In *White Collar Crime and Risk* (pp. 231–251). Palgrave Macmillan. 10.1057/978-1-137-47384-4_9

Sakyi-Nyarko, C., Ahmad, A. H., & Green, C. J. (2022). The gender-differential effect of financial inclusion on household financial resilience. *The Journal of Development Studies*, 58(4), 1–21. 10.1080/00220388.2021.2013467

Singleton, T. W., & Singleton, A. J. (2007). Why don't we detect more fraud? *Journal of Corporate Accounting & Finance*, 18(4), 7–10. 10.1002/jcaf.20302

Slemrod, J. (2007). Cheating ourselves: The economics of tax evasion. *The Journal of Economic Perspectives*, 21(1), 25–48. 10.1257/jep.21.1.25

Srivastava, S., Srivastava, G., & Bhatnagar, R. (2019, December). Analysis of process mining in audit trails of organization. In *International Conference on Information Management & Machine Intelligence* (pp. 611-618). Springer, Singapore.

Sun, G., Li, T., Ai, Y., & Li, Q. (2023). Digital finance and corporate financial fraud. *International Review of Financial Analysis*, 87, 102566. 10.1016/j.irfa.2023.102566

Tomal, A., & Johnson, L. (2008). Earnings determinants for self-employed women and men in the informal economy: The case of Bogotá, Colombia. *International Social Science Review*, 83(1/2), 71–84.

Tran, H. T. T., Le, H. T. T., Nguyen, N. T., Pham, T. T. M., & Hoang, H. T. (2022). The effect of financial inclusion on multidimensional poverty: The case of Vietnam. *Cogent Economics & Finance*, 10(1), 2132643. 10.1080/23322039.2022.2132643

Wang, L., Wang, Y., Sun, Y., Han, K., & Chen, Y. (2022). Financial inclusion and green economic efficiency: Evidence from China. *Journal of Environmental Planning and Management*, 65(2), 240–271. 10.1080/09640568.2021.1881459

Wang, R., & Luo, H. R. (2022). How does financial inclusion affect bank stability in emerging economies? *Emerging Markets Review*, 51, 100876. 10.1016/j.ememar.2021.100876

West, J., & Bhattacharya, M. (2016). Intelligent financial fraud detection: A comprehensive review. *Computers & Security*, 57, 47–66. 10.1016/j.cose.2015.09.005

Yang, X., Huang, Y., & Gao, M. (2022). Can digital financial inclusion promote female entrepreneurship? Evidence and mechanisms. *The North American Journal of Economics and Finance*, 63, 101800. 10.1016/j.najef.2022.101800

Younas, Z. I., Qureshi, A., & Al-Faryan, M. A. S. (2022). Financial inclusion, the shadow economy and economic growth in developing economies. *Structural Change and Economic Dynamics*, 62, 613–621. 10.1016/j.strueco.2022.03.011

Zakaria, P. (2023). Financial Inclusion to Digital Finance Risks: A Commentary on Financial Crimes, Money Laundering, and Fraud. In *Financial Technologies and DeFi: A Revisit to the Digital Finance Revolution* (pp. 123–130). Springer International Publishing. 10.1007/978-3-031-17998-3_9

Chapter 2
Automated Wealth Management:
Exploring the Evolution and Impact of Robo-Advisors in Finance

Mani Tyagi
https://orcid.org/0000-0002-6469-7041
Manav Rachna International Institute of Research and Studies, India

Kirti Khanna
https://orcid.org/0000-0002-0093-9451
Manav Rachna International Institute of Research and Studies, India

ABSTRACT

This paper presents a comprehensive investigation into the transformative landscape of wealth management through the lens of robo-advisors. The evolution of automated wealth management strategies is examined, tracing the historical trajectory from inception to technological advancements. A comparative analysis of traditional wealth management practices and robo-advisor-driven approaches is conducted, assessing their efficacy, performance, and risk management capabilities. Furthermore, this research explores the market adoption rates, demographic trends, and geographical variances in the utilization of robo-advisors, shedding light on the factors influencing their widespread acceptance. Technological innovations such as artificial intelligence, machine learning algorithms, and predictive analytics are scrutinized for their pivotal This comprehensive exploration provides a foundational understanding of the evolution, impact, and implications of robo-advisors in finance, offering insights that contribute to the ongoing dialogue on the future of wealth management.

DOI: 10.4018/979-8-3693-3633-5.ch002

1. INTRODUCTION

In recent years, the financial landscape has witnessed a transformative shift with the advent and proliferation of robo-advisors—automated systems designed to assist in wealth management and investment decisions. These digital platforms, driven by sophisticated algorithms and technological advancements, have reshaped traditional paradigms of financial planning, offering streamlined and accessible solutions to investors of varying backgrounds and portfolios.

The emergence of robo-advisors marks a pivotal moment in the evolution of wealth management practices. A robot advisor is a type of fintech that boosts the presence of an investment advisor in the financial markets (Chong, D., 2017). This paper seeks to explore the profound impact and evolutionary trajectory of these automated systems within the realm of finance. By examining their historical roots, technological underpinnings, market adoption, regulatory frameworks, and their implications for both financial institutions and individual investors, this research aims to provide a comprehensive understanding of the role and significance of robo-advisors in contemporary finance.

AI has moved from simple rule-based systems to complex data-driven systems (Tyagi & et al, 2022). The evolution of financial technology (FinTech) has propelled the development of robo-advisors, enabling these systems to leverage artificial intelligence (AI), machine learning algorithms, and predictive analytics to offer personalized investment strategies and portfolio management. Such advancements have not only democratized access to wealth management tools but also raised pertinent questions about the efficiency, risks, and ethical considerations surrounding these automated systems.

Furthermore, as robo-advisors continue to gain traction across diverse demographics and geographic regions, exploring the factors influencing their adoption and assessing their comparative effectiveness against traditional wealth management strategies becomes imperative. This paper endeavours to delve into these facets, elucidating the opportunities and challenges presented by robo-advisors and forecasting potential trajectories for their future integration within financial landscapes.

By illuminating the evolution and impact of robo-advisors in finance, this research aims to contribute to the ongoing discourse surrounding automated wealth management strategies, providing insights that aid in comprehending their role in shaping the financial future.

This introduction outlines the context, significance, and overarching themes your paper aims to explore regarding automated wealth management through robo-advisors in finance.

a. Historical Evolution of Wealth Management:-

The historical evolution of wealth management is an intricate journey that has transformed significantly over time. Wealth management traces back to ancient civilizations, where affluent individuals employed advisors or stewards to manage their wealth, often in the form of land, livestock, or commodities. These advisors handled investments, estates, and financial affairs. The concept evolved during the Renaissance when banking emerged, allowing individuals to store wealth and seek financial advice. Merchant banking and private banks catered to wealthy clients, offering investment advice and facilitating trade. The 18th and 19th centuries witnessed the Industrial Revolution, leading to the accumulation of significant wealth. Investment banks, stock exchanges, and modern financial systems began to take shape, shifting the focus from land and commodities to stocks, bonds, and securities. Wealth management expanded rapidly in the 20th century, becoming more formalized. The Great Depression in the 1930s prompted the establishment of regulations and agencies like the SEC, laying the groundwork for modern investment regulations.

The latter part of the 20th century saw technological advancements, leading to the emergence of mutual funds, hedge funds, and pension funds. The advent of computers brought about a shift in investment strategies, introducing quantitative analysis and algorithm-based decision-making. The early 2000s witnessed the advent of robo-advisors, a disruptive force in wealth management. These automated platforms leverage algorithms and technology to offer low-cost, accessible investment solutions, democratizing wealth management for a broader audience.

Throughout this evolution, wealth management has shifted from an exclusive service accessible to the ultra-rich to a more democratized industry catering to a wider range of investors. Robo-advisors represent the latest chapter in this history, challenging traditional models by offering algorithm-driven, low-cost investment management services to the masses.

b. Ethical implications of robo advisor

The demand for financial guidance and the high expense of hiring human advisors to provide it led to the development of robot advisors (Fisch, J. et al., 2019). The integration of robo-advisors in finance introduces several ethical considerations that warrant attention. Robo-advisors rely on algorithms to make investment decisions. Ensuring transparency regarding how these algorithms function, the criteria used for recommendations, and the underlying assumptions is crucial. Investors should understand the limitations and risks associated with automated advice.

Robo-advisors aim to provide objective advice based on algorithms, ensuring that they act in the best interest of clients (fiduciary duty) is vital. There could be concerns regarding conflicts of interest in the algorithms' recommendations, favoring certain financial products or providers. Robo-advisors gather and process substantial amounts of sensitive financial data. Ensuring robust data protection measures to safeguard client information from breaches or misuse is imperative to maintain trust and confidentiality. Algorithms used in robo-advisors might inadvertently incorporate biases present in historical data, leading to unfair or discriminatory outcomes. Ensuring these algorithms are regularly audited for biases and ensuring fairness across diverse demographics is crucial.

Despite being automated, having human oversight and accountability for the decisions made by robo-advisors is essential. This includes accountability for errors, malfunctions, or unexpected market behavior that the algorithms may not anticipate. Investors might rely solely on robo-advisor recommendations without fully comprehending the underlying investment strategies. Educating users about the limitations, risks, and benefits of automated advice is crucial to prevent over-reliance and misplaced trust. As robo-advisors operate within the financial industry, adhering to existing regulations and staying updated with evolving regulatory frameworks is essential. Compliance with standards ensuring investor protection, suitability, and fair practices is crucial.

Addressing these ethical considerations requires collaboration between regulators, industry stakeholders, and technology developers to establish guidelines, ensure transparency, and maintain ethical standards in the implementation and operation of robo-advisors in wealth management.

2. REVIEW OF LITERATURE

Robo-advisors, a product of the ever-evolving financial technology landscape, have garnered significant attention in recent academic discourse and industry reports. Studies by Tokic, D. et al. (2018) and Rossi, A. G., & Utkus (2020) highlight the emergence and rapid evolution of robo-advisors, emphasizing their role in democratizing investment access and disrupting traditional wealth management practices.

The technological underpinnings of robo-advisors have been extensively explored. Research by Méndez et al. (2019) discusses the integration of artificial intelligence and machine learning algorithms, elucidating how these technologies drive personalized investment strategies and portfolio optimization. Additionally, Zhang et al. (2021) delve into predictive analytics and its implications in augmenting decision-making processes within robo-advisor platforms.

Market adoption rates and user preferences have been focal points in numerous studies. Research conducted by Linnainmaa (2020) and Yang et al. (2016) analyze the demographic trends and factors influencing the adoption of robo-advisors among various investor segments. They identify cost-effectiveness, ease of use, and customization as pivotal factors driving user engagement and satisfaction.

Regulatory frameworks governing robo-advisors have also been scrutinized. Gupta et al. (2019) and Hossain et al. (2019) examine the legal and ethical considerations surrounding automated wealth management, highlighting compliance challenges, potential risks, and the need for robust regulatory oversight to safeguard investor interests.

Furthermore, comparative analyses conducted by Cheng (2021) and Lee (2017) contrast the performance and risk management capabilities of robo-advisors with traditional wealth management strategies. These studies offer insights into the strengths and limitations of automated approaches, shedding light on their efficacy in different market conditions.

While existing literature provides a foundational understanding of robo-advisors and their impact on finance, areas remain for further exploration. This paper aims to contribute to this body of knowledge by comprehensively examining the evolution, implications, and future trajectories of automated wealth management facilitated by robo-advisors.

This review synthesizes findings from various studies, identifying key themes such as technological advancements, market adoption, regulatory considerations, and comparative analyses. It serves as a starting point for your paper, providing a framework to build upon and further explore these themes in the context of automated wealth management through robo-advisors in finance.

3. RESEARCH OBJECTIVE AND METHODOLOGY

The aim of the study is to trace the historical development of robo-advisors, exploring their inception, technological advancements, and the evolution of their role in wealth management. This research is an exploratory study, considering the new marvel Robo Advisor. There is little research available on robo-advisory services in finance. Secondary data was collected to achieve the objective of this study. According to Abraham et al. (2019), Digital services known as "robo-advisors" use artificial intelligence (AI) to create and manage user portfolios automatically. They are designed to be an affordable alternative to conventional human consultants. Since their inception as FinTech companies following the global financial crisis, robo-advisors have become more established in the financial services sector, especially with the entry of more conventional financial institutions into the robo-advisory space.

4. DISCUSSION AND CONCLUSION

The emergence and rapid evolution of robo-advisors have fundamentally transformed the landscape of wealth management within the financial industry. This research aimed to comprehensively explore the multifaceted aspects of automated wealth management facilitated by robo-advisors, shedding light on their evolution, impact, and implications for various stakeholders. In this competitive business era, the leaders need to have all type of skills to set good example of leadership and decision maker. Their ability to judge the real time situation in most effective manner enables them to take strong successive decisions (Khanna, K. & Sharma, V., 2023).

The historical journey of robo-advisors, from their nascent stages to the sophisticated automated systems of today, underscores their pivotal role in democratizing investment access and redefining traditional wealth management paradigms (Fig 1). Technological advancements in artificial intelligence, machine learning algorithms, and predictive analytics have empowered these systems to offer personalized investment strategies, optimizing portfolio management and risk mitigation strategies.

Figure 1. Studies reflecting the development of AI in finance

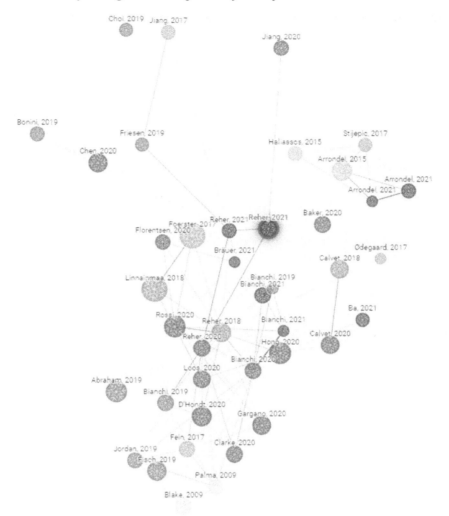

Robo-advisors have transformed the wealth management market by democratizing access to sophisticated financial services. These digital platforms use cutting-edge technology to automate and optimize many parts of investment management, providing a variety of benefits to both novice and experienced investors. One of the critical benefits of robo-advisors is their accessibility. They cater to investors with varied portfolio sizes using algorithms and automated processes, making wealth management services available to a broader clientele. This inclusivity provides financial and professional advice to individuals who may have previously been excluded due to high entrance hurdles. Market adoption trends and demographic analyses revealed the diverse factors influencing the acceptance of robo-advisors among different investor segments. In its essence, green finance denotes financially sustainable and socially responsible investments (Sharma, V. & et al., 2023).

However, while the promise of robo-advisors in enhancing accessibility and efficiency in wealth management is evident, regulatory and ethical considerations remain paramount. The complex regulatory landscape governing automated wealth management demands robust frameworks to ensure compliance, protect investors, and mitigate potential risks associated with algorithmic decision-making. Another distinguishing feature of robo-advisors is their cost-effectiveness. Using low-cost investment vehicles such as exchange-traded funds (ETFs) and automating processes, these platforms usually charge lower fees than traditional financial advisors. This cost-effectiveness puts professional wealth management services within the reach of a broader range of investors.

Looking ahead, the future trajectory of automated wealth management through robo-advisors appears promising yet nuanced. Anticipated advancements in technology, regulatory adaptations, and evolving investor preferences are poised to shape the continued integration and evolution of these systems within financial landscapes.

In conclusion, this research underscores the transformative impact of robo-advisors in reshaping wealth management practices. The insights gleaned from this exploration contribute to the ongoing dialogue on the future of finance, emphasizing the need for a balanced approach that harnesses technological innovation while preserving ethical considerations and human expertise in pursuing optimal financial outcomes. Robo-advisors have made financial management more accessible, less expensive, and more customized. Their incorporation of cutting-edge technology simplifies investing procedures and gives investors the confidence and ease to negotiate the intricacies of the financial markets.

REFERENCES

Abraham, F. (2019). *Robo-advisors: Investing through machines.* World Bank Research and Policy Briefs 134881.

Cheng, Y. M. (2021). Will robo-advisors continue? Roles of task-technology fit, network externalities, gratifications, and flow experience in facilitating continuance intention. *Kybernetes*, 50(6), 1751–1783. 10.1108/K-03-2020-0185

Chong, D. (2017). *All Faculty Scholarship.*, 3120. 10.1093/oso/9780198845553.003.0002

Gupta, K. P., Manrai, R., & Goel, U. (2019). Factors influencing adoption of payments banks by Indian customers: Extending TAUT with perceived credibility. *Journal of Asia Business Studies*, 13(2), 173–195. 10.1108/JABS-07-2017-0111

Hossain, A., Quaresma, R., & Rahman, H. (2019). Investigating factors influencing the physicians' adoption of electronic health record (EHR) in the healthcare system of Bangladesh: An empirical study. *International Journal of Information Management*, 44(1), 76–87. https://www.researchgate.net/publication/351019909_Ethics_on_Robo-advisors_and_its_big_data_Introduction_and_background. 10.1016/j.ijinfomgt.2018.09.016

Khanna, K., & Sharma, V. (2024). Business Decision Making with an Analytical Approach: A New Leadership Pattern. In Taneja, S., Ozen, E., Kumar, P., & Kumar, S. (Eds.), *Global Financial Analytics and Business Forecasting.* Nova. 10.52305/NART0833

Linnainmaa, J. T., Melzer, B. T., & Previtero, A. (2020). The misguided beliefs of financial advisors. *The Journal of Finance*, 76(2), 587–621. 10.1111/jofi.12995

Méndez, S., Mariano, F., García, F., & Fernando, G. (2019). Artificial intelligence modeling framework for financial automated advising in the copper market. *Journal of Open Innovation*, 5(4), 81. https://s-space.snu.ac.kr/bitstream/10371/150835/1/000000154956.pdf. 10.3390/joitmc5040081

Rossi, A. G., & Utkus, S. P. (2020). *The needs and wants in financial advice: Human versus robo-advising.* 10.2139/ssrn.3759041

Sharma, V., Taneja, S., Jangir, K., & Khanna, K. (2023). Green Finance- An Integral Pathway to Achieving Sustainable Development. In Taneja, S., Ozen, E., & Kumar, P. (Eds.), *Sustainable Investment in Green Finance. IGI Global Publishers (Nov. 2023)* (pp. 49–63)., Retrieved from https://www.igi-global.com/chapter/green-finance/33397210.4018/979-8-3693-1388-6.ch003

Tokic, D. (2018). BlackRock robo-advisor 4.0: When artificial intelligence replaces human discretion. *Strategic Change*, 27(4), 285–290. 10.1002/jsc.2201

Tyagi, M., Ranjan, S., & Gupta, A. (2022). Transforming Education System through Artificial Intelligence and Machine Learning. *3rd International Conference on Intelligent Engineering and Management (ICIEM)*. IEEE. 10.1109/ICIEM54221.2022.9853195

Yang, S. H., Hwang, Y. S., & Park, J. L. (2016). A study on using fintech payment services based on the UTAUT model. *Journal of Vocational Rehabilitation*, (3), 183–209.

Zhang, L., Pentina, I., & Fan, Y. (2021). Who do you choose? Comparing perceptions of human vs robo-advisor in the context of financial services. *Journal of Services Marketing*, 35(5), 628–640. 10.1108/JSM-05-2020-0162

Chapter 3
An Empirical Study on Awareness of Ponzi Schemes in India

Jagruti Patni
School of Behavioural Sciences and Forensic Investigations, Rashtriya Raksha University, India

Naveen Kumar Singh
https://orcid.org/0000-0001-7133-900X
School of Behavioural Sciences and Forensic Investigations, Rashtriya Raksha University, India & INTI International University, Malaysia

ABSTRACT

The given point of view on how Indians perceive and relate to Ponzi is taken up for consideration. The rather classic sampling model employed in the study is alarming as it shows that despite the information imbalance between the urban and village areas, there are huge knowledge gaps left in the villages. The survey showcases a scary picture—Indian people are highly attracted to this preposterous rhetoric and speculative investments that underutilize financial rationality. The research points out that celebrity endorsement is a major issue requiring immediate legal action. Scapegoating public figures who had the audacity to lend their dignity to Ponzi schemes means that the public is more trusting of the unknown, the never-heard-of-before enterprises. A highly valuable conclusory statement was developed, which formed the basis for the development of a blueprint for improving public education and financial literacy initiatives. Using this, Indians are allowed to avoid that narrow bridge, which often leads to the drainage of their savings through the wrong investment schemes.

DOI: 10.4018/979-8-3693-3633-5.ch003

INTRODUCTION

Ponzi schemes have grown to be a significant financial danger in India, affecting people from all socioeconomic backgrounds. Along with other financial frauds, Ponzi schemes is one that has been on the rise in India recently (Bhadra and Singh, 2023; Madhavan and Kalabaskar, 2023). Investors are drawn into a web of deceit with the promise of quick and lucrative returns, which leaves them open to significant financial losses (Lee and Keathley, 2022). A victim of such Ponzi scheme loses their job, their financial condition becomes unstable which impacts their general well-being. (Wang et al., 2023). Therefore, it is crucial to discover awareness gaps on Ponzi schemes among ordinary investors to develop regulations to protect them and decrease the impact of these schemes' detrimental consequences. Fraudsters use such loopholes to gain undue advantage and profit out of the apparent ignorance of small investors, luring them by spreading false information, among other dishonest tactics at their behest.

According to a poll conducted by Local Circles, alarming information about financial theft within India was revealed. The survey indicated that 74% of those respondents could not get their money back from their investments. In the last three years, 42% of the respondents have been a victim of some financial fraud. According to RBI data in 2021–2022, frauds worth 60,414 crore were reported. In the last seven years, these scams have cost India a distressing figure of 100 crore per day. It is important to understand that this, like many other problems, has been besetting India for quite some time now. The issue of Ponzi schemes cannot be solved by legislation alone. It is critical now, more than ever, to spread financial information and educate the masses on a massive scale. For example, any organization offering unrealistic returns should be shunned as a red flag. Alternatively, investors could consider diversifying among various financial instruments, as banks and other regulated financial institutions are only permitted to charge a maximum interest rate of 6-7% on savings accounts. However, mutual funds and equity markets have varying degrees of risk but can provide returns of up to 18% if invested diligently.

The increasing frequency of financial frauds necessitates the identification of gaps in awareness among investors in order to implement investor protection strategies. The purpose of this study is to research consumer awareness and education on Ponzi schemes, subsequently offer ways to mend these fissures among investing community. The current level of knowledge/awareness on Ponzi schemes among the Indians would be assessed from the sampled demographics like age, gender, educational background and geographical regions they belong.

LITERATURE REVIEW

According to the study of economic journalist Dr. Bindra(2020), "A staggering 2 lakh credulous investors were defrauded" clearly demonstrates the sheer number of issues and sufferings brought about by financial scams involving Ponzi schemes, unregulated deposit programs, and collective investment schemes (CIS). Over the years, India has experienced a number of fraudulent schemes that have negatively impacted the country's financial and economic stability. This essay looks at the factors that led to the increase in popularity of investment schemes like Ponzi and CIS, how these schemes have operated throughout time, and potential protections for investors' interests. Cerasoli, S., & Porporato, A. (2023) concede that many desire to become affluent with the least amount of work. Both the con artists and the purported victims of these get-rich schemes exhibit questionable morality. Ponzi schemes illustrate the ethical disparities between business and government while also offering insights into individual scams.

A large body of research studies has been carried out over the years to gain insight into the Ponzi Schemes' awareness in India. Studies shows that more than 70% of Indian investors were watchful of Ponzi schemes but still succumbed to it, which was due to the prospect of unrealistic gains (Assocham, 2021). This thereby brings to light to the fact that the governing bodies need to introduce more comprehensive investor education and protection policies.

Grover and Gupta (2020) investigated awareness of Ponzi schemes among college-going students in Punjab, India. They found people who enrolled in financial literacy programs, having a family background in finance discipline and the having personal experience in the field of investments were predictors of Ponzi schemes. It thus seems that educational initiatives will be successful in decreasing risk-taking behaviour by focusing on the susceptible young audience groups. Agarwal and Chakrabarti (2019) in the next step investigated the link between digital financial inclusion and understanding of Ponzi schemes. They identified that digital banking and investment platforms had high level of access for the youth who have undergone financial literacy trainings thereby enhancing their ability to identify such financial frauds. Raghavan and Rajendran (2019) reviewed the media coverage of Ponzi schemes in India. They concluded that news reports frequently discussed these schemes as been prevalent however they failed to capture the details which would have aided investors in making better investment decisions suggesting the necessity of media becoming an active contributor in imparting investors' awareness programmes in the future.

The regulation law of Ponzi schemes was unchecked as per Sinha and Ghosh (2016), saying that even though the government made some steps to eliminate loopholes and gaps in the system, very often, criminals were still able to find ways to defraud people using fraudulent schemes. Indian authorities advocate for stricter requirements, increased monitoring, and joint operational control among the regulators at the national level.

Dey and Mukhojee (2018) conducted another study that focused on psychological and behavioural factors that determine people who are susceptible to these Ponzi schemes. Their research pointed out obstacles like overconfidence, optimism bias, and less finance knowledge. All these economic factors that the investors had were the key contributors to their risk susceptibility. This emphasizes the importance of considering the peculiarities of cognitive biases while developing interventions. Social media had been examined before as a tool for proliferating Ponzi schemes during the times of Verma and Sharma (2017). However, their data showed that many brands used the internet to impersonate trusted web sources and social media influencers to accomplish their deceptive aim. They also spoke about the need to boost digital financial literacy and stricter rules on investment promotion over social networks.

Building on individual awareness, however, Chatterjee and Bose (2016) sought to understand how institutions in India handle Ponzi schemes. They observed that regulatory entities like SEBI, has taken steps to control these frauds as well; lack of resources, coordination, and specific skills to deal with this kind of fraud are, however, the major hurdles. Along the same line, Rao and Menon (2015) delineated the case-specific problems faced by law enforcement labs in cracking such escapades. They demonstrated that there is a need for extensive training, better investigative tools, and a high degree of cooperation between law enforcement agencies at a regional level to be able to fight financial crime efficiently.

Choudhury and Dasgupta (2014) analysed what features of society and economy lead to the birth of Ponzi schemes in India. They realized that lack of financial inclusion and the absence of formal financial services in mostly rural and semi-urban areas are some of the fundamental reasons why many do not engage in financial activities beyond basic subsistence. A significant point made by the authors is need of a system which promotes financial inclusivity to mitigate this problem.

From the point of view of journal writer Basu, K. (2016) in Markets and Manipulation, he mentioned that anyone who saw the Madoff scandal is undoubtedly of the opinion that elaborate frauds such as Ponzi schemes exist. The basic premise of Ponzi schemes is that a con artist takes money from new investors to pay interest to previous ones rather than employing investor funds to launch a profitable business enterprise. However, economists are beginning to recognize that when one assumption feeds into another, it can also happen naturally, even by accident, resulting in a speculative frenzy and an economy that grows but eventually collapses. Experts in behavioural economics and finance believe that Ponzi-like activities are closely linked to fluctuations in the world's financial markets. This holds true whether or not one considers the markets to be natural phenomena, like moon eclipses or ocean tides. In the study on "How can financial literacy reduce the risk of participation in a Ponzi scheme" by Sharma and Khurana (2013) affirmed this fact by proving that those with money knowledge showed themselves to be least affected by fraudulent schemes. This, therefore, should fuel the process of coming up with intensive financial literacy programs that should focus on both the urban and the rural inhabitants. Through these studies, Bose and Mukerji (2012) evaluated investor awareness campaigns carried out by different agencies that can help restore investor confidence, such as regulatory bodies as well as non-governmental organizations (NGOs). They identified that these projects brought a positive change with regard to Kiambi and other members of the community, acknowledging that it was a Ponzi scheme. However, their reach and sustainability still remain limited.

Last but not least, Gupta and Sharma's (2011) research involved a comparative study of the Ponzi scheme's awareness and regulatory framework spanning across many states in India. The research results demonstrated that the incorporation of the nation-wide concerted efforts will help close down the gaps based on geography. They aim to induce a strong integration perspective, including a national action plan to fight Ponzi schemes and shield investors from vulnerabilities.

Several research papers were gathered from various databases for the literature review. Using the advanced search option, the research paper was found using keywords like "Ponzi schemes" and "awareness." For accurate, current information and to expedite this investigation, research publications from the years 2000–2024 were chosen. Considering the literature, enhancement is urgently required, with a particular emphasis on data analysis connected to financial management literacy. It's critical to comprehend the mind set of people who make financial decisions to protect themselves from fraud. We can shield people against fraud and give them the information they need to deal with difficult financial circumstances by raising people's financial literacy. Hence, the objective of this study is to examine Indian people's awareness of Ponzi schemes and to recommend that stakeholders safeguard their finances. Generally, research says that the awareness of Ponzi schemes is low in the Indian market. However, the authorities have to double their efforts to provide ordinary investors with basic financial education so as to help them make right decision while choosing investment avenues. This holistic financial education approach could help in tightening regulations, improved monitoring, help investors detect fraudulent acts and report them to the concerned authorities. Collective and coordinated efforts between government, media, and financial institutions is the fundamental ingredient that could significantly help us dealing with this chronic problem.

An Empirical Study on Awareness of Ponzi Schemes in India

Research Design

Ponzi schemes have been one of the persistent issues in India resulting in honest investors losing their hard-earned money. The research is based on the descriptive research design of the study, involving the particular use of quantitative methods for the simultaneous collection of accurate and detailed information. The quantitative method involves conducting a state-wide survey, collecting responses from a large representative sample of individuals from geographically distributed areas and groups differing in their educational levels, social statuses, and age groups. The questionnaire will encompass the questions that have been specifically developed to evaluate the participants' proficiency in identifying warning signs along with their percentage of readiness for the prevention of Ponzi scheme fraud.

Sampling Strategy

Diversified individual group populations dispersed all over India will be materialized in our data collection process through an applied approach. This contributes to the chance of getting the findings, if not totally; at least, it will give a picture of the different campus populations. The study looks at the people living in different urban and rural pockets of the country. Here, we will mention various strata of society, including young and old people with different levels of education and income bracket, many among them who are engaged in various jobs. For our research, we have used convenient sampling. For instance, the people may have various groups in the traditional setup, such as those being separated based on age: 18-30, 30-40, 40-50 over 50, education level: less than high school and high school, graduated and postgraduate, and income group: low, lower - middle, upper – middle and high.

Data Analyses and Interpretation

The scope of the study was to discover the level of awareness of Ponzi schemes in India by determining the responses of 61 individuals as samples. The data collected spanned a range of things, such as gender, age, education, work, etc.

Table 1. Descriptive analysis (Source: SPSS v26 Output)

Construct	Parameter	No. of Response	Percentage
Gender	Male	28	45.9
	Female	33	54.1
Age	18 - 30 yrs	50	82

continued on following page

Table 1. Continued

Construct	Parameter	No. of Response	Percentage
	30 - 40 yrs	8	13.1
	40 - 50 yrs	3	4.9
	Above 50 yrs	0	0
Occupation	Business Person	5	8.2
	Employee	9	14.8
	Retired	1	1.6
	Student	45	73.8
	Unemployed	1	1.6
Location	Andhra Pradesh	3	4.9
	Assam	1	1.6
	Bihar	1	1.6
	Chhattisgarh	1	1.6
	Delhi (National	1	1.6
	Goa	1	1.6
	Gujarat	32	52.5
	Karnataka	1	1.6
	Kerala	6	9.8
	Maharashtra	1	1.6
	Manipur	2	3.3
	Puducherry	1	1.6
	Punjab	1	1.6
	Rajasthan	1	1.6
	Tamil Nadu	1	1.6
	Telangana	1	1.6
	West Bengal	6	9.8
Total		61	100.00

Based on Table 1, here are some additional points for data analysis on awareness about Ponzi schemes across Indian states: Gujarat stands out from the rest of the states with a population of 32 responses, whereas the other states depict the response scale of not more than 20 per state as depicted the table. This is probably the case of a high-profile Ponzi scheme investment.

This shows that the respondents belonging to different categories of gender are present. Among 61 participants, 28(45.9%) said they were males, and 33 (54.1%) responded that they were females. This distribution states that females have a slightly higher rate of participation in the study group, which could indicate that women have a higher interest or concern level about Ponzi schemes.

An Empirical Study on Awareness of Ponzi Schemes in India

Analysis of the sample of participants of different ages shows that there is almost no ambivalent pattern, but most of them are from younger age groups. Talking about the specifics, 50 respondents (82%) ranged from 18 to 30 years old, followed by 8 respondents (13.1%) who were in the age group of 30-40, and 3 respondents (4.9%) were found in the category of age group over 40. A considerable piece of information shows that no response was recorded for people 50 years and above. Demographic analysis shows that the younger population may have a higher level of awareness regarding Ponzi schemes. A range of issues could be involved here like better affordability and/or access to financial or other services, financial education among youths, or the prevalence of fraudulent schemes aimed at specific age groups. As per the data, the great majority of students' 45 (73.8%) familiarity may be used to underline the conclusion that the students are more aware of this issue in general. At the top of the list, there are conclusions that the 9 respondents (14.8%) who are deprived of jobs are involved in Ponzi schemes. However, for those who could achieve permanent employment, missing are not only the 5 business persons (8.2%), who have the only unrevealed percentage share, but also the 1 retired respondent (1.6%). By so doing, these classifications might show that television programs was preferred a lesser proportion of people. There is 1 unemployed respondent (1.6%) also involved in this issue.

Figure 1. Count of understanding of the Ponzi scheme concept

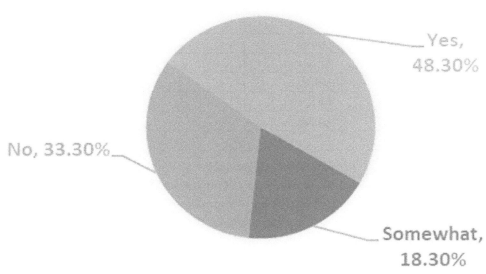

(Source: MS Excel 2019 Output)

An Empirical Study on Awareness of Ponzi Schemes in India

Fig 1 shows that a significant portion of the population (around 46.7%) understands the concept of Ponzi schemes and their functionality, as shown in this image. However, a considerable percentage (33.3%) still do not understand this concept.

Figure 2. Count of familiarity with the term Ponzi scheme

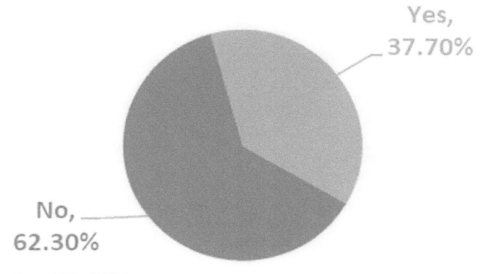

(Source: MS Excel 2019 Output)

Fig 2 indicates that a majority (62.3%) have not heard of the term "Ponzi" before, while only 37.7% have heard of it. This suggests a lack of widespread awareness about this specific terminology.

Figure 3. Number of victims of the Ponzi scheme

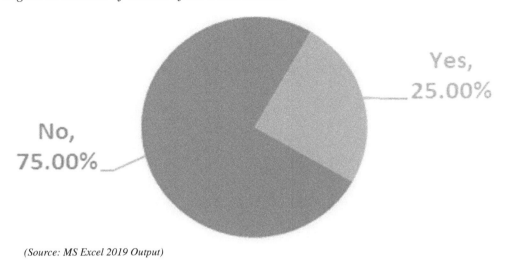

(Source: MS Excel 2019 Output)

Fig 3, a substantial majority (75.9%) have not been victims of a Ponzi scheme themselves, which is a positive sign. However, a notable minority (24.1%) have fallen victim to such fraudulent schemes.

Figure 4. Awareness of red flags of fraudulent Ponzi scheme

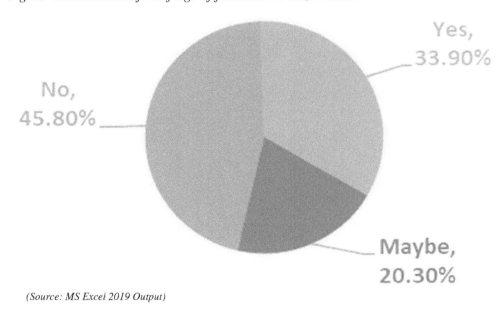

(Source: MS Excel 2019 Output)

Fig 4, we can see that while a significant portion (45.8%) are not aware of any red flags associated with Ponzi schemes, a considerable percentage (33.9%) are aware of these warning signs. Additionally, 20.3% are uncertain about their awareness of red flags.

Figure 5. Reporting of the fraud schemes

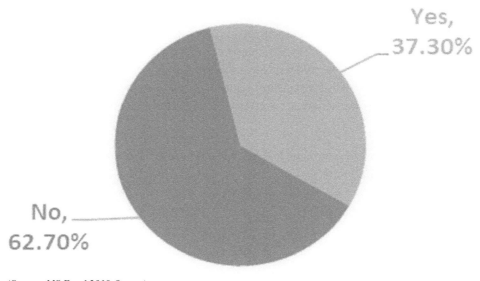

(Source: MS Excel 2019 Output)

Figure 5 reveals that only 37.3% of the population know how to report a Ponzi scheme fraud, while a larger percentage (62.7%) do not know the proper reporting channels.

Overall, these pie charts suggest that while there is some level of awareness about Ponzi schemes among the population, there is also a significant lack of knowledge and understanding about the specifics, red flags, and reporting mechanisms related to these fraudulent schemes. This highlights the need for further education and awareness campaigns to protect individuals from becoming victims of such financial fraud.

Table 2. Cross-tabulation of age category and reporting of fraud (Source: SPSS v26 Output)

		Have you reported a suspected Ponzi scheme to the relevant authorities?			
			No	Yes	Total
Age	18 - 30 yrs	4	35	11	50
	30 - 40 yrs	0	4	4	8
	40 - 50 yrs	0	2	1	3
Total		4	41	16	61

Table 2 depicts that a high percentage of respondents in the 18-30 years age group have not reported a suspected Ponzi scheme which suggests that younger individuals may not be properly aware of detecting and reporting potential fraudulent activities. This could be valuable information for authorities and regulators in understanding the dynamics of Ponzi scheme reporting and target their efforts accordingly.

Table 3. Cross-tabulation of age category and availability of educational resources (Source: SPSS v26 Output)

		Do you believe enough educational resources are available to help individuals identify Ponzi schemes in India?			
			No	Yes	Total
	18 - 30 yrs	1	28	21	50
	30 - 40 yrs	0	5	3	8
	40 - 50 yrs	0	1	2	3
Total		1	34	26	61

Above data shows the count of respondents across age groups (18-30 years, 30-40 years, and 40-50 years) and their belief on whether enough educational resources are available to identify Ponzi schemes in India (No or Yes).

The high proportion of respondents in the 18-30 years age group who believe there are not enough educational resources suggests that younger individuals may be more conscious of the need for improved financial literacy to help identify and prevent Ponzi schemes.

Table 4. Cross-tabulation of age category and checking the legitimacy of the scheme (Source: SPSS v26 Output)

		Have you ever checked the legitimacy of a Ponzi scheme before investing in it?			
		No	Sometimes	Yes	Total
	18 - 30 yrs	3	26	6	15	50
	30 - 40 yrs	0	5	1	2	8
	40 - 50 yrs	0	0	2	1	3
Total		3	31	9	18	61

Here, most respondents (31 out of 61, or 50.8%) haven't checked the legitimacy of a Ponzi scheme before investing in it. Among the age groups, the 18-30 years age group had the highest number of respondents who never checked the legitimacy of a Ponzi scheme (26 out of 31, of all respondents who never checked).

On the basis of Table 4, we can conclude that the people of India do not check the legitimacy of investment schemes. This is evident from the proportion of the respondents, especially those in the younger age group, who confirm investment in such schemes as a habit and also reveal a fairly noticeable number who do not. This goes a long way in shedding more light on the importance of having strong training programs, which will enable people to acquire the necessary information and skills to exercise their own vigilance and likely escape from being duped into Ponzi schemes. Through the development of a financial literacy culture and encouragement of critical thinking, people can take a better look at the compensated practices and build themselves up for the right actions and not fall victim to the scam.

DISCUSSION AND RESEARCH IMPLICATION

By investigating the level of awareness and understanding of Ponzi schemes among the samples collected from Indian population, this research aims to contribute to the following areas:
1. Exploring the literature on Ponzi schemes and financial fraud, developing body of knowledge, particularly in the Indian context, due to lack of research in this area.
2. Offering empirical data and information to could be utilized in future research about different types of fraud people are prone to committing and psychological factors that persuade them to engage in such deceptive acts.
3. Proposing theoretical guidelines for comprehending patterns of Ponzi-scribed phenomenal studies and devising the counteractive measures.
4. Identifying the weak spots and problematic areas in the current school educational curriculum and targeted information campaigns so that the new tactics can be built for the better familiarity about Ponzi schemes.

5. Providing regulatory authorities and law enforcement agencies with the techniques which could be used while monitoring the activities of various stakeholders. Moreover, consumer protection organizations could also benefit from the insights regarding the perspectives and experiences of these stakeholders.
6. Improving the monitoring capacities of the financial system's participants, such as banks, investment companies, and fund managers, by providing those tools for the detection of suspicious signs and making them responsible for the protection of their clients from financial fraud schemes.
7. Making available fact-and-reason-based recommendations with doable implementation instructions to officials and regulatory agencies for reinforcement of legal basis, rigors of law enforcement, and investor's protection acts against Ponzi schemes.
8. Providing adequate reference actions and plans in areas of financial literacy and consumer education programs with a specific focus on regions or groups with low awareness levels. Participating in building the basis for the creation of efficient public campaigns for raising the level of awareness and programs, which are devoted to the target population of Indian society and its unique traits.
9. Ultimately, the data from this research represents a crucial step in minimizing the risks to financial systems and negative occurrences aroused by Ponzi schemes.

Recommendations and Limitations

Educational Campaign

The Ministry of Finance, jointly with the SEBI and the RBI, should be given the lead in day-to-day coordination for a national campaign sharing information about the need for an economic nation since that is the goal. The campaign should focus on educating the entire public; they will be enlightened with the features of Ponzi schemes, tricks, and the idea of financial banter. The Ministry of Education must, therefore, introduce a compulsory financial literacy course within the school and college curriculum, which should cover introductory topics on investment, risk assessment, and the early detection of fraudulent behaviour.

Regulatory Reinforcement

Both SEBI and RBI can strengthen the current regulatory system and enforcement systems to make sure that they are more robust and thorough when inspecting the practices of all investment firms and their financial activity. The regulatory authorities need to create a framework in which the proper vetting of investment offers and the timely containing of any suspicious behaviours are performed seamlessly.

Investor Safeguards

The Ministry of Corporate Affairs is to develop the necessary investor protections such as whistle-blower policies, independent audit framework, and compensation mechanisms to cover the damages a victim of a Ponzi scheme may suffer. These should be measures that would rather enable those people and organizations to report any possible cases of fraudulent activities; additionally, they should give them support from authorities.

Coordination and Collaboration

The Ministry of Finance, simultaneously working with law enforcement and international bodies, should enhance mechanisms of coordination and information sharing to assist in the cessation of effective crossed-border Ponzi schemes. This cooperation will be centered on pinpointing and closely monitoring Ponzi scheme partners, as well as transferring experiences and measures for preventing and solving cases.

Evaluation and Improvement

Finance Minister together with SEBI and other relevant agencies, should undertake to conduct a thorough research to assess the adequacy of the ongoing awareness creation process. In conclusion, from the results, the regulatory body should have new designs of strategies and initiatives to cover any punctures or drawbacks in the existing anti-Ponzi scheme fraud programs.

The gathered data embodies the attitudes and perceptions of the repliers that might have varied from their own experiences, preconceptions, or their level of awareness about Ponzi schemes. The selected sample, and also the respondents' geographic distribution, could not be so generalized as a reflection of the Indian population in total, so this restricts the generalizability of the results. This study methodology included only a collection of responses, but it did not involve deeper surveys or revelations of the full understanding of Ponzi schemes or the true source of information.

CONCLUSION AND REMARKS

The results presented above portray the views of the sampled Indian population towards the measures to prevent and detect the Ponzi scheme fraud. Equipped with this understanding, interested parties can create focused and effective initiatives to enhance financial literacy and fortify barriers against unscrupulous financial conduct.

Responses indicate that stricter rules are a necessity; investors should be allowed to verify that investment firms' credibility; there is a need to promote financial literacy, enforce stricter penalties for violations and encourage investors to diversify their portfolios. The research, moreover, manifests the authority's deficiency in comprehending the intricacies in the process of detecting and mitigating such financial frauds.

REFERENCES

Agarwal, S., & Chakrabarti, R. (2019). Digital financial inclusion and Ponzi scheme awareness in India. *Financial Counseling and Planning*, 30(2), 279–291.

Anggriawan, R., Susila, M. E., Sung, M. H., & Irrynta, D. (2023). The Rising Tide of Financial Crime: A Ponzi Scheme Case Analysis. *Lex Scientia Law Review*, 7(1), 307–346. 10.15294/lesrev.v7i1.60004

Assocham. (2021). *Awareness about Ponzi Schemes and Pyramids in India*. Associated Chambers of Commerce and Industry of India.

Basu, K. (2018). Markets and Manipulation: Time for a Paradigm Shift? *Journal of Economic Literature*, 56(1), 185–205. 10.1257/jel.20161410

Bhadra, S., & Singh, K. N. (2023). Ponzi scheme like investment schemes in India–causes, impact and solution. *Journal of Money Laundering Control*, 27(2), 348–362. 10.1108/JMLC-02-2023-0040

Bose, S., & Mukherjee, P. (2012). Investor awareness campaigns by regulatory bodies and non-governmental organizations: Impact and implications. *IIMB Management Review*, 24(3), 139–150.

Bosley, S., & Knorr, M. (2018). Pyramids, Ponzis and fraud prevention: Lessons from a case study. *Journal of Financial Crime*, 25(1), 81–94. 10.1108/JFC-10-2016-0062

Chatterjee, C., & Bose, G. K. (2016). Institutional response to Ponzi schemes in India. *Journal of Financial Crime*, 23(1), 194–209.

Choudhury, R., & Dasgupta, R. (2014). Socioeconomic factors behind the prevalence of Ponzi schemes in India. *Journal of Financial Crime*, 21(3), 365–381.

Dey, S., & Mukherjee, A. (2018). Behavioral biases and Ponzi scheme participation: Evidence from India. *Behavioral Science*, 8(2), 19.

Goyal, A., & Kumar, S. (2020). Factors influencing Ponzi scheme awareness among college students in Punjab, India. *International Journal of Bank Marketing*, 38(5), 1165–1181.

Gupta, L., & Sharma, A. (2011). Comparative analysis of Ponzi scheme awareness and regulatory frameworks across different states in India. *Journal of Financial Regulation and Compliance*, 19(4), 387–401. 10.1108/JFRC-07-2020-0067

Hidajat, T., Primiana, I., Rahman, S., & Febrian, E. (2020). Why are people trapped in Ponzi and pyramid schemes? *Journal of Financial Crime*, 28(1), 187–203. 10.1108/JFC-05-2020-0093

Raghavan, T. S., & Rajendran, K. (2019). Media coverage of Ponzi schemes in India: An exploratory study. *Journal of Financial Crime*, 26(3), 810–824.

Raj, K., & Aithal, P. S. (2018). Digitization of India-impact on the BOP sector. [IJMTS]. *International Journal of Management, Technology, and Social Sciences*, 3(1), 59–74. 10.47992/IJMTS.2581.6012.0036

Rao, K. S., & Menon, V. (2015). Investigating and prosecuting Ponzi schemes in India: Challenges and the way forward. *Journal of Financial Crime*, 22(2), 246–259.

Sharma, E., & Khurana, N. (2013). Influence of financial literacy on investment decisions of employees. *Anvesha*, 6(2), 12–19.

Sinha, P. K., & Ghosh, A. (2016). Ponzi schemes in India: Challenges in regulation and the way forward. *IIMB Management Review*, 28(1), 30–40.

Verma, S., & Sharma, R. (2017). The role of social media in the proliferation of Ponzi schemes in India. *Journal of Financial Crime*, 24(2), 306–320.

Wang, L., Cheng, H., Zheng, Z., Yang, A., & Xu, M. (2023). Temporal transaction information-aware Ponzi scheme detection for ethereum smart contracts. *Engineering Applications of Artificial Intelligence*, 126, 107022. 10.1016/j.engappai.2023.107022

Williams, J. M., Strauch, S., & Duncan, D. (2018). *Ponzi Schemes and the Awareness of South Carolina Students to Financial Fraud*. Research Gate.

Chapter 4
Data Management in the Digital Age:
A Financial Institution Case Study

Firdous Mohd Farouk
Taylor's University, Malaysia

ABSTRACT

This chapter illustrates the data management in a large financial institution in Malaysia during a major technology implementation phase. The case organisation implemented big data analytics (BDA) as a strategic move towards better decision-making through a better understanding of market needs. The case bank was, at the time of this research being conducted, actively involved in implementing BDA through various planned activities. To begin with, the implementation of BDA was a strategic decision, and it was incorporated as a four-year plan in the bank. While there were many aspects to BDA implementation in the bank, one major aspect was data itself because the way data is used in the financial institution is subject to scrutiny. BDA enables a vast amount of data to be analysed to gain actionable insights, however, the case organisation was heavily regulated. This chapter will revolve around issues in data management and data protection in the case organisation.

INTRODUCTION

The financial services industry plays a major role in the financial-economic activity in modern economics by executing a range of functions that primarily deal with facilitating financial and monetary transactions such as deposits, loans, investments, and currency exchange. The industry has been fairly stable largely at least until the 2008 financial crisis. Since then, regaining stability and trust has been a core challenge for players within this industry. This mission has been further complicated by the rapid deployment of financial and technological innovation that disrupts the usual landscape of how business is done, nudging this mostly traditional sector to embrace digital transformation. As digital disruption is happening at an unimaginable pace, invoking the innovative capability has now become more important than ever for players in this field making innovation, business transformation and strategic change imperative (Deloitte 2019). The industry is responding by investing heavily in technology (Greer, Gareth, Mazzini, & Eiichiro, 2019) with data and analytics being the top three in the focus list (PWC 2017) and forming alliances (PWC 2016).

Financial services institutions, namely banks, generally use a highly sophisticated ensemble of information technologies in supporting their business and are characterised by high volumes of transactions that bring about immense growth in data (Eastburn and Boland 2015). One of the biggest technological advancements that is radically redesigning the financial services industry is the ongoing shift from depending on human judgement to the automated analysis of consumer data. Access to real-time information provided by "big data" and analytics (BDA) enables management to make a better-informed decision to meet customer expectations. In this age of the digital revolution, BDA has received considerable attention from practitioners and researchers in the quest for smarter business insights (Davenport et al. 2012) as it has been touted as the next frontier for innovation, competition and productivity (Manyika et al. 2011). Capitalising the use of analytical tools enables managers to make sense of large amounts of data in order to be better acquainted with their business and channel that knowledge into improved decision-making and consequently, performance (Abbasi, Sarker, & Chiang, 2016; Chen, Chiang, & Storey, 2012). However, the value-creation process, i.e. from data to enhanced performance, is very subjective and studies identify that one of the biggest barriers to realising value from data is information management and cyber security (Kache and Seuring 2017). Similarly, Dai et al. (2020) suggest more studies on data privacy and security concerns.

The business and IS literature provide varied perspectives on BDA implementation and benefits, focusing on BDA resource orchestration and outcomes (Gupta and George 2016; Wamba et al. 2017). However, the central aspect of data management in implementing BDA and the necessary organisational actions in data protection have received less theoretical attention and empirical investigation in the literature. There seems to be an implied understanding that the prescribed orchestration of resources and capabilities will lead to the realisation of BDA outcomes (Gupta and George 2016; Akter et al. 2016; Wamba et al. 2017). In contrast, recent IS studies have distinguished between the potential of BDA and the necessary actions taken by actors to achieve desired BDA outcomes (Tim et al. 2020; Dremel et al. 2020). The distinction between the potential provided by BDA and actions required to achieve outcomes has paved the way for further research that attempts to understand the value realisation process of BDA. This study aims to unpack the actions of actors within the financial services industry to manage data during the BDA implementation process. More specifically, this study aims to illustrate the efforts of data management and data protection in a large financial institution in Malaysia during BDA implementation.

METHODOLOGY

This study employed a single, in-depth case study approach due to its ability to provide causal explanations underlying the phenomena being investigated. The intensive research strategy allowed detailed examination of data management and data protection during BDA implementation within the specific context. Single case studies are well-established in top information systems (IS) journals, offering deep insights into IS usage in socially embedded contexts. According to Yin (1994), a single case study is suitable when the case represents a critical test of theory, an extreme or unique instance, a revelatory inquiry, a common everyday situation, or a longitudinal study. The study of data management during new technology implementation in the banking industry aligns with Yin's revelatory inquiry criteria, as it seeks to unpack the contextual conditions involved in the technology implementation process, making a single in-depth case study well-suited.

Case Context

The case organisation, BankX, is a leading ASEAN universal bank, one of the largest Asian investment banks, and among the world's largest Islamic banks. Headquartered in Kuala Lumpur, Malaysia, it offers consumer banking, commercial banking, wholesale banking, Islamic banking, and asset management products and services. After completing its four-year target to enhance its ASEAN presence and drive sustainable growth in 2018, BankX embarked on a new strategy to accelerate growth and future-proof itself. In the face of the fourth industrial revolution, BankX aims to be the disruptor rather than the disrupted by growing its business differently to remain relevant in the changing financial industry landscape. One of its key strategies for future-proofing is leveraging big data analytics (BDA) in every aspect of decision-making to enable a differentiated approach to providing financial services. With the core principle of enhancing customer experience, BankX strives to provide customers with simple and convenient access to financial services. In line with this mission, BankX leveraged BDA to gain a better understanding of their customers and optimize processes. They aggressively started streamlining

Data Management in the Digital Age

their activities regarding data through various measures, including upskilling staff, integrating data into a central data warehouse, and starting a sandbox incubator program. BankX made several significant changes to its operating environment and structure alongside the implementation of BDA.

Data Collection

Following case study best practices, the study commenced with a pilot study including an open-ended online survey and two interviews. The pilot results supported fine-tuning of the survey and interview guide to remove redundancies and allow probing. As BDA implementation and data management is a strategic phenomenon, study participants were senior executives, primarily C-level (Vice Presidents, Senior Vice Presidents, Assistant Vice Presidents, and departmental heads) and C-1 level managers reporting to C-level executives.

Table 1. Case database summary

Method	Data source	Purpose
Open-ended online survey	Pilot study: 3 C-level and C-1 level managers and senior executives, 1 external service provider.	Familiarisation with BDA attributes & constraints. Identify processes and routines. Support theory gleaning.
	Main study: 26 C-level and C-1 level managers and senior executives, 9 external service providers.	
Telephone interviews	1 C-level executive, 1 C-1 level executive, 1 external service provider.	Familiarisation with BDA attributes. Identify processes and routines. Support theory gleaning.
In-depth online interviews	Pilot study: 4 C-level and C-1 level executives, 2 external service providers.	Gain insight into BDA processes & constraints. Theory refinement and consolidation. Triangulation with other data sources.
	Main study: 24 C-level and C-1-level executives, 6 external service providers.	
Secondary sources	20 industry reports 18 press releases 6 Bank Negara Malaysia Guidelines 3 annual reports- 2018-20 12 newspaper reports	Triangulation and corroboration. Gain insight into corporate strategy. Identification of contextual constraints.

The survey explored BDA implementation, data usage, issues and management and business outcomes. The survey link was emailed to 50 BankX executives engaged in BDA implementation, both as users and senior operations managers. Following that, online interviews were conducted to support the development of emergent concepts. Sampling continued until data saturation was reached, and new informants produced no new information. Similar studies achieved saturation between 15 and 32 participants. Overall, the case database represents the views of a difficult-to-reach elite cadre of senior managers and technology innovation providers in a leading financial services business. Secondary sources, including industry reports, press releases, regulatory guidelines, annual reports, and newspaper reports, were used for triangulation, corroboration, gaining insight into corporate strategy, and data-related issues.

FINDINGS

The explication of the case study data revealed four major themes revolving around data management and data protection during BDA implementation in BankX, namely: regulatory oversight, data governance and architecture, compliance and risk management and data partnership and ecosystem.

Regulatory Oversight

Central Bank Guidelines

While BDA enables a vast amount of data to be analysed to gain actionable insights, the way data is used is subject to scrutiny in the banking industry as it is bound by regulation. Some of the relevant guidelines are:
1. Data Management and MIS Framework,
2. Risk Management in Technology (RMiT),
3. Management of Customer Information and Permitted Disclosure, and
4. Personal Data Protection Act 2010

The data management and MIS framework from BNM specifically lists out guiding principles on; (i) having an effective data management framework, (ii) sound data governance structure, (iii) comprehensive data and system architecture, (iv) accessing and monitoring data quality, (v) effective control over data security and privacy and (vi) MIS functions that are robust to provide timely access to critical data for decision-making, analysis and control purposes. The RMiT guidelines, also from BNM, set out banks' requirements to manage technology risks. The Management of Customer Information and Permitted Disclosure and Personal Data Protection Act 2010 guidelines generally dictate the protection of customer data and call for security controls to be in place as financial services-providing institutions handle a significant amount of customer data and information (Laws of Malaysia 2010; BNM 2017). Details on how and where data is to be used and with whom it is shared must

Data Management in the Digital Age

be specified (BNM 2017). Furthermore, approval must be obtained for its usage (BNM 2017). These guidelines exhibit that the unauthorised use of customer data and information is strictly prohibited: e.g.,

...it is very restricted to internal use and to benefit the client. It's very specific in that way. So now you see in Europe, the GDPR[1] coming in and all that they cannot just use customer information because that is not what you intended for. So this is going to be a key challenge coming up, and we see it more and more in Singapore and South Korea. (P16, Managing Director)

In line with data protection and privacy, any data used for a new product or any process in the bank needs to be approved by the central bank (BNM). One example cited by a VP in BankX is the approval needed for data usage for the cross-selling activity of the bank:

There could be many things you can use big data for, any fancy way of exploiting customer data but you are not necessarily allowed to do so because all this is new. When you need to launch a cross-selling effort using customer data, you need to seek Central Bank approval. (P20, Director- Investment Banking).

Data Residency and Cross-border Restrictions

Restrictions regarding the usage and sharing of data that contains personally identifiable information (PII) of customers cause unintentional data silos in banks. These restrictions are in place to protect customers' privacy. Besides that even data sharing between departments is restricted (BNM 2017). As a senior manager in the bank states, *"I cannot be accessing someone else's or some other department's customers. That is not allowed"* (P7, Senior Manager- Data Strategy).

Within the realms of data usage and management, the regulation within the banking industry also restricts the movement of customer data from one country to another, ensuring that customer data stays within the country of residency. Even data within the same group that operates in different countries cannot be moved across borders due to customer-sensitive information. For example, a banking group with branches in other countries cannot bring data from their overseas branches to be modelled in Malaysia:

Domestic customer data is all restrained to domestic countries. So you will not be able to sit in Malaysia and analyse your Singapore or Vietnam customer data. Each country protects their citizens and customer data on [its] shores. (P20, Director- Investment Banking)

Cloud Infrastructure Governance

BDA requires advanced infrastructure capability to enable the storage and processing of a large amount of data (Akter et al. 2016; Mikalef et al. 2019). With the increasing amount of data, the cost of on-premise storage hardware increases, and it may not accommodate the volume, velocity and variability of big data (Gandomi and Haider 2015). While it may still be possible to get large on-premises hardware for this function, it may take a long time to set it up. As such, cloud migration is an important infrastructure set-up by many companies involved in BDA endeavours, especially with the data integration efforts towards having a single data repository to synchronise data from various systems in various geographic locations. However, there are restrictions and regulations concerning cloud migration in the banking industry. For example, a data scientist in the risk department of BankX said, *"BNM is not yet ready for banks to embrace cloud infrastructure"* (Survey respondent).

However, while there is a restriction on cloud migration, it is to be noted that cloud migration is not prohibited in its entirety (BNM 2019). As adapting to the changing landscape of business and the technology needs of new business models, BNM released regulations on outsourcing, including guidelines for cloud service providers:

Increasing digitalisation and advancement in financial technologies have further spurred financial institutions to continuously adapt their business models and processes through outsourcing in order to have access to and reap the benefits of these technologies. This has led to growing interest in recent years in using cloud service providers to improve business agility in responding to customer needs and achieving economies of scale. (BNM 2019)

The central concern about cloud migration in the banking industry is about data protection and safety as banking data involves sensitive information of customers, and the financial impact of any breach of security is enormous. While restrictions are needed to ensure data protection and security, there are some grey areas regarding what is allowed and what is not, which brings the issue of ambiguity; as the director of BankX said:

And that's where the struggle can be because there is not a single, very clear guideline... but it's more in terms of recommended practices... challenge is to understand; Why can't we put it on the cloud....sometimes you also need a lot of time to understand what is the spirit of that Bank Negara's guidelines or regulation. (P28, Director, Analytics Service Provider)

Data Governance and Architecture

Data Governance Department

BankX established a data architecture department, a data committee and a Chief Data Officer (CDO) to oversee data security and protection in the organisation. The data governance framework was drawn to ensure compliance with governance standards. With data integration efforts, a data governance layer was built with well-defined metrics on domain and data access. As said by a director, *"We have a data governance layer, we have a layer for metadata and services, and also we have a layer where we can store physical data into different data zones"* (P19, Director- Lead Analytics Architect).

Data with personally identified information (PII) of customers were only accessible by managers of a certain level, such as heads of departments. This architecture was managed by group technology and internal control and access were built to ensure privacy. The refining of the governance by BankX has paved the way toward a single data repository system that enhances data integration with proper governance in place. The data architecture department ensures proper integration of data and systems across the institution according to BNM guidelines, as illustrated below.

A comprehensive data and systems architecture should facilitate the proper integration of data and systems across the institution and should generally address the following elements: (i) standards, guidelines or common criteria and data definitions to be applied in the development of systems, data repositories and interfaces, and controls over data flow. Such protocols should be designed to ensure that common data and MIS systems are implemented consistently, thereby mitigating the increased cost and risk of fragmented and disconnected flows of data within the organisation. (The Edge 2019)

Data Access Controls and Anonymisation

Matters about data usage and sharing were one consistent challenge in BDA implementation in the banking industry. While integrating data from various sources is vital in getting a wholesome picture to gain relevant insights, data sharing restrictions were cumbersome for data scientists as they need as much data as possible for modelling purposes. Across border data sharing is restricted as per data residency regulation. While these regulations can be challenging, adhering to them is a given, especially in the banking industry. Any data privacy and sharing restrictions were strictly adhered to by BankX. Data were anonymised to ensure that the PII of customers were kept private. These anonymised data were used for modelling purposes as privacy was maintained and no personal information was visible. Data was also anonymised when it was to be shared with a third party. Anonymisation of data ensures that privacy is maintained, and at the same time, data can be used for modelling purposes for the onboarding of customers and other processes, *"You can move data, but you have to anonymise the data with hashing, or masking, then you can move. Most of the use cases do not require the customer data"* (P19, Director- Lead Analytics Architect).

Similarly, anonymised data could be transferred across the border, and sometimes modellers were sent to respective countries to deal with data that could not be moved. BankX has data partnerships with telecommunication companies, payment wallets and online shopping platforms. Data acquired from these organisations were also anonymised to ensure privacy until a particular customer was onboarded. Until then, PII is not visible. In this way, data availability increased, but governance was in place to ensure regulatory compliance: e.g.,

We have agreements with several parties, but we cannot reveal who the customer is, and they don't reveal it either. So normally what happens is like, they will give you some sort of like profiles of customers. And then, we will build a model to determine the creditworthiness based on that profile. And then basically it is a thing where they provide us with the leads, and we provide the financing. Because we are not allowed to transfer customer data, I mean personally identifiable information. It is once the customer is on board with us that we know who the customer is, but until that point, we do not. (P24, Vice President- Data Governance)

Compliance and Risk Management

Regulatory Approval Processes

Due to the central bank's regulations, PDPA and data usage guidelines, the regulatory body must approve data used for BDA-enabled activities such as cross-selling. Even though it may appear to be a long process, actors meticulously acquired the related approvals and ensured that all proposals prepared for cross-selling activities were adequate and data usage was specified. Appropriate processes were in place to ensure all guidelines and regulations were complied with. Similarly, individual pricing proposals were also appropriately justified, *"I don't believe that the data is a big issue, regulation is a big issue, as long as you do it responsibly, and you don't compromise the data information about a client"* (P18, Head of Retail).

As insights from BDA were slowly integrated within the core business function and its operations and processes, it became part of the decision-making culture in BankX and allowed innovation. As regulations are there to preserve the interest of various stakeholders and the economy at large, careful considerations are necessary. Within the banking industry, any new products and services, models for processes and new organisational forms have to be approved by the regulation. Actors in BankX carefully followed protocols and ensured that regulations were adhered to and strived to protect customer data and privacy at any given time. At the same time, as guidelines were ambiguous and contained some grey areas, actors also attempted to redefine and take actions within the ambit of regulation rather than holding back. The innovation team head in BankX commented on the importance of being able to capitalise on opportunities that lie within regulation and not be laid back blaming regulation: e.g:

There are always opportunities within the ambit of regulation. Regulations exist because they are trying to protect the people's money so that banks do not end up going and gambling with that and taking undue risks. But regulations always have grey areas that you need to know. What is the underlying principle around which the regulation has been set and proceed true to that rather than creating checklists? (P17, Head of Innovation)

However, the senior executive clarified that working around regulation is not to be mistaken as finding loopholes but more about understanding the premise of regulation or guideline and working within it, "I'm not talking about grey areas in the sense of trying to find loopholes. I'm talking about grey areas to move the needle. To move the needle within the principle on why the regulation existed in the first place" (P17, Head of Innovation).

Continuous Engagement with Authorities

In the BDA implementation cloud is an important infrastructure for data storage and management. The inability to utilise the cloud reduces infrastructure capability and affects data integration efforts, speed and accessibility, negatively affecting the realisation of BDA value. While managing only on-premises systems, the bank's managing director constantly engaged with regulators in discussions of cloud safety and the need for cloud migration. The bank's information technology specialist is included in these continuous engagements with the relevant authorities to discuss and explain security protocols to justify data protection and safety: e.g.,

Every time I go to see them [central bank], my IT guys are part of the team because they can explain in a very not-so-technical way how the data is protected. How is it not so different from what we are doing already on-premises? What is the cost that we can take if anything goes wrong? (P16, Managing Director)

In October 2019, BNM released the outsourcing guidelines, which specifically include regulation on cloud usage and security protocols (BNM 2019):

Increasing digitalisation and advancement in financial technologies have further spurred financial institutions to continuously adapt their business models and processes through outsourcing in order to have access to and reap the benefits of these technologies. This has led to growing interest in recent years in using cloud service providers to improve business agility in responding to customer needs and achieving economies of scale. (BNM 2019)

Within this guideline, cloud usage is permitted but with guidelines attached to service providers' geographical location and data security. It also outlines the protocols for engaging these services. However, the ambiguity regarding cloud usage persists in terms of "what is allowed" and "what can be allowed", as there is a lack of a definitive rule. The guideline is more of a guideline of best practice. Frequent engagement with regulators clarified ambiguity and safe system migration to the cloud; for example, a senior manager said, *"So I hear it from my boss how frequently he needs to go to the Bank Negara to explain things."* (P21, Senior Manager- Web Analytics).

BankX managed to migrate to the cloud in stages where the non-critical systems were moved with the view of more migration in the future. BankX had its HR system on the cloud and was using a cloud-based data management platform and Adobe Analytics.

Data Management in the Digital Age

While the partial movement to the cloud with the potential for more system migration increased infrastructure capacity in BDA implementation efforts, the onus of data security lay on the bank: e.g.,

Where the outsourcing arrangement involves a cloud service provider, a financial institution should take effective measures to address risks associated with data accessibility, confidentiality, integrity, sovereignty, recoverability and regulatory compliance. This is particularly important as cloud service providers often operate a geographically dispersed computing infrastructure with regional or global distribution of data processing and storage. (BNM 2019)

Proper safety protocols and governance to ensure data safety was ensured by BankX actors as the cost for breach of compliance is hefty: e.g.,

Bank Negara said we could move even our critical system to the cloud. Critical means core banking system. But they put the responsibility on the organisation. So, they say the bank should have a clear cloud strategy, which needs clear security protocols on how we should protect our data. For example, what VPN[2] and what security framework we should have so that the data is protected? (P19, Director-Lead Analytics Architect)

Third-party Tracking and Usage Approvals

BankX's digital data analytic team engaged in website tracking activity to optimise websites to enhance the customer journey, i.e., from the time they arrive at the website until they are converted into a customer. However, certain data usage from the website and data tracking method was restricted, limiting data availability for a complete analysis. A senior manager said, *"We were looking to implement third-party tracking, maybe something like tabs on Google. To check on user behaviour, maybe to check all the way up until that transaction, but yeah, we were not allowed to"* (P21, Senior Manager- Web Analytics).

When actors were not allowed to implement third-party tracking, the managing director had to make several trips to the regulator and hold negotiations and a series of explanations on the nature of this activity and how it does not infringe on privacy matters. The senior manager explained, *"My direct boss needed to go to Bank Negara to explain to them how it works and how we cannot leak any of our customers' PII. So, all these slow down the whole process of implementing something that we think is important to us"* (P21, Senior Manager- Web Analytics). Eventually, third-party tracking was allowed when the regulators understood the process and were satisfied with its security. With these continuous efforts to negotiate and advocate their purpose, more analytical activities were performed to serve customer needs better to enhance their experience. Compliance with regulation and adequate governance are vital in the banking industry. However, in the case of a new, evolving technology, frequent engagement that allowed approval, safe analytics methods and data usage was made possible.

Secure Ecosystem

External Data Partnership

Data partnership to combine internal and external data is an important practice to leverage big data analytics effectively. BankX partners with other companies such as telecommunication companies and online shopping platforms: e.g.,

We have a partnership with X, and X has got a lot of information on tolls and parking. Similarly, we are also in partnerships with Y and Z as they have data different from ours. The main thing here is that, as a bank, we see the last mile of any transaction. And they see the first mile. So, with data partnership, we are trying to stitch that together. (P16, Managing Director)

For example, a telecommunication company knows when a customer searches for an airline ticket, but they would not know if it was purchased. The bank will know when the purchase is done but not the search process. Combining the knowledge of the telecommunication company and the bank allows a complete understanding of the customer journey. While data partnership allowed better visibility to serve customers better, BankX ensured data handling and sharing was done in compliance with the regulation. Compliance with regulation with regards to data sharing and usage ensured the smooth operation of the business, *"You hear a lot of data partnerships going on, but they are not easy at this stage. Because there are a lot of privacy issues. You need to protect the privacy of your customers. So there is a lot that still needs to be worked through, but there is a lot of potential on the data partnership side of things"* (P16, Managing Director).

Regulatory Sandbox for Testing and Validation

As collaboration with promising start-ups further enhanced and hastened BDA implementation and innovative efforts at BankX, BankX sourced for these start-ups to accelerate their efforts. Once a promising start-up was identified, they were placed in a "regulatory sandbox"[3] to test suitability regarding regulatory compliance of data sharing and usage. Once the bank and the regulator were satisfied with protocols and regulatory compliance, it was "graduated" from the sandbox and joined in as a venture or any other form of partnership deemed fit by both parties: e.g.,

The innovation team is given a set of money to go and find companies that are worth investing in... like an incubator. This company is run as a separate entity. It works as a FinTech. It builds its program and everything; once it can run and it's something that the bank sees as worth doing in the long term, then the bank talks about equity...the bank can take a certain percentage; it depends on how they negotiate it. So in that way, of course, you can come up with something with lesser governance. (P5, Assistant Vice President, Modelling & Portfolio Analytics)

DISCUSSION

The finalised model in this study is illustrated in Figure 1.

Figure 1. Data Management in BDA Implementation

While studies exemplify that BDA resources capabilities lead to various outcomes and performance gains (e.g., Akter et al., 2016; Mikalef, 2019; Müller, Fay, & vom Brocke, 2018); there has been considerably less research on the data management aspect in this value realisation process. While extant literature discusses BDA resource configurations and beneficial BDA outcomes, it does not explicate the central issue in BDA, i.e. the data itself. While the limited number of literature discusses the actions of actors in the BDA implementation (Dremel et al. 2020; Tim et al.

2020; Zeng et al. 2020), the existing scholarly knowledge on data management and protection during the implementation process is still in a nascent stage and lacks empirical evidence.

The study framework (Figure 1) shows that to derive outcomes from BDA resources and capabilities, data management and protection play a central role. To begin with, the regulatory environment displays the necessity of regulations to protect customer privacy and ensure ethical data usage. The importance of security measures is recognised as any breach could significantly impact various stakeholders and the economy. The activities at the case organisation demonstrate proactive measures to align BDA implementation efforts with the regulatory environment. Secondly, comprehensive data governance and architecture protocols are vital to legitimise data usage and enable the realisation of BDA benefits. A robust data governance framework was established in the case organisation, and the data architecture team worked diligently to monitor data needs, usage, and quality in achieving their objectives.

Thirdly, while data integration into a central warehouse is essential for leveraging BDA resources and capabilities, it needs to be carried out in compliance with regulations and appropriate risk management efforts. An inbuilt governance layer monitored data access to ensure protection and security. The case organisation ensured adherence to data-sharing regulations by anonymising data and complying with relevant guidelines. Additionally, necessary approvals were obtained for new products, services, and processes. Models created using data were carefully evaluated as regulatory compliance remained a top priority for case organisations to maintain a positive rapport with regulators and warrant legitimacy. However, regulations need not necessarily impede the realisation of BDA benefits. The case organisation increased engagement with regulators, advocating for policy changes and seeking clarity and further approvals where regulations seemed ambiguous.

Finally, a secure ecosystem ensures safe data sharing with third-party service providers and partners. The case organisation also utilised a "regulatory sandbox" to test the suitability of data sharing and usage practices regarding regulatory compliance. Rather than allowing regulations to constrain innovative efforts, the "regulatory sandbox" provided a controlled approach to data sharing for innovative initiatives.

The regulatory oversight, data governance and architecture, compliance and risk management and the establishment of a secure ecosystem resulted in increased legitimacy in acquiring BDA-related resources, capabilities, data, infrastructure, and innovative capacity. BankX's proactive approach demonstrates how banks might legitimately mobilise resources in the face of an evolving regulatory environment. By proactively addressing data management and protection concerns BankX can effectively leverage the benefits of data-driven technologies while maintaining the highest standards of data security, privacy, and regulatory compliance within the stringent banking industry regulatory environment.

CONCLUSION

By drawing on data from a case study in the financial services industry, this study explains the process of data management and data protection in BDA implementation. While the BDA resources and capabilities are integral in producing business value, the role of regulatory oversight, data governance and architecture, compliance and risk management and establishment of a secure ecosystem are equally vital in ensuring data protection in the digital age. Answering calls for industry-specific research explaining how BDA can support competitive advantage (Abbasi, Sarker, and Chiang 2016; Mikalef 2019), this work makes important contributions to the IS literature. This research is timely and significant, considering the building pressure in the financial services industry to respond to the changing landscape of business.

The findings also have several implications for industry practitioners. Practitioners should improve the elements surrounding BDA implementation that facilitate positive BDA outcomes. Thus, practitioners should prioritise issues such as data protection raised in BDA implementation and work on potential solutions. The constant effort and strategy used by BankX to overcome various barriers can be replicated by other organisations implementing BDA in their business model. Organisations should not just concentrate on building novel BDA-related resources but on improvisation of the existing environment within the context. As finance is a facilitator of many production and consumption activities, accomplishments in the financial sector will directly affect the economy (Frame & White, 2004). The importance of financial innovation for economic growth is amplified as it brings new and improved products, processes, and organisational structures that reduce costs, reduce risks, and better respond to customer demand. Understanding the importance of innovation in the financial industry, the findings from this research may also assist in policy development for future framework development concerning innovation, risk management, and technology use.

Like any research undertaking, this study contains several limitations that can be addressed in future research. The first limitation is that the study findings are based in the context of a developing country where the legal technology framework is not fully advanced. While this is an important contribution as developed Western countries' context dominates the literature, the actualisation practices derived in this context can differ from those organisations in a developed nation. As the literature lacks an empirical-based investigation of BDA implementation in the banking industry, future research could conduct a similar study on banks in developed economies and compare the findings.

The next set of limitations relates to data collection. While this study's intensive case study approach provided grounds for uncovering mechanisms (Bygstad, Munkvold, and Volkoff 2016; Sayer 2002), it restricted the range and diversity of empirical material. This research design did not capture every possible BDA implementation. However, given that the central premise of this research is to understand data management and protection in BDA implementation, the case organisation was carefully selected. Thus, the findings of this research, while not generalisable in terms of statistical generalisation, offer analytical generalisability based on their connection to theory (Yin, 2014).

Further, although data collection (interviews, survey) took place over several months, this study did not cover a large enough period to enable a first-hand longitudinal observation of organisational transformation. Rather, the transformation was analysed through the retrospective accounts of activities occurring prior to the data collection period and the analysis of archival documents. Nevertheless, given the interest of this thesis in exploring data management in BDA implementation, the narrative of the interview participants on events and actions responds adequately to the research questions. Although it may be argued that perception and interpretations may change over time, it is suggested that participants of organisational processes do not easily forget key events (Leonard-Barton 1990). Hence, given the salience of the BDA projects in the case organisation, this limitation is not regarded to risk the validation of the analysis. Nonetheless, future studies could employ a longitudinal research design that may result in more accurate accounts of events as they occur. In addition to that, future research could build on this study and apply quantitative techniques to provide statistical descriptions of the data management to construct robust meta-inferences (Mingers et al., 2013; Volkoff & Strong, 2017).

REFERENCES

Abbasi, A., Sarker, S., & Chiang, R. (2016). Big Data Research in Information Systems: Toward an Inclusive Research Agenda. *Journal of the Association for Information Systems*, 17(2), I–XXXII. 10.17705/1jais.00423

Akter, S., Wamba, S. F., Gunasekaran, A., Dubey, R., & Childe, S. J. (2016). How to Improve Firm Performance Using Big Data Analytics Capability and Business Strategy Alignment? *International Journal of Production Economics*, 182, 113–131. 10.1016/j.ijpe.2016.08.018

BNM. (2017). *Management of Customer Information and Permitted Disclosures*. BNM. https://www.bnm.gov.my/index.php?ch=57&pg=146&ac=633&bb=file

Bygstad, B., Munkvold, B. E., & Volkoff, O. (2016). Identifying Generative Mechanisms through Affordances: A Framework for Critical Realist Data Analysis. *Journal of Information Technology*, 31(1), 83–96. 10.1057/jit.2015.13

Chen, H., Chiang, R. H. L., & Storey, V. C. (2012). Business Intelligence and Analytics: From Big Data to Big Impact. *Management Information Systems Quarterly*, 36(4), 1165–1188. 10.2307/41703503

Dai, H. N., Wang, H., Xu, G., Wan, J., & Imran, M. (2020). Big Data Analytics for Manufacturing Internet of Things: Opportunities, Challenges and Enabling Technologies. *Enterprise Information Systems*, 14(9–10), 1279–1303. 10.1080/17517575.2019.1633689

Davenport, T. (2012). How 'Big Data' Is Different. *MIT Sloan Management Review*, 54(1), 21–25.

Dremel, C., Herterich, M. M., Wulf, J., & vom Brocke, J. (2020). Actualizing Big Data Analytics Affordances: A Revelatory Case Study. *Information & Management*, 57(1), 103121. 10.1016/j.im.2018.10.007

Eastburn, R. W., & Boland, R. J.Jr. (2015). Inside Banks' Information and Control Systems: Post-Decision Surprise and Corporate Disruption. *Information and Organization*, 25(3), 160–190. 10.1016/j.infoandorg.2015.05.001

Frame, W. S., & White, L. J. (2004). Empirical Studies of Financial Innovation: Lots of Talk, Little Action? *Journal of Economic Literature*, 42(1), 116–144. 10.1257/002205104773558065

Gandomi, A., & Haider, M. (2015). Beyond the Hype: Big Data Concepts, Methods, and Analytics. *International Journal of Information Management*, 35(2), 137–144. 10.1016/j.ijinfomgt.2014.10.007

Gupta, M., & George, J. F. (2016). Toward the Development of a Big Data Analytics Capability. *Information & Management*, 53(8), 1049–1064. 10.1016/j.im.2016.07.004

Kache, F., & Seuring, S. (2017). Challenges and Opportunities of Digital Information at the Intersection of Big Data Analytics and Supply Chain Management. *International Journal of Operations & Production Management*, 37(1), 10–36. 10.1108/IJOPM-02-2015-0078

Leonard-Barton, D. (1990). A Dual Methodology for Case Studies: Synergistic Use of a Longitudinal Single Site with Replicated Multiple Sites. *Organization Science*, 1(3), 248–266. 10.1287/orsc.1.3.248

Manyika, J., & Brown Chui, M. (2011). *Big Data: The next Frontier for Innovation, Competition and Productivity*. McKinsey Global Institute.

Mikalef, P. (2019). Exploring the Relationship between Big Data Analytics Capability and Competitive Performance : The Mediating Roles of Dynamic and Operational Capabilities. *Information & Management*, 2018(February). 10.1016/j.im.2019.05.004

Mikalef, P., Boura, M., Lekakos, G., & Krogstie, J. (2019). Big Data Analytics Capabilities and Innovation: The Mediating Role of Dynamic Capabilities and Moderating Effect of the Environment. *British Journal of Management*, 30(2), 272–298. 10.1111/1467-8551.12343

Müller, O., Fay, M., & vom Brocke, J. (2018). The Effect of Big Data and Analytics on Firm Performance: An Econometric Analysis Considering Industry Characteristics. *Journal of Management Information Systems*, 35(2), 488–509. 10.1080/07421222.2018.1451955

PWC. (2016). *Catching the Fintech Wave- A Survey of Fintech in Malaysia*. PWC. https://www.pwc.com/my/en/assets/publications/2016-pwc-aicb-catching-the-fintech-wave.pdf

PWC. (2017). *Global Fintech Report 2017*. PWC.

Sayer, A. (2002). Critical Realist Methodology: A View from Sweden. *Journal of Critical Realism*, 1(1), 168–170. 10.1558/jocr.v1i1.168

Tim, Y., Hallikainen, P., Pan, S. L., & Tamm, T. (2020). Actualizing Business Analytics for Organizational Transformation: A Case Study of Rovio Entertainment. *European Journal of Operational Research*, 281(3), 642–655. 10.1016/j.ejor.2018.11.074

Wamba, S. F., Gunasekaran, A., Akter, S., Ren, S. J., Dubey, R., & Childe, S. J. (2017). Big Data Analytics and Firm Performance: Effects of Dynamic Capabilities. *Journal of Business Research*, 70, 356–365. 10.1016/j.jbusres.2016.08.009

Zeng, D., Tim, Y., Yu, J., & Liu, W. (2020). Actualizing Big Data Analytics for Smart Cities: A Cascading Affordance Study. *International Journal of Information Management*, 54(3), 102156. 10.1016/j.ijinfomgt.2020.102156

ENDNOTES

1. GDPR is The General Data Protection Regulation in the European Union (EU) and the European Economic Area (EEA) concerning data protection and privacy.
2. A virtual private network, or VPN, is an encrypted connection over the Internet from a device to a network. The encrypted connection helps ensure that sensitive data is safely transmitted.
3. A regulatory sandbox is a framework set up by a regulator that allows Fin-Tech start-ups and other innovators to conduct live experiments in a controlled environment under a regulator's supervision.

Chapter 5
Compliance Challenges and Tech-Driven Solutions in Combating Financial Crime Within the Fintech Ecosystem

Mushtaq Ahmad Shah
https://orcid.org/0000-0002-3177-9622
Lovely Professional University, India

B. Udaya Bhaskara Ganesh
https://orcid.org/0000-0002-9122-4565
Lovely Professional University, India

ABSTRACT

The fast-growing Fintech industry has become a battleground for financial crime, posing significant challenges to regulators and business stakeholders. This chapter investigates financial crime threats and regulatory implications in the changing FinTech environment. The study looks into the awareness of financial crimes and examines the major Fintech risks that businesses face. Employing an exploratory research approach, the study examines public awareness of financial crimes through a survey questionnaire sent to the target respondents. Moreover, the recent regulatory actions against FinTech companies are examined, illustrating the growing emphasis on consumer protection and compliance. The chapter concludes by emphasising the importance of an exclusive global legislative framework for combating financial crimes in FinTech. This chapter advances understanding of financial crime risks and regulatory considerations in FinTech, providing significant insights for scholars, regulators, and FinTech enterprises.

INTRODUCTION

Financial crime is a pervasive and multidimensional problem that continues to plague the financial industry despite the utmost efforts of regulators and compliance experts.(Ghazi-Tehrani & Pontell, 2022). The nature of the relationship between the recent emergence of networks of corruption and the related problem of financial crimes is little understood at present (Hardy & Bell, 2020). Depending on the area and context, the phrase financial crime can refer to a variety of issues. Nevertheless, (Henning, 2009) argues that financial crime encompasses a wide range of property crimes involving the unauthorised transformation of another's property for one's own personal use and benefit, most commonly involving fraud but also "bribery, corruption, money laundering, embezzlement, insider trading, tax violations, cyber-attacks", and the like. These crimes not only directly injure persons and organisations, but they also endanger the overall soundness of the financial system, causing a ripple effect with enormous economic effects (Gottschalk, 2010). Previous research has found that economic and financial crimes have increased despite harsh legislative measures implemented in both rich and developing nations. Bribes, for example, are estimated to cost between $1.5 trillion and $2 trillion per year (or around 2% of world GDP) in both developing and rich countries (Lagarde, 2016). According to a survey performed by a private business, "LocalCircles", 42% of Indian respondents encountered financial fraud in the previous three years, and 74% of those who experienced it did not recover their money. Illegal advantage for personal gain appears to be a key feature of financial fraud. Within businesses, financial crimes such as fraud, theft, and corruption occur frequently. (Acquaah-Gaisie, 2000). It is the core responsibility of the company board and top management to prevent such crimes (Perera-Aldama et al., 2009)

With the rise of new fintech startups in recent years, the financial industry has experienced substantial changes. These firms have disrupted traditional financial services by introducing new and more efficient methods of dealing with and managing money. The rise of technology has had an impact on how financial transactions are done as well as compliance with anti-money laundering legislation, among other things. (Arner et al., 2019). While this interruption has provided several advantages to both consumers and businesses, it has also provided novel likelihoods for financial criminals (Milanesi, 2022). Opportunities include more customer-centric goods, convenience, and the creation of safekeeping measures to combat increasing cyber and information menaces, while vulnerabilities include "money laundering, which threatens the integrity of financial services, cyber security, and national security

(Fulop et al., 2022). The increased vulnerabilities of the financial sector due to digital innovations can result in financial instability and failure to protect consumers.

Innovative fintech firms operate in a digital world with innovative and complicated business models that may not precisely fit into established regulatory frameworks. This can lead to compliance loopholes, making these businesses vulnerable to financial fraud. Many fintech companies, for example, operate across several jurisdictions, each with its own requirements for regulation, making it difficult to maintain a uniform strategy for adherence. Financial crime poses a significant threat to the financial system, and emerging fintech businesses are not immune. The current study was carried out in order to comprehend and address financial crimes in the fintech ecosystem through a rigorous literary assessment in a methodical approach based on the issue inquiries of finance and technology, anti-money laundering, financial crimes, and due diligence. Section 1 provides an overview of financial crimes and the fintech landscape. Section 2 investigates the related literature on the topic. Section 3 discusses the study's research material and methods. Section 4 contains the results and commentary, as well as a visual representation of the results. Section 5 concludes the chapter and gives policy recommendations.

LITERATURE REVIEW

Financial crime is a persistent issue that continues to pose significant risks to the financial industry. This risk has only increased with the emergence of innovative fintech companies, which operate in a digital environment that creates new opportunities for financial criminals. The following review of literature provides an overview of the current research on financial crime in the context of the innovative fintech landscape, focusing on compliance gaps. Nowadays, banks are working on digitization to speed up processes. The major risks faced by the techno-finance sector and the reasons why applications, software and systems should be implemented against vulnerabilities and hacking (Sahay et al., 2020). Several studies have already been carried out that analyse the risk of money laundering linked to the use of cryptocurrencies and, more generally, to FinTech systems, however these researches have focused on each specific aspect, such as criminal investigations Fintech forensic (Nikkel, 2020). (Kumari & Devi, 2022)) examine the risks of financial crimes in the fintech industry, highlighting the use of new technologies, such as blockchain and cryptocurrencies, which make it easier to conceal illicit transactions. The authors suggest that regulators need to stay ahead of these developments and create effective policies to combat money laundering in the fintech sector.

Song et al., (2023) reviews the risks of money laundering and terrorist financing in fintech, with a particular focus on the use of virtual currencies. The authors argue that the anonymity and decentralization of virtual currencies make them particularly vulnerable to illicit activity. The paper concludes that regulatory frameworks need to be updated to account for new technologies and that fintech companies need to implement effective AML and counter-terrorist financing measures. In a study by (Salerno, 2019) it was found that fintech companies in Europe and Asia have a high risk of being used for money laundering due to weak AML regulations. The study recommended that fintech companies should be subject to stricter AML regulations and that regulators should work together to create a consistent global regulatory framework. Ferreira et al., (2020) systematic literature review identifies and analyzes the existing research on fraud prevention in fintech. The authors found that most of the research focuses on developing new fraud detection and prevention techniques, such as machine learning algorithms and biometric authentication. The paper concludes that fintech companies need to adopt a multi-layered approach to fraud prevention to ensure the security of their platforms. According to the Financial Action Task Force (FATF), fintech companies should be subject to the same anti-money laundering (AML) regulations as traditional financial institutions. However, many fintech companies operate in countries with weak AML regulations or may not be subject to regulations at all. This has led to concerns about the use of fintech for money laundering. Mishra (2019) reviews the challenges of cybersecurity in the fintech industry, which include the protection of sensitive customer data and the risk of cyberattacks. The authors argue that fintech companies must take proactive measures to mitigate these risks, such as implementing two-factor authentication, using encryption, and conducting regular security audits. Adebayo & Thomas, (2021) reviews the regulatory frameworks for fintech in various regions around the world, including North America, Europe, Asia, and Africa. The authors found that many countries are still in the process of developing regulatory frameworks for fintech, and that there is a need for greater international cooperation to establish consistent standards. The paper concludes that effective regulation is essential to mitigate the risks of financial crimes in the fintech industry. In a study by the (*Cambridge Centre for Alternative Finance*, 2020) it was found that fraud was the most commonly reported type of financial crime in the fintech industry. The study recommended that fintech companies should invest in better fraud prevention measures, such as multi-factor authentication and biometric identification, to reduce the risk of fraud.

In a study by KPMG (2021), it was found that cybercrime was the biggest risk facing fintech companies. The study recommended that fintech companies should invest in cybersecurity measures, such as encryption and two-factor authentication, to reduce the risk of cybercrime. Financial crimes in growing fintech are a significant concern for both customers and fintech companies. Money laundering, fraud, and cybercrime are all risks associated with fintech. Regulatory frameworks for fintech are still developing, and there is a need for a consistent global regulatory framework to reduce the risk of financial crimes. Fintech companies should invest in better AML, fraud prevention, and cybersecurity measures to reduce In general, all of these studies emphasise the importance of good regulatory frameworks and the use of innovative technology to reduce the dangers of financial crime in the rapidly rising fintech industry. Countries are still in the process of developing regulatory frameworks for fintech, and that there is a need for greater international cooperation to establish consistent standards. The paper concludes that effective regulation is essential to mitigate the risks of financial crimes in the fintech industry

MATERIAL AND METHODS

This study aimed to understand the level of financial crime awareness, major fintech risks facing by FinTech companies, and the role of technology in combating financial crime. The study is based on exploratory research-based approach, collecting data through a questionnaire survey targeting three distinct demographic segments: the general public, professionals within financial services, and academic researchers specializing in finance and technology to have holistic view of the financial crime awareness. A total of 90 complete questionnaires were found suitable for the study. The questionnaire was distributed electronically, utilizing email and online survey platforms, which facilitated efficient data collection and allowed participants to respond at their convenience. Additionally, the researchers conducted an extensive literature review using scientific databases Shah et al. (2023), {Citation}academic journals, industry reports, and regulatory documents, with a special emphasis on sources discussing the implications of FinTech innovations on financial crime and regulation.

DATA ANALYSIS AND DISCUSSION

History and Evolution of Financial Fraud

The history of financial fraud is practically intertwined with the creation of financial institutions themselves. From the calculating plot of Greek merchant Hegestratos in 300 BC, who attempted to sink his empty ship and collect insurance on a nonexistent cargo, to the complex schemes of modern insider trading and market manipulation, fraudulent techniques have constantly adapted and grown more complicated. While the core motive of manipulating financial systems for personal gain remains constant, the methods have undergone a dramatic transformation. Early attempts involved exploiting weaknesses in newly formed financial instruments. As financial products became more complex and markets globalized, new opportunities emerged for sophisticated scams. The invention of computers and the internet further propelled this evolution, creating a digital landscape ripe for cybercrime and identity theft. This ever-evolving threat landscape poses a significant challenge for modern businesses, demanding constant vigilance and adaptation.

Impact on Modern Business Environments

The repercussions of financial fraud on contemporary business environments are substantial. Not only does fraud undermine trust and integrity, but it also poses significant economic risks. Businesses globally suffer considerable losses due to fraudulent activities, with estimates suggesting an average annual loss of around 5% of profits to fraud. The banking sector, in particular, faces heightened vulnerability to fraudulent schemes, leading to financial instability and reputational harm. The advent of new technologies and changing wealth dynamics has introduced further complexities to the landscape of financial fraud. As financial systems become increasingly interconnected, the consequences of a major fraud can ripple outwards, affecting entire sectors and even triggering economic crises. Despite these negative effects, the fight against financial fraud continues, with advancements in technology and stricter regulations playing a crucial role in safeguarding financial institutions and businesses. However, the ever-inventive minds of fraudsters mean this will be an ongoing battle, requiring constant vigilance and adaptation.

Financial Crime in Context of Fintech

Financial crime, particularly in the context of Fintech, refers to illegal activities that involve the use of financial systems and institutions to facilitate illegal transactions, such as money laundering, terrorist financing, and fraud. These crimes pose significant risks to the integrity of the financial system and can have severe consequences for individuals, businesses, and the economy as a whole. Money laundering, fraud, theft, market manipulation, and ransomware attacks are all examples of financial crime in the fintech sector A number of illegal activities can occur in both the commercial and public sectors. So long as there are weaknesses that can be exploited for gain, companies and other organizations as well as private individuals will be taken advantage of (Pickett & Pickett, 2002). Therefore, we find a great variety of criminal activities that are classified as financial crime. Financial crimes refer to a wide range of illegal activities (Figure 1) that involve the use of financial systems and institutions to commit fraud, theft, or other criminal activities

Figure 1. Categories of financial crimes

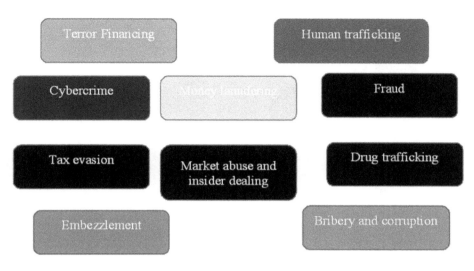

Source: Author's Compilation

Financial crimes can be broadly categorized into three main groups: crimes committed by individuals, crimes committed by organizations, and crimes committed by the government or public officials. These crimes including fraud, money laundering, embezzlement, bribery, insider trading, cybercrime, counterfeiting, and tax evasion. Each of these categories involves specific types of criminal activities that can cause significant harm to individuals, businesses, and society as a whole. Understanding these categories can help individuals and organizations protect themselves from financial crimes and take steps to prevent them.

Figure 2. Awareness of financial crime

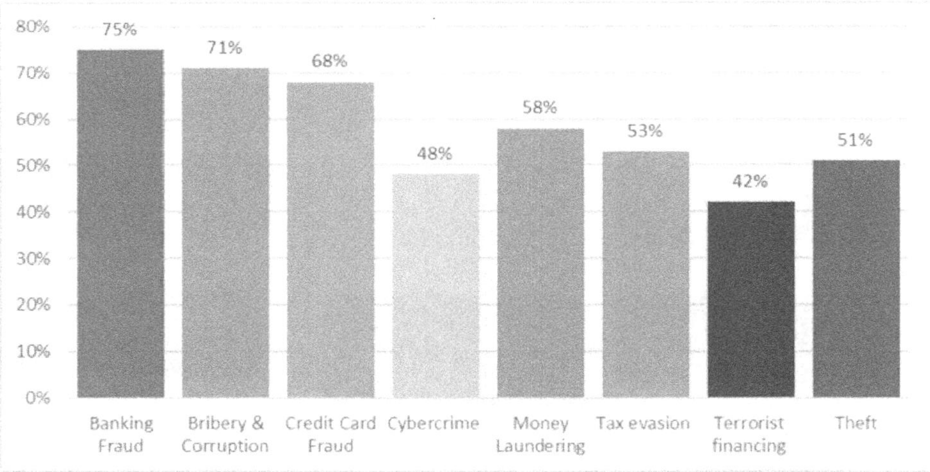

[Bar chart showing: Banking Fraud 75%, Bribery & Corruption 71%, Credit Card Fraud 68%, Cybercrime 48%, Money Laundering 58%, Tax evasion 53%, Terrorist financing 42%, Theft 51%]

Source: Author's Compilation

As depicted in Figure 2, Banking Fraud, followed by Bribery & Corruption and Credit Card Fraud, demonstrate notable awareness levels across all demographic groups, indicating a widespread comprehension of these common financial offenses. Terrorism financing and cybercrime exhibit a moderate level of awareness, potentially showing a slight waning among professionals and researchers compared to the general public. This could be attributed to terrorism financing being a broader concept, not always immediately associated with financial crimes. Nonetheless, Cybercrime registers the lowest awareness overall, though one might anticipate a higher level of awareness among professionals and researchers owing to their specialized expertise.

Fintech Ecosystem

To understand the competitive and collaborative dynamics in fintech innovation, we must first analyze the ecosystem. A stable symbiotic fintech ecosystem is instrumental in the growth of the fintech industry. Albarrak & Alokley (2021) suggested that entrepreneurs, government, and financial institutions are the participants in a fintech ecosystem. Five elements of the fintech ecosystem (figure 3) were identified 1. "Fintech startups (such as payment, portfolio management, lending, crowdsourcing, investment market, and insurance fintech companies); 2. Technologists (such as big data analytics, cloud computing, and social media developers); 3. Government (such as financial regulators and legislation); 4. Financial customers (such as individuals and organisations); and 5. Traditional financial institutions (such as traditional banks, insurance companies, and stock brokerage firms)". These elements symbiotically contribute to the innovation, stimulate economy, facilitate collaboration and competition in the financial industry, and ultimately benefit consumers in the financial industry.

Figure 3. Elements of the fintech ecosystem

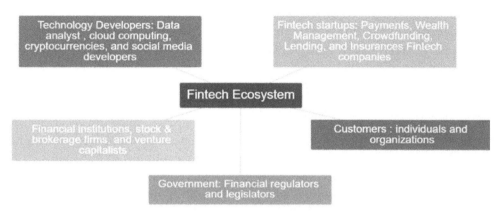

Source: Lee & Shin (2018)

Fintech startups are at the core of the ecosystem. Startups in the fintech industry use technology to offer cutting-edge financial services and solutions. By providing customers and companies with quicker, less expensive, and more convenient options, they want to upend the status quo in the financial sector. In India, the fintech sector has been rapidly growing in recent years, driven by factors such as increasing smartphone penetration, the government's push towards a digital economy, and the need for financial inclusion. By incurring lower operating costs, focusing on more niche markets, and offering more customised services than traditional financial firms, these companies, which are primarily innovative, have driven significant innovations in the fields of payment, "wealth management, lending, crowdfunding, capital markets, and insurances". They are driving the financial services unbundling trend, which has severely disrupted banks (Lee & Shin, 2018). One of the key factors influencing growth in the fintech industry is the capacity to unbundle services since traditional financial institutions are at a disadvantage in this scenario.

Technology developers: provide digital platforms for social media, big data analytics, cloud computing, artificial intelligence, smart phones, and mobile services. Technology developers create a favourable environment for fintech startups to launch innovative services rapidly. Technology developers are professionals or companies that design, develop, and maintain software and hardware products (Shah & Uddin, 2023). They play a critical role in the technology industry by creating new technologies that enable innovation and progress in various sectors.

Favourable regulatory environments: Since the 2008 financial crisis, governments have created favourable regulatory environments for fintech. (Feyen et al., 2021). Governments around the world play an essential role in shaping the growth and development of the fintech industry. In India, the government has been actively involved in promoting fintech startups and facilitating the adoption of digital financial services. Depending on the national economic development plans and economic policies, different governments provide different levels of regulation (e.g., licensing of financial services, relaxation of capital requirements, tax incentives) for fintech startups to stimulate fintech innovation and facilitate global financial competitiveness. For example, the government has invested in building digital infrastructure such as the Unified Payments Interface (UPI) and Aadhaar, a biometric identification system. These initiatives have made it easier for fintech companies to offer digital financial services and enabled financial inclusion for millions of Indians.

Financial customers: in fintech refer to individuals, businesses, or organizations that use digital financial services provided by fintech companies. These customers are an essential component of the fintech industry, as they drive demand for new and innovative financial products and services. Financial customers are the source of revenue generation for fintech companies. While large organizations are important sources of revenue, the predominant revenue source for fintech companies are individual customers and small and medium sized enterprises (SMEs). A survey found that the use of fintech services is greatest among younger, wealthier customers (Lee & Shin, 2018). In fintech, individuals are the most prevalent financial consumers. They manage their accounts and conduct transactions using digital financial services including mobile banking, digital wallets, and online investing platforms. Early adopters of fintech are often younger, more tech-savvy, urban, and more affluent people. Millennials, or those between the ages of 18 and 34, now make up a large share of fintech consumption in the majority of nations.

Conventional financial services providers compete favourably with fintech firms in terms of economies of scale and financial resources. However, conventional financial organisations favour combined services over separated specialised ones, offering consumers a one-stop shop for all financial products and services. Although these rapidly expanding fintech companies were initially viewed as threats by traditional financial institutions, they have since shifted their attention to working with fintech startups with a variety of funding options. They are allowed to use the startup firms' insights in return for investment, which helps them stay at the cutting edge of technology. (Mirchandani et al., 2020)

FINANCIAL RISK IN FINTECH ECOSYSTEM

Digital financial technologies' growth and use have contributed to reshaping economic and financial processes worldwide, but they have also exposed people, systems, and administration to new risks that undermine the efficiency of procedures and current rules (Ashta & Herrmann, 2021; Kujur & Shah, 2015). Fintech provides easier and more effective ways to make payments. However, there are dangers associated with the innovation in the digital economy(Zhao & Chen, 2021). The financial sector has undoubtedly profited from technology improvements on a worldwide scale, but they also pose significant risks to competitiveness, privacy, and financial stability(Mishchenko et al., 2021). As a result, many people are concerned about issues like privacy, system dependability, cyber security, and the possibility for cyberattacks. Evidence suggests that cyber risk in the Fintech industry is the most recent and probably significant threat to the existing environment (Duran & Griffin, 2020). Due to the global COVID-19 and an increase in cashless transactions and business digitization, cyber dangers are increasing. (Fabris, 2022). Duran & Griffin (2020) examine the risks presented by smart contracts, a game-changing development in financial technology, and decide if they may eventually endanger the stability of the global financial system. Other challenges facing this sector include regulatory ambiguity, illegal activity, and data exploitation. Hua & Huang, 2021) developed a model to assess users' intentions for using digital financial technologies while taking into account four distinct categories of hazards, including financial, legal, security, and operational risks. He discovered that customers' intents to keep using fintech were most negatively impacted by legal risk. The research also revealed that early and late adopters commonly experience various distinct advantages and risks. Fintech, like any other emerging technology, comes with its own set of risks table 1. Here are some of the major fintech risks to consider

Table 1. Major fintech risks

Type of risk	Description	Sources
Regulatory compliance risk	Fintech companies fail to comply with regulatory requirements	(Hua & Huang, 2021; Ryu, 2018)
Cyber-security risk	As fintech companies rely heavily on technology to store sensitive data and conduct transactions, they are vulnerable to cyber-attacks	(Fabris, 2022; Mishchenko et al., 2021)
Operational risks	Fintech companies must have adequate backup and disaster recovery plans in place in case of system failures or disruptions.	(Hollanders, 2020)

continued on following page

Table 1. Continued

Type of risk	Description	Sources
Financial crimes and lack of investor protection	As it is simpler to assume false identities online, fintech channels are prone to far higher fraud rates	(Jamil et al., 2021; Sapkauskienė & Višinskaitė, 2020)
Legal risks	Fintech companies may face legal risks due to intellectual property rights infringement, consumer protection, and contract disputes.	(Gozman & Willcocks, 2019)
Lack of financial literacy	Due to financial illiteracy, customers in developing countries fear using financial technologies and prefer traditional method	(Ozili, 2021)
Money laundering and finance terrorism	Due to accessibility through the internet, criminals have developed advanced technologies for money laundering.	(Arner et al., 2019)

Source Author's Compilations

Fintech firms must cope with a variety of risks, including the above-mentioned financial and regulatory issues. Depending on the specific areas of fintech expertise, the financial risk may change. For instance, a fintech that provides financial services for student loans or mortgages can encounter counterparty risk that a financial institution with significant resources can handle but that a smaller business would be unable to do. Customers may be exposed to financial risk if robo-advisors are used to manage their bonds, treasury bills, and stock portfolios, and fintech companies may be held accountable for any losses incurred as a result of robo-advisor algorithmic failure. FinTech's will not be immune to the liabilities emerging from robo-advisors' flawed investment advice, according to recent lawsuits and a number of settlements resulting from the improper sales of derivative products by top-tier banks. Fintech organisations should establish strong security measures, adhere to legal regulations, have dependable and resilient operations, maintain a positive reputation, undertake risk assessments, and have backup plans in place to reduce these risks.

RECENT REGULATORY ACTIONS INVOLVING FINTECH'S

Innovative fintech products are posing a threat to a variety of traditional banking services, including payments and financial advice. With greater assurance of transactions, quicker currency swaps, and cheaper transaction costs both locally and internationally, fintech is revolutionising many traditional banking services. Many fintechs have effectively achieved these results by delivering disruptive solutions that transform payments, lending, wealth management, and more. However, recent regulatory and industry developments suggest a potential blurring of the lines between fintechs and other financial institutions. The ingenious services provided by fintech such as NFTs, stablecoins, DeFi, and other unregulated financial products using virtual assets are now the target of greater regulatory attention following the collapse of crypto businesses like Terra/Luna and FTX. Stablecoin regulatory frameworks are being considered by nations including the US and Canada. A consultation paper on proposed regulatory changes was also released by the Singapore Monetary Authority. The regulatory community is recognizing that fintech's are offering services similar to those from traditional institutions. As a result, some fintech's are abandoning the "not financial institutions" mantra to consider or pursue bank charters, both to compete more broadly and to avoid having to address disparate regulatory requirements. FinTech's can no longer claim that they are different from traditional financial institutions in their product delivery since the future will bring additional dangers connected to rising regulatory requirements, along with possible penalties and legal proceedings for non-compliance. Recent regulatory measures figure 4 that are particular to fintech's have a variety of origins and fact patterns, but they all have several characteristics

Figure 4. Recent regulatory actions involving FinTech's

Modern fintech's don't make distinctions based on company size or reputation; some feature well-known fintech's, while others focus on less well-known firms. The oldest action was started in 2015, and they are all current and indicative of the regulatory action being taken now. Notably, they draw attention to the reputational, operational, and regulatory risks that fintech's confront. Similar risks routinely put the security and integrity of banks and other financial organisations in jeopardy in these situations. About half of these actions involved mistreating customers, one out of every five involved privacy violations, and the remaining cases involved Know Your Customer violations, intellectual property thefts, and other issues, according to an analysis of about two dozen such incidents. The danger that fintech companies confront with their consumers was recently brought to light by an FBI investigation into possible terrorist funding being carried out through a well-known marketplace fintech business. At the same time, it's important to note the emphasis on customer service. Consumers may anticipate regulatory protection for fintech goods and services that resemble those offered by banks but are supplied through non-traditional channels that prioritise speed and simplicity of access based on the number of actions concentrating on customer care.

REGULATORY RESPONSES AND PREVENTIVE MEASURES

In light of the pervasive threat of financial fraud, regulatory bodies have implemented measures to combat fraudulent activities and safeguard investors. Institutions like the Securities and Exchange Commission (SEC), established in response to the 1929 stock market crash, play a crucial role in defining market rules and deterring fraudulent practices. These regulatory frameworks aim to protect investor interests, maintain market integrity, and deter fraudsters from engaging in illicit activities. Different regulatory bodies currently approach fintechs and banking innovation in different ways, but many are moving closer to supervision. The Office of the Comptroller of the Currency (OCC) released a white paper in March 2016 that discussed its "vision for responsible innovation in the federal banking system." By collaborating with authorities to provide solutions tailored to the regulation of their product offerings, fintech's may now continue their quest of growth as a consequence of this endeavour. Having strong risk management procedures in place may help fintech businesses succeed in regulated markets regardless of how they choose to approach them whether by becoming chartered institutions or staying as they are. A compliance firm may well be more appealing to the public given the growing regulatory scrutiny and the requirement to have controls in place to both know and treat consumers well. The opportunity for market share and revenue development may arise from this distinction. Additionally, it might provide some level of comfort to a number of stakeholders, such as the clients the business serves, the board of directors and management of the business, analysts (both equity and rating agencies) who value the openness of businesses' risk management procedures, and any regulatory bodies that might be interested in the firm.

CONCLUSION AND POLICY RECOMMENDATION

Financial crimes in growing fintech are a significant concern for both customers and fintech companies. Money laundering, fraud, and cybercrime are all risks associated with fintech. Regulatory frameworks for fintech are still developing, and there is a need for a consistent global regulatory framework to reduce the risk of financial crimes. Fintech companies should invest in better anti-money laundering, fraud prevention, and cybersecurity measures to reduce the emergence of fintech, which has brought significant advancements to the financial sector by providing innovative and convenient services to customers worldwide. Regulatory authorities should establish clear guidelines and regulations that fintech companies must follow to prevent and detect financial crimes. These guidelines should include AML and KYC procedures and measures to prevent cyber-attacks and data breaches. Fintech companies should collaborate with regulators, law enforcement agencies, and other financial institutions to share information and prevent financial crimes Fintech companies should educate their employees and customers about financial crimes and how to detect and prevent them. They should also raise awareness about the importance of cybersecurity and data protection. Fintech companies should conduct due diligence on their customers and partners to prevent money laundering and fraud. They should also monitor and analyse customer transactions to detect suspicious activities. Fintech companies play a vital role in the financial sector, and the risks associated with financial crimes should not be overlooked. This chapter offers a comprehensive analysis of financial crime risks and regulatory considerations in FinTech, providing valuable insights for researchers, policymakers, and FinTech companies to navigate the evolving landscape and ensure a secure and sustainable future for the industry. By implementing effective policies and measures, fintech companies can mitigate these risks and continue to provide innovative financial services to customers worldwide.

REFERENCES

Acquaah-Gaisie, G. (2000). Fighting Public Officer and Corporate Crimes. *Journal of Financial Crime*, 8(1), 12–20. 10.1108/eb025962

. Adebayo, O. S., & Thomas, A. W. (2021). *Impact of regulation of financial technology (fintech) services on the performance of deposit money banks in Nigeria.* Research Gate.

Albarrak, M. S., & Alokley, S. A. (2021). FinTech: Ecosystem, Opportunities and Challenges in Saudi Arabia. *Journal of Risk and Financial Management*, 14(10), 10. 10.3390/jrfm14100460

Arner, D. W., Zetzsche, D. A., Buckley, R. P., & Barberis, J. N. (2019). The Identity Challenge in Finance: From Analogue Identity to Digitized Identification to Digital KYC Utilities. *European Business Organization Law Review*, 20(1), 55–80. 10.1007/s40804-019-00135-1

Ashta, A., & Herrmann, H. (2021). Artificial intelligence and fintech: An overview of opportunities and risks for banking, investments, and microfinance. *Strategic Change*, 30(3), 211–222. 10.1002/jsc.2404

Cambridge Centre for Alternative Finance. (2020). Cambridge Judge Business School. https://www.jbs.cam.ac.uk/faculty-research/centres/alternative-finance/

Duran, R. E., & Griffin, P. (2020). Smart contracts: Will Fintech be the catalyst for the next global financial crisis? *Journal of Financial Regulation and Compliance*, 29(1), 104–122. 10.1108/JFRC-09-2018-0122

Fabris, N. (2022). Impact of Covid-19 Pandemic on Financial Innovation, Cashless Society, and Cyber Risk. *ECONOMICS*, 10(1), 73–86. 10.2478/eoik-2022-0002

Ferreira, C. M. S., Oliveira, R. A. R., Silva, J. S., & da Cunha Cavalcanti, C. F. M. (2020). Blockchain for Machine to Machine Interaction in Industry 4.0. In da Rosa Righi, R., Alberti, A. M., & Singh, M. (Eds.), *Blockchain Technology for Industry 4.0: Secure, Decentralized, Distributed and Trusted Industry Environment* (pp. 99–116). Springer. 10.1007/978-981-15-1137-0_5

. Feyen, E., Frost, J., Gambacorta, L., Natarajan, H., & Saal, M. (2021). *Fintech and the digital transformation of financial services: Implications for market structure and public policy.*

Fulop, M. T., Topor, D. I., Ionescu, C. A., Căpu neanu, S., Breaz, T. O., & Stanescu, S. G. (2022). Fintech accounting and Industry 4.0: Future-proofing or threats to the accounting profession? *Journal of Business Economics and Management*, 23(5), 5. 10.3846/jbem.2022.17695

Ghazi-Tehrani, A. K., & Pontell, H. N. (2022). Comparative CriminologyComparative criminology and White-Collar CrimeWhite-collar crime. In Ghazi-Tehrani, A. K., & Pontell, H. N. (Eds.), *Wayward Dragon: White-Collar and Corporate Crime in China* (pp. 33–49). Springer International Publishing. 10.1007/978-3-030-90704-4_2

Gottschalk, P. (2010). Categories of financial crime. *Journal of Financial Crime*, 17(4), 441–458. 10.1108/13590791011082797

Gozman, D., & Willcocks, L. (2019). The emerging Cloud Dilemma: Balancing innovation with cross-border privacy and outsourcing regulations. *Journal of Business Research*, 97, 235–256. 10.1016/j.jbusres.2018.06.006

Hardy, J., & Bell, P. (2020). Resilience in sophisticated financial crime networks: A social network analysis of the Madoff Investment Scheme. *Crime Prevention and Community Safety*, 22(3), 223–247. 10.1057/s41300-020-00094-7

Henning, J. (2009). Perspectives on financial crimes in Roman-Dutch law: Bribery, fraud and the general crime of falsity (falsiteyt). *Journal of Financial Crime*, 16(4), 295–304. 10.1108/13590790910993771

Hua, X., & Huang, Y. (2021). Understanding China's fintech sector: Development, impacts and risks. *European Journal of Finance*, 27(4–5), 321–333. 10.1080/1351847X.2020.1811131

Jamil, A. H., Mohd Sanusi, Z., Yaacob, N. M., Mat Isa, Y., & Tarjo, T. (2021). The Covid-19 impact on financial crime and regulatory compliance in Malaysia. *Journal of Financial Crime*, 29(2), 491–505. 10.1108/JFC-05-2021-0107

Kujur, T., & Shah, M. A. (2015). *Electronic Banking: Impact*. Risk and Security Issues.

Kumari, A., & Devi, C. (2022). The Impact of FinTech and Blockchain Technologies on Banking and Financial Services. *Technology Innovation Management Review*, 12(1/2), 22010204. 10.22215/timreview/1481

Lagarde, C. (2016). Addressing Corruption Openly. In *The Power of Partnership: Selected Speeches by Christine Lagarde, 2011-2019*. eLibrary. https://www.elibrary.imf.org/display/book/9781513509907/ch09.xml

Lee, I., & Shin, Y. J. (2018). Fintech: Ecosystem, business models, investment decisions, and challenges. *Business Horizons*, 61(1), 35–46. 10.1016/j.bushor.2017.09.003

. Milanesi, D. (2022). *Buy Now, Pay Later ("BNPL") Under Regulatory Scrutiny – The Evolving Regulatory Landscape for BNPL in the United States, the United Kingdom, and Europe.*

Mirchandani, A., Gupta, N., & Ndiweni, E. (2020). UNDERSTANDING THE FINTECH WAVE: A SEARCH FOR A THEORETICAL EXPLANATION. *International Journal of Economics and Financial Issues*, 10(5), 331–343. 10.32479/ijefi.10296

Mishchenko, S., Naumenkova, S., Mishchenko, V., & Dorofeiev, D. (2021). Innovation risk management in financial institutions. *Investment Management and Financial Innovations*, 18(1), 190–202. 10.21511/imfi.18(1).2021.16

Mishra, D. R. N. (2019). *Dynamics of Operational Risk Management in Digital Arena Regulatory Panacea or Overkill?* (*SSRN* Scholarly Paper 3407160). 10.2139/ssrn.3407160

Nikkel, B. (2020). Fintech forensics: Criminal investigation and digital evidence in financial technologies. *Forensic Science International Digital Investigation*, 33, 200908. 10.1016/j.fsidi.2020.200908

Perera-Aldama, L., Amar, P., & Trostianki, D. (2009). Embedding corporate responsibility through effective organizational structures. *Corporate Governance (Bradford)*, 9(4), 506–516. 10.1108/14720700910985043

Pickett, K. H. S., & Pickett, J. M. (2002). *Financial Crime Investigation and Control*. John Wiley & Sons.

Ryu, H.-S. (2018). What makes users willing or hesitant to use Fintech?: The moderating effect of user type. *Industrial Management & Data Systems*, 118(3), 541–569. 10.1108/IMDS-07-2017-0325

Sahay, M. R., von Allmen, M. U. E., Lahreche, M. A., Khera, P., Ogawa, M. S., Bazarbash, M., & Beaton, M. K. (2020). *The Promise of Fintech: Financial Inclusion in the Post COVID-19 Era*. International Monetary Fund.

Salerno, A. C. F. (2019). Regulating the Fintech Revolution: How Regulators Can Adapt to Twenty-First Century Financial Technology. *Annual Survey of American Law*, 75, 365.

Sapkauskienė, A., & Višinskaitė, I. (2020). Initial Coin Offerings (ICOs): Benefits, risks and success measures. *Entrepreneurship and Sustainability Issues*, 7(3), 1472–1483. 10.9770/jesi.2020.7.3(3)

. Shah, M. A., Kumar, S., Shah, M. A., & Rasool, A. (2023). Examining the relationship among critical success factors (CSFs) for delivery of sustainable public-private partnership projects. *Journal of Financial Management of Property and Construction*. 10.1108/JFMPC-12-2022-0064

Shah, M. A., & Uddin, F. (2023). Leveraging Blockchain Technology in the Construction Industry. In *Building Secure Business Models Through Blockchain Technology: Tactics, Methods, Limitations, and Performance* (pp. 50–65). IGI Global. 10.4018/978-1-6684-7808-0.ch004

Song, Y., Chen, B., & Wang, X.-Y. (2023). Cryptocurrency technology revolution: Are Bitcoin prices and terrorist attacks related? *Financial Innovation*, 9(1), 29. 10.1186/s40854-022-00445-336712148

Zhao, Y., & Chen, X. (2021). The relationship between the withdrawal of the digital economy's innovators, government interventions, the marketization level and market size based on big data. *Journal of Enterprise Information Management*, 35(4/5), 1202–1232. 10.1108/JEIM-01-2021-0050

Chapter 6
Securing the Future Through AI, Green Finance, and Sustainable Development in the Digital Age

Numan Khan
Sunway University, Malaysia

Sitara Karim
https://orcid.org/0000-0001-5086-6230
Sunway University, Malaysia

Farah Naz
https://orcid.org/0000-0002-4707-5443
Kinnaird College for Women, Lahore, Pakistan

ABSTRACT

Climate change has become one of the pressing challenges in the 21st century. Ensuring and devising strategies to combat climate change is necessary and for this purpose, this study discusses the relationship between artificial intelligence, green finance, and sustainable development. Moreover, this study analyzes the role of green finance and its connection with AI and sustainable development. Green bonds, stocks, and cryptocurrencies are analyzed with the objective of its support towards sustainable development. The study further discussed that AI has key role in sustainable development through green finance and the interplay of these factors can achieve sustainable development goals. Furthermore, the chapter sheds light

DOI: 10.4018/979-8-3693-3633-5.ch006

Copyright © 2024, IGI Global. Copying or distributing in print or electronic forms without written permission of IGI Global is prohibited.

on challenges in the data for green finance and sustainable development where AI stands in between which generates data through its different technologies. This chapter offers various insights and implications for policymakers and government officials to help reshape sustainable development in the long run.

INTRODUCTION

The issue of climate change has been a pressing challenge for the world in recent decades. From the increasing sea levels to the food shortage and damaging concerns, to the rising sea levels, and increase in temperature has influenced mother nature drastically and adversely. Without tacking any drastic steps to change the scenario of the current climate crisis, will remain persistent and even more catastrophic in future. In the words of Guy McPherson "if you think that the environment is less important than the economy, try holding your breath while you count your money". Climate change refers to the changes in the weather patterns due to the changes in the natural environment i.e. Sun's activity or volcanic eruptions in the long term (UNEP,2018). The issue of climate change will not stop until the whole world takes responsibility for dealing with it while tackling its issues which causes it in the first place. The adverse effects of climate change around the world need serious consideration from the community, policy makers, and political leaders (Z. et al., 2023). Importance has been given in most part of the world particularly in the advanced economies and in some parts of the developing world in terms of Paris Agreement 2015 which includes Nationally Determined Contributions (NDCs) objectives for each country to reach the target of net zero emissions and in general achieve the sustainable development goals in 2030 (Yu et al., 2024; Goodell et al., 2024; Rao et al., 2024).

However, the rapid economic growth of developing economies, aimed at alleviating poverty, heavily relies on the substantial use of natural resources such as coal, oil, gas, and minerals. This dependency on fossil fuels leads to significant pollution of air and water. Additionally, the extraction of resources for rapid economic growth raises carbon dioxide (CO_2) and greenhouse gas (GHG) emissions (Rao et al., 2024). This surge in emissions contributes to environmental degradation, biodiversity loss, iceberg melting, and deforestation. These issues, in turn, lead to higher temperatures and exacerbate global warming (Z. Wang et al., 2023; Husain et al., 2024).

To address and limit the gap between the existing policies and the future sustainable options, the temperature needs to be reduced further and should not be increased more than 1.5 degrees. For these the greenhouse gas emissions will have to be sustained and more than its neutral behavior, it must be reduced in all sectors of economies particularly in the sectors of economy. Moreover, the target countries should be least developed because these economies rely more on fossil fuels than advanced economies. According to the Inter-governmental panel of climate change (IPCC), data of the most affected areas must be collected to build a climate resilient program and to adapt these economies towards more resilient climate programs (United nations, 2022). Without data and information systems, deep learning, and machine learning algorithms, most of the countries are facing difficulties in dealing with climate crisis. For instance, Middle East and African regions have lack of data among the least developed countries and faces issues in dealing with the sustainable development goals. The basic and most important facilities such as access to clean water and energies which can enhance women and children's lives, mapping of deforestation to avoid pollution in the air and water, low carbon electrification and avoid health hazard activities to promote high standard of living which could be beneficial in terms of socio-economic and environmental sustainability initiatives in the regions. Without data availability in most of the least developed regions, it hinders the possibility of sustainable development because the policy makers, political leaders and world organizations navigating the issues in the dark (Li et al., 2023). At the same time the region faces pressing challenges and finds difficulties in achieving the basic sustainable goals in the regions. Henceforth, to resolve the issue of data collection, mapping of issues in the region, artificial intelligence comes into play for the informed decisions making based on the data that could revolutionize the sustainability efforts which leads to sustainable development.

Artificial intelligence (AI) has gained tremendous significance in recent years as a transformative technology to target the issues of sustainable development. Generative AI is the technology that learns and senses the environment and acts upon that sense to provide the response based on that sense related to their programming objectives. These computer systems include diverse technologies which includes block chain (a distributed database that manages records in a growing number), machine learning (represents the collection of data and algorithms to act upon that data to imitate similarly to humans and gradually improves in the long run). Artificial intelligence targets the climate crisis in different ways. As discussed earlier, Arab, and African regions are data scarce regions which covers the area of 22.4% of the world have strong implications for climate crisis. AI can play its role in the data scarcity issues in these regions along with other regions where the data is scarce and policy makers find it difficult to promote sustainable environment and development initiatives in the regions. AI holds the upper hand in this category through its data mapping techniques, tracking system and machine learning algorithms can help the climate crisis issues and can pave the way for climate resilient policies.

Figure 1. The graphical illustration of blockchain technology globally and its share in the economic sectors

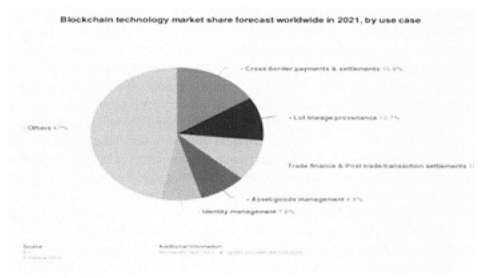

Source (Statista, 2022)

Moreover, cutting-edge technologies and applications i.e. block chain, internet of things, and machine learning algorithms. AI is known for creating its synthetic data sets and data augmentation which can imitate human and real data sets and bootstrapping these data sets through different algorithms to provide timely solutions for climate change. Besides, AI is supporting the initiatives of deforestation mapping through generative AI technologies, data sensing through satellite imagery networks, track natural disasters, evaluate water resources, and efficiency of natural resources extraction and utilization through its big data techniques and machines learning algorithms. Nevertheless, on a micro (i.e. firms' level) block chain technology has revolutionized the artificial intelligence industry by combining blocks and chains which creates chains of blocks, and unlike centralized database, it's a decentralized ones providing access to every stakeholder. Comparatively, Blockchain technology is more secured than any other traditional databases due its hashing and digital signatures which holds importance in accessing the data and tampering them would lead to change the hash of the block every time in the database (Ali et al., 2016; Khan et al., 2017). This technology users have access to cryptographic keys to get each time new passwords and validate digital signatures further boosting digital security of the users.

The advantageous nature of blockchain technology, it targets climate change and global warming its unique perspective. Renewable energy trading and peer to peer energy trading efficiently manages the selling and buying of renewable energy without the involvement of traditional brokers and intermediaries to create the deal between the two parties. Since there is no third-party involvement in the trading of clean energy systems and technologies, blockchain has enhanced efficiency in the clean energy areas and have further expanded the financial opportunities which increases sustainable finance and targets climate change. Blockchain reduces material footprints and carbon emissions in the industry level by tracking each party involved in the supply chain is compliant with the sustainable environment and any violation alerts the firm to stop the payment of a party involving in unsustainable activities through its smart contracts. Hence, generative AI (machine learning and Blockchain) technologies play a key role in enhancing sustainable development initiatives (Acemoglu & Restrepo, 2019). Figure 1 shows the share of blockchain technologies globally which indicates how fast economic sectors have adopted blockchain and its significance will further increase in the long run.

Consistent with the AI and sustainable development, sustainable finance is one of the leading determinants of sustainable development index. Green finance refers to the financial flows which can be directed towards the sustainable development activities from the public, private and non-profitable sectors (UNEP). The key part of this finance is to deal with the environmental and social risks along with sustainable returns for the investors to engage in a win-win situation. The organizations on climate change have been striving to connect and direct the financial inflows from every sector towards renewable energy sectors, enhance investments in efficient technologies, production and manufacturing activities which could lead to sustainability and efficiency in using of resources in the long run. UN environments remain relevant in this area and its sister organizations have been constantly engaged in trying to allocate capital to shape today's financial eco-system for better consumption and production in the future. Hence, in today's world, the current initiatives and advancement in technology suggests that AI, green finance, and sustainable development have strong interplay and can shape the sustainable future of the world. To support the low carbon economy and backing up of the economies and its economic sectors for their transition towards renewable and efficient technologies, generative AI and sustainable finance should be taken into the limelight for sustainable development.

The remaining part of the study is organized in the following manner. Section 2 of this study comprehensively explains the role of artificial intelligence, challenges, and opportunities for sustainable development. Section 3 discusses the evolution of green finance and its connection with artificial intelligence and sustainable development. Section 4 provides important case studies while Section 5 concludes the study along with the future research directions for the further enhancement of the linkages of AI and financial sector towards sustainability.

THE IMPORTANCE OF ARTIFICIAL INTELLIGENCE IN PROTECTING FINANCIAL SUSTAINABLE DEVELOPMENT

Artificial intelligence has evolved over the years from mere conceptual understandings to practical applications, and we have witnessed its revolutionary impact on technological advancements in recent decades. Artificial intelligence term was coined in 1950 by mathematicians which could help in solving algebra problems till to the 20th century which evolves as the advanced technologies supporting different aspects of the economy and environment. AI first evolved as the language which solved problems in the 70's and 60's and enhanced into the machine learning algorithms in the 90's which is way more powerful and can imitate human capabilities. In the early 20th and the 21st century AI has been evolving constantly with the pace towards more advancement and learning methods shifting its focus from robots and tradition AI technologies towards more sophisticated and complex methods (Agrawal et al., 2019). Block chain and Cloud computing kind of applications have been considered the cutting-edge technologies applications which help in ensuring the safety and smooth process of businesses along with its focus on the sustainable operations globally. Moreover, internet of things and quantum computing helps the industries to enhance connectivity and solve advance problems face by the firms in the industries. Besides, the introduction of voice assistance programs developed through machine learning programs, robots, that are dissimilar to the traditional robots because of its usage of clean energy, vehicles and industrial machineries are evident of increased role in efficiency and sustainable operations (Kaack et al., 2022).

Nevertheless, understanding of the machine learning, block chain, cloud computing, machine learning for sustainable development is mainly represented using renewable and energy efficient technologies such as the robots which use cleaner energy systems to drive and perform operations. In the earlier days, using the AI technologies such as robots would emit large amount of carbon emissions and causing material footprint, however, the investments and increasing role of green finance initiatives in the economies stimulates the process of renewable energy technologies and clean energy which supports these robots. Proper assessment of these robots decreases pollution and carbon emissions which effectively combats climate change (Karanth et al., 2023). The usage of artificial intelligence technologies and machine learning applications have been increasing which supports these robots and similar projects. Figure 2 explains the corporate investments by the companies in artificial intelligence globally by different stakeholders such as investments done through

Securing the Future Through AI, Green Finance, Sustainable Development

mergers and acquisitions have remained very high which shows that companies around the globe are joining the bandwagon of AI (Artificial Intelligence - Our World in Data, 2023). It should be noted that in the last previous decade alone—despite of the pandemic crisis Covid-19, Russian-Ukrainian conflict, oil crisis in 2014– (these are the major volatile which effects the investment ratios in the world by companies and individuals) has seen the significant increase in the evolution and rise of investments in artificial intelligence around the globe.

Figure 2. The investments of different stakeholders in AI from 2013-2022

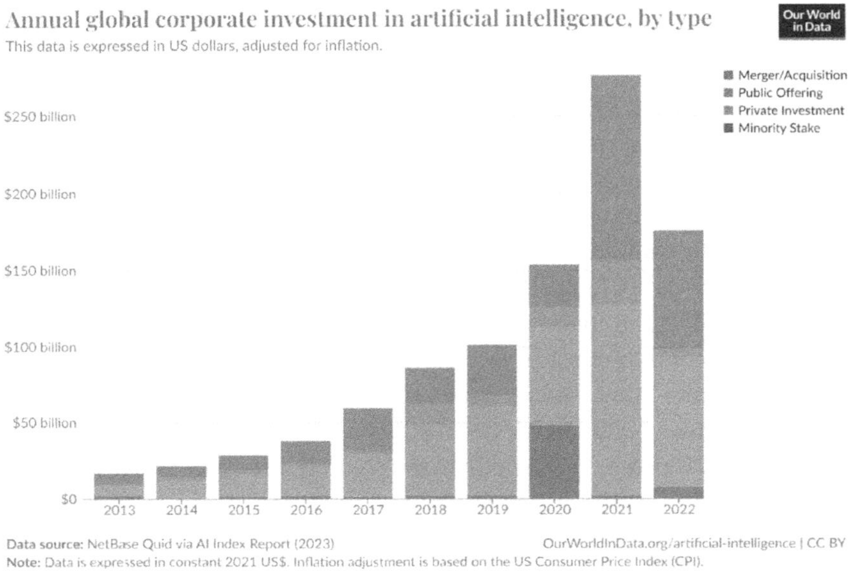

Annual global corporate investment in artificial intelligence, by type
This data is expressed in US dollars, adjusted for inflation.

- Merger/Acquisition
- Public Offering
- Private Investment
- Minority Stake

Data source: NetBase Quid via AI Index Report (2023)
OurWorldInData.org/artificial-intelligence | CC BY
Note: Data is expressed in constant 2021 US$. Inflation adjustment is based on the US Consumer Price Index (CPI).

Source (Artificial Intelligence - Our World in Data, 2023).

With these intensive and rising in investments in AI shows significant changes in the field of sustainable development and combating climate crisis. The changes occurred from the energy intensive robots which uses high energy to perform the tasks and causes environmental degradation towards to more clean energy robots to use renewable energies. More energy efficient designs are developing and to further decrease emissions, the world particularly, advanced, and emerging economies are applying for patents of new robots which could emerge from the recycling of electronic products (Z. Wang et al., 2023). The traction of recycling items has been getting attention to achieve high level of sustainability in the regions across the world.

Moreover, the big data concepts which comprise of structured and unstructured data, audios, videos, and text messages and compiling and analyzing data to grab the efficient outputs have been an important aspect of AI which stimulates sustainable development. Big data is analyzed and supported using machine learning algorithms which provide the outputs related to the climate crisis and can be significantly tackled through strong policy recommendations and implications. Despite of this raw data in different forms and structures, machine learning has been one of the important tools execute this data, analyze the historical patterns of the data, and predict the future outcomes for the policy makers and authorities through which decisions can be taken for sustainable future and initiatives that targets sustainable environment around the world (Dwivedi et al., 2023; Hofmann et al., 2008).

When discussing the role of AI in sustainable development, it is argued that AI utilizes various technologies (as previously mentioned) to combat climate change globally. Despite of the negative influence of AI on the environment in some respects due to traditional robots and technologies, the world is adopting and adapting the concepts of generative AI technologies, applications, and methods in particular machine learning, cloud computing and Block chain which has remained at the forefront of sustainability (Kumar et al., 2022). For this reason, policy makers and global leaders should pay heed to the artificial intelligence which is still an emerging area due to its importance that it could be considered the as strong weapon many areas to combat the climate crisis hanging over the world. For this, the sustainable finance initiatives should also be promoted (discussed in the next section) which has been proven as the game changer in the clean energy and efficient technologies area to further strengthened the environmental objectives and promote sustainable socio-economic development in the region (Dhar, 2020). However, transparency and avoidance of green washing issues should be ensured to promote the fair process and implementation of AI in the field of sustainability.

OVERVIEW OF GREEN FINANCE-SUSTAINABLE DEVELOPMENT NEXUS IN PROTECTING DATA

Green finance after becoming one of the leading determinants has been increasing since 2013 because the green bonds were formulated and issued by economies in their struggle against climate change and it has now reached to 21.3 trillion dollars in 2021-2022. Fortunately, despite the pandemic, the amount of sustainable finance increased by 439 billion dollars alone in 2021-2022 (Sachs et al, 2023). This formulates that the policies have been in place for the sustainable development and achievement of SDGs, however, the critiques claim that most of the increase has been possible due to the artificial intelligence which improves the sources and data collection and since new data is pouring in the database, the figures of green finance increased in the recent years. This shows that a lot of improvements and struggle is required to improve the level of green finance for sustainable development (Rasoulinezhad & Taghizadeh-Hesary, 2022; Zhang et al., 2022). Another strong reason for the improvements in green finance is due to the methodological reasonings which shows significant improvements in the public and private sector because of improving their regulations structures, policies and operations which attracts more finances in this area to increase environmental quality.

Despite the improvements and drastic changes in the financial development structure, a substantial gap is present in between green finance and sustainable development. While the developed and advanced economies have been prominent in this sustainability, they are causing externalities in the developing and emerging economies which keep and lags these countries (R. Wang et al., 2023). Most of the economies in developing world such as India, Pakistan, China, African regions require extreme focus to improve the indicators of sustainable finance to reduce the greenhouse gas emissions. Without lowering pollution in Air and Water in the developing regions, the climate change will persist and despite of the improvements in the advanced economies, the large part of the world is still in dire need of finance because these regions would be a game changer in combating a climate change. According to the Asian development bank and Asian policy makers that the developing economies in Asia require 1.6 trillion dollars per year with a total of 26 trillion dollars till 2030 to eradicate poverty, combat climate crisis, improve environmental quality and enhance sustainable development. it is evident that most of the economies in the developing Asia are dependent on the natural resource's extraction and its utilization and consumption for energy generation makes it worse and creates a dilemma to deal with both the poverty eradication and carbon emissions. These economies use 66% of coal to generate electricity and energy for production and manufacturing for rapid economic expansion. However, the lesser use of renewable energy and efficient technologies have left behind these countries in terms of SDGs. In terms of green investments, most of the economies are taking because of the global pressure such as China is one of the leading economies in Asia which has invest billions of dollars, started new initiatives such as carbon financing and pilot carbon trading schemes, however, despite of these large initiatives, the economy still requires huge investments depending on its economy size to reduce greenhouse gas emissions (Z. Wang et al., 2023; Razi et al., 2024).

To promote the initiatives in Asian regions many governing bodies are taking drastic measures and devising policies for them such as Asian development bank, World Bank, United Nations, and African development Bank. The Asian economies generates large amounts of finances through green bonds, environment related taxes, and related long term debts finances with the help of priorly mentioned bodies to tackle the menace of climate change and improve sustainable development in addition to long-term debt, Asian governments should increase levies and taxes on intensive and traditional technology users to reduce carbon emissions and promote environmental sustainability. New programs should be developed at the micro-level to raise awareness among corporations about sustainable initiatives. Furthermore, higher taxes should be imposed on corporations using traditional energy sources to boost revenue, which can then be invested in sustainable initiatives.

Usefulness of Green Finance and Its Instruments in Overcoming the Issues in Financial Sustainable Development

Sustainable finance in general and green finance in particular is recognized as one of the crucial elements in sustainable development. Green finance includes activities and financial instruments which are directed towards environmental sustainability and reduction of CO_2 emissions vis-à-vis GHG emissions. Environmental bodies and institutions like Inter-governmental panel for climate change (IPCC), UN-environmental Program and similar organizations have recognized the need for financial tools and instruments which needs to be targeted at the reduction of CO_2 emissions and more importantly its urgency is stressed in many areas of operations. Many governing bodies specific to countries and to the world such as UNFCCC which conducted the Paris climate agreement, clearly specifies to focus on the green initiatives and combat climate change by reducing the temperature and limit it to 1.5 degree centigrade. Furthermore, policy makers are recognizing the need for green finance and thereby promoting it by incentivizing the renewable energy projects, taxing the operations which causes CO_2 and GHG emissions. Moreover, to promote sustainable development objectives, most of the countries have adopted the regulations of compulsory regulations and disclosures for the industries and firms which ultimately leads to the promotion of green finance. These disclosures come in different perspectives which includes ESG (environmental social governance) requirements for companies and carbon taxes, for the companies involved in causing carbon emissions by using fossil fuels in production processes.

Moreover, the private and non-profit organizations sector also played a major role in the promotion of green finance since last decade. Stakeholders demands the private corporations and institutions include sustainable options in their operations which are measured through ESG (environmental social governance) scores. Moreover, the public institutions started green bonds in 2013 which specifically target the environment and the funds through these bonds are raised specifically for the environmental concerns and projects related to sustainable development.

Other than discussing the background of green finance, its usefulness is recognized in a sense that it channelizes funds through financial instruments which includes green bonds, carbon finance, climate finance and similar kinds of finances targeted at the sustainable initiatives and economic development (Zhang, 2023). Green finance supports projects such as renewable energy projects such as installation of solar and wind projects. Besides, the increasing of energy efficient technologies in industries to enhance sustainable economic progression, it also increases jobs and employment opportunities, promoting other sectors of the economy and creating long term economic resilience.

Given the green finance usefulness, it has emerged one of the stable finance initiatives directly after the global financial crisis and has remained stable in events such as oil crisis 2014 and Covid-19 pandemic. Nevertheless, investors prefer green financial products because of long term economic and financial resilience which makes it suitable even for prospective customers as well. Green finance is more related to the sustainability because its ultimate objectives are related to the reduction of environmental pollution and promote sustainability whereas its resilience comes from the idea that it reduces the reliance on fossil fuels and diminishes the risks of the volatility in the natural resources. Moreover, green finance helps the economy in transitions towards low or zero carbon economy because it finances projects which are energy efficient, clean, and innovative in a sense that emit zero or very lesser carbon emissions. Furthermore, green finance provides the opportunities to the administrations and companies attracting collectively sensible investors invest and finance these companies because of their focus on the sustainability and therefore, it leads these companies towards getting a strong position in the market and grab these companies into more fruitful competitive advantages in the future. Companies having lesser access to traditional finance might attract more investments when they have a focus on the SDGs and environmental quality because they can offer bonds which matures in a very long term and that benefits ultimately both the companies and environment, creating a win-win situation. Figure 2 provides the data of climate related finances from 2012-2022 which shows how the investments and financing have been increased in one decade, but still a lot more must be done to enhance it further and help the least developed economies to achieve the SDGs in 2030. Finally, green finance is increasing through new financial technologies ("fintech") which can further enhance the role of financing and financial investments (Karim & Lucey, 2024). Three broad areas that come under AI are blockchain technologies, Internet of things (IoT) and big data which helps in the accessibility and feasibility of green finance and channelize its impact on the sustainable development. Sustainable development is not just a wish or a slogan; it offers the right path to achieving green growth and high employment. Therefore, it is time to give it the focus and attention it truly deserves.

Figure 3. The green finance initiatives (investments) from 2011-2022

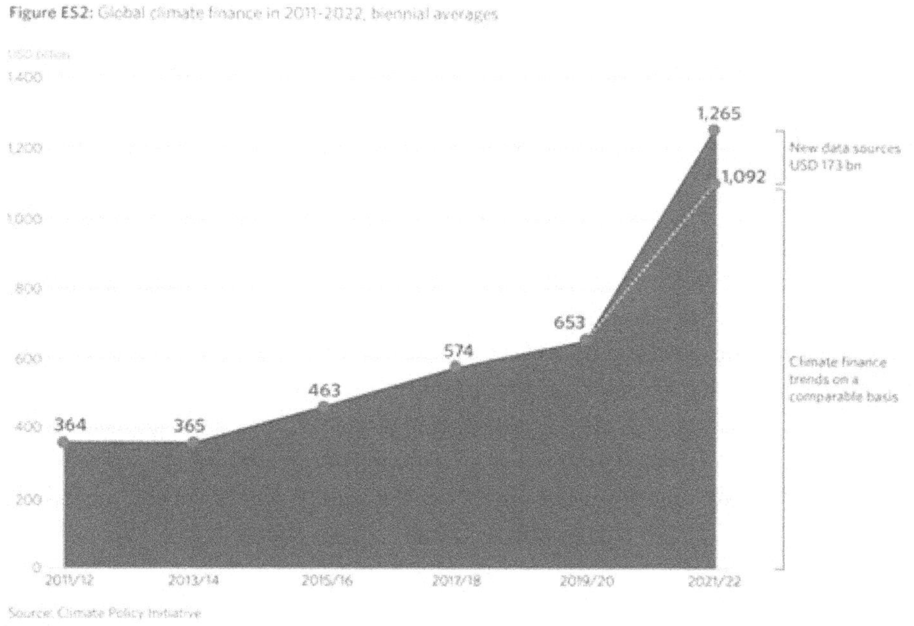

Source: (Climate Policy Initiative, 2023).

Nexus of AI, Green Finance, and Sustainable Development in Safeguarding Data

Artificial intelligence along with green finance provides different yet dynamic experience in the sustainable development. Given the urgency of climate crisis in the world, AI technologies and methods predict the places and the urgency of green finance through its different tools. On the other hand, green finance initiatives stimulate financing in technologies that advance, energy efficient and sustainable which includes artificial technologies as well (J. Wang et al., 2023). By advancing the green investments in these areas enhance research and development, new technologies that could enhance the purpose of generative AI and overall level of sustainable development. Moreover, the rise of electronic finance and financial technologies (Fintech) has been the game changer in green finance dimension and AI because fintech uses both sides of the systems which includes blockchain technologies for securing of payments and finance which is used in the sustainable activities (Della Valle et al., 2024; Naz et al., 2023; Siddique et al., 2022; 2023). Financial technologies in the field of AI have developed and are still advancing with pace in recent years particularly after the pandemic.

In addition, it is evident from the previous work of financial companies that AI improves sustainability through green finance which indicates that AI is one of the main drivers of green finance. Climate investing and green investments are especially important (as discussed in the previous sections), in this regard, AI provides the ways and methods such as machine learning and deep learning techniques and algorithms to help the corporations and governments to correctly make the decision of investing or financing projects, calculate the risks of that financial investments and find out the responsibilities and regulations of the companies to avoid green washing. While performing these steps and channelizing the influence of AI towards green finance indicates that it could strengthen the green finance decisions, promote sustainable development, and enhance its role in the attainment of SDGs. Moreover, with the expansion in the capabilities of AI, it is now more powerful which can calculate the output of renewable energy consumption and provides decision makers the outcomes through which further expansion in clean energy technologies are possible in the future. Henceforth, these outcomes provide long-term benefits for society and environment along with sustainable economic progression.

Besides predicting the outcomes of green finance through AI, helps the policy makers to invest and adopt renewable energy technologies for production and household consumption which further leads towards the step of achieving green economic progression and improves the environment by reducing the reliance on fossil fuels consumption. Hence, it can be concluded that AI, green finance, and sustainable development are interrelated factors which cause each in the long run and have strong equilibrium exists among these variables. Furthermore, AI's advanced capabilities and green financial instruments develop a strong framework which channelizes its impact towards to sustainable development by increasing efficiency in the process, reliability, and accountability in the pursuit of sustainable future. The synergistic role of these factors together can form and reshape a new and dynamic relationship not only supports sustainable economic growth but also play its role in protecting planetary health.

CASE STUDIES OF THE COMPANIES

Several companies across the world have adopted technologies related to artificial intelligence which have revolutionized the operating system of their companies. The adoption and integration of AI technologies helps in reducing fraudulent activities, tracking and ensuring of sustainability across the operations of the firm, enhancing transparency in the operations, providing accessibility in easy way and promoting their safety in the long run. This section expands into the companies which have adopted several technologies artificial intelligence.

Tech Mahindra

Tech Mahindra is one of the leading companies in the technology sphere, having a vast network in more than 90 countries with 152,000 in workforce. Tech Mahindra provides its services in the field of artificial intelligence, 5G, Meta Verse and quantum computing. The company serves and aspires firms most of which comes in the list of fortune 500 companies. These firms are mostly engaged in oil and gas, manufacturing, government firms and health care industries (Forbes,2024). Tech Mahindra has adopted blockchain technology called "Block Ecosystem" which has positioned this company as one of the leading in the field of AI and serving the firms efficiently and effectively through its advanced AI technologies. TM uses Hyperledger fabric, Quorum and Ripple kinds of protocols —depending on the company's requirements— which ensures scalability, wider applications of customized blockchain technologies for the client firms and ensures in activities such as transaction processes, cross border payments and health care services (Jan et al., 2024; Nygaard & Silkoset, 2023). From building customized applications for companies to ready technologies for companies checking their own technologies, TM has ensured the transparency, safety and security of transactions and digital identities of firms and customers.

TM is helping in implementation of block chain and cloud computing technologies with its several protocols enhancing the efficiency and transparency of discounting invoices, cross border transactions, and international payments. Blockchain and cloud computing has made it easier for companies to reduce the margins of errors and to ensure smooth and tidy outcomes of their operations.

PayPal

PayPal has differentiated itself from the traditional financial companies and online banking system. PayPal is designed in a way which has made the online shopping, digital payments, and cross border transactions so smooth with a vision that everyone has the right to take part in the global economy. PayPal is famous for international payments and has a more transparent and worthy system which keeps the user's money secure and safe (Mbaidin et al., 2023). Similar to Mahindra Tech, PayPal uses three important protocols which are Bitcoin, Ethereum and Litecoin, these support the easy payments for customers in a most secure and efficient fashion. Bitcoin is one of the leading cryptocurrencies which supports the transactions of PayPal through its proof of Work mechanism to make the transactions secure and reliable (Böhmecke-Schwafert & García Moreno, 2023). The advantage of Bitcoin is that it is the largest and highly known cryptocurrency which makes it the perfect choice for PayPal consumers.

PayPal through its blockchain technologies users a digital record through its Bitcoins with encrypting the information and track the digital transactions makes it impossible to corrupt in the long run. The company provides more support and information to provide users with learning and has made it easy for them where they can transfer Bitcoin in and to other digital wallets and exchanges.

Samsung Group

One of the giant industry leaders in the telecom industry in the past years has faced security and safety concerns regarding customer data around the world. In 2022, Samsung, has actively invested in blockchain technologies, similar AI technologies and Metaverse to provide their customers with advanced security solutions and excellent experience of using Samsung Digital Wallets. Samsung has remained committed to the security of operations in their devices and have also introduced the virtual asset management program through blockchain in their wallet systems which reduces the possibilities of frauds and corrupt transactions. The Samsung Block Chain wallet is one of its kind which accepts transactions and transfers it smoothly to other digital wallets in an easy and more reliable way. Other than Bitcoin, Samsung uses protocols like Tron (TRX) and TRC-20 tokens. For the developers, the company has expanded its blockchain technology through the protocols of Ledger Nano S and Ledger Nano X enables the developers to import its assets into Samsung in more secure ways.

Besides, the company has further expanded its blockchain technologies into newsfeed where they consumers and Samsung users can get new information, guidance and learning of advancements in blockchain technology within the Samsung to make the customers satisfied for its security in using the company products. Once known for lesser secure companies than its competitors, Samsung has pushed itself in the arena of safe and sound environment where the customers lesser feel to be hacked or face fraudulent activities while transforming their experience into new dimensions.

Oracle

Conversely, to the prior mentioned case studies, Oracle along with blockchain technology is more related to the cloud computing and in this area, the firm is highly involved in creating software's and technologies with an efficient infrastructure which enhances firms' performance more efficiently and effectively. Moreover, with the provision of software for data processing and securing it, Oracle has decentralized software based on blockchain technology with cloud computing which provides secure and safe access to customers. Moreover, Oracle blockchain provides a collaborative network and platform for the customers to store their data securely and safely with digital key access and specific wallets. Nevertheless, Oracle has revolutionized the supply chain and specifically the transportation industry where they have launched SaaS application tracks and collect data for the users(Saurabh et al., 2024). Such applications are operated through cloud on premises and hybrid blockchain options. Figure 4 provides the global SaaS application investments till 2025 which indicates that investments in these applications becoming necessaity and to deal with the challenges of sustainability, cloud computing for efficient data processing is necessary.

Figure 4. Illustrates the investments in cloud computing and its applications

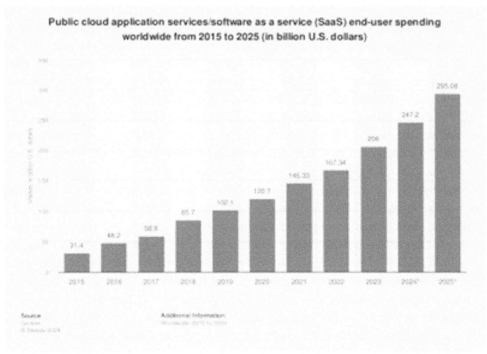

Source (Statista,2024)

Nonetheless, Oracle follows Hyperledger blockchain protocols which runs and is supported through Linux foundations and frameworks (Singh et al., 2023). This protocol mainly oversees the security of user data and ensures authorized access to databases.

Having said that, these case studies focused on the tracking of the data, its security, ensuring it to be non-corrupted and safety of the data. All these provide that when countries and firms have corrected data and secure through blockchain, it can provide several opportunities and plans for achieving sustainable development and more importantly it can track the performance of companies and countries towards sustainable development.

CONCLUSION AND RECOMMENDATIONS

This study examines the interplay of Artificial intelligence, green finance, and sustainable development. The qualitative nature of this study provided different insights related to the artificial intelligence and green finance and its theoretical and practical connection with the sustainable development globally. Artificial intelligence presents opportunities for sustainability and tackling the issue of harmful emissions generated through fossil fuels and dirty sources of energy consumption. We have discussed that Artificial intelligence promotes technologies and methods such as blockchain technology, Internet of things (IoT) and cloud computing while machine learning and its algorithms, deep learning and big data related methods prominently play its role in the reduction of environmental degradation and promotion of sustainability practices around the globe. Blockchain technologies are considered the most secured decentralized technologies which tracks the sustainability practices of each company through its sophisticated tracking and secure methods from manufacturing to the transportation of products towards final consumers. Cloud computing and IoT provide relevant and related support in the achievement of SDGs. Moreover, Machine learning algorithms helps in analyzing the data on its historical backgrounds and predict the future events related to climate crisis which can be reduced through its future data observations. To promote the methods and technologies of AI which are sustainable, the world needs more financial support which is supported through green finance and its different instruments from green bonds to green securities and carbon trading activities. Green finance targets efficient technologies, clean and renewable energy technologies which indirectly promote AI technologies and directly reduce environmental degradation and in turn promote sustainable development. Green finance and AI significantly play its role in sustainable development and providing opportunities for the policy makers and authorities to promote these determinants in the future.

This study provides the following recommendations and implications based on the discussion and conclusions. First, the use AI applications should be enhanced particularly in the least developed regions such as Middle East and African regions to garner and nourish the data possibilities which are related to the future climate changes. Moreover, these applications should be adopted globally in ethical framework considerations to focus on the correct data and its measures. Second, authorities should promote the AI certifications which must ensure reliability, safety and validity of the data and its affiliation, consistency and dependability with the sustainable development and SDGs. Third, policy makers should recognize the benefits of green finance in the Asia pacific and African regions to further invest in it which could directly enhance the use of renewable energy products, efficient technologies in production and manufacturing while could indirectly pave the way for AI technologies which are also advantageous for the promotion of sustainable development. Fourth, Policy makers should strengthen and enhance the green financial instruments by increasing regulations and environmental taxes which would further create climate resilience in the future and enhance sustainable initiatives. In this way, combating climate crisis can be ensured and future economic resilience will be ensured through the strengthening of policies in AI and green finance initiatives globally. Lastly, AI, green finance and sustainable development eco-system should be the top priority of policy makers and government officials which should focus on these aspects, increase investments in these areas to advance the sustainable practices in the regions with more correction, efficiency, and reliability.

REFERENCES

Acemoglu, D., & Restrepo, P. (2019). Artificial Intelligence, Automation, and Work. *The Economics of Artificial Intelligence*, 197–236. 10.7208/chicago/9780226613475.003.0008

Agrawal, A., Gans, J., & Goldfarb, A. (2019). *The Economics of Artificial Intelligence*. University of Chicago Press. 10.7208/chicago/9780226613475.001.0001

Ali, K., Khan, Z., Khan, N., Alsubaie, A.-H. I., Subhan, F., & Kanadil, M. (2016). Performance Evaluation of UK Acquiring Companies in the Pre and Post-Acquisitions Periods. *Asian Journal of Economics and Empirical Research*, 3(2), 130–138. https://ideas.repec.org/a/aoj/ajeaer/v3y2016i2p130-138id220.html. 10.20448/journal.501/2016.3.2/501.2.130.138

Böhmecke-Schwafert, M., & García Moreno, E. (2023). Exploring blockchain-based innovations for economic and sustainable development in the global south: A mixed-method approach based on web mining and topic modeling. *Technological Forecasting and Social Change*, 191, 122446. 10.1016/j.techfore.2023.122446

Climate Policy Initiative. (n.d.). *Expertise in climate finance and policy analysis*. CPI. https://www.climatepolicyinitiative.org/

Della Valle, N., D'Arcangelo, C., & Faillo, M. (2024). Promoting pro-environmental choices while addressing energy poverty. *Energy Policy*, 186, 113967. 10.1016/j.enpol.2023.113967

Dhar, P. (2020). The carbon impact of artificial intelligence. *Nature Machine Intelligence*, 2(8), 423–425. 10.1038/s42256-020-0219-9

Dwivedi, D., Batra, S., & Pathak, Y. K. (2023). A machine learning based approach to identify key drivers for improving corporate's esg ratings. *Journal of Law and Sustainable Development*, 11(1), e0242. 10.37497/sdgs.v11i1.242

Goodell, J. W., Gurdgiev, C., Karim, S., & Palma, A. (2024). Carbon emissions and liquidity management. *International Review of Financial Analysis*, 95, 103367. 10.1016/j.irfa.2024.103367

Husain, A., Karim, S., & Sensoy, A. (2024). Financial fusion: Bridging Islamic and Green investments in the European stock market. *International Review of Financial Analysis*, 94, 103341. 10.1016/j.irfa.2024.103341

Jan, A., Salameh, A. A., Rahman, H. U., & Alasiri, M. M. (2024). Can blockchain technologies enhance environmental sustainable development goals performance in manufacturing firms? Potential mediation of green supply chain management practices. *Business Strategy and the Environment*, 33(3), 2004–2019. 10.1002/bse.3579

Kaack, L. H., Donti, P. L., Strubell, E., Kamiya, G., Creutzig, F., & Rolnick, D. (2022). Aligning artificial intelligence with climate change mitigation. *Nature Climate Change, 12*(6), 518–527. 10.1038/s41558-022-01377-7

Karanth, S., Benefo, E. O., Patra, D., & Pradhan, A. K. (2023). Importance of artificial intelligence in evaluating climate change and food safety risk. *Journal of Agriculture and Food Research*, 11, 100485. 10.1016/j.jafr.2022.100485

Karim, S., & Lucey, B. M. (2024). BigTech, FinTech, and banks: A tangle or unity? *Finance Research Letters*, 64, 105490. 10.1016/j.frl.2024.105490

Khan, N., Ali, K., Kiran, A., Mubeen, R., Khan, Z., & Ali, N. (2017). Factors that Affect the Derivatives Usage of Non-Financial Listed Firms of Pakistan to Hedge Foreign Exchange Exposure. *Journal of Banking and Financial Dynamics*, 1(1), 9–20. 10.20448/journal.525/2017.1.1/525.1.9.20

Kumar, S., Sharma, D., Rao, S., Lim, W. M., & Mangla, S. K. (2022). Past, present, and future of sustainable finance: Insights from big data analytics through machine learning of scholarly research. *Annals of Operations Research*. 10.1007/s10479-021-04410-835002001

Li, M., Zhang, K., Alamri, A. M., Ageli, M. M., & Khan, N. (2023). Resource curse hypothesis and sustainable development: Evaluating the role of renewable energy and R&D. *Resources Policy*, 81, 103283. 10.1016/j.resourpol.2022.103283

Mbaidin, H. O., Alsmairat, M. A. K., & Al-Adaileh, R. (2023). Blockchain adoption for sustainable development in developing countries: Challenges and opportunities in the banking sector. *International Journal of Information Management Data Insights*, 3(2), 100199. 10.1016/j.jjimei.2023.100199

Naz, F., Karim, S., Houcine, A., & Naeem, M. A. (2024). Fintech growth during COVID-19 in MENA region: Current challenges and future prospects. *Electronic Commerce Research*, 24(1), 371–392. 10.1007/s10660-022-09583-3

Nygaard, A., & Silkoset, R. (2023). Sustainable development and greenwashing: How blockchain technology information can empower green consumers. *Business Strategy and the Environment*, 32(6), 3801–3813. 10.1002/bse.3338

Rao, A., Kumar, S., & Karim, S. (2024). Accelerating renewables: Unveiling the role of green energy markets. *Applied Energy*, 366, 123286. 10.1016/j.apenergy.2024.123286

Rasoulinezhad, E., & Taghizadeh-Hesary, F. (2022). Role of green finance in improving energy efficiency and renewable energy development. *Energy Efficiency*, 15(2), 1–12. 10.1007/s12053-022-10021-435529528

Razi, U., Karim, S., & Cheong, C. W. (2024). From Turbulence to Resilience: A Bibliometric Insight into the Complex Interactions Between Energy Price Volatility and Green Finance. *Energy*, 304, 131992. 10.1016/j.energy.2024.131992

Saurabh, K., Rani, N., & Upadhyay, P. (2024). Towards novel blockchain decentralised autonomous organisation (DAO) led corporate governance framework. *Technological Forecasting and Social Change*, 204, 123417. 10.1016/j.techfore.2024.123417

Siddique, M. A., Nobanee, H., Karim, S., & Naz, F. (2022). Investigating the role of metal and commodity classes in overcoming resource destabilization. *Resources Policy*, 79, 103075. 10.1016/j.resourpol.2022.103075

Siddique, M. A., Nobanee, H., Karim, S., & Naz, F. (2023). Do green financial markets offset the risk of cryptocurrencies and carbon markets? *International Review of Economics & Finance*, 86, 822–833. 10.1016/j.iref.2023.04.005

Singh, A. K., Kumar, V. R. P., Shoaib, M., Adebayo, T. S., & Irfan, M. (2023). A strategic roadmap to overcome blockchain technology barriers for sustainable construction: A deep learning-based dual-stage SEM-ANN approach. *Technological Forecasting and Social Change*, 194, 122716. 10.1016/j.techfore.2023.122716

Wang, J., Wang, W., Liu, Y., & Wu, H. (2023). Can industrial robots reduce carbon emissions? Based on the perspective of energy rebound effect and labor factor flow in China. *Technology in Society*, 72, 102208. 10.1016/j.techsoc.2023.102208

Wang, R., Destek, M. A., Weimei, C., Albahooth, B., & Khan, Z. (2023). Drivers of Sustainable Green Finance: Country's Level Risk and Trade Perspective for OECD Countries. *Journal of Environment & Development*. 10.1177/10704965231217046/ASSET/IMAGES/LARGE/10.1177_10704965231217046-FIG2.JPEG

Wang, Z., Alamri, A. M., Mawad, J. L., Zhang, M., & Khan, N. (2023). Sustainable growth and green environment? Evidence from nonparametric methods provincial data of China. *Ekonomska Istrazivanja*, 36(3), 2152070. 10.1080/1331677X.2022.2152070

Yu, S., Liang, Y., Zhu, Z., Olaniyi, O. N., & Khan, N. (2024). Dutch disease perspective of energy sector: Natural resources and energy sector nexus with the role of renewable energy consumption. *Resources Policy*, 90, 104740. 10.1016/j.resourpol.2024.104740

Zhang, D. (2023). Does green finance really inhibit extreme hypocritical ESG risk? A greenwashing perspective exploration. *Energy Economics*, 121, 106688. 10.1016/j.eneco.2023.106688

Zhang, D., Mohsin, M., & Taghizadeh-Hesary, F. (2022). Does green finance counteract the climate change mitigation: Asymmetric effect of renewable energy investment and R&D. *Energy Economics*, 113, 106183. 10.1016/j.eneco.2022.106183

Chapter 7
Navigating Fintech Disruptions:
Safeguarding Data Security in the Digital Era

Maizaitulaidawati Md Husin
https://orcid.org/0000-0002-2789-8274
Universiti Teknologi Malaysia, Malaysia

Shahab Aziz
https://orcid.org/0000-0003-1275-3061
King Fahd University of Petroleum and Minerals, Saudi Arabia

ABSTRACT

The rise of financial technology (fintech) has revolutionized the landscape of financial services, offering innovative solutions that streamline transactions, enhance accessibility, and transform traditional banking processes. However, amidst the rapid expansion of fintech, the issue of data security emerges as a paramount concern. This chapter explores the disruptive impact of fintech on traditional financial systems and the profound implications for data security in the digital age. By analyzing the technological advancements driving fintech innovation and the evolving regulatory landscape, this chapter examines the challenges and opportunities in safeguarding sensitive financial data. This chapter also identifies key vulnerabilities and threats to data security within fintech ecosystems and proposes strategic approaches to mitigate risks and strengthen cybersecurity measures. In sum, this chapter contributes to the ongoing dialogue surrounding the intersection of financial innovation, technology, and cybersecurity in the contemporary digital economy.

DOI: 10.4018/979-8-3693-3633-5.ch007

Copyright © 2024, IGI Global. Copying or distributing in print or electronic forms without written permission of IGI Global is prohibited.

INTRODUCTION

The rise of financial technology (fintech) has revolutionized the landscape of financial services, offering innovative solutions that streamline transactions, enhance accessibility, and transform traditional banking processes. The evolution of fintech traces back to the early 21st century, marked by the emergence of online banking, electronic payments, and peer-to-peer lending platforms. Over the years, fintech has evolved beyond its nascent stages, leveraging cutting-edge technologies such as artificial intelligence, blockchain, and big data analytics to revolutionize financial services. The proliferation of smartphones and digital devices has accelerated the adoption of fintech solutions, enabling users to conduct transactions, manage investments, and access financial information anytime, anywhere. From crowdfunding platforms to digital wallets, fintech innovations span a wide spectrum of services, offering tailored solutions to diverse consumer needs.

As fintech continues to disrupt the financial industry, one critical aspect that demands attention is data security (Ebrahim et al., 2021; Zhang et al., 2023). In an increasingly interconnected and data-driven world, the protection of sensitive financial information has become a top priority for individuals, businesses, and regulatory authorities alike. The digitization of financial transactions and the aggregation of personal and financial data present lucrative targets for cybercriminals seeking to exploit vulnerabilities in fintech platforms. Data breaches, identity theft, ransomware attacks and phishing scams are among the threat landscape facing fintech companies around the world. In the US, 1.4 million identity theft cases were reported in 2024 (IdentityTheft.org, 2024). Moreover, the interconnected nature of fintech ecosystems amplifies the potential impact of security breaches, posing systemic risks to financial stability and consumer trust. According to Statista (2023), 3,205 cases of data compromises has been reported in the US in 2023. Meanwhile, over 353 million individuals were affected in the same year by data compromises, including data breaches, leakage, and exposure. As the numbers of data compromises are alarming, effective data security in fintech requires a multifaceted approach that encompasses technological innovation, regulatory compliance, and risk management strategies. Fintech companies must implement robust cybersecurity measures to safeguard sensitive financial data and protect against emerging threats. Encryption techniques, multi-factor authentication, and intrusion detection systems are among the tools used to fortify fintech platforms against cyber-attacks. Furthermore, adherence to regulatory standards such as the General Data Protection Regulation (GDPR) and the Payment Card Industry Data Security Standard (PCI DSS) is essential for ensuring compliance and fostering consumer trust (Williams and Adamson, 2022). Looking ahead, the future of fintech hinges on innovation, collaboration, and adaptability in the face of evolving threats and regulatory challenges. As fintech continues to disrupt traditional financial models, the integration of advanced technologies such as biometrics, machine learning, and quantum encryption holds promise for enhancing data security and privacy in fintech applications. Moreover, the emergence of regulatory sandboxes and collaborative initiatives aimed at promoting cybersecurity innovation and information sharing are critical steps towards building a more secure and resilient fintech ecosystem.

Mitigating risks and strengthening cybersecurity resilience are imperative for the long-term viability of fintech ecosystems. Collaboration between industry stakeholders, regulatory authorities, and cybersecurity experts is key to addressing emerging threats and promoting best practices in data security. Fintech companies must adopt a proactive stance towards cybersecurity, investing in robust infrastructure, conducting regular security audits, and implementing incident response plans to mitigate the impact of security breaches. Furthermore, raising awareness among consumers about cybersecurity risks and promoting digital literacy is essential for fostering a culture of cyber resilience.

This chapter explores the disruptive impact of fintech on traditional financial systems and the profound implications for data security in the digital age. By analyzing the technological advancements driving fintech innovation and the evolving regulatory landscape, this study examines the challenges and opportunities in safeguarding sensitive financial data. Drawing on case studies and industry insights, the chapter identifies key vulnerabilities and threats to data security within fintech ecosystems and proposes strategic approaches to mitigate risks and strengthen cybersecurity measures. Through a multidimensional analysis of fintech disruptions and their implications for data security, this chapter contributes to the ongoing dialogue surrounding the intersection of financial innovation, technology, and cybersecurity in the contemporary digital economy.

LITERATURE REVIEW

Fintech

Definition of Fintech

Fintech, short for financial technology, encompasses a broad spectrum of innovative digital solutions that aim to streamline and enhance financial services (Varga, 2017). At its core, fintech leverages cutting-edge technology, data analytics, and digital platforms to revolutionize traditional banking and financial processes. This includes but is not limited to mobile banking apps, peer-to-peer lending platforms, robo-advisors, cryptocurrency exchanges, and blockchain technology. In recent years, fintech companies and startups focus on providing efficient, user-friendly, and accessible financial services to individuals, businesses, and institutions (Harsono & Suprapti, 2024; Lee et al., 2021). Example. The key characteristic of fintech lies in its ability to democratize access to financial products and services, promote financial inclusion, and drive efficiencies across the financial ecosystem (Morgan, 2022). Fintech has reshaped the way people manage, invest, and interact with money in the digital age.

Evolution of Fintech

The evolution of fintech represents a dynamic and multifaceted journey that has reshaped the financial landscape in profound ways. Initially emerging in the early 21st century, fintech gained momentum with the proliferation of online banking, electronic payments, and peer-to-peer lending platforms. These early innovations disrupted traditional banking models by offering consumers greater convenience, accessibility, and cost-effectiveness in managing their finances (Harsono & Suprapti, 2024; Kumar & Kaur, 2023). As technology continued to advance, fintech expanded its reach and scope, embracing emerging technologies such as artificial intelligence, machine learning, and big data analytics (Ashta & Herrmann, 2021; Stojanović et al., 2021). Mobile banking apps has revolutionized the way individuals transfer money, pay bills, and manage their accounts, enabling seamless transactions from the palm of one's hand. Additionally, digital wallets like PayPal and Apple Pay provided users with secure and convenient payment options both online and in-store (Muhtasim et al., 2022). Also, the emergence of robo-advisors democratized investment management, offering algorithm-driven portfolio management and personalized financial advice at a fraction of the cost of traditional wealth management services. According to Shanmuganathan (2020), robo-advisors are recognized as most disruptive trend in asset and wealth management. Furthermore, the rise of cryptocurrencies and blockchain technology has paved the way for decentralized finance (DeFi) platforms, enabling peer-to-peer lending, decentralized exchanges, and automated smart contracts without the need for intermediaries (Karin et al., 2022). For examples, decentralized lending protocols like Compound and Aave, decentralized exchanges such as Uniswap and SushiSwap, and yield farming platforms like Yearn Finance has automate the process. In sum, the evolution of fintech represents a convergence of innovation, accessibility, and disruption, transforming the way individuals, businesses, and institutions engage with financial services in the digital age.

Overview of Fintech Disruptions

Fintech disruptions have ushered in a new era of innovation and transformation within the financial industry, revolutionizing traditional banking and financial services. At its core, fintech disruptions encapsulate a spectrum of technological advancements, digital platforms, and innovative business models that challenge the status quo and redefine the way individuals and businesses interact with financial services (Pizzi et al., 2021; Mărăcine et al., 2021). One of the key disruptions brought about by fintech is the democratization of financial services, enabling greater access and inclusion for underserved populations. Through mobile banking apps, digital wallets, and peer-to-peer lending platforms, fintech has empowered individuals to manage their finances more conveniently and affordably, irrespective of geographical barriers or socioeconomic status (Friedline and Chen, 2021; Friedline et al., 2020).

Moreover, fintech disruptions have fundamentally altered the landscape of payments and transactions, introducing faster, more secure, and efficient payment solutions (Liang, 2023). Digital payment platforms like PayPal, Square, and Stripe have streamlined online transactions, facilitating seamless payment processing for e-commerce merchants and consumers worldwide. Additionally, blockchain technology and cryptocurrencies have introduced decentralized and peer-to-peer payment systems, challenging traditional banking infrastructure and offering alternatives to fiat currencies. The emergence of cryptocurrencies like Bitcoin and Ethereum has spurred a wave of innovation in digital assets, smart contracts, and decentralized finance (DeFi) applications, providing users with greater financial autonomy and control over their assets.

Furthermore, fintech disruptions have catalyzed a paradigm shift in investment management and wealth advisory services. Robo-advisors, powered by algorithms and artificial intelligence, have democratized investment advice and portfolio management, offering personalized financial guidance and automated investment strategies to investors of all backgrounds. Platforms like Betterment, Wealthfront, and Robinhood have democratized access to investment opportunities, allowing users to invest in stocks, bonds, and exchange-traded funds (ETFs) with minimal fees and barriers to entry. Additionally, crowdfunding platforms and peer-to-peer lending networks have revolutionized capital formation and access to funding for startups, small businesses, and entrepreneurs, bypassing traditional banking institutions and democratizing access to capital.

In conclusion, fintech disruptions represent a seismic shift in the financial industry, driving innovation, democratization, and accessibility across a myriad of financial services and products. As fintech continues to evolve and expand its footprint, its disruptions will continue to reshape the financial landscape, empowering individuals, businesses, and institutions to navigate the complexities of the digital economy with greater efficiency, transparency, and inclusivity.

Emergence Of Digital Banking And Payment Systems

The emergence of digital banking and payment systems has revolutionized the way individuals and businesses conduct financial transactions, marking a significant shift towards digitization and convenience in the financial industry. Digital banking encompasses a range of services and platforms that enable customers to manage their finances online or through mobile applications, without the need for physical bank branches. From account management to fund transfers and bill payments, digital banking offers users a seamless and accessible way to access and control their financial assets from anywhere, at any time.

One of the key drivers behind the rise of digital banking is the increasing adoption of smartphones and internet connectivity worldwide (Pavithra, 2021). With the proliferation of mobile devices and high-speed internet access, consumers have come to expect instant access to their financial accounts and services. Mobile banking apps provided by traditional banks as well as digital-only banks offer a user-friendly interface that allows customers to check balances, transfer funds, pay bills, and deposit checks with just a few taps on their smartphones. This convenience has transformed the way individuals manage their finances, making banking services more accessible and convenient than ever before.

In addition to digital banking, the emergence of digital payment systems has revolutionized the way people transact and exchange value. Digital payment solutions enable individuals and businesses to make secure and convenient transactions without the need for physical cash or checks (Ahmed and Sur, 2021; Najib and Fahma, 2020). For example, Ahmed and Sur (2021) found out that convenience is one of the factors that leads SMEs to adopt digital banking services. Online payment platforms such as PayPal, Venmo, and Square Cash have simplified peer-to-peer payments, enabling users to send money to friends, family, or merchants with ease. Moreover, digital wallets and mobile payment apps like Apple Pay, Google Pay, and Samsung Pay have transformed the way consumers make in-store purchases, allowing them to pay securely with their smartphones or other mobile devices.

Furthermore, the COVID-19 pandemic has accelerated the adoption of digital banking and payment systems, as consumers increasingly seek contactless and remote options for conducting financial transactions. A study conducted by Baicu et al. (2020) has highlighted that the COVID-19 pandemic effect on consumers' lifestyle has a direct and positive influence on the attitude toward internet and mobile banking services. With social distancing measures in place and concerns about the spread of the virus through physical currency, digital payments have become the preferred method of payment for many individuals and businesses. This shift towards digital banking and payment systems is increasing in the post-pandemic era, as consumers embrace the convenience, security, and flexibility offered by digital financial services. In conclusion, the emergence of digital banking and payment systems represents a transformative shift in the way people manage and transact with their finances, paving the way for a more connected, accessible, and efficient financial ecosystem.

UNDERSTANDING DATA SECURITY IN FINTECH

Key Concepts and Principles

Data security stands as a fundamental pillar underpinning the trust and integrity of financial transactions and interactions in fintech. Key concepts and principles of data security in fintech encapsulate a multifaceted approach to safeguarding sensitive financial information across digital platforms. Encryption serves as a cornerstone principle, where data is encoded into unreadable formats, ensuring that even if intercepted, it remains indecipherable to unauthorized entities. Advanced encryption algorithms like AES (Advanced Encryption Standard) and RSA (Rivest-Shamir-Adleman) are commonly employed to secure data both during transit and at rest, fortifying the confidentiality and integrity of financial data (Alsaffar et al., 2020; Rapolu et al., 2022).

Authentication mechanisms represent another pivotal aspect of data security in fintech, wherein users are required to verify their identities before accessing financial services or conducting transactions. Biometric authentication, leveraging unique physiological traits such as fingerprints, facial features, or iris patterns, offers a robust and user-friendly method for verifying user identities (Sarkar and Singh, 2020). Additionally, multi-factor authentication combines multiple authentication factors such as passwords, biometrics, and one-time passcodes to enhance security and thwart unauthorized access attempts, adding layers of protection to fintech systems and platforms.

Data privacy and regulatory compliance constitute essential principles in fintech data security, ensuring that financial institutions adhere to strict guidelines and standards governing the collection, storage, and processing of personal and financial data. Moreover, continuous monitoring and threat intelligence play a crucial role in maintaining the security posture of fintech systems and networks. By leveraging advanced threat detection technologies and security analytics, fintech companies can proactively identify and mitigate potential security threats and vulnerabilities in real-time. Security incident response plans enable organizations to respond swiftly and effectively to security incidents, minimizing the impact of data breaches and ensuring business continuity. Overall, the adherence to key concepts and principles of data security in fintech is paramount to fostering trust, resilience, and stability in the digital financial ecosystem, safeguarding the interests of stakeholders and customers alike.

Innovations in Data Security Technologies

Innovations in data security technologies have become indispensable in the digital age, where the protection of sensitive information is paramount. As cyber threats continue to evolve and proliferate, organizations are constantly seeking advanced solutions to safeguard their data assets and mitigate the risks of cyber-attacks. One of the most significant innovations in data security technologies is the adoption of encryption techniques, which enable organizations to protect data by encoding it into unreadable formats that can only be decrypted by authorized users with the appropriate encryption keys (Seth et al., 2022; Hasan et al., 2021). Advanced encryption algorithms such as AES (Advanced Encryption Standard) and RSA (Rivest-Shamir-Adleman) have become standard practices for securing data both in transit and at rest, ensuring confidentiality and integrity in digital communications and storage.

Another key innovation in data security technologies is the development of biometric authentication systems, which utilize unique physiological or behavioral characteristics such as fingerprints, facial recognition, and voice patterns to verify the identity of users (Sarkar and Singh, 2023). Biometric authentication offers a more secure and convenient alternative to traditional password-based authentication methods, reducing the risk of unauthorized access and credential theft (Bodepudi and Reddy, 2020). By integrating biometric authentication into digital systems and devices, organizations can enhance security measures and strengthen access controls, ensuring that only authorized users can access sensitive information and resources.

Furthermore, innovations in machine learning and artificial intelligence (AI) have revolutionized the field of cybersecurity by enabling proactive threat detection and response capabilities (Apruzzese et al., 2023; Dasgupta et al., 2022). AI-powered security solutions leverage machine learning algorithms to analyze vast amounts of data and identify patterns indicative of cyber threats and malicious activities. By continuously monitoring network traffic, user behavior, and system logs, AI-driven security platforms can detect anomalies and suspicious activities in real-time, enabling organizations to respond swiftly and effectively to potential threats before they escalate into full-blown security incidents. Additionally, AI-powered threat intelligence platforms enable organizations to stay ahead of emerging threats by analyzing global threat data and identifying trends and patterns that may indicate impending cyber-attacks (Mallikarjunaradhya et al., 2023).

In conclusion, innovations in data security technologies play a crucial role in helping organizations navigate the complex and evolving landscape of cybersecurity threats. By embracing encryption techniques, biometric authentication, and AI-driven threat detection capabilities, organizations can strengthen their defenses against cyber attacks and protect their data assets from unauthorized access, theft, and manipulation. As cyber threats continue to evolve, the importance of investing in advanced data security technologies cannot be overstated, as they serve as the frontline defense against the ever-present risks of cybercrime and data breaches in the digital age.

Importance of Data Security in The Digital Era

In the digital era, data security holds paramount importance due to the exponential growth of digital transactions, online interactions, and data storage. As businesses and individuals increasingly rely on digital platforms for communication, financial transactions, and storage of sensitive information, the protection of data becomes essential to safeguard privacy, prevent fraud, and maintain trust in digital systems. Data security encompasses measures and protocols designed to ensure the confidentiality, integrity, and availability of data, protecting it from unauthorized access, theft, or manipulation.

One of the primary reasons for the importance of data security in the digital era is the sheer volume and sensitivity of data being generated and transmitted across digital networks (Febiryani et al., 2021). From personal information such as names, addresses, and financial details to confidential business data and intellectual property, digital platforms store and transmit vast amounts of sensitive information that can be exploited by malicious actors if not adequately protected (Bracken et al., 2022; Casino et al., 2021). Data breaches and cyber attacks pose significant risks to individuals and organizations, resulting in financial loss, reputational damage, and legal liabilities.

Moreover, data security is crucial for maintaining compliance with regulatory requirements and industry standards governing the protection of sensitive information. Regulatory frameworks such as the General Data Protection Regulation (GDPR) in Europe and the Health Insurance Portability and Accountability Act (HIPAA) in the United States mandate strict guidelines for the collection, storage, and processing of personal data, imposing hefty fines and penalties for non-compliance (Ke and Sudhir, 2023; Serrado et al., 2020). By implementing robust data security measures, organizations can mitigate the risk of regulatory violations and demonstrate their commitment to protecting customer privacy and confidentiality.

Furthermore, data security is essential for fostering trust and confidence in digital transactions and online services (Zang and Kim, 2023). In an increasingly interconnected and data-driven world, consumers expect their personal information to be handled with care and diligence by the organizations they interact with. By investing in advanced encryption techniques, multi-factor authentication, and secure communication protocols, businesses can enhance the security of their digital infrastructure and reassure customers that their data is safe from unauthorized access or misuse.

In conclusion, the importance of data security in the digital era cannot be overstated, as it serves as the foundation for trust, privacy, and integrity in digital transactions and communications. By prioritizing data security and adopting best practices in information security management, organizations can mitigate the risks associated with cyber threats, protect sensitive information, and preserve the integrity of their digital assets in an increasingly interconnected and data-driven world.

FINDINGS

Implications of Fintech Disruptions

Advantages and Opportunities

Fintech disruptions bring forth a myriad of advantages and opportunities that reshape the landscape of financial services and drive innovation across various sectors. One of the primary advantages of fintech disruptions lies in enhanced accessibility and inclusivity, as these innovations break down barriers to traditional banking services and financial products (Dogan et al., 2021). Fintech solutions, such as mobile banking apps and digital wallets, enable individuals and businesses to access financial services conveniently from anywhere with an internet connection, fostering financial inclusion and empowerment, particularly for underserved populations and those in remote areas (Hasan et al., 2023; Kong and Loubere, 2021)

Moreover, fintech disruptions offer cost-effective alternatives to traditional financial services, reducing overhead costs associated with brick-and-mortar branches and manual processes (Ebrahim et al., 2021; Kou et al., 2021). By leveraging digital platforms and automation technologies, fintech companies can streamline operations, improve efficiency, and pass on cost savings to consumers through lower fees and competitive rates. This cost-effectiveness makes financial services more accessible to a broader spectrum of consumers and businesses, democratizing access to banking, lending, investment, and insurance products.

Furthermore, fintech disruptions drive innovation and spur entrepreneurship by creating new opportunities for startups and emerging fintech companies to enter the market (Adam, 2021; Akyuwen et al., 2022). The low barriers to entry and the availability of open banking APIs enable fintech innovators to develop and launch innovative solutions that address unmet needs and pain points in the financial industry. From peer-to-peer lending platforms to robo-advisors and blockchain-based solutions, fintech disruptions catalyze a wave of creativity and innovation, driving competition and pushing incumbents to innovate and adapt to changing consumer preferences and market dynamics.

Additionally, fintech disruptions enable financial institutions to harness the power of data analytics and artificial intelligence to deliver personalized and tailored financial services to customers. By leveraging data-driven insights and predictive analytics, fintech companies can gain a deeper understanding of customer needs and behaviors, offering customized solutions and recommendations that enhance the overall customer experience (Cao et al., 2021). This personalized approach not only fosters customer loyalty and engagement but also enables financial institutions to cross-sell and upsell relevant products and services, driving revenue growth and profitability in an increasingly competitive market.

In conclusion, fintech disruptions offer a plethora of advantages and opportunities that redefine the way individuals and businesses access, manage, and interact with financial services. From enhanced accessibility and cost-effectiveness to driving innovation and personalization, fintech disruptions hold the potential to transform the financial industry, create new business models, and empower consumers to achieve their financial goals in the digital age.

Challenges and Risks to Data Security

Fintech disruptions, while promising significant advancements in financial services, also introduce a host of challenges and risks to data security that demand vigilant attention (Najaf et al., 2021). One of the primary challenges is the escalating threat landscape posed by cybercriminals who exploit vulnerabilities in fintech systems and networks to perpetrate data breaches, financial fraud, and identity theft (Saluja, 2024; Stojanović et al., 2021). The interconnected nature of digital platforms and the proliferation of sensitive financial data make fintech companies prime targets for cyber-attacks, highlighting the critical need for robust cybersecurity measures and proactive risk management strategies.

Furthermore, the rapid pace of fintech innovation often outpaces regulatory frameworks and compliance standards, leaving gaps in data protection and privacy laws that expose consumers to potential risks and vulnerabilities. Fintech companies must navigate a complex and evolving regulatory landscape characterized by disparate regulations across jurisdictions, compliance burdens, and regulatory uncertainty. Various legal frameworks have been developed worldwide which will help to accelerate fintech growth. For example, Kapsis (2020) makes recommendations for legal improvements in the European legal frameworks. Aulia et al. (2020) analyse the existing regulatory framework of Islamic fintech in Indonesia while Bu and Wu (2022) presented the effective regulations of finTech innovations in China. Failure to adhere to regulatory requirements and industry standards can result in hefty fines, legal liabilities, and reputational damage, undermining consumer trust and confidence in fintech platforms and services.

Moreover, the reliance on third-party vendors and partners introduces additional risks to data security, as fintech companies often share sensitive data and infrastructure with external entities. Supply chain vulnerabilities, inadequate due diligence, and weak vendor management practices can compromise the security and integrity of fintech systems, exposing them to supply chain attacks, data breaches, and service disruptions (Despotović et al., 2023). Hence, fintech companies must implement robust vendor risk management programs and contractual safeguards to mitigate the risks associated with third-party relationships and ensure the security of shared data and resources.

Additionally, the evolving threat landscape and sophistication of cyber-attacks necessitate continuous investment in cybersecurity technologies, threat intelligence, and employee training to stay ahead of emerging threats and vulnerabilities. Human error and insider threats pose significant challenges to data security, as employees may inadvertently disclose sensitive information, fall victim to social engineering attacks, or engage in malicious activities. Therefore, fintech companies must foster a culture of security awareness and accountability, providing employees with regular training and education on cybersecurity best practices and risk mitigation strategies.

In conclusion, the challenges and risks to data security in fintech disruptions underscore the importance of proactive risk management, robust cybersecurity measures, and regulatory compliance initiatives. By addressing the complexities of the threat landscape, enhancing regulatory compliance efforts, and fostering a culture of security awareness, fintech companies can mitigate risks, safeguard sensitive data, and uphold the trust and confidence of consumers in the digital financial ecosystem.

CONCLUSION

This chapter underscores the critical importance of addressing data security challenges amidst the transformative changes brought about by fintech disruptions. This chapter delves into the multifaceted landscape of fintech innovations, recognizing their potential to democratize access to financial services, drive operational efficiencies, and foster financial inclusion. However, it also highlights the inherent risks and vulnerabilities associated with fintech disruptions, particularly in terms of data security and privacy. Through a comprehensive analysis of key concepts, principles, and emerging technologies in data security, this chapter emphasizes the need for proactive measures to mitigate risks and safeguard sensitive financial information. Encryption techniques, biometric authentication, and robust cybersecurity frameworks emerge as critical components in fortifying the integrity and confidentiality of data within fintech ecosystems. Moreover, regulatory compliance and adherence to industry standards play a pivotal role in ensuring transparency, accountability, and trust in fintech platforms and services.

Furthermore, this chapter underscores the importance of fostering a culture of security awareness and continuous learning within fintech organizations, empowering employees to recognize and respond effectively to emerging threats and vulnerabilities. By investing in advanced technologies, threat intelligence, and employee training, fintech companies can enhance their resilience against cyber attacks and mitigate the impact of security breaches on customers, stakeholders, and the broader financial ecosystem.

In conclusion, this chapter advocates for a holistic approach to navigating fintech disruptions, one that balances innovation with risk management and prioritizes the protection of customer data and privacy. As fintech continues to evolve and reshape the financial landscape, it is imperative for stakeholders to collaborate, innovate, and adapt to emerging challenges and opportunities in the digital era. Through collective efforts and proactive initiatives, the financial industry can harness the transformative potential of fintech disruptions while safeguarding the integrity and security of financial data in an increasingly interconnected and digitized world.

REFERENCES

Adam, H. (2021). Fintech and entrepreneurship boosting in developing countries: A comparative study of India and Egypt. In *The Big Data-Driven Digital Economy: Artificial and Computational Intelligence* (pp. 141–156). Springer International Publishing. 10.1007/978-3-030-73057-4_12

Ahmed, S., & Sur, S. (2021). Change in the uses pattern of digital banking services by Indian rural MSMEs during demonetization and Covid-19 pandemic-related restrictions. *Vilakshan-XIMB Journal of Management*, 20(1), 166–192.

Akyuwen, R., Nanere, M., & Ratten, V. (2022). Technology entrepreneurship: Fintech lending in Indonesia. *Entrepreneurial Innovation: Strategy and Competition Aspects*, 151-176.

Alsaffar, D. M., Almutiri, A. S., Alqahtani, B., Alamri, R. M., Alqahtani, H. F., Alqahtani, N. N., & Ali, A. A. (2020, March). Image encryption based on AES and RSA algorithms. In *2020 3rd International Conference on Computer Applications & Information Security (ICCAIS)* (pp. 1-5). IEEE. 10.1109/ICCAIS48893.2020.9096809

Apruzzese, G., Laskov, P., Montes de Oca, E., Mallouli, W., Rapa, L. B., Grammatopoulos, A. V., & Di Franco, F. (2023). The role of machine learning in cybersecurity. *Digital Threats : Research and Practice*, 4(1), 1–38. 10.1145/3545574

Ashta, A., & Herrmann, H. (2021). Artificial intelligence and fintech: An overview of opportunities and risks for banking, investments, and microfinance. *Strategic Change*, 30(3), 211–222. 10.1002/jsc.2404

Aulia, M., Yustiardhi, A. F., & Permatasari, R. O. (2020). An overview of Indonesian regulatory framework on Islamic financial technology (fintech). *Jurnal Ekonomi & Keuangan Islam*, 64-75.

Baicu, C. G., Gârdan, I. P., Gârdan, D. A., & Epuran, G. (2020). The impact of COVID-19 on consumer behavior in retail banking. Evidence from Romania. *Management & Marketing. Challenges for the Knowledge Society*, 15(s1), 534–556.

Bodepudi, A., & Reddy, M. (2020). Cloud-Based Biometric Authentication Techniques for Secure Financial Transactions: A Review. *International Journal of Information and Cybersecurity*, 4(1), 1–18.

Bracken, B. K., Wolcott, J., Potoczny-Jones, I., Mosser, B. A., Griffith-Fillipo, I. R., & Areán, P. A. (2022). Detection and Remediation of Malicious Actors for Studies Involving Remote Data Collection. In *HEALTHINF* (pp. 377-383). ACM. 10.5220/0010805500003123

Bu, Y., Li, H., & Wu, X. (2022). Effective regulations of FinTech innovations: The case of China. *Economics of Innovation and New Technology*, 31(8), 751–769. 10.1080/10438599.2020.1868069

Cao, L., Yang, Q., & Yu, P. S. (2021). Data science and AI in FinTech: An overview. *International Journal of Data Science and Analytics*, 12(2), 81–99. 10.1007/s41060-021-00278-w

Casino, F., Lykousas, N., Katos, V., & Patsakis, C. (2021). Unearthing malicious campaigns and actors from the blockchain DNS ecosystem. *Computer Communications*, 179, 217–230. 10.1016/j.comcom.2021.08.023

Dasgupta, D., Akhtar, Z., & Sen, S. (2022). Machine learning in cybersecurity: A comprehensive survey. *The Journal of Defense Modeling and Simulation*, 19(1), 57–106. 10.1177/1548512920951275

Despotović, A., Parmaković, A., & Miljković, M. (2023). Cybercrime and Cyber Security in Fintech. In *Digital Transformation of the Financial Industry: Approaches and Applications* (pp. 255–272). Springer International Publishing. 10.1007/978-3-031-23269-5_15

Dogan, H., Whittington, P., Apeh, E., & Ki-Aries, D. (2021, July). 1 st Workshop on Diversity, Accessibility and Inclusivity in Cyber Security. In *34th British HCI Workshop and Doctoral Consortium* (pp. 1-4). BCS Learning & Development.

Ebrahim, R., Kumaraswamy, S., & Abdulla, Y. (2021). FinTech in banks: opportunities and challenges. *Innovative strategies for implementing fintech in banking*, 100-109.

Febiryani, W., Kusumasari, T. F., & Fauzi, R. (2021, November). Analysis and Design Of Implementation Guidelines Data Security Management Assessment Techniques Based On DAMA-DMBOKv2. In *2021 IEEE 5th International Conference on Information Technology, Information Systems and Electrical Engineering (ICITISEE)* (pp. 371-375). IEEE. 10.1109/ICITISEE53823.2021.9655782

Friedline, T., & Chen, Z. (2021). Digital redlining and the fintech marketplace: Evidence from US zip codes. *The Journal of Consumer Affairs*, 55(2), 366–388. 10.1111/joca.12297

Friedline, T., Naraharisetti, S., & Weaver, A. (2020). Digital redlining: Poor rural communities' access to fintech and implications for financial inclusion. *Journal of Poverty*, 24(5-6), 517–541. 10.1080/10875549.2019.1695162

Harsono, I., & Suprapti, I. A. P. (2024). The Role of Fintech in Transforming Traditional Financial Services. [COUNT]. *Accounting Studies and Tax Journal*, 1(1), 81–91. 10.62207/gfzvtd24

Hasan, M., Noor, T., Gao, J., Usman, M., & Abedin, M. Z. (2023). Rural consumers' financial literacy and access to FinTech services. *Journal of the Knowledge Economy*, 14(2), 780–804. 10.1007/s13132-022-00936-9

Hasan, M. K., Islam, S., Sulaiman, R., Khan, S., Hashim, A. H. A., Habib, S., Islam, M., Alyahya, S., Ahmed, M. M., Kamil, S., & Hassan, M. A. (2021). Lightweight encryption technique to enhance medical image security on internet of medical things applications. *IEEE Access: Practical Innovations, Open Solutions*, 9, 47731–47742. 10.1109/ACCESS.2021.3061710

IdentityTheft.org© (2024). *2024 Identity Theft Facts and Statistics*. Identity Theft. https://identitytheft.org/statistics/

Kapsis, I. (2020). A truly future-oriented legal framework for fintech in the EU. *European Business Law Review*, 31(3), 475–514. 10.54648/EULR2020020

Karim, S., Lucey, B. M., Naeem, M. A., & Uddin, G. S. (2022). Examining the interrelatedness of NFTs, DeFi tokens and cryptocurrencies. *Finance Research Letters*, 47, 102696. 10.1016/j.frl.2022.102696

Ke, T. T., & Sudhir, K. (2023). Privacy rights and data security: GDPR and personal data markets. *Management Science*, 69(8), 4389–4412. 10.1287/mnsc.2022.4614

Kong, S. T., & Loubere, N. (2021). Digitally down to the countryside: Fintech and rural development in China. *The Journal of Development Studies*, 57(10), 1739–1754. 10.1080/00220388.2021.1919631

Kou, G., Olgu Akdeniz, Ö., Dinçer, H., & Yüksel, S. (2021). Fintech investments in European banks: A hybrid IT2 fuzzy multidimensional decision-making approach. *Financial Innovation*, 7(1), 39. 10.1186/s40854-021-00256-y35024283

Kumar, T., & Kaur, S. (2023). Evolution of Fintech in Financial Era. *Fintech and Cryptocurrency*, 1-12.

Lee, C. C., Li, X., Yu, C. H., & Zhao, J. (2021). Does fintech innovation improve bank efficiency? Evidence from China's banking industry. *International Review of Economics & Finance*, 74, 468–483. 10.1016/j.iref.2021.03.009

Liang, S. (2023). The future of finance: Fintech and digital transformation. *Highlights in Business. Economics and Management*, 15, 20–26.

Mallikarjunaradhya, V., Pothukuchi, A. S., & Kota, L. V. (2023). An overview of the strategic advantages of AI-powered threat intelligence in the cloud. *Journal of Science and Technology*, 4(4), 1–12.

Mărăcine, V., Voican, O., & Scarlat, E. (2020, July). The digital transformation and disruption in business models of the banks under the impact of FinTech and BigTech. In *Proceedings of the International Conference on Business Excellence* (Vol. 14, No. 1, pp. 294-305). IEEE. 10.2478/picbe-2020-0028

Morgan, P. J. (2022). Fintech and financial inclusion in Southeast Asia and India. *Asian Economic Policy Review*, 17(2), 183–208. 10.1111/aepr.12379

Muhtasim, D. A., Tan, S. Y., Hassan, M. A., Pavel, M. I., & Susmit, S. (2022). Customer satisfaction with digital wallet services: An analysis of security factors. *International Journal of Advanced Computer Science and Applications*, 13(1), 195–206. 10.14569/IJACSA.2022.0130124

Najaf, K., Mostafiz, M. I., & Najaf, R. (2021). Fintech firms and banks sustainability: Why cybersecurity risk matters? *International Journal of Financial Engineering*, 8(02), 2150019. 10.1142/S2424786321500195

Najib, M., & Fahma, F. (2020). Investigating the adoption of digital payment system through an extended technology acceptance model: An insight from the Indonesian small and medium enterprises. *International Journal on Advanced Science, Engineering and Information Technology*, 10(4), 1702–1708. 10.18517/ijaseit.10.4.11616

Pavithra, C. B. (2021). Factors Affecting Customers' perception Towards Digital Banking Services. [TURCOMAT]. *Turkish Journal of Computer and Mathematics Education*, 12(11), 1608–1614.

Pizzi, S., Corbo, L., & Caputo, A. (2021). Fintech and SMEs sustainable business models: Reflections and considerations for a circular economy. *Journal of Cleaner Production*, 281, 125217. 10.1016/j.jclepro.2020.125217

Rapolu, R. T., Gopal, M. K., & Kumar, G. S. (2022, April). A Secure method for Image Signaturing using SHA-256, RSA, and Advanced Encryption Standard (AES). In *2022 IEEE International Conference on Distributed Computing and Electrical Circuits and Electronics (ICDCECE)* (pp. 1-7). IEEE. 10.1109/ICDCECE53908.2022.9792989

Saluja, S. (2024). Identity theft fraud-major loophole for FinTech industry in India. *Journal of Financial Crime*, 31(1), 146–157. 10.1108/JFC-08-2022-0211

Sarkar, A., & Singh, B. K. (2020). A review on performance, security and various biometric template protection schemes for biometric authentication systems. *Multimedia Tools and Applications*, 79(37-38), 27721–27776. 10.1007/s11042-020-09197-7

Serrado, J., Pereira, R. F., Mira da Silva, M., & Scalabrin Bianchi, I. (2020). Information security frameworks for assisting GDPR compliance in banking industry. *Digital Policy. Regulation & Governance*, 22(3), 227–244. 10.1108/DPRG-02-2020-0019

Seth, B., Dalal, S., Jaglan, V., Le, D. N., Mohan, S., & Srivastava, G. (2022). Integrating encryption techniques for secure data storage in the cloud. *Transactions on Emerging Telecommunications Technologies*, 33(4), e4108. 10.1002/ett.4108

Shanmuganathan, M. (2020). Behavioural finance in an era of artificial intelligence: Longitudinal case study of robo-advisors in investment decisions. *Journal of Behavioral and Experimental Finance*, 27, 100297. 10.1016/j.jbef.2020.100297

Stojanović, B., Božić, J., Hofer-Schmitz, K., Nahrgang, K., Weber, A., Badii, A., Sundaram, M., Jordan, E., & Runevic, J. (2021). Follow the trail: Machine learning for fraud detection in Fintech applications. *Sensors (Basel)*, 21(5), 1594. 10.3390/s2105159433668773

Varga, D. (2017). Fintech, the new era of financial services. *Vezetéstudomány-Budapest Management Review*, 48(11), 22–32. 10.14267/VEZTUD.2017.11.03

Williams, B., & Adamson, J. (2022). *PCI Compliance: Understand and implement effective PCI data security standard compliance*. CRC Press. 10.1201/9781003100300

Zang, H., & Kim, J. (2023, July). A Comprehensive Study on Blockchain-based Cloud-Native Storage for Data Confidence. In *2023 Fourteenth International Conference on Ubiquitous and Future Networks (ICUFN)* (pp. 106-108). IEEE. 10.1109/ICUFN57995.2023.10200136

Zhang, W., Siyal, S., Riaz, S., Ahmad, R., Hilmi, M. F., & Li, Z. (2023). Data Security, Customer Trust and Intention for Adoption of Fintech Services: An Empirical Analysis From Commercial Bank Users in Pakistan. *SAGE Open*, 13(3), 21582440231181388. 10.1177/21582440231181388

KEY TERMS AND DEFINITIONS

Cybersecurity: Protection of computer systems and data from theft or damage to ensure confidentiality, integrity, and availability.
Digital: Relating to electronic devices and data.
Fintech: Financial services delivered through innovative technology.
Technology: Tools and techniques used to create, process, and store information.

Chapter 8
Revolutionizing Financial Data Security Through Blockchain and Distributed Ledger Technology

Misal Ijaz
https://orcid.org/0009-0008-2636-9400
Kinnaird College for Women, Lahore, Pakistan

Farah Naz
https://orcid.org/0000-0002-4707-5443
Kinnaird College for Women, Lahore, Pakistan

Sitara Karim
https://orcid.org/0000-0001-5086-6230
Sunway University, Malaysia

ABSTRACT

In the digital age, safeguarding financial data has become paramount amid increasing cyber threats and data breaches. This chapter explores the transformative role of blockchain and distributed ledger technology (DLT) in enhancing financial data security. Through practical applications and detailed case studies, the chapter illustrates the real-world implementation and efficacy of blockchain and DLT in the financial sector. Security features intrinsic to these technologies, such as decentralization, cryptographic hashing, and consensus mechanisms, are explored in depth, highlighting their contributions to a more secure financial ecosystem. Furthermore,

DOI: 10.4018/979-8-3693-3633-5.ch008

Copyright © 2024, IGI Global. Copying or distributing in print or electronic forms without written permission of IGI Global is prohibited.

the chapter addresses the regulatory landscape surrounding blockchain and DLT, discussing both the challenges and opportunities posed by these innovations. By presenting a comprehensive analysis of the current state and future potential of blockchain and DLT, this chapter aims to provide valuable insights into how these technologies are reshaping the approach to financial data security and resilience.

INTRODUCTION

In the contemporary digital economy, financial data security has become a paramount concern for institutions, regulators, and consumers alike (Oyewole, Oguejiofor, Eneh, Akpuokwe, & Bakare, 2024). Traditional financial systems, reliant on centralized databases, are increasingly vulnerable to a range of sophisticated cyber threats, including hacking, data breaches, fraud, and insider threats (Olweny, 2024). These vulnerabilities not only jeopardize the integrity and confidentiality of sensitive financial information but also undermine public trust and the stability of financial markets. As digital transactions and the volume of financial data continue to surge, existing security measures often prove inadequate in addressing the evolving landscape of cyber risks (Evren & Milson, 2024). Furthermore, financial institutions are subject to stringent regulatory requirements, such as anti-money laundering (AML) and know your customer (KYC) regulations, which necessitate robust mechanisms for data integrity, transparency, and auditability. Traditional systems frequently struggle to meet these regulatory demands efficiently, resulting in high compliance costs and operational inefficiencies. Additionally, the reliance on multiple intermediaries in financial transactions introduces delays, increases costs, and further exposes systems to risks of data tampering and fraud (Javaid, Haleem, Singh, Suman, & Khan, 2022).

Having said that, the rapid digitization of financial services, coupled with the increasing sophistication of cyber threats, has necessitated the development of robust mechanisms to protect sensitive information (Olweny, 2024). Blockchain and Distributed Ledger Technology (DLT) have garnered significant attention as transformative tools, offering innovative solutions that enhance the security, transparency, and integrity of financial data (Macharia, 2023). Blockchain technology, initially conceptualized as the underlying framework for Bitcoin, has evolved far beyond its cryptocurrency roots. Its decentralized nature and immutable record-keeping capabilities provide a formidable defense against data tampering and unauthorized access (Panwar & Bhatnagar, 2020). By distributing data across a network of nodes, blockchain eliminates single points of failure, making it exceptionally resistant to hacking attempts. Each transaction is encrypted and linked to the previous one, creating a chronological chain that is virtually impossible to alter retroactively. Distributed

Ledger Technology extends these principles beyond blockchain, encompassing various architectures that can be tailored to specific financial applications (Sunyaev & Sunyaev, 2020). Whether through permissioned or permission less ledgers, DLT offers versatile solutions for ensuring data consistency and security across diverse platforms. Financial institutions are increasingly adopting these technologies to safeguard transactions, streamline processes, and comply with regulatory standards (Farahani, Firouzi, & Luecking, 2021).

This chapter focuses on the role of blockchain and DLT in safeguarding financial data against the backdrop of an ever-evolving digital landscape. It explores the foundations, practical applications, security features and the regulatory implications of these innovations. By examining case studies and current implementations, the chapter aims to provide a comprehensive understanding of how blockchain and DLT are reshaping the financial sector's approach to data security and integrity. Through this exploration, we will uncover the potential and challenges of these technologies in creating a safer and more resilient financial ecosystem.

CYBER THREATS IN DIGITAL FINANCE

The digital transformation has revolutionized the management of financial transactions, assets, and services. Despite these advancements, the financial sector is increasingly facing cyber-attacks that compromise the security and integrity of financial systems (Nish, Naumann, & Muir, 2022). Cyber threats such as data breaches, identity theft, ransomware attacks, and financial fraud pose significant risks to the safety and reliability of digital finance (Vadiyala, 2021). One of the major cyber threats is data breaches, where unauthorized individuals gain access to financial institutions' records (Talesh, 2018). These breaches can expose sensitive information such as bank account numbers, credit card details, and personally identifiable information (PII), leading to identity theft, fraud, and financial losses for both individuals and companies (Aswathy & Tyagi, 2022). The repercussions of data breaches extend beyond financial losses, causing reputational damage, regulatory fines, and legal liabilities for the affected institutions.

Identity theft is another prevalent cyber threat, exploiting vulnerabilities in digital finance systems to obtain personal information and steal identities (Mugari, Gona, Maunga, & Chiyambiro, 2016). Cybercriminals employ tactics such as phishing emails, social engineering, and malware to capture login credentials, social security numbers, and biometric data. This stolen information can then be used to impersonate victims, open fraudulent accounts, and conduct unauthorized transactions, leading to both financial and reputational harm (Baddam et al., 2023). Financial institutions are also increasingly targeted by ransomware attacks, where sensitive data is encrypted, and a ransom is demanded for its release. These attacks can disrupt financial operations, compromise customer data, and incur significant financial costs (Tao et al., 2019). By denying access to critical data and services, ransomware attacks can cause extensive disruptions within financial systems (Chisty, Baddam, & Amin, 2022).

Financial fraud is another major concern in the realm of digital finance, with cybercriminals exploiting weaknesses in authentication, transaction processing, and regulatory frameworks (Al-Hashedi & Magalingam, 2021). Common types of financial fraud include account takeovers, payment card fraud, investment scams, and business email compromise (BEC). These fraudulent activities target individuals, corporations, and financial institutions, resulting in substantial economic losses and diminishing trust in digital financial services (Siddique & Vadiyala, 2021). The proliferation of mobile banking, online payments, and digital wallets has expanded the attack surface for cybercriminals, introducing new opportunities for fraud and exploitation. Mobile banking applications, for example, are vulnerable to threats such as malware, unsecured connections, and phishing attacks (Vadiyala, Baddam, & Kaluvakuri, 2016). As cyber threats become more sophisticated, traditional centralized banking systems struggle to mitigate risks and prevent attacks. Centralized databases and servers are susceptible to hacking, data breaches, and denial-of-service (DoS) attacks (Baddam, Vadiyala, & Thaduri, 2018). The reliance on intermediaries and trusted third parties further complicates the financial ecosystem, introducing additional vulnerabilities.

Blockchain technology, with its decentralized and distributed ledger system, offers a transformative approach to managing cyber threats in digital finance. By distributing control across a network of nodes, they eliminate the single point of failure inherent in centralized systems (Kaluvakuri & Vadiyala, 2016). Each transaction is secured through cryptographic techniques and recorded immutably, preventing tampering and fraud. The consensus mechanism ensures that transactions are validated and confirmed by the majority of network participants, thereby enhancing trust and transparency without the need for intermediaries (Dwivedi, Amin, & Vollala, 2020).

BACKGROUND OF BLOCKCHAIN AND DISTRIBUTED LEDGER TECHNOLOGY (DLT)

Blockchain technology was first conceptualized in 2008 by an anonymous person or group of people using the pseudonym Satoshi Nakamoto. Nakamoto (2008) white paper, "Bitcoin: A Peer-to-Peer Electronic Cash System," introduced the world to blockchain as the underlying technology for Bitcoin, the first decentralized cryptocurrency. The primary innovation of blockchain was to enable digital transactions without the need for a trusted third party, such as a bank (Nakamoto, 2008). The initial blockchain, which underpins Bitcoin, is a decentralized and public ledger that records all transactions across a network of computers. Each transaction is grouped into a block, and these blocks are linked together in a chronological chain, hence the term "blockchain" (Komalavalli, Saxena, & Laroiya, 2020). The decentralized nature of this technology ensures that no single entity has control over the entire network, promoting transparency and security.

Since the inception of Bitcoin, blockchain technology has evolved significantly. It has expanded beyond cryptocurrencies to encompass a wide range of applications, including supply chain management, healthcare, voting systems, and financial services (Shukurov, 2022). The development of Ethereum in 2015 introduced smart contracts, which are self-executing contracts with the terms directly written into code, further broadening the potential uses of blockchain. Distributed Ledger Technology (DLT) is a broader term that encompasses blockchain but also includes other types of distributed ledgers (Hughes, Park, Kietzmann, & Archer-Brown, 2019). While blockchain is a specific type of DLT that organizes data into blocks and chains them together, other DLT systems may use different structures and consensus mechanisms to achieve similar goals of decentralization, security, and transparency.

ROLE OF BLOCKCHAIN AND DLT IN SAFEGUARDING FINANCIAL DATA

The current digital financial landscape is marked by rapid innovation, with new technologies and business models emerging at an unprecedented pace. Blockchain and DLT are at the forefront of this transformation, driving the development of new financial products and services (Collomb & Sok, 2016). These technologies enable the creation of decentralized finance (DeFi) platforms, which offer financial services without traditional intermediaries. DeFi platforms can provide more inclusive access to financial services, particularly for individuals and businesses that are underserved by conventional financial institutions (Popescu, 2020). This democratization of financial services is a significant step forward in promoting financial inclusion and economic empowerment globally. The key ways in which these technologies safeguard financial data are as follows:

Enhanced Security

One of the foundational security features of blockchain technology is its immutability (Pilkington, 2016). Once data is added to the blockchain, it cannot be altered or deleted. This is achieved through a process called hashing, where each block of data contains a cryptographic hash of the previous block, creating a chain of interlinked blocks. This immutability ensures the integrity of financial records by preventing unauthorized modifications (Rahardja, Hidayanto, Lutfiani, Febiani, & Aini, 2021). For example, any attempt to alter a transaction would require altering all subsequent blocks, which is computationally impractical in a well-secured network. Additionally, Blockchain employs advanced cryptographic techniques to secure data (Le Nguyen et al., 2020). Each transaction is encrypted and linked to the previous one using cryptographic hashes. This ensures that the data remains confidential and secure from tampering. Public-key cryptography, which uses pairs of public and private keys, ensures that only authorized parties can access or validate transactions, providing an additional layer of security (Farahani et al., 2021). Furthermore, unlike traditional centralized databases, a blockchain is maintained across multiple nodes (computers) in a network. This distribution reduces the risk of a single point of failure. In a decentralized system, even if some nodes are compromised, the integrity of the data remains intact because other nodes can validate and maintain the correct version of the ledger (Bodó & Giannopoulou, 2019).

Transparency and Accountability

Public blockchains offer a high degree of transparency, as all transactions are visible to all participants. This transparency helps in preventing fraud and ensures that all parties have access to the same information. For instance, Bitcoin's blockchain allows anyone to view the complete history of transactions, ensuring that no double-spending or unauthorized transactions occur (Sedlmeir, Lautenschlager, Fridgen, & Urbach, 2022). Moreover, Blockchain technology provides a clear and traceable history of all transactions. This traceability is crucial for tracking the origin and movement of funds, which is essential for detecting and preventing fraudulent activities. For example, in supply chain finance, blockchain can track the journey of a product from its origin to the final consumer, ensuring authenticity and preventing counterfeiting (Sarmah, 2018).

Operational Efficiency

Smart contracts are self-executing contracts with the terms of the agreement directly written into code. These contracts automatically enforce and execute the terms of the agreement when predefined conditions are met. This automation reduces the need for intermediaries, such as brokers or escrow services, minimizing the risk of human error and manipulation. For instance, in derivatives trading, smart contracts can automatically execute trades based on market conditions, ensuring timely and accurate settlements (Madir, 2020). Having said that, DLT allows for real-time updates and synchronization across all nodes in the network. This ensures that all participants have the most up-to-date information, reducing discrepancies and the need for reconciliation. For example, in interbank payments, blockchain can enable real-time gross settlement (RTGS), where transactions are processed and settled immediately, improving liquidity and reducing counterparty risk (Farahani et al., 2021).

Data Integrity and Reliability

Blockchain employs consensus mechanisms, such as Proof of Work (PoW) and Proof of Stake (PoS), to validate transactions. These mechanisms ensure that all participants agree on the validity of transactions before they are added to the ledger. This consensus process prevents fraudulent transactions and ensures the reliability of financial data. For instance, PoW requires nodes to solve complex mathematical problems to validate transactions, making it costly and time-consuming to manipulate the ledger (Sharma, 2021). Additionally, since the ledger is replicated across multiple nodes, blockchain inherently provides data redundancy. This replication acts as a backup, ensuring data is not lost even if some nodes fail. In financial systems, this redundancy is critical for disaster recovery and business continuity. For example, in the event of a cyberattack or hardware failure, the distributed nature of blockchain ensures that data can be recovered from other nodes, maintaining the availability and integrity of financial records (Dinh et al., 2018).

Privacy and Confidentiality

For financial institutions requiring privacy, permissioned blockchains restrict access to authorized participants only. These blockchains ensure that sensitive financial data is shared only among trusted parties. Permissioned blockchains, such as Hyperledger Fabric, allow institutions to maintain control over who can access and participate in the network, providing a secure environment for confidential transactions (Androulaki et al., 2020). Moreover, Zero-knowledge proofs (ZKPs) are cryptographic techniques that enable one party to prove to another that a statement is true without revealing any specific information about the statement itself. In the context of blockchain, ZKPs can be used to verify transactions without disclosing the underlying data. This ensures that privacy is maintained while still proving the validity of transactions. For instance, Zcash, a privacy-focused cryptocurrency, uses ZKPs to enable private transactions on its blockchain (Zhou, Diro, Saini, Kaisar, & Hiep, 2024).

Regulatory Compliance

The immutable nature of blockchain provides a reliable audit trail, which is invaluable for regulatory compliance. Regulators can access a transparent and tamper-proof history of financial transactions, making it easier to monitor compliance with financial regulations. For example, blockchain can be used to track and audit the flow of funds in anti-money laundering (AML) efforts, ensuring that all transactions are accounted for and comply with regulatory standards (Gokoglan, Cetın, & Bılen, 2022). However, blockchain can enhance Know Your Customer (KYC) processes by providing a secure and verifiable digital identity. This helps financial institutions comply with AML regulations and other regulatory requirements. For instance, blockchain-based digital identity platforms can store and verify customer identities, reducing the risk of identity theft and ensuring compliance with KYC regulations (Parate, Josyula, & Reddi, 2023).

KEY FEATURES OF BLOCKCHAIN AND DLT

Blockchain technology is revolutionizing financial security in the digital age by offering robust solutions to safeguard financial systems against cyberattacks, fraud, and data breaches (Yerram et al., 2021). This section focuses on the key blockchain innovations that enhance economic security and integrity in today's digital landscape.

o Decentralization: In traditional centralized systems, a single entity or a group of entities has control over the data. In contrast, blockchain and DLT distribute the data across multiple nodes in a network. This decentralization removes the need for intermediaries and reduces the risk of a single point of failure (Raval, 2016).
  o Consensus Mechanisms: To ensure the integrity and validity of the data, blockchain and DLT rely on consensus mechanisms. These are protocols that all nodes in the network must follow to agree on the state of the ledger. Common consensus mechanisms include Proof of Work (PoW), Proof of Stake (PoS), and Practical Byzantine Fault Tolerance (PBFT) (Lashkari & Musilek, 2021).
    o Immutability: Once data is recorded on a blockchain, it cannot be altered or deleted. This immutability is achieved through cryptographic hashing and the chaining of blocks. Any attempt to change a block would require altering all subsequent blocks, which is computationally infeasible in a secure network (Hofmann, Wurster, Ron, & Böhmecke-Schwafert, 2017).
o Transparency: Public blockchains allow anyone to view the entire

history of transactions, providing transparency and enabling auditability. Even in permissioned or private blockchains, where access is restricted, transparency can be maintained among authorized participants (Hellani, Sliman, Samhat, & Exposito, 2021).

o	Cryptographic Security: Blockchain uses cryptographic techniques to secure data. Each transaction is encrypted, and each block contains a cryptographic hash of the previous block, ensuring data integrity and security (Dasgupta, Shrein, & Gupta, 2019).

o	Interoperability and Integration: It facilitates smooth communication and cooperation between a variety of parties by integrating with financial systems. Blockchain uses open-source frameworks and defined protocols to enable data transfer and interoperable activities between financial institutions. Due to their modular architecture and APIs that interface with the current financial infrastructure, blockchain solutions can be installed without causing any disruptions to ongoing operations (Belchior, Vasconcelos, Guerreiro, & Correia, 2021).

o	Smart Contracts: Self-executing contracts containing programmed terms remove middlemen and streamline contractual procedures by automating predetermined actions based on conditions. For financial security, smart contracts can automate trade settlements, insurance claims, and escrow (Nowiński & Kozma, 2017). By automating contractual processes and enforcing compliance without requiring human intervention, smart contracts improve efficiency and confidence in financial transactions by lowering errors, delays, and conflicts.

IMPORTANCE OF BLOCKCHAIN AND DLT IN FINANCIAL DATA SECURITY

Cyber threats are becoming increasingly sophisticated and pervasive in today's digital landscape, posing significant risks to financial systems (Parn & Edwards, 2019). Traditional financial infrastructures are often vulnerable to breaches, fraud, and other forms of cybercrime. Blockchain and Distributed Ledger Technology (DLT) offer robust defenses against these evolving threats. By leveraging decentralization and advanced cryptographic techniques, these technologies make financial data much harder to alter or steal. The immutable nature of blockchain ensures that once a transaction is recorded, it cannot be changed or erased, which significantly reduces the risk of fraudulent activities and ensures the integrity of financial records (Collomb & Sok, 2016).

Trust is a foundational element in the financial sector, and blockchain significantly enhances this trust by providing a transparent and verifiable record of transactions (Kshetri, 2021). In an era where financial fraud and scandals can quickly erode public confidence, the transparency offered by blockchain is invaluable. Public blockchains allow all participants to see the entire history of transactions, ensuring that activities can be monitored and audited in real-time. This level of transparency helps build trust among consumers and stakeholders while also facilitating better regulatory oversight, making it easier to detect and prevent illegal activities such as money laundering (Lu, Liu, Wang, Qu, & Liu, 2018).

Furthermore, regulatory compliance is a critical concern for financial institutions, especially in a global market characterized by diverse and stringent regulations. Blockchain and DLT provide powerful tools for meeting these compliance requirements efficiently (Giannino, Di Maio, & Vianelli, 2020). The immutable audit trails created by blockchain ensure that all transactions are accurately recorded and easily accessible for audits. This transparency simplifies the process of regulatory reporting and enhances the ability of institutions to comply with laws such as anti-money laundering (AML) and know your customer (KYC) regulations (Xu, Liu, Nie, & Gai, 2021). Additionally, the use of smart contracts can automate compliance with regulatory requirements, reducing the risk of human error and ensuring that financial activities adhere to the necessary legal standards (Mik, 2017). This capability is particularly relevant in the current landscape, where regulatory scrutiny is intensifying.

Moreover, operational efficiency and cost reduction are major priorities for financial institutions, especially as they navigate the highly competitive and fast-paced digital financial market. Blockchain and DLT can significantly streamline financial operations by automating processes and eliminating the need for intermediaries (Petrov, 2019). For example, in cross-border payments, blockchain can reduce the time and costs associated with currency conversion and transfer fees by facilitating direct transactions between parties. This operational efficiency is crucial in a market where speed and cost-effectiveness are key differentiators. By reducing the reliance on intermediaries, financial institutions can offer faster and cheaper services to their customers, enhancing their competitive edge (Isaksen, 2018).

CASE STUDIES

Numerous financial institutions and organizations worldwide have adopted blockchain to enhance security, efficiency, and transparency (Yerram et al., 2021). This technology is revolutionizing the banking industry, impacting banks, payment processors, insurance companies, and investment firms alike. This section explores notable cases of blockchain adoption in the finance sector and examines how blockchain technology is bolstering financial security amid the digital transformation.

JPMorgan Chase's Quorum Blockchain

JPMorgan Chase, one of the largest financial institutions in the world, recognized the need to enhance the security and efficiency of its financial transactions (Yerram et al., 2021). The traditional banking systems were increasingly vulnerable to cyber threats, data breaches, and fraud. To address these challenges, JPMorgan Chase developed Quorum, an enterprise-focused blockchain platform built on the Ethereum protocol. Quorum was designed to support both public and private transactions, providing enhanced privacy for sensitive financial data while maintaining the transparency and immutability inherent in blockchain technology. It employs advanced cryptographic techniques and consensus mechanisms to ensure the integrity and security of financial transactions. Quorum allows for the creation of permissioned networks where only authorized participants can access and verify transactions, reducing the risk of unauthorized access and fraud (Espel, Katz, & Robin, 2017).

Since its implementation, Quorum has significantly improved the security and efficiency of JPMorgan Chase's financial transactions. The decentralized nature of the blockchain has eliminated single points of failure, making the system more resilient to cyberattacks. The cryptographic security measures ensure that transaction data is tamper-proof, providing a reliable and transparent audit trail. Moreover, Quorum's permissioned structure has enhanced compliance with regulatory requirements, ensuring that only authorized parties can access sensitive financial data. This has led to a reduction in fraud and operational costs, demonstrating the potential of blockchain technology in safeguarding financial data (Mazzoni, Corradi, & Di Nicola, 2022).

HSBC's Use of Blockchain for Trade Finance

HSBC, a leading global bank, faced challenges in its trade finance operations, including fraud, lack of transparency, and inefficient processes. Trade finance involves multiple parties and complex documentation, making it susceptible to fraud and errors. To address these issues, HSBC turned to blockchain technology to enhance the security and efficiency of its trade finance transactions (Sahay & Tiwari, 2023). HSBC implemented a blockchain-based trade finance platform called Voltron, developed in collaboration with other major financial institutions and technology partners. Voltron leverages the distributed ledger technology of blockchain to digitize and streamline the entire trade finance process. It provides a secure and transparent platform where all parties involved in a trade transaction can access and verify documents and transaction details in real-time (Ton, 2022). However, the implementation of Voltron has revolutionized HSBC's trade finance operations. The blockchain platform has significantly reduced the risk of fraud by providing an immutable record of all trade transactions and related documents. This transparency ensures that all parties can verify the authenticity of the documents and the terms of the trade, reducing the likelihood of disputes and fraud. Additionally, the digitization of trade documents has streamlined the process, reducing the time and costs associated with trade finance transactions. Voltron's success has demonstrated the effectiveness of blockchain technology in enhancing the security and efficiency of financial operations (Ton, 2022).

The Australian Securities Exchange (ASX) and DLT

The Australian Securities Exchange (ASX) sought to modernize its clearing and settlement system, known as CHESS (Clearing House Electronic Subregister System), which was becoming outdated and inefficient. The existing system faced challenges related to data integrity, security, and operational inefficiencies. To address these issues, ASX decided to implement a Distributed Ledger Technology (DLT) solution (Babones, 2017). ASX partnered with Digital Asset Holdings to develop a DLT-based system to replace CHESS. The new system leverages DLT to provide a secure, transparent, and efficient platform for clearing and settlement of securities transactions. It uses a permissioned ledger to ensure that only authorized participants can access and validate transactions, enhancing security and compliance with regulatory requirements (van der Elst & Lafarre, 2024).

The DLT-based system has significantly improved the security and efficiency of ASX's clearing and settlement operations. The decentralized nature of the DLT has eliminated single points of failure, reducing the risk of cyberattacks and data breaches. The immutable ledger provides a transparent and tamper-proof record of all transactions, ensuring data integrity and enhancing trust among market participants (Hossain, Steigner, Hussain, & Akther, 2024). Additionally, the new system has streamlined operations, reducing the time and costs associated with clearing and settlement processes. The successful implementation of DLT by ASX highlights the potential of blockchain technology in transforming financial market infrastructures and safeguarding financial data (Priem, 2020).

Santander's One Pay FX

Santander, a major global bank, identified inefficiencies and security vulnerabilities in its cross-border payment services. Traditional cross-border transactions were often slow, expensive, and prone to errors and fraud. To enhance the security and efficiency of its cross-border payment services, Santander turned to blockchain technology (Dalal & Samal, 2022). Santander developed One Pay FX, a blockchain-based international payment service built on Ripple's blockchain technology. One Pay FX leverages Ripple's decentralized ledger to provide fast, secure, and transparent cross-border payments. The platform enables real-time tracking of payments and ensures that transaction data is immutable and tamper-proof (Morgan, 2016).

The implementation of One Pay FX has transformed Santander's cross-border payment services. The blockchain-based platform has significantly reduced the time and costs associated with international payments, providing customers with faster and more affordable services. The transparency and immutability of the blockchain ledger have enhanced the security of transactions, reducing the risk of fraud and errors (Mahajan & Nanda, 2024). Customers can track their payments in real-time, enhancing trust and satisfaction. Santander's successful deployment of blockchain technology in cross-border payments demonstrates its potential to enhance the security and efficiency of financial transactions.

Having said that, these case studies illustrate how blockchain and distributed ledger technology can address the security challenges faced by financial institutions, enhancing the integrity, transparency, and efficiency of financial transactions in the digital age.

DISCUSSION

Several significant insights have emerged from exploring how blockchain technology can enhance financial security during the digital transformation. The outcomes of this chapter underscore the transformative potential of blockchain technology in tackling the evolving challenges of financial security. These insights also emphasize the regulatory considerations and future prospects for employing blockchain technology in the financial industry.

One crucial finding is that blockchain technology offers innovative solutions for securing digital financial transactions against cyber threats. By leveraging a decentralized architecture, immutable ledger, cryptographic security, and smart contracts, blockchain enhances the reliability, security, and transparency of financial transactions (Prasad, Rao, & Lanka, 2022). Blockchain's cryptographic security measures protect against data breaches, identity theft, and fraud, while its decentralized consensus mechanism ensures resilience against cyber-attacks. Additionally, smart contracts automate contractual processes and ensure compliance with obligations, thereby reducing the chances of errors, delays, and disputes in financial transactions (Hamledari & Fischer, 2021).

Another key finding is the critical role of regulatory considerations in the implementation of blockchain technology within the financial sector (Yeoh, 2017). Varying regulatory frameworks across different jurisdictions pose challenges for blockchain developers and financial institutions striving to comply with industry-specific laws and regulations. Careful attention to data privacy, cybersecurity, anti-money laundering (AML), know-your-customer (KYC) standards, and consumer protection is necessary to ensure compliance and mitigate regulatory risks (Baddam et al., 2018). The chapter also underscores the importance of collaboration and integration for blockchain adoption in the financial sector. Collaboration among regulators, financial institutions, and technology providers is essential to develop regulatory frameworks that facilitate the responsible deployment of blockchain technology in the financial sector, balancing innovation with risk management (Davradakis & Santos, 2019).

Moving on, effective implementation requires cooperation among various stakeholders, including financial institutions, technology providers, regulators, and others, to create interoperable and secure blockchain solutions that address the diverse needs of the financial sector (Ali, Ally, & Dwivedi, 2020). Integrating blockchain technology with existing financial infrastructure and regulatory frameworks is essential for its seamless adoption and scalability. Furthermore, ongoing research and development in areas such as scalability, interoperability, and governance are vital to overcoming the current technical and regulatory challenges faced by blockchain-based financial systems (Zachariadis, Hileman, & Scott, 2019).

Looking ahead, the future of blockchain technology in enhancing financial security amid the digital revolution is both promising and complex. While the adoption of blockchain technology is accelerating, several significant obstacles hinder its mainstream implementation (Toufaily, Zalan, & Dhaou, 2021). These challenges include regulatory uncertainties, technological scalability, interoperability, and governance. Despite these hurdles, the potential benefits of blockchain technology necessitate ongoing investment and innovation in the financial sector. Such benefits include enhanced security, efficiency, and transparency in financial transactions (Cocco, Pinna, & Marchesi, 2017).

The chapter however highlights the transformative potential of blockchain technology in bolstering financial security during digital transformation. By offering innovative solutions to cyber threats, addressing regulatory considerations, promoting collaboration and integration, and charting a promising yet intricate future outlook, blockchain technology stands to revolutionize the financial sector. This could usher in a new era of trust, transparency, and efficiency in financial transactions (Baddam et al., 2023).

REGULATORY PERSPECTIVES AND FUTURE OUTLOOK

As blockchain technology becomes increasingly prevalent in finance, regulatory considerations are crucial for its acceptance, governance, and integration within existing financial systems (Upadhyay, 2020). Regulators worldwide must strike a balance between fostering innovation and managing risks to ensure that blockchain solutions comply with regulatory standards while promoting competitiveness and innovation in the financial sector (Ross, 2016). This section examines the regulatory landscape and the potential of blockchain technology to enhance financial security amid digital transformation.

1. The lack of standardized regulatory frameworks poses challenges for blockchain adoption in finance. While some regulatory bodies are open to innovation, others remain cautious about regulating blockchain technology. Key regulatory concerns include data privacy, cybersecurity, anti-money laundering (AML), know your customer (KYC) requirements, and consumer protection (Vadiyala, 2021). Financial institutions and blockchain developers must navigate a complex regulatory environment to ensure compliance with various laws and regulations while leveraging blockchain technology.

2. Although blockchain offers robust security features such as cryptographic encryption and decentralized consensus, it also raises data privacy and compliance issues, particularly with regulations like the EU's General Data Protection Regulation (GDPR). It is essential for regulators and financial institutions to establish stringent data privacy policies, encryption standards, and access controls to safeguard sensitive financial information and adhere to regulatory requirements (Schwerin, 2018). Ensuring cybersecurity and preventing fraud are top priorities, given the immutable nature of blockchain records and the potential vulnerabilities to cyberattacks. Collaboration between regulators, industry stakeholders, and technology providers is necessary to set cybersecurity standards, best practices, and incident response protocols.

3. Adhering to AML and KYC regulations is vital for the adoption of blockchain technology in banking. While blockchain can enhance transaction transparency and traceability, it also presents challenges in identifying and verifying transaction participants (Sander, Semeijn, & Mahr, 2018). Implementing rigorous AML and KYC protocols, including due diligence, monitoring, and reporting, is essential to prevent money laundering, terrorist financing, and other illicit activities. Financial institutions and blockchain developers must work together to develop robust AML and KYC frameworks that ensure compliance and protect customer data.

4. Ensuring consumer protection is a primary concern for regulators to safeguard the interests of retail investors and consumers in blockchain-based financial products and services. It is crucial to educate consumers about the risks and benefits associated with blockchain technology, including potential financial losses, security breaches, and regulatory compliance issues (Gikay, 2019). Financial institutions and blockchain developers must adhere to consumer protection laws, such as disclosure requirements, fair lending practices, and dispute resolution mechanisms, to maintain transparency, fairness, and trust in blockchain-based financial transactions.
5. The future of blockchain technology in enhancing financial security during digital transformation is promising yet complex. Regulators and financial institutions must collaborate to develop innovative, risk-managed regulatory frameworks as blockchain usage expands. Addressing technical and regulatory challenges in blockchain-based financial systems requires ongoing research and development in areas such as scalability, interoperability, and governance. Blockchain technology has the potential to revolutionize finance by increasing efficiency, transparency, and trust in financial transactions, reducing risks, and strengthening financial security in the digital era (Mandapuram, Mahadasa, & Surarapu, 2019).

By addressing these regulatory considerations and fostering collaboration among stakeholders, blockchain technology can effectively transform the financial landscape, offering a more secure, transparent, and efficient system for managing financial transactions and data.

LIMITATIONS AND IMPLICATIONS

Despite its potential, blockchain technology in finance comes with several limitations and policy implications that must be addressed to maximize its benefits and minimize risks. Blockchain technology faces issues related to scalability, interoperability, and energy consumption. Scalability challenges arise from network congestion, leading to delays and higher transaction costs. Interoperability issues stem from the inability of different blockchain networks to communicate and share data effectively. Moreover, the energy-intensive consensus mechanisms used in blockchain mining raise environmental concerns (Verhoeven, 2022). Continuous research and development are needed to enhance blockchain systems' scalability, interoperability, and energy efficiency. The regulatory landscape for blockchain is complex and rapidly evolving. Financial institutions and blockchain developers face regulatory uncertainties that complicate compliance with existing laws. Unclear regulatory frameworks can impede the advancement and adoption of blockchain technology in finance. Policymakers must work together to create clear, harmonized regulatory standards that foster innovation while protecting against money laundering, fraud, and ensuring consumer protection.

Although blockchain technology offers cryptographic encryption and decentralized consensus, these mechanisms are not impervious to breaches. The immutability of blockchain transactions can pose problems in cases of errors or fraud (Shrimali & Patel, 2022). Furthermore, the transparency inherent in blockchain transactions raises privacy concerns regarding sensitive financial data. Policymakers need to find a balance between transparency, security, and privacy to protect users from fraud, identity theft, and data breaches in blockchain-based financial systems (Hussein, Taha, & Khalifa, 2018). Blockchain technology in finance also faces challenges related to education, awareness, and infrastructure. Many stakeholders lack familiarity with blockchain technology and its applications in financial services. Integrating blockchain technology into the financial infrastructure may require significant efforts in education, training, and infrastructure development. Policymakers can promote blockchain adoption by engaging stakeholders, providing innovative incentives, and supporting research and development initiatives.

REFERENCES

Al-Hashedi, K. G., & Magalingam, P. (2021). Financial fraud detection applying data mining techniques: A comprehensive review from 2009 to 2019. *Computer Science Review*, 40, 100402. 10.1016/j.cosrev.2021.100402

Ali, O., Ally, M., & Dwivedi, Y. (2020). The state of play of blockchain technology in the financial services sector: A systematic literature review. *International Journal of Information Management*, 54, 102199. 10.1016/j.ijinfomgt.2020.102199

Androulaki, E., Camenisch, J., Caro, A. D., Dubovitskaya, M., Elkhiyaoui, K., & Tackmann, B. (2020). Privacy-preserving auditable token payments in a permissioned blockchain system.*Paper presented at the Proceedings of the 2nd ACM Conference on Advances in Financial Technologie*s. ACM. 10.1145/3419614.3423259

Aswathy, S., & Tyagi, A. K. (2022). *Privacy Breaches through Cyber Vulnerabilities: Critical Issues, Open Challenges, and Possible Countermeasures for the Future Security and Privacy-Preserving Techniques in Wireless Robotics*. CRC Press. 10.1201/9781003156406-14

Babones, S. (2017). *The Australian Securities Exchange endorses the distributed ledger—but don't call it blockchain.*

Baddam, P. R., Vadiyala, V. R., & Thaduri, U. R. (2018). Unraveling Java's Prowess and Adaptable Architecture in Modern Software Development. *Global Disclosure of Economics and Business*, 7(2), 97–108. 10.18034/gdeb.v7i2.710

Baddam, P. R., Yerram, S. R., Varghese, A., Ande, J., Goda, D., & Mallipeddi, S. (2023). From Cashless Transactions to Cryptocurrencies: Assessing the Impact of Digitalization on Financial Security. *Asian Accounting and Auditing Advancement*, 14(1), 31–42.

Belchior, R., Vasconcelos, A., Guerreiro, S., & Correia, M. (2021). A survey on blockchain interoperability: Past, present, and future trends. *ACM Computing Surveys*, 54(8), 1–41. 10.1145/3471140

Bodó, B., & Giannopoulou, A. (2019). *The logics of technology decentralization–the case of distributed ledger technologies Blockchain and Web 3.0*. Routledge.

Chisty, N. M. A., Baddam, P. R., & Amin, R. (2022). Strategic Approaches to Safeguarding the Digital Future: Insights into Next-Generation Cybersecurity. *Engineering International*, 10(2), 69–84. 10.18034/ei.v10i2.689

Cocco, L., Pinna, A., & Marchesi, M. (2017). Banking on blockchain: Costs savings thanks to the blockchain technology. *Future Internet*, 9(3), 25. 10.3390/fi9030025

Collomb, A., & Sok, K. (2016). Blockchain/distributed ledger technology (DLT): What impact on the financial sector? *Digiworld Economic Journal,* (103).

Dalal, A., & Samal, B. (2022). Transforming Financial Landscapes: Case Studies on the Positive Disruption of Cross-Border Payments through Ripple. *International Journal of Research Radicals in Multidisciplinary Fields, ISSN: 2960-043X, 1*(2), 77-82.

Dasgupta, D., Shrein, J. M., & Gupta, K. D. (2019). A survey of blockchain from security perspective. *Journal of Banking and Financial Technology*, 3(1), 1–17. 10.1007/s42786-018-00002-6

Davradakis, E., & Santos, R. (2019). *Blockchain, FinTechs and their relevance for international financial institutions.* EIB Working Papers.

Dinh, T. T. A., Liu, R., Zhang, M., Chen, G., Ooi, B. C., & Wang, J. (2018). Untangling blockchain: A data processing view of blockchain systems. *IEEE Transactions on Knowledge and Data Engineering*, 30(7), 1366–1385. 10.1109/TKDE.2017.2781227

Dwivedi, S. K., Amin, R., & Vollala, S. (2020). Blockchain based secured information sharing protocol in supply chain management system with key distribution mechanism. *Journal of Information Security and Applications*, 54, 102554. 10.1016/j.jisa.2020.102554

Espel, T., Katz, L., & Robin, G. (2017). Proposal for protocol on a quorum blockchain with zero knowledge. *Cryptology ePrint Archive.*

Evren, R., & Milson, S. (2024). *The Cyber Threat Landscape: Understanding and Mitigating Risks.* EasyChair.

Farahani, B., Firouzi, F., & Luecking, M. (2021). The convergence of IoT and distributed ledger technologies (DLT): Opportunities, challenges, and solutions. *Journal of Network and Computer Applications*, 177, 102936. 10.1016/j.jnca.2020.102936

Giannino, A., Di Maio, D., & Vianelli, A. (2020). Innovation through regulation: A comprehensive regulatory framework for blockchain-based services and products. *Journal of Financial Compliance*, 3(2), 147–157.

Gikay, A. A. (2019). *European consumer law and blockchain based financial services: a functional approach against the rhetoric of regulatory uncertainty.*

Gokoglan, K., Cetın, S., & Bılen, A. (2022). Blockchain technology and its impact on audit activities. *Journal of Economics Finance and Accounting*, 9(2), 72–81. 10.17261/Pressacademia.2022.1567

Hamledari, H., & Fischer, M. (2021). Role of blockchain-enabled smart contracts in automating construction progress payments. *Journal of legal affairs and dispute resolution in engineering and construction, 13*(1), 04520038.

Hellani, H., Sliman, L., Samhat, A. E., & Exposito, E. (2021). On blockchain integration with supply chain: Overview on data transparency. *Logistics*, 5(3), 46. 10.3390/logistics5030046

Hofmann, F., Wurster, S., Ron, E., & Böhmecke-Schwafert, M. (2017). The immutability concept of blockchains and benefits of early standardization. *Paper presented at the 2017 ITU Kaleidoscope: Challenges for a Data-Driven Society.* ITU K. 10.23919/ITU-WT.2017.8247004

Hossain, M. I., Steigner, D. T., Hussain, M. I., & Akther, A. (2024). Enhancing Data Integrity and Traceability in Industry Cyber Physical Systems (ICPS) through Blockchain Technology: A Comprehensive Approach. *arXiv preprint arXiv:2405.04837*.

Hughes, A., Park, A., Kietzmann, J., & Archer-Brown, C. (2019). Beyond Bitcoin: What blockchain and distributed ledger technologies mean for firms. *Business Horizons*, 62(3), 273–281. 10.1016/j.bushor.2019.01.002

Hussein, D. M. E.-D. M., Taha, M. H. N., & Khalifa, N. E. M. (2018). A blockchain technology evolution between business process management (BPM) and Internet-of-Things (IoT). *International Journal of Advanced Computer Science and Applications*, 9(8). 10.14569/IJACSA.2018.090856

Isaksen, M. (2018). *Blockchain: The Future of Cross Border Payments*. University of Stavanger.

Javaid, M., Haleem, A., Singh, R. P., Suman, R., & Khan, S. (2022). A review of Blockchain Technology applications for financial services. *BenchCouncil Transactions on Benchmarks. Standards and Evaluations*, 2(3), 100073.

Kaluvakuri, S., & Vadiyala, V. R. (2016). Harnessing the Potential of CSS: An Exhaustive Reference for Web Styling. *Engineering International*, 4(2), 95–110. 10.18034/ei.v4i2.682

Komalavalli, C., Saxena, D., & Laroiya, C. (2020). *Overview of blockchain technology concepts Handbook of research on blockchain technology*. Elsevier.

Kshetri, N. (2021). Blockchain technology for improving transparency and citizen's trust. *Advances in Information and Communication: Proceedings of the 2021 Future of Information and Communication Conference (FICC)*. Springer. 10.1007/978-3-030-73100-7_52

Lashkari, B., & Musilek, P. (2021). A comprehensive review of blockchain consensus mechanisms. *IEEE Access: Practical Innovations, Open Solutions*, 9, 43620–43652. 10.1109/ACCESS.2021.3065880

Le Nguyen, B., Lydia, E. L., Elhoseny, M., Pustokhina, I., Pustokhin, D. A., Selim, M. M., & Shankar, K. (2020). Privacy preserving blockchain technique to achieve secure and reliable sharing of IoT data. *Computers, Materials & Continua*, 65(1), 87–107. 10.32604/cmc.2020.011599

Lu, Z., Liu, W., Wang, Q., Qu, G., & Liu, Z. (2018). A privacy-preserving trust model based on blockchain for VANETs. *IEEE Access: Practical Innovations, Open Solutions*, 6, 45655–45664. 10.1109/ACCESS.2018.2864189

Macharia, D. N. (2023). *Distributed Ledger Technology (DLT) Applications in Payment, Clearing, and Settlement Systems: A Study of Blockchain-Based Payment Barriers and Potential Solutions, and DLT Application in Central Bank Payment System Functions*. University of Huddersfield.

Madir, J. (2020). Smart Contracts-Self-Executing Contracts of the Future? *Int'l. In-House Counsel J., 13*, 1.

Mahajan, S., & Nanda, M. (2024). Revolutionizing Banking with Blockchain: Opportunities and Challenges Ahead. *Next-Generation Cybersecurity: AI, ML, and Blockchain*, 287-304.

Mandapuram, M., Mahadasa, R., & Surarapu, P. (2019). Evolution of Smart Farming: Integrating IoT and AI in Agricultural Engineering. *Global Disclosure of Economics and Business*, 8(2), 165–178. 10.18034/gdeb.v8i2.714

Mazzoni, M., Corradi, A., & Di Nicola, V. (2022). Performance evaluation of permissioned blockchains for financial applications: The ConsenSys Quorum case study. *Blockchain: Research and applications, 3*(1), 100026.

Mik, E. (2017). Smart contracts: Terminology, technical limitations and real world complexity. *Law, Innovation and Technology*, 9(2), 269–300. 10.1080/17579961.2017.1378468

Morgan, R. (2016). It's All About the BLOCKCHAIN. *American Bankers Association.ABA Banking Journal*, 108(2), 51.

Mugari, I., Gona, S., Maunga, M., & Chiyambiro, R. (2016). Cybercrime-the emerging threat to the financial services sector in Zimbabwe. *Mediterranean Journal of Social Sciences*, 7(3), 135–143. 10.5901/mjss.2016.v7n3s1p135

Nakamoto, S. (2008). Bitcoin: A peer-to-peer electronic cash system.

Nish, A., Naumann, S., & Muir, J. (2022). *Enduring cyber threats and emerging challenges to the financial sector*. Carnegie Endowment for International Peace.

Nowiński, W., & Kozma, M. (2017). How can blockchain technology disrupt the existing business models? *Entrepreneurial Business and Economics Review*, 5(3), 173–188. 10.15678/EBER.2017.050309

Olweny, F. (2024). Navigating the nexus of security and privacy in modern financial technologies. *GSC Advanced Research and Reviews*, 18(2), 167–197. 10.30574/gscarr.2024.18.2.0043

Oyewole, A. T., Oguejiofor, B. B., Eneh, N. E., Akpuokwe, C. U., & Bakare, S. S. (2024). Data privacy laws and their impact on financial technology companies: A review. *Computer Science & IT Research Journal*, 5(3), 628–650. 10.51594/csitrj.v5i3.911

Panwar, A., & Bhatnagar, V. (2020). Distributed ledger technology (DLT): the beginning of a technological revolution for blockchain. *Paper presented at the 2nd International Conference on Data, Engineering and Applications (IDEA)*. IEEE. 10.1109/IDEA49133.2020.9170699

Parate, S., Josyula, H. P., & Reddi, L. T. (2023). Digital identity verification: Transforming KYC processes in banking through advanced technology and enhanced security measures. *International Research Journal of Modernization in Engineering Technology and Science*, 5(9), 128–137.

Parn, E. A., & Edwards, D. (2019). Cyber threats confronting the digital built environment: Common data environment vulnerabilities and block chain deterrence. *Engineering, Construction, and Architectural Management*, 26(2), 245–266. 10.1108/ECAM-03-2018-0101

Petrov, D. (2019). The impact of blockchain and distributed ledger technology on financial services. *Industry 4.0*, 4(2), 88-91.

Pilkington, M. (2016). *Blockchain technology: principles and applications Research handbook on digital transformations*. Edward Elgar Publishing.

Popescu, A.-D. (2020). Transitions and concepts within decentralized finance (Defi) Space. *Research Terminals in the social sciences*.

Prasad, S., Rao, A. N., & Lanka, K. (2022). Analysing the Barriers for Implementation of Lean-Led Sustainable Manufacturing and Potential of Blockchain Technology to Overcome These Barriers: A Conceptual Framework. *International Journal of Mathematical. Engineering and Management Sciences*, 7(6), 791–819. 10.33889/IJMEMS.2022.7.6.051

Priem, R. (2020). Distributed ledger technology for securities clearing and settlement: Benefits, risks, and regulatory implications. *Financial Innovation*, 6(1), 11. 10.1186/s40854-019-0169-6

Rahardja, U., Hidayanto, A. N., Lutfiani, N., Febiani, D. A., & Aini, Q. (2021). Immutability of Distributed Hash Model on Blockchain Node Storage. *Sci. J. Informatics*, 8(1), 137–143. 10.15294/sji.v8i1.29444

Raval, S. (2016). *Decentralized applications: harnessing Bitcoin's blockchain technology*. O'Reilly Media, Inc.

Ross, E. S. (2016). Nobody puts blockchain in a corner: The disruptive role of blockchain technology in the financial services industry and current regulatory issues. *Cath. UJL & Tech*, 25, 353.

Sahay, A., & Tiwari, T. (2023). *HSBC: Facilitating Trade Finance Through Blockchain*. Indian Institute of Management Ahmedabad.

Sander, F., Semeijn, J., & Mahr, D. (2018). The acceptance of blockchain technology in meat traceability and transparency. *British Food Journal*, 120(9), 2066–2079. 10.1108/BFJ-07-2017-0365

Sarmah, S. S. (2018). Understanding blockchain technology. *Computing in Science & Engineering*, 8(2), 23–29.

Schwerin, S. (2018). Blockchain and privacy protection in the case of the european general data protection regulation (GDPR): A delphi study. *The Journal of the British Blockchain Association*, 1(1), 1–77. 10.31585/jbba-1-1-(4)2018

Sedlmeir, J., Lautenschlager, J., Fridgen, G., & Urbach, N. (2022). The transparency challenge of blockchain in organizations. *Electronic Markets*, 32(3), 1779–1794. 10.1007/s12525-022-00536-035602109

Sharma, A. (2021). Consensus Mechanisms in Blockchain Networks: Analyzing Various Consensus Mechanisms Such as Proof of Work (PoW), Proof of Stake (PoS), and Practical Byzantine Fault Tolerance (PBFT). *Blockchain Technology and Distributed Systems*, 1(1), 1–11.

Shrimali, B., & Patel, H. B. (2022). Blockchain state-of-the-art: Architecture, use cases, consensus, challenges and opportunities. *Journal of King Saud University. Computer and Information Sciences*, 34(9), 6793–6807. 10.1016/j.jksuci.2021.08.005

Siddique, S., & Vadiyala, V. (2021). Strategic Frameworks for Optimizing Customer Engagement in the Digital Era: A Comparative Study. *Digitalization & Sustainability Review*, 1(1), 24–40.

Sunyaev, A., & Sunyaev, A. (2020). Distributed ledger technology. *Internet computing: Principles of distributed systems and emerging internet-based technologies*, 265-299.

Talesh, S. A. (2018). Data breach, privacy, and cyber insurance: How insurance companies act as "compliance managers" for businesses. *Law & Social Inquiry*, 43(2), 417–440. 10.1111/lsi.12303

Tao, H., Bhuiyan, M. Z. A., Rahman, M. A., Wang, G., Wang, T., Ahmed, M. M., & Li, J. (2019). Economic perspective analysis of protecting big data security and privacy. *Future Generation Computer Systems*, 98, 660–671. 10.1016/j.future.2019.03.042

Ton, T. (2022). *Blockchain-Transforming the Future of Trade Finance*.

Toufaily, E., Zalan, T., & Dhaou, S. B. (2021). A framework of blockchain technology adoption: An investigation of challenges and expected value. *Information & Management*, 58(3), 103444. 10.1016/j.im.2021.103444

Upadhyay, N. (2020). Demystifying blockchain: A critical analysis of challenges, applications and opportunities. *International Journal of Information Management*, 54, 102120. 10.1016/j.ijinfomgt.2020.102120

Vadiyala, V. R. (2021). Byte by Byte: Navigating the Chronology of Digitization and Assessing its Dynamic Influence on Economic Landscapes, Employment Trends, and Social Structures. *Digitalization & Sustainability Review*, 1(1), 12–23.

Vadiyala, V. R., Baddam, P. R., & Kaluvakuri, S. (2016). Demystifying Google Cloud: A Comprehensive Review of Cloud Computing Services. *Asian Journal of Applied Science and Engineering*, 5(1), 207–218. 10.18034/ajase.v5i1.80

van der Elst, C., & Lafarre, A. (2024). *The Viability of Blockchain in Corporate Governance Board-Shareholder Dialogue: Best Practices, Legal Constraints and Policy Options*. Cambridge University Press.

Verhoeven, P. (2022). *Management model for social and environmental impact in logistics through blockchain technologies*. Universitätsverlag der Technischen Universität Berlin.

Xu, C., Liu, C., Nie, D., & Gai, L. (2021). How can a blockchain-based anti-money laundering system improve customer due diligence process? *Journal of Forensic & Investigative Accounting*, 13(2), 273–287.

Yeoh, P. (2017). Regulatory issues in blockchain technology. *Journal of Financial Regulation and Compliance*, 25(2), 196–208. 10.1108/JFRC-08-2016-0068

Yerram, S. R., Goda, D. R., Mahadasa, R., Mallipeddi, S. R., Varghese, A., Ande, J., Surarapu, P., & Dekkati, S. (2021). The role of blockchain technology in enhancing financial security amidst digital transformation. *Asian Bus. Rev*, 11(3), 125–134. 10.18034/abr.v11i3.694

Zachariadis, M., Hileman, G., & Scott, S. V. (2019). Governance and control in distributed ledgers: Understanding the challenges facing blockchain technology in financial services. *Information and Organization*, 29(2), 105–117. 10.1016/j.infoandorg.2019.03.001

Zhou, L., Diro, A., Saini, A., Kaisar, S., & Hiep, P. C. (2024). Leveraging zero knowledge proofs for blockchain-based identity sharing: A survey of advancements, challenges and opportunities. *Journal of Information Security and Applications*, 80, 103678. 10.1016/j.jisa.2023.103678

Chapter 9
Protecting Investor Sentiment by Detecting Financial Fraud With the Help of ML and AI Applications

Anumita Chaudhury
Garden City University, India

ABSTRACT

Investors, in spite of their vigilant moves, often are observed to fall victim to financial fraud. There are several machine learning algorithms both supervised and unsupervised which exists and continue to serve the objective of detecting financial fraud like under supervised machine learning random forest, k-nearest neighbours (KNN), logistic regression and support vector machine (SVM) and unsupervised machine learning includes K-means and SOM (self-organizing map).AI will help in mitigating the impact of volatility in the financial market. There is a necessity to adopt new-age machine learning and Artificial Intelligence which will promptly process millions of data and also identify dubious patterns has become very crucial to evade the losses caused by fraudulent activities.

INTRODUCTION

We have seen a sharp rise in fraud in the previous several years in the globalized and liberalized corporate climate, particularly in India's financial sectors. Over the past ten years, the Indian financial industry has experienced exponential expansion.

DOI: 10.4018/979-8-3693-3633-5.ch009

However, this progress has not been without its challenges, since there has been a spike in fraud instances. Fraud causes the public coffers to suffer large losses, which has a negative impact on industry. To mitigate the threat of financial fraud, a protocol needs to be framed for early financial detection which is commonly witnessed within various service providers. The easy target of financial fraud in particular are the financial institutions in particular such as banks, fintech etc. The tactics adopted by the fraudsters are very dynamic in nature and hence continuous monitoring is required. Also, with the growth of the population of investment avenues, protecting investors' sentiments has progressively become a vital importance linked to global economic growth and people's lives. Financial fraud is a huge industry, causing direct losses of over USD 20 billion a year. Experts in the field believe that this number is actually considerably higher because businesses and investors find it difficult to properly detect and quantify damages resulting from fraud. Financial frauds mostly affect foreign direct investment (FDI) into India (ASSOCHAM, 2024). It is now necessary for the regulators to develop an internal fraud management strategy that is more strategic and technical in nature. They require disciplined and targeted action to overcome this obstacle.

This paper addresses a practical problem and makes several contributions to the body of knowledge on financial fraud detection. First of all, it discusses the most advanced method of financial fraud detection available in artificial intelligence and machine learning, which has excellent performance accuracy. Since traditional systems mostly depended on human interaction, they are unable to adjust to potential changes or circumstances. Adjuster inspections, agent inquiries, and internal auditor examinations were formerly used to combat fraud. However, traditional approaches have grown cumbersome and slow as the industry generates and processes more records, papers, and data on a Terabyte and Petabyte scale. As a result, practitioners and academics can better grasp this topic by using machine learning and artificial approaches as a road map.

The findings of this study are helpful for the finance industry, investors, and policy makers to obtain a better understanding of fraudulent activities and for detecting it using a predictive model. The remainder of the paper is as follows: section 2 discusses the past relevant studies; section 3 includes the materials and methods that are being used to build the solution for fraud detection. Moreover, data preprocessing, feature computation, and predictive models are being described here. Section 4 covers the overall discussion and concludes the paper where the it also includes the theoretical implications, practical implications, discussion, and conclusion of the study.

STATEMENT OF THE PROBLEM

In today's financial system, financial fraud is a major worry as it may result in substantial losses for people, businesses, and economies. The accuracy, speed, and flexibility of conventional techniques for identifying financial fraud, like rule-based systems, statistical analysis, expert systems, and others, are constrained. The need for increasingly complex and advanced techniques for detecting financial fraud is rising as a result. The shortcomings of conventional fraud detection techniques may be addressed using artificial intelligence (AI) and machine learning (ML). But the successful application of AI and ML in financial fraud detection necessitates a deep comprehension of the tools, methods, and algorithms employed, as well as the difficulties and constraints related to their employ. The current project intends to investigate financial fraud detection using AI and ML systems.

BACKGROUND OF THE STUDY

Researchers and academics are working to create a reliable method for identifying and preventing financial frauds because these crimes are resulting in large losses. A four-category taxonomy of financial fraud was established by Ngai et al. (2011) and included securities and commodities fraud, bank fraud, insurance fraud, and other financial fraud. The possible repercussions of undiscovered abnormalities on the sector and on daily life have led to a significant increase in awareness of financial fraud throughout the last 10 years. These crimes can take many different forms and have the potential to destabilize economies, raise living expenses, and undermine consumer confidence (Syeda, Zhang, & Pan, 2002). The existence of various theories and some empirical evidence on stock price manipulation in the United States is presented in many expert research work. There are two categories of people in stock market namely manipulators and information seekers and their influence on stock market (Agarwal & Wu, 2003). These information seekers push prices up to where information from a knowledgeable party suggests they should, which manifestly increases market efficiency in a market free of manipulators. Information seekers have a more unclear position in a market where there are manipulators. Increased competition for shares, which facilitates the entry of manipulators into the market and may decrease market efficiency, is implied by an increase in information seekers. The persons who may have knowledge, such as market makers, brokers, underwriters, business insiders, and major shareholders, are probably manipulators (Agarwal & Wu, 2003). Their result suggest that stock market manipulation may have important impacts on market efficiently. Therefore, there is a need of strong financial fraud detection model which will assists the genuine investors to detect the fraud and also foresee the financial distress popularly called as financial distress prediction model. Determining the importance of data mining applications to capital markets becomes the vital process to prevent fraud. Financial performance applications, such as anticipating company bankruptcies and failures, spotting transaction manipulation, determining financial risk management, and determining customer profiles and depth management, are especially helpful in the finance sector (Akaya & Ceren,2011). They suggest that the disclosure of hidden values and useful information amongst a vast volume of data might be characterized as data mining. The goal of data mining is to develop decision-making models for forecasts based on historical activity analysis. Supervised and unsupervised data mining techniques are two different categories. Target variables are not identified in unsupervised approaches. Rather, the data mining program looks for structure and trends in all the variables. Clustering is the most often used unsupervised data mining technique. Thus, data mining techniques have applications in the finance sector, especially in identifying financial failure early on and financial information manipulation. Further investigating the fraud detection technique Analytics India Magazine (2020) and Satyam Misra (2020) discusses anomaly detection and behaviour analytics in payment fraud risk management. It is very vital to know the effect of anomaly and its detection importance for economy of the country (Satyam Misra,2020; Analytics India Magazine,2020). In continuation with stock market anomaly detection, Rakesh Deshmukh (2024) provides an interesting insight on identifying red flags in financial statements as a guide for investors safeguarding their investments. Businesses frequently attempt to present themselves in a more favourable position than reality dictates (Rakesh Deshmukh,2024). This is where red flags become valuable, they serve as indicators that there may be underlying issues with a company's financial status. Stock market frauds are going to unthinkable heights as the Hindu flashes the news on how Hyderabad citizens conned of 1.16 crore in two major stock trading frauds. This number flashes an importance of importance of well-equipped fraud detection techniques (by Ravinder Shah,2024). Ted talk forum furnishes the valuable technique of Investing with Anomaly Detection and Timing. Systematic identification of market inconsistencies can derive profitable investments (TED,2024). The conversation touches upon the price momentum anomaly, post earnings announcement drift and the importance of timing in the stock market. Nearly 45 short articles on individual companies from the Dutch East India Co. in the 1600s to Donald Trump's two failed companies that went bankrupt were identified. This book provides valuable insight on stock corners in which someone gained control of all the shares in a company forcing shorts to sell at whatever price they asked. In most cases, cornering the market ended up bankrupting the speculator owning the corner when the price of the stock dropped (Bryan Taylor,2018). World Economic Forum publishes n eyebogler information in their report. Some of the most severe risks we may face over the next decade, against a backdrop of rapid technological change and economic uncertainty, as the world is plagued by a duo of dangerous crises: climate and conflict (Global Risk Report,2024). They further state that owing to the rise in adversity of the two crisis the fraudsters are taking advantage of the situation and manipulating the stock market. Applied standard set of anomaly detection techniques, used in big data based on nearest-neighbours, clustering and statistical approaches, to detect rare anomalies present within the historical daily trading information for five years (i.e., 2009--2013) for each stock listed on the Australian Security Exchange (ASX) were investigated. LOF (Local Outlier Factor) and CMGOS (Clustering-based Multivariate Gaussian Outlier Score) are the best performing anomaly detection techniques (Mohiuddin Ahmed et al.,2017).

Numerous researchers have examined numerous strategies and contrasted their ability to forecast outcomes (Singh and Jain, 2021). In a survey on machine learning and nature-inspired fraud detection techniques, Adewumi and Akinyelu (2017) evaluated the efficacy of several techniques. In a comparison of three machine learning techniques, Random Forest (RF), Logistic Regression (LR), and Support Vector Machine (SVM), Carneiro et al. (2017) found that RF performed the best. However, a significant body of research has shown that decision trees (DT) are superior to other algorithms in the identification of fake news (Muhammad et al., 2020) and building insurance fraud (Hassan and Abraham, 2016). In contrast, Awoyemi et al. (2017) and Ain et al. (2020) discovered that K closest neighbour (KNN) performed better for credit card fraud detection than Naïve Bayes (NB), LR, RF, DT, SVM, J48, and Binary Classification Technique (BCT).

REAL-WORLD EXAMPLES OF FRAUD DETECTION

Artificial intelligence and machine learning are being used by companies in a variety of industries, including banking, online gaming, healthcare, and e-commerce, to identify financial fraud. Whatever your sector, you can always take use of AI and ML's capacity to process massive volumes of data, identify trends, and thwart fraud. For instance, by identifying trends in client behaviour, ML and AI in banking are able to identify account takeovers, unauthorized access, and other fraud. PayPal and Mastercard are a few actual instances of businesses that are already making use of machine learning's ability to detect financial fraud.

CURRENT METHODS OF DETECTING FINANCIAL FRAUD AND THEIR LIMITATIONS

a) Rule based systems: These systems recognize suspicious transactions based on pre-established rules and criteria. These systems' drawbacks include their propensity for false alarms, their inability to identify novel and unidentified types of fraud, and their inability to adjust to shifting patterns in fraudulent activity.
b) Statistical Analysis: Using this technique, a lot of financial data is analysed to find trends and abnormalities that can point to fraud. This method's drawbacks include its inability to identify fraud in real time and its reliance on a substantial volume of past data for optimal performance.
c) Expert systems: In order to detect fraud, these systems rely on human expertise and knowledge. Its drawbacks include requiring a lot of time, being subject to human mistake, and being constrained by the level of experience of those engaged.

MATERIAL AND METHODS

Prior research has documented using supervised, unsupervised, and hybrid algorithms for fraud detection, as was previously recognized and thoroughly addressed. The types and patterns of fraud are constantly changing, thus it's critical to comprehend the technology involved in fraud detection. In order to find the optimal model that can accurately forecast fraud claims, this study gives a conceptual framework in which many algorithms are discussed which are commonly adopted to prevent financial fraud because of their predictive analyses' nature. The fact that current detection systems rely on predetermined standards or learned records makes it challenging to identify novel assault patterns. In this study, machine learning techniques based on supervised learning and unsupervised learning have been intensively researched in an effort to find new patterns and increase detection accuracy.

Understanding the many forms of financial fraud, looking into the shortcomings of the techniques now in use for spotting it, and investigating the possibility of utilizing AI and ML algorithms for financial fraud detection are the goals of the current study. To fulfil these goals, the study employs a descriptive methodology and uses secondary data gathered from publications and papers that have been published. This Study considers qualitative approach to gain an understanding of various AI/ML tools for financial fraud. Also, survey on existing financial fraud detection methods based on the technical development routes is adopted. This survey article has explored the state -of-the-art fraud detection systems in financial sector. Furthermore, the fraud detection approaches and techniques have been categorized

Detecting Financial Fraud With the Help of ML and AI Applications

and reviewed. In this survey, we provided a comprehensive overview of financial fraud detection practices. This is done by streamlining of two main dimensions which has become very vital for regulators namely technological and infrastructural dimensions for financial fraud detection.

Financial Fraud Detection Using Technological Dimension

Developing technological framework will enhance the financial fraud detection in a systematic way as this framework follows the stepwise process of implementation of technology. Structured and stepwise technological framework for fraud detection should be adopted which includes;

Step 1: Collection of data: Regulated industries can always fetch any transactional data with personal information in order to develop strong trustworthy profiles as per KYC and AML regulations. Financial fraud can be prohibited to a greater extent if regulators construct strong rules and regulation which will not give any scope for financial frauds like money laundering. To design a proper regulation, it is very important to systematically follow KYC process and understand your customers before taking them onboard and thereafter scrutinize their financial transactions. Systematic collection of data will allow one to identify the customer properly which in turn will help in determination of risk level of the customers. Periodic review of KYC will regulate the dubious activities. Apart from collecting the general information about the customer one needs to keep the track of transaction and also updating them. This can be done with the help of the system called as customers due diligence which will authenticate and validate the process of collection of data.

Figure 1.

Step 2: Information Processing: Next step is to systematically process the data by properly cleaning and labelling which will make input data ready for the software. As the raw data may contain missing values, inconsistencies and outliers, cleaning of data possesses the challenge of scaling errors. The strong build software will assist in accurately detect and label the fraud transactions. As per use case the amount of data processing will be decided upon. CatBoost is the apt example of the information processing as it permits only minimal pre-processing. Accurate information processing assists the data to achieve the systematic format which helps in representing the relationship and patterns. This eases out the job of machine learning model and learns about the data in better way. Proper cleaning and labelling make the data informative and meaningful. Information processing in combination with machine learning will process large volume of data with optimal accuracy and computation.

Figure 2. Cleaning of the data

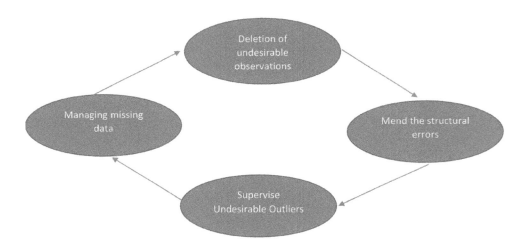

Figure 3. Labelling of the data

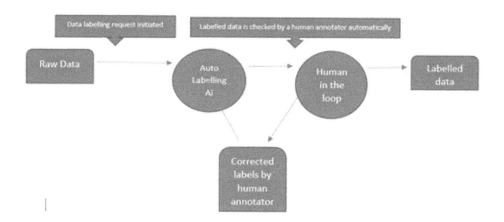

Step 3: Selection of Machine learning model: Comprehensive Machine learning model should be selected depending on the nature of the data. One can complete the task efficiently with minimal human effort with the help of machine learning algorithms. Algorithms are capable of responding to situations very quickly based on their past learnings even if they are not programmed for the same explicitly. Efficient machine learning model identifies the hidden patterns from the data and computes rapidly as compared to traditional process. The selection process of machine learning should be precise and based on the objective. Our aim is to protect the investor's sentiment with the use relatable historical data. Therefore, the efficient machine learning model will use the historical data and attempts to understand the relation and patterns followed by creating logical model. Machine learning model not only reduces cost but mitigate risk by detecting frauds or dubious activity in financial market. The most popular application of machine learning models is detecting spam mails which will also help us in detecting fraudulent activities as machine learning models are self-driven and self-reliant. Hence selection of Machine learning model is very vital for financial experts using data science knowledge. While selecting the model one needs to explore all three types of machine learning namely supervised, unsupervised and reinforcement learning.

Figure 4. Machine learning model

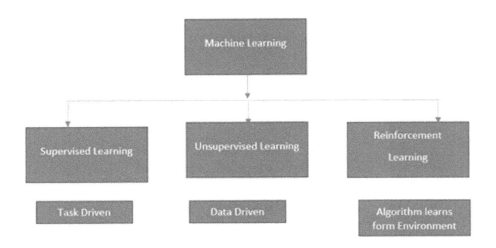

Step 4: Training of Machine learning model: The extensive data created is considered to train the ML algorithm. This step is very vital as this model will analyse both licit and fallacious transactions by searching for patterns that exist between both. During training phase, the selected algorithms look for connections and patterns. The internal parameters are repeated in the training data to avoid the disparity between actual output and expected output. The financial expertise of a financial experts lies while selecting training data which should be relevant, uniform, representative, comprehensive but most importantly diverse.

Figure 5. Training of Machine learning model

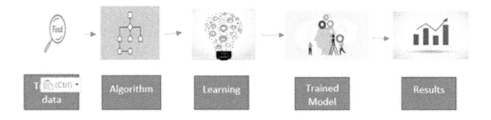

Step 5: Stationing: After training the software should be amalgamated in a way such that it is approachable by all team members. This helps in proper review whenever necessary. For stationing the software, the most vital requisite is to implement various types of risk alerts and threshold so that whenever necessary the manual reviews can be conducted. Ideal stationing of the software should be such that it ensures as well as assist in optimum security, maximum compatibility and optimization. This is possible only when circumstances are less disruptive to an organizations workforce and also offer post deployment support. Productive big data management facilitates the ability to collect and interpret large amount of data after analysing different types of metrics and identifying patterns in fraud detection.

Step 6: Surveillance: This step is very crucial for any type of structured system. Continuous monitoring helps in maintaining the safe environment for investors. Also, the provision of easy updates to risk alerts and threshold assists in systematic surveillance of the system. The surveillance conducts regular checks on companies, transactions etc to certain their compliance with laws and regulations with respect to financial frauds like money laundering, theft, financial terrorism etc. It should be noted that surveillance is not a one-time effort but a continuous process. Methodical training for employees is required to ensure that they are aware of all regulations and best practices. Internal and external audits is one of the best of surveillance tactics to address any areas of improvement.

Figure 6. Structured and stepwise technological framework for fraud detection

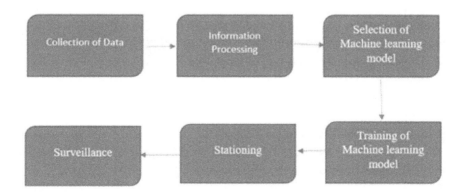

Financial Fraud Detection using Infrastructural dimension

Deployment of systematic infrastructural dimension should include;

1) **Fraud detection team:** Unlike Cybersecurity task force trained professionals who are experts in large data analytics are required so that they can detect fraud at early stage. The team should be harnessed with competent software solution along with appropriate resources with relevant communication channels which should be easily accessible. The investigators of fraud detection team will be able to identify pattern and connections which are critical in order for prompt action against fraudulent activity. The time spent by the analyst and the speed with which frauds are detected is directly proportional to each other. Therefore, the strong fraud detection team is vital for the organisation.

2) **Active policies:** Possibility of risk should be recognised by all the organisational member. Hence strong and defined policies should be constructed so that all are aware of the threshold of risk acceptance. Policy maker should be prepared to accept risk vis-à-vis be very carefully determine the risk. Strong and activities policies on fraud not only need to be developed but also promoted among staffs. A document with defined responsibilities and procedures helps to early detection of fraud. Strong policies raise awareness among staffs and also minimise the impact of damage caused by dubious activities. Active policies should clearly define fraudulent action to avoid any complexity.

3) **Awareness among organization:** All the fraud detection and prevention measures need to communicated to all the members of the organisation. Hence, the awareness will be created which will help them not be susceptible to the fraud. If employees are aware of risk and scam tactics many dubious activities like phishing can be controlled and can prevent massive leaks of data as this leak can create fraud. Post-pandemic has put forth many challenges and different types of novel fraud is one among them. Ignorance on the same will cost heavily to the economy of any country. Therefore, awareness among organisation should exist by staying informed and be updated on various scam.

4) **Encouraging reporting of malicious activity:** Malicious acts like insider information, bribery etc can be prohibited by adopting and encouraging the act to promoting the creation of Suspicious Activity Reports (SARs) if any such malicious transaction is witnessed. Staff can be trained to report about such pervasive threats irrespective of their positions in the organisation.

5) **Collaboration:** Collaborating with potential business partners and maintain a good relationship with fraud prevention provider is a very crucial part of security. Appraising potential business partner is a vital part of security. Like KYC there is a concept of KYB which stresses on know your business and also a part of due diligence. Such partners bring along with them their own robust framework for fraud

prevention which will help in preventing intense information leaks which otherwise would sprung if we have untrustworthy affiliates.

6) **Surveillance:** Regular updating and refreshment of above-mentioned processes is required for documentation and staff awareness. Best practices and new threats evolve simultaneously. Hence the strong protocols should also emerge alongside, persistence training on this is the compulsory requirement.

Impact of Artificial Intelligence and Machine Learning for Effective Fraud Detection with Algorithms and Techniques

Investors can be protected from the financial fraud with the help of early detection which is only possible in current scenario through the concept of artificial intelligence and machine learning. The vital part of fraud detection process is to identify the anomalies in dataset. Machine learning is widely used because it promptly classifies the data systematically and assists in prediction. This can be done with the help of both supervised and unsupervised machine learning.

Fraud Detection Using Machine Learning Algorithms: Supervised Methods

a) Random Forest

This machine learning model develops decision trees on samples of the data thereby getting predictions from each of them and finally selects the best solution. One of the key features of Random Forest algorithm is its diversity and simplicity. Multiple decision trees are built and then merged together to achieve accuracy in predictions. Moreover, Random Forest algorithm can be also used for regression. In finance random forest algorithm will assist in detecting fraudsters who are out too scam the bank or the companies who are in verge to liquidate but investors are unaware of the same.

Figure 7. Random forest algorithm

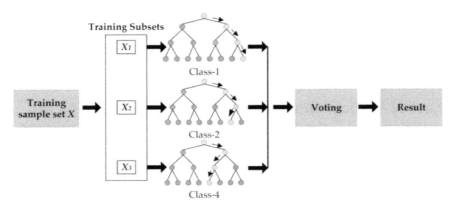

Random forest is a one of the supervised methods of machine learning. Therefore, as discussed earlier it follows the process of data collection, model training, evaluation and deployment. To begin with data set is extracted from the trading platform of particular time period which includes both listed and delisted companies. The dataset contains all the information of the trading activities along with the names of delisted companies. Before processing, the data is cleaned in order to get complete data. Thereafter multiple decision tree is constructed and merged together as individual trees are tagged as weak learner owing to its low predictive power. The steps begin with selection of random samples from a given data (training set). Random forest will construct a decision tree for every training data and then voting takes place by average technique of the decision tree. Finally, the selection of most voted prediction result as a final prediction. This method is suitable for fraud detection as it considers binary classifier for the detection. The financial transactions are classified as 0 and 1 which represents fraud or not a fraud.

b) <u>K-nearest neighbours (KNN)</u>

Taking the advantage of the similarity concept, this model predicts the value of new data point by taking inti account K closest neighbours in the training dataset. As the name suggest it tries to identify the similarities with the help of classifier and then gives the output which is very closest to the training set. The most vital feature which makes K-NN Algorithm unique is that it is non-parametric in nature which implies that there is no assumption on underlying data and therefore it is distribution free and can be applied for non-normal variables. As our basic aim is fraud detection this feature becomes very important as most of the data will be in the form of non-normal variables. This algorithm is also termed as lazy algorithm as this model simply looks for the solution only when outside classifiers are introduced rather than constructing the internal structure of the training set. For example, if we have an image of an object which seems like a fruit similar to papaya or watermelon but we are not sure of it. Here we can K-NN Algorithm as it works on the concept of similarity. We use K-NN classifier as shown in the figure and this model will identify similar features of the new data set to papaya and watermelon images and based on most similar feature the output will be obtained of either papaya or watermelon category.

Figure 8.

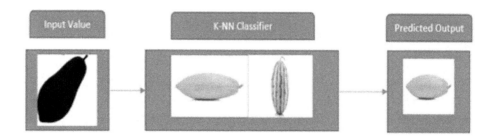

Similarly, when we are discussing about fraud detection analysis the entire financial database can be divide into two namely, suspicious pattern and normal pattern. The association rules namely Apriori algorithm is applied for both the patterns simultaneously and this process is applied repeatedly to determine the transactions with high frequency. To do this Euclidean distance function is created which determines new cases closeness to which of the two mentioned patterns. It all begins by calculating best value K from suspicious and normal financial pattern. However, there is no particular way to determine the K but generally number 5 is taken as most preferred value. If the new data point is close to any one the pattern than it is concluded that new data point is close to that particular pattern therefore new data belongs to normal pattern or suspicious pattern and therefore, we can detect the fraud transaction accordingly. The Process is explained in the figure below as to how the new data point with the help of K-NN Algorithm is assigned to the respective (normal) pattern

Figure 9.

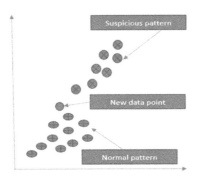 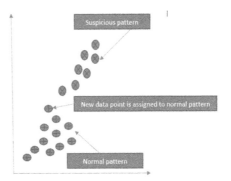

Logistic Regression

This model supports the concept of probability as the dependent variable is bounded between 0 and 1. In short, it analyses the relationship between independent and dependent variable set as the logistic regression is a predictive analysis. Logistic regression helps in building the classifier which assists detecting fraud and non-fraud zone. Logistic regression is based on sigmoid function and builds an S curve by squeezing the straight line. The advantage of logistic regression algorithm over linear regression is that the predicted output lies within 0 and 1 range. To begin with the large data is divided into two training set and testing set. Model one can be used for training set and the model two can be used for testing set wherein few more variables which is the combination of the already selected variables is added. To detect fraud in logistic regression, one can select "n" independent variables while keeping dependant variable as "FRAUD". Thereby, based on p-value (higher or lower than 0.05) and type of correlation (negative or positive) the effectiveness of the variables can be determined. Later the training model is used to predict the testing data (model two) for evaluating the accuracy of the prediction.

c) Support Vector Machine

SVM separates the datapoints in different classes by finding the optimal hyperplane. The main objective of the constructing the hyperplane is to maximise the margin between the closest points of different classes.

Figure 10.

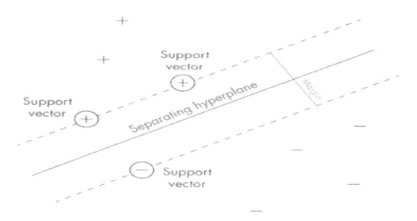

Source: Mathworks (Sector vector machine)

As shown in the figure one class of datasets is separated from another class of datasets with the help of hyperplane. The transaction which are not fraudulent are termed as + and the transaction which are fraudulent are termed as -. Like all other algorithm in SVM also the large datasets are divided into training set and testing data but only the support vectors selected from the training data are used to construct the decision surface. This Machine learning uses kernel system wherein complex dataset is mapped to higher dimension is a way that it makes the separation of data point easier. In fraud detection SVM as an anomaly detector assists in determining whether the particular object in the dataset belongs to the normal class or they behave as outliers.

Fraud Detection Using Machine Learning Algorithms: Unsupervised Methods

a) K-means

This machine learning model assist in solving the clustering problems in machine learning or data science. Data are divided into clusters that share similarities and dissimilar data belongs to another cluster. The "K" refers to the numbers of clusters to be created. In fraud detection based on data obtained divide the data into two namely fraud and non-fraud.

Figure 11.

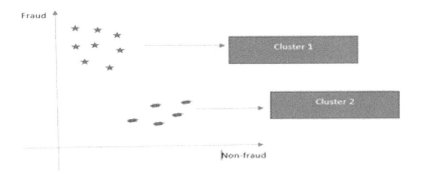

As shown in figure above, two clusters are created. In Cluster 1 we can see the data with high fraud cases and in Cluster 2 we can see the data with non-fraud. The allocation of two centroids is initiated because in our case we have created two clusters. Initially the centroid is randomly selected and not necessarily a central point of a given data set. Secondly distance between each of the randomly assigned centroids is determined. The point whose distance is less from both the centroids is assigned to that centroid. The distance calculation and repositioning of the centroid continuous until final cluster is obtained. After the solid cluster formation of historical data, it becomes possible to detect prospective fraud based its proximity to clusters that indicate fraudulent patterns.

b) Self-Organizing Map (SOM)

This machine learning model emphasizes on competitive learning. According to the concept some criteria select the winning process element and then weights are assigned accordingly to come to the conclusion. This algorithm can be applied on large and complex dataset and can detect fraud patterns efficiently. The Initial step for fraud detection using SOM is proper selection of dataset and then convert the data into numerical data set. Thereby apply SOM and conclude the process with review and decision making. As mentioned before, to begin with fraud detection the data set needs to be accurately divided into three namely Account related data (account number, currency of account etc), customer related data (customer id, customer type etc) and transaction related data (transaction no, location etc). Few of data like location, name needs to be converted into numeric one because all this data is required to be in the form of normal distribution. Thereafter implementation of SOM is initialised where in input vector matrix is created. Finally, after assigning weight vector neuron matrix is created which gives the output of SOM in patterns and cluster formation. The cluster so formed in fraud detection will be in the form of fraudulent and genuine set. Finally, the cluster formation obtained shows the categories of transactions performed as well as rarely performed more frequently as well as rarely. If there is a case of dubious activity which exceeds a certain threshold value than the transaction is sent for review. In this way processing time and complexity can be reduced.

DISCUSSION AND CONCLUSION

The struggle to fight fraud is primitive but recent development in digitalisation has made it lot tougher. Digitalisation has witnessed the increase in threat actors with advance sophisticated techniques. AI will play a key role in future of fraud detection process because human error will account for high numbers of false positives. AI is preferred over traditional method like prediction analysis because AI can learn from its own analyses which outstands unchanging protocols. The more they learn the more they are familiar with the system that threat actors can adopt to crack them and the more AI models become effective. AI initially is assisted by historical data but over the time due to repetitive and continuous process AI can see fraudulent behaviour long before it actually occurred. Fraud detection and prevention mechanism through machine learning has been proposed both by supervised and unsupervised process. The supervised relies on showcasing the genuine transaction continuously during training so that identification of malicious transactions is possible. In unsupervised captures normal data distribution during training unlike supervised methods. Later both the models determine whether the sample is valid or malicious based on patterns and structures. The various AI Algorithm discussed in this chapter addresses the key feature of AI that it analyses large volumes of data quickly and accurately also it identifies dubious transactions and patterns that may indicate fraudulent activity. Financial institutions can now use advanced methodologies to better serve their clients and consumers thanks to the growth in data availability and its use, as well as advancements in machine learning and artificial intelligence. The goal of machine learning (ML) is to maximize operational efficiency, save expenses, and gain a competitive edge—not to completely replace human resources. The institutions using it will benefit from the value combination of traditional methodologies, behavioural/sentiment analysis, and machine learning techniques. The ability to process vast amounts of data in less time with high precision, minimize behavioural errors, and make decisions based on earlier learning experiences are the main benefits of machine learning. Financial institutions may be able to maintain their financial stability through more effective processing of data on credit risks, fraud detection and prevention, and the possibility to boost regulatory compliance. However, new technologies' scalability and network improvements could lead to the emergence of new dependencies. It's possible that many of the present AI and ML suppliers are unaware of the regulatory laws or operate outside of the framework. Because ML and AI are not interpretable, there is a chance that the impacts won't be predicted or identified, but the algorithms can still be trained to provide the best answers in low-volatility scenarios. The usage of opaque models that could have unforeseen implications is not advised. Another problem that the institutions would have is the lack of resources with the necessary training and expertise. It is important to keep an eye on the usage, developments, security, and regulatory ramifications of machine learning and artificial intelligence applications.

We have reviewed 6 ML models in this chapter. But still there is a need of some process that tells without research and experimentation which model suits one's processes and data science in a particular setting. Nevertheless, through AI the world has achieved milestones like AI assist in Automated anomaly detection and identification of patterns like unusual transaction amount, from the same device if multiple transaction has been made etc. AI can assist in behavioural analyses like customer behaviour pattern. AI can use natural language processing for customer communications like emails to identify fraud. Finally, AI ensures continuous learning which ensures that the fraud detection system is updated with the latest fraud trends and tactics. To conclude, AI-powered financial fraud detection is vital for identifying and preventing fraudulent activity. Financial transactions continue to grow, the use of AI and ML will become increasingly important for detecting sophisticated and complex fraud schemes.

REFERENCES

Agarwal, A., Gans, J., & Goldfarb, A. (2018) *Economic policy for artificial intelligence. National Bureau of Economic Research.* University of Chicago Press. https://doi.org/10.1086/699935

Azulay, D. (2019). *Artificial Intelligence in Finance – a Comprehensive Overview.* Boston: Emerj: The AI Research and Advisory Company. 10.1007/s43546-023-00618-x

Bahrammirzaee, A. (2010). A Comparative Survey of Artificial Intelligence in Finance: Artificial Neural Network, Expert System and Hybrid Intelligence System. *Neural Comput & Applic.* Springer.10.1109/IC3I56241.2022.10073077

Barboza, F., Kimura, H., & Altman, E. (2017). Machine learning models and bankruptcy prediction. *Expert Systems with Applications*, 83, 405–417. 10.1016/j.eswa.2017.04.006

Barboza, F., Kimura, H., & Altman, E. (2017). Machine learning models and bankruptcy prediction. *Expert Systems with Applications*, 83, 405–417. 10.1016/j.eswa.2017.04.006

Bharti Kumari, J. K. (January 2021). *System Dynamics Approach for Adoption of Artificial Intelligence in Finance.* Springer Nature Singapore.10.1007/978-981-15-8025-3_54

Brédart, X., & Cultrera, L. (2016). Bankruptcy prediction: The case of Belgian SMEs. *Review of Accounting and Finance*, 15(1), 101–119. 10.1108/RAF-06-2014-0059

Bui, T. H., & Nguyen, V. P. (2022). The Impact of Artificial Intelligence and Digital Economy on Vietnam's Legal System. *International Journal for the Semiotics of Law.* 10.1007/s11196-022-09927-036189171

Chandra, D., Ravi, V., & Ravisankar, P. (2010). Support vector machine and wavelet neural network hybrid: Application to bankruptcy prediction in banks. *International Journal of Data Mining. Modelling and Management*, 2(1). 10.1504/IJDMMM.2010.031019

(2021). Federal Register (n.d.), *Request for Information and Comment on Financial Institutions' Use of Artificial Intelligence, Including. Machine Learning.*

Gensler, G., & Bailey, L. (2020). Deep Learning and Financial Stability. SSRN *Electronic Journal.* 10.2139/ssrn.3723132

Grice, J. S., & Ingram, R. (2001). Tests of the Generalizability of Altman's Bankruptcy Prediction Model. *Journal of Business Research*, 54(1), 53–61. 10.1016/S0148-2963(00)00126-0

Huang, S.-Y., Tsaih, R.-H., & Yu, F. (2014). Topological pattern discovery and feature extraction for fraudulent financial reporting. *Expert Systems with Applications*, 41(9), 4360–4372. 10.1016/j.eswa.2014.01.012

Kemmler, M., Rodner, E., Wacker, E.-S., & Denzler, J. (2013). One-class classification with gaussian processes. *Pattern Recognition*, 46(12), 3507–3518. 10.1016/j.patcog.2013.06.005

Larcker, D. F., Richardson, S. A., & Tuna, I. (2007). Corporate governance, accounting outcomes, and organizational performance. *The Accounting Review*, 82(4), 963–1008. https://www.jstor.org/stable/30243484. 10.2308/accr.2007.82.4.963

Li, H., & Sun, J. (2012). Forecasting business failure: The use of nearest-neighbour support vectors and correcting imbalanced samples – Evidence from the Chinese hotel industry. *Tourism Management*, 33(3), 622–634. 10.1016/j.tourman.2011.07.004

Meir, L., Van de Geer, S., & Bühlmann, P. (2008). The group lasso for logistic regression. *Journal of the Royal Statistical Society. Series B, Statistical Methodology*, 70(1), 53–71. 10.1111/j.1467-9868.2007.00627.x

Ngai, E. W., Hu, Y., Wong, Y. H., Chen, Y., & Sun, X. (2011). The application of data mining techniques in financial fraud detection: A classification framework and an academic review of literature. *Decision Support Systems*, 50(3), 559–569. 10.1016/j.dss.2010.08.006

Nourani, M. (2020), *The Effects of Meaningful and Meaningless Explanations on Trust and Perceived System Accuracy in Intelligent Systems*,

http://www.aaai.org

OECD. (2020). *OECD Business and Finance Outlook 2020: Sustainable and Resilient Finance*. OECD Publishing. 10.1787/eb61fd29-

Perols, L., & Lougee, B. A. (2011). The relation between earnings management and financial statement fraud. *Advances in Accounting*, 27(1), 39–53. 10.1016/j.adiac.2010.10.004

Shi, Y., & Li, X. (2019). An overview of bankruptcy prediction models for corporate firms: A systematic literature review. *Intangible Capital*, 15(2), 114–127. 10.3926/ic.1354

Sun, J., Li, H., Huang, Q., & He, K. (2014). Predicting financial distress and corporate failure: A review from the state-of-the-art definitions, modelling, sampling, and featuring approaches. *Knowledge-Based Systems*, 57, 41–56. 10.1016/j.knosys.2013.12.006

Tian, S., Yu, Y., & Guo, H. (2015). Variable selection and corporate bankruptcy forecasts. *Journal of Banking & Finance*, 52, 89–100. 10.1016/j.jbankfin.2014.12.003

Tobback, E., Bellotti, T., Moeyersoms, J., Stankova, M., & Martens, D. (2017). Bankruptcy prediction for SMEs using relational data. *Decision Support Systems*, 102, 69–81. 10.1016/j.dss.2017.07.004

Wang, L., & Wu, C. (2017). Business failure prediction based on two-stage selective ensemble with manifold learning algorithm and kernel-based fuzzy self-organizing map. *Knowledge-Based Systems*, 121, 99–110. 10.1016/j.knosys.2017.01.016

Xiao, Z., Yang, X., Pang, Y., & Dang, X. (2012). The prediction for listed companies' financial distress by using multiple prediction methods with rough set and Dempster–Shafer evidence theory. *Knowledge-Based Systems*, 26, 196–206. 10.1016/j.knosys.2011.08.001

Yu, T., Chen, S.-H., & Kuo, T.-W. (2005). A Genetic Programming Approach to Model International Short-Term Capital Flow. *Advances in Econometrics*, 19, 45–70. 10.1016/S0731-9053(04)19002-6

Zmijewski, M. (1984). Methodological Issues Related to the Estimation of Financial Distress Prediction Models. *Journal of Accounting Research*, 22, 59–86. 10.2307/2490859

Chapter 10
Vertical Assimilation of Artificial Intelligence and Machine Learning in Safeguarding Financial Data

Bhupinder Singh
https://orcid.org/0009-0006-4779-2553
Sharda University, India

Christian Kaunert
https://orcid.org/0000-0002-4493-2235
Dublin City University, Ireland & University of South Wales, UK

ABSTRACT

The rapid evolution of technology has revolutionized the financial industry with digital banking and financial services becoming increasingly prevalent. The prevailing trend in the contemporary financial services sector centers around the transition to digital platforms, particularly mobile and online banking. In an age marked by unparalleled convenience and speed, consumers no longer prefer visiting physical bank branches for their transactions. As banks strive to introduce new features to attract and retain customers, disruptive banking technologies from startups and neo banks are emerging. The integration of artificial intelligence (AI) and machine learning (ML) in the banking sector holds the potential to transform operational processes and enhance services which leads to improved efficiency, productivity and customer experience. This chapter explores the role of AI and ML in addressing information privacy and security concerns in the arena of digital banking and

DOI: 10.4018/979-8-3693-3633-5.ch010

financial services in digital age.

INTRODUCTION AND BACKGROUND

The cloud platforms are essential to modern organizations in order to grow, stay flexible and boost productivity (Ray et al., 2024). However, there is an increased danger of cybersecurity risks with the growing trend of cloud adoption (Dinesh Arokia Raj et al., 2024). Cyberattacks targeting cloud infrastructure can provide significant risks to data confidentiality, security and uptime (Yue & Shyu, 2024). Organisations utilising cloud services face a serious danger from adversaries that possess a deep grasp of cloud-specific features (Mithas et al., 2022). These actors are known as "cloud-conscious" attacker and there was a significant 95% rise in cloud exploitation cases compared to 2022 (Ivanov et al., 2019). The number of events where attackers targeted cloud settings nearly tripled, indicating a 288% increase in yearly rates (Munirathinam, 2020). This increasing trend illustrates a larger pattern in which nation-state actors and cybercriminals modify their methods and expertise to more successfully take use of cloud systems (Javaid et al., 2022). These days, adversaries concentrate on breaking into endpoints and exploiting access to go into the cloud, transforming it into a vital theater of operations for stopping security lapses (Trung et al., 2021).

There is a pressing need for creative ways to safeguard sensitive data since sophisticated cloud infrastructures are more vulnerable to cyberattacks (Trakadas et al., 2020) (Radanliev et al., 2021). Businesses must have sophisticated security measures in place to guard against such intrusions and guarantee the integrity of their operations (Sigov et al., 2022) (Rymarczyk, 2020). To address security concerns, organizations are adopting more sophisticated machine learning (ML) and artificial intelligence (AI) technologies (Mhlanga, 2020). These technological advancements are essential for bolstering cybersecurity defenses against ever-changing threats. Businesses may improve their capacity to identify and address cyber risks in a number of ways by employing AI and ML tools (Javaid et al., 2020). These include thwarting hostile AI, reacting to threats instantly, and anticipating possible future assaults (Ahmad et al., 2022). Employing machine learning algorithms makes it possible to spot irregularities and potential security breaches, giving companies early warning systems that can help avert disastrous data breaches (Sakhawat et al., 2024). Businesses' security architectures become increasingly complicated as they implement multi-cloud platforms to handle a variety of workloads (Karisma, 2024). In particular, generative AI is a powerful tool for defenders, allowing them to automate repetitive operations and use generative processes to improve their abilities, reduce time and boost speed (Sobb et al., 2020). With increasing productivity in security operations centers, automation helps to implement cybersecurity measures that are more effective and efficient (Wan et al., 2020).

Significance of Study

It is harder to manage security across different cloud platforms in an efficient manner, particularly when it comes to network visibility (Fraga-Lamas et al., 2021). To provide accurate detection and real-time security, a unified platform strategy is crucial, seamlessly integrating workloads, identities, data, and telemetry from client endpoints (Kumar et al., 2019). AI and ML-powered security technologies are scalable and adaptive, protecting companies in a variety of cloud settings (Felsberger et al., 2022). These solutions are adaptable to the unique needs of every platform, guaranteeing smooth security without sacrificing effectiveness (Rath et al., 2024). Unnoticed security breaches are becoming more likely as cloud computing grows in breadth (Asadollahi-Yazdi et al., 2020). Using the right technologies is essential for developing proactive security management and obtaining critical insights into security status (Meyendorf et al., 2023). Although the leading cloud platforms provide cutting-edge native Cloud Security Posture Management (CSPM) solutions, they frequently have platform-specific restrictions (Zhong et al., 2017). Consequently, in hybrid or multi-cloud systems, incorporating specialist tools is advised for complete security visibility (Angelopoulos et al., 2019). Also, in recognizing and addressing dangers, AI and ML both have critical responsibilities to play (Lu et al., 2020).

The data issue of cybersecurity has always involved the difficult effort of finding minute signs of adversarial activity among billions of data points (Chander et al., 2022). The single-agent architecture for effective data intake into the platform and a strong cloud-native data platform that can manage enormous data volumes are required to resolve this problem (Kasowaki & Ahmet, 2024). The system combines artificial intelligence (AI) and machine learning (ML) with fast detection to quickly identify hidden risks and simplify challenging operations (Sima et al., 2020). This is how the Falcon platform was created from the ground up. Although AI and ML have revolutionized cybersecurity, concerns exist about the possible abuse of generative AI (Tseng et al., 2021). The potential of Generative AI to produce phony information that appears realistic enough to be taken seriously is a serious risk (Anastasi et al., 2021). It makes more difficult to discern between actual and modified content, especially in emails (Dwivedi et al., 2021).

Objectives of the Chapter

Artificial intelligence and Machine learning is more than just a catchphrase; in the financial sector, it has revolutionary potential (Majstorovic & Mitrovic, 2019). Its effects range from strengthening financial security against fraud to improving customer care through chatbots, radically altering the way banks operate. In the future, the combination of machine learning and artificial intelligence (AI) promises even more exciting developments (Badri et al., 2018). AI works in the background to make your banking experience safe and easy, whether you're applying for a loan, checking your account balance, or getting investing advice (Xu et al., 2018). This chapter has the following objectives to:

- analyze the current state of information privacy and security in digital banking.
- explore the applications of AI and ML in enhancing data security.
- assess the effectiveness of AI and ML in identifying and preventing financial fraud.
- discuss ethical considerations and potential risks associated with the use of AI and ML in financial services.

Figure 1. Shows the objectives of the chapter

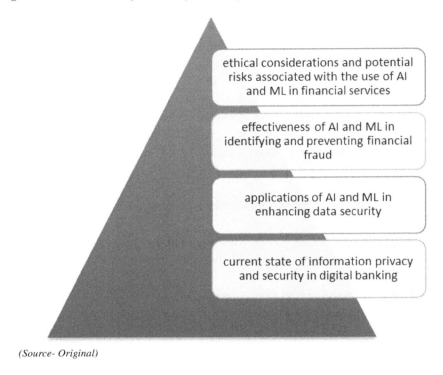

(Source- Original)

Structure/ Flow of the Chapter

This chapter expressly specifies the Assimilation of Artificial Intelligence and Machine Learning in Safeguarding Financial Data for Information Privacy- Security Concerns in Digital Banking and Financial Services. Section 2 elaborates the Artificial Intelligence and Machine Learning in Safeguarding Financial Data. Section 3 explores the Information Privacy and Security in Digital Banking. Section 4 lays down the Artificial Intelligence and Machine Learning Applications. Section 5 scrutinizes the Ethical Considerations and Risks. Finally, Section 6 Conclude the Chapter with Future Scope.

Figure 2. Displays the structure/flow of the chapter

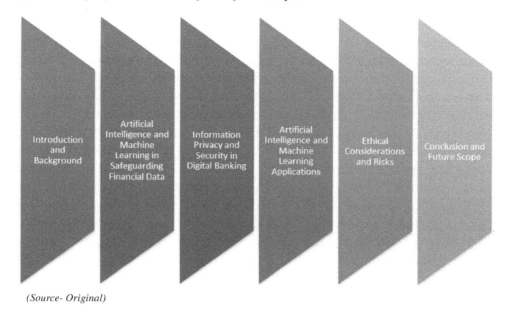

(Source- Original)

ARTIFICIAL INTELLIGENCE AND MACHINE LEARNING IN SAFEGUARDING FINANCIAL DATA

AI/ML systems have advanced significantly in the last ten years although it will take time for a computer to be developed that can grasp or learn every intellectual work that a human can (Bhuiyan et al., 2020). The current artificial intelligence (AI) systems are excellent at well specified activities that normally need human intelligence (Reier Forradellas & Garay Gallastegui, 2021). A key component of most AI systems is the learning process, or machine learning (ML), which is based on concepts from decision theory, statistics, and mathematics (Singh Rajawat et al., 2021). Facial recognition, digital assistants, and self-driving cars are just a few of the achievements made possible by recent machine learning (ML) advances, notably in deep learning algorithms (Leng et al., 2020). The financial industry has significantly grown its use of AI/ML systems, led by financial technology businesses 9Javaid et al., 2021). The adoption of technology breakthroughs by the financial industry such as cloud computing and big data, together with the expansion of the digital economy, has made it easier to use AI/ML systems efficiently (Hassoun et al., 2023).

The banking industry is undergoing a change thanks to AI/ML's capabilities (Aoun et al., 2021). Through the use of chatbots and other similar technologies, AI/ML systems are changing the way that financial service providers communicate with their clients (Arden et al., 2021). Also, they are improving identity verification via the use of technologies like image recognition, simplifying mortgage underwriting, and impacting investing processes with the advent of robo-advisors (Rane, 2023). These technologies are also changing the way financial institutions operate by automating procedures, saving a lot of money using predictive analytics to provide better products, and improving risk and fraud management procedures in addition to regulatory compliance (Awan et al., 2021). In the end, AI/ML systems give central banks and agencies in charge of prudential supervision new means of bolstering prudential monitoring and improving systemic risk surveillance (Kumar et al., 2020).

The digital divide between developed and developing nations can get worse due to the rapid improvements in AI/ML research (Li et al., 2017). The use of AI/ML and its benefits have mostly benefited developed nations and a small number of emerging economies (Kurniawan et al., 2022). Even while these technologies might greatly help emerging economies by lowering the cost of credit risk assessments, for example many of these nations are still falling behind because of a lack of funding, restricted access to research, and a shortage of human resources (Jakka et al., 2022). The creation of a digitally friendly policy framework built around four essential policy pillars is required to close this gap: spending money on infrastructure (Xing et al., 2021).

INFORMATION PRIVACY AND SECURITY IN DIGITAL BANKING

The financial industry is using artificial intelligence (AI) approaches more and more in sectors including asset management, credit underwriting, algorithmic trading and blockchain-based finance (Shi et al., 2020). The wealth of publicly available data and the accessibility of computational power are factors supporting this development (Finance, 2015). Without the need for human programming, machine learning (ML) models use huge data to automatically learn and improve performance and predictability over time through experience and data. Financial institutions are expected to gain competitive benefits from the use of AI in finance. This entails raising the caliber of services and goods provided to customers while also increasing efficiency by cutting expenses and raising production (Saeed et al., 2023). As a result, by evaluating the creditworthiness of customers with little credit history, financial consumers may gain access to insights generated from data for well-informed investment strategies and possibly even greater financial inclusion (Kumar & Mallipeddi, 2022). The use of AI applications in finance, however, may potentially bring about or worsen problems related to money and non-money matters, raising issues with investor and consumer protection (Bag & Pretorius, 2022). These hazards may include worries about data handling and utilization, as well as skewed, unjust or discriminating customer consequences. The absence of transparency in AI model processes might pose a threat to internal governance and financial supervisory frameworks, as well as the technology-neutral approach to policymaking (Morgan et al., 2021). It could also increase the likelihood of pro-cyclicality and systemic risk in markets. Although many of the hazards related to artificial intelligence (AI) in finance are not unique to this breakthrough, the use of such techniques might amplify these vulnerabilities because of the intricacy, dynamic flexibility and degree of autonomy of the techniques used (Singh et al., 2022).

Through digitalization and the ability to successfully compete with FinTech companies, the integration of Artificial Intelligence (AI) in the banking sector offers a transformational edge. According to a survey done in conjunction with Narrative Science and the National Business Research Institute, 32% of financial service providers have already adopted AI technology like voice recognition and predictive analytics (Nica & Stehel, 2021). The banking sector now relies heavily on artificial intelligence, a technology that allows robots to mimic human intelligence (Ahmad et al., 2021). Artificial Intelligence (AI) is no longer just a science fiction notion; it is a real technology that is changing the way banks operate and interact with their customers (Wamba-Taguimdje et al., 2020). AI is the collective term for a variety of technologies that analyze data, make judgments, and automate procedures. These technologies include computer vision, natural language processing, and machine learning. AI is being used in banking to provide individualized financial solutions, strengthen security protocols, and improve customer service (Popov et al., 2022).

AI is used in banking to improve client experiences, security, and efficiency. It lowers operating expenses by streamlining repetitive operations like fraud detection and data input. AI-powered chatbots provide round-the-clock customer assistance, while machine learning algorithms examine client data to provide tailored services and spot anomalous transactions, which improves security (Lu, 2019). AI is used by credit scoring models to make more accurate creditworthiness assessments. AI also helps with portfolio management by maximizing investment plans (Blobel, 2020). For better product creation, natural language processing (NLP) helps analyze client input. All things considered, artificial intelligence (AI) transforms the banking industry by optimizing processes, reducing risks, and offering customized services to clients (Borowski, 2021).

In the financial industry, security is crucial, and artificial intelligence is a potent weapon in the continuous fight against fraud. Large amounts of data are quickly evaluated in real-time using AI algorithms to spot odd trends or suspect activity (Lim et al., 2021). As a result, banks are frequently able to identify fraudulent transactions before their clients are aware of them, protecting their hard-earned money. The days of needing to make an appointment with a financial advisor in order to talk about investing are long gone (Vogt et al., 2021). By evaluating financial history, risk tolerance, and investing objectives to deliver tailored advise, artificial intelligence has revolutionized this process. This guarantees that investments are in line with each person's financial goals while also saving time (Gadekar et al., 2022).

Artificial Intelligence streamlines a range of banking processes in the background (Tao et al., 2021). By automating repetitive processes like document verification and data entry, it lowers the possibility of human mistake. This increased effectiveness reduces operating expenses and saves time, which might result in better products for customers. Banks must evaluate an applicant's creditworthiness before approving a loan or credit card (Chen et al., 2022). Through its analysis of credit history, spending trends, and financial behavior, AI is essential to this judgment. This makes it possible for banks to decide on loans more quickly and accurately (Mourtzis et al., 2022).

ARTIFICIAL INTELLIGENCE AND MACHINE LEARNING APPLICATIONS IN FRAUD DETECTION AND PREVENTION: BIOMETRIC AUTHENTICATION IN BANKING AND FINANCIAL SECTOR

Since the digital revolution throughout sectors, banking has evolved beyond simple deposits to take on a full role as suppliers of financial services (Wan et al., 2018). Digital assistants, smartphone applications, and internet banking are increasingly commonplace (Cioffi et al., 2020). This growth brings with it new difficulties as well as conveniences, most notably those related to data security and privacy. A significant amount of created data is the outcome of the transition to a more digitally oriented lifestyle (Laskurain-Iturbe et al., 2021). Banks save this frequently private and sensitive information in order to improve services, offer individualized goods and learn more about the behavior of their clients. Innovation in the banking sector entails more than just implementing new technology; it also entails recognizing how client demands are evolving and making necessary adjustments (Brock et al., 2019). Through improving AI algorithms, investigating the possibilities of blockchain technology, or implementing new biometric security measures, entrepreneurs and innovators have a tremendous chance to revolutionize the banking industry (Nguyen et al., 2022). It is important to approach innovation from a customer-centric perspective. Any technology development in banking should start with data security and privacy as its top priorities. Rebuilding trust is difficult after it has been eroded, thus it is imperative to preserve it (Hassoun et al., 20220.

The financial sector is changing as a result of the capacity to gather massive volumes of data from the environment and process it using machine learning (ML) and artificial intelligence (AI) (Nahavandi, 2019). In addition to reshaping financial markets, enhancing risk management and compliance, fortifying prudential supervision, and arming central banks with new instruments to carry out their monetary and macro-prudential mandates, AI/ML offers improved capacity to foresee economic, financial, and risk events (Zhou et al., 2021). The multifarious applications of artificial intelligence and machine learning in digital banking and financial data as-

A. Predicting

AI/ML systems are used in the financial industry to anticipate financial and macroeconomic factors, satisfy client requests, determine payment capacity and keep an eye on company circumstances (de la Pena Zarzuelo et al., 2020). Compared to conventional statistical and economic models, these models are more flexible, allowing for the investigation of otherwise difficult-to-detect correlations between variables and extending the toolkits utilized by institutions (Sanchez-Sotano et al., 2020). Machine learning techniques frequently perform better than linear regression-based techniques in terms of forecast resilience and accuracy. Although there are advantages to using AI/ML in predicting, there are drawbacks as well (Bokhari & Myeong, 2023). Finding novel correlations between variables can benefit from the use of atypical data in AI/ML, such as location, browser history and social media data. In a similar vein, unstructured data such as information found in email texts can be included into the forecasting process through the use of artificial intelligence (AI) natural language processing (NLP) (Ali et al., 2022). There are issues with the legal and regulatory environment, privacy and ethical issues and data quality in terms of correctness, relevance, cleanliness and possible biases when using unconventional data in financial forecasting (Kuzior, 2022).

B. Banking and Investment Services

Recent developments in AI and ML have had a big influence on the financial sector's investment management business (Bongomin et al., 2020). Although the industry has been using technology for decades in back-office operations, trading, and client services, AI/ML and related technologies are revolutionizing the industry by bringing in new players to the market like- product customization, improving client interfaces like chatbots boosting analytics and decision-making techniques and cutting costs through automated procedures (Pivoto et al., 2021). The banking sector has been slower to implement AI/ML than the investment management sector. The banking sector, which has always been at the forefront of technology innovation, has encountered difficulties since financial data is proprietary and secret (Gupta, 2023). However, the use of AI and ML in banking has expanded recently, in part due to heightened competition from fintech (financial technology) businesses, such as fintech lenders (Dorfleitner & Braun, 2019). The potential of AI/ML to optimize product placement (e.g., through behavioral and personalized insights analytics), improve client relations (e.g., through chatbots and AI/ML-powered mobile banking), support back-office operations, improve risk management, enhance credit underwriting and realize significant cost savings is what is driving this adoption (Nassiry, 2018).

C. Management of Risk and Compliance

As a result of tighter rules and rising compliance costs in the wake of the 2008 global financial crisis, recent developments in AI and ML are changing the technological landscape in regulatory compliance and elevating the significance of regulatory technology. At first, technology was primarily used to automate reporting and compliance procedures (Singh, 2024). But in the last several years, AI/ML development has revolutionized risk and compliance management by automating compliance decisions and using large datasets, frequently in real-time (Chen & Volz, 2021). This change has decreased related expenses and improved compliance quality. The technology adoption in the financial sector might be further accelerated by the continued maturation of AI/ML technologies (Yang et al., 2021). A recent global poll indicates that businesses are primarily considering AI/ML as their top technology (Zhang et al., 2018). It increased integration of AI/ML has greatly expanded its application in banking, securities, insurance and other financial services, covering a wide range of tasks like identity verification, risk management, fraud detection, micro-prudential and macro-prudential reporting, anti-money laundering and combating the financing of terrorism (Migliorelli & Dessertine, 2019).

Figure 3. Applications of AI and ML in digital banking sector and financial data services

(Source- Original)

Benefits of Artificial Intelligence and Machine Learning for Fraud Identification

Even with the availability of sophisticated analytics tools, fraud detection and data analysis still require human participation, which leaves potential for problems like processing delays and human mistake. Some of these issues are resolved by integrating machine learning, which has various advantages for banks (Naderi & Tian, 2022).

Accuracy: After being taught, machine learning algorithms are able to carefully examine and spot patterns in seemingly unimportant data. They are particularly good at picking up on subtle or illogical patterns that are difficult or impossible for others to notice. This considerably improves the accuracy of fraud detection by lowering false positives and undetected frauds (Singh, 2023).

Speed: Machine learning algorithms are able to evaluate large volumes of data quickly, gathering and processing new data in real time. With the volume and pace of eCommerce rising, speed becomes more and more important for efficient fraud detection (Thomason et al., 2018).

Scalability: Human analysis and rules-based systems are under pressure from the growing amount of transactions in banks, which drives up expenses, slows down processing times, and reduces accuracy (Liu et al., 2022). Machine learning algorithms, on the other hand, benefit greatly from increased data. As the software develops, they get better with more data, allowing for quicker and more precise fraud detection (Yan et al., 2022).

Efficiency: Machine learning algorithms are very good at carrying out repeated operations and identifying minute differences in patterns across large datasets. This effectiveness is essential for detecting fraud far more quickly than is possible with human skills (Bayram et al., 2022). Algorithms are able to examine hundreds of thousands of payments each second, which is more than several human analysts could do in the same amount of time. Because of its efficiency, transaction analysis becomes less expensive and takes less time (Sachs et al., 2019).

Figure 4. Shows the benefits of AI and ML for fraud identification

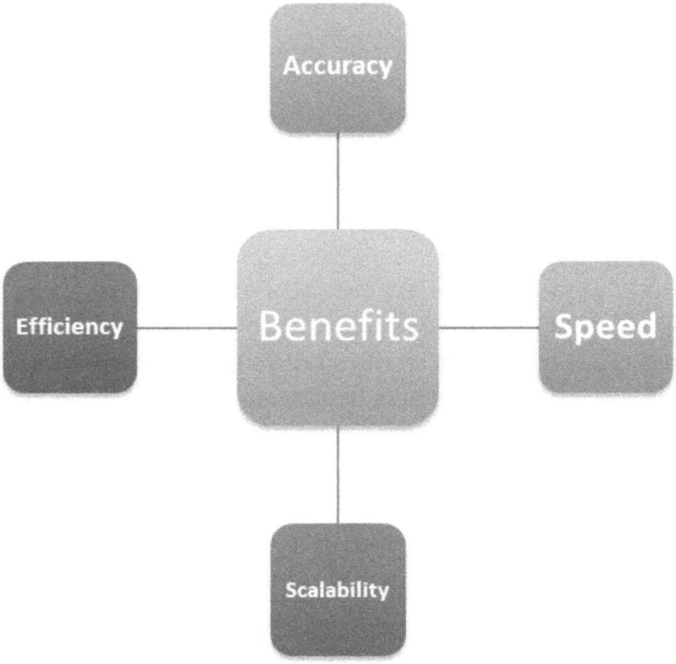

(Source- Original)

The need for fraud risk management and anomaly detection has increased due to the rise in financial frauds, which result in larger yearly fraud losses for banks and clients (Campbell-Verduyn, 2023). The old-fashioned rule-based fraud detection methods are insufficient nowadays (Singh, 2023). Adoption of AI and machine learning is not only faster, more precise, and more efficient than rule-based systems, but it also saves a significant amount of human labour. In order to stay competitive and resistant to fraud, machine learning systems will be more advantageous in the future (Schulz & Feist, 2021).

ETHICAL CONSIDERATIONS AND RISKS

There are hazards related to supervision and control systems as well, which could require modifications in light of this new technology (Kalaiarasi & Kirubahari, 2023). The unexpected effects of AI-based models and systems on the integrity and stability of the market are one of the particular hazards associated with its application. The difficulty in comprehending how AI-based algorithms produce outcomes presents challenges (Chueca Vergara & Ferruz Agudo, 2021). The financial system's ability to withstand difficult times may be threatened by a number of operational hazards associated with the growing use of AI in finance (Schoenmaker & Volz, 2022). These risks might also enhance market interconnectivity because AI can learn on its own and adapt to changing situations, its incorporation into finance might amplify current dangers in the financial markets (Singh, 2022). It can also bring with it new general hazards and problems (Sharma & Singh, 2022). The hazards that are now present are associated with the inappropriate use of data or the use of low-quality data, which may lead to biases and discriminatory consequences that will eventually hurt financial customers (Marke, 2018. The need for investment in AI approaches may lead to concerns about concentration and competitiveness, ultimately resulting in a reliance on a small number of dominant firms (Hoang et al., 2022). Insufficient model governance that is adapted to the particularities of AI might lead to issues related to market integrity and compliance as well as unclear accountability structures (Schloesser & Schulz, 2022).

Enhance the Role of Government in Regulatory Focus: Customer Insights to Provide Analysis on Customer Trust and Adoption

Big data may be a major source of nonfinancial risk when used in AI-driven applications (Singh, 2022). These risks and difficulties arise from issues with data privacy and confidentiality, cybersecurity, fairness considerations and quality of the data used (Harris, 2018). AI techniques may lessen prejudice in interpersonal relationships or increase prejudice, unfair treatment, and discrimination in the financial services, depending on how they are used (Shih et al., 2023). Intentional inference and proxies e.g., determining gender from purchase activity data or the use of low-quality, faulty or inadequate data in machine learning models can lead to biases and prejudice in AI (Ozili, 2023). In addition to possible competitive challenges, such as higher risks of tacit collusion or excessive market concentration among providers in specific areas, there are worries about financial consumer protection associated with the use of big data and machine learning models (Bayram et al., 2022).

The failure to offer an explanation puts financial service providers' internal governance, risk management, and control systems in jeopardy in addition to current rules and regulations (Singh, 2022). This restriction makes it more difficult for users to understand how their models affect markets or cause market shocks which might increase the systemic risks related to pro-cyclicality (Micaroni, 2020). Crucially, users' failure to modify their tactics in times of stress might intensify market turbulence and result in illiquidity occurrences, exacerbating situations that resemble flash crashes (Dell'Erba, 2021). Explainability problems are made worse by a general lack of technical literacy and by the discrepancy between the requirements of human-scale reasoning and interpretation that is in line with human cognition and the intrinsic complexity of AI models. Additional regulatory obstacles include those pertaining to transparency and such audits (Bin Amin et al., 2022).

CONCLUSION AND FUTURE SCOPE

AI will play a pivotal role in the future of banking by utilizing its powerful data analytics skills to prevent fraudulent transactions and improve compliance (Voigt & von dem Bussche, 2017) (Tikkinen-Piri et al., 2018). Artificial intelligence algorithms enable the rapid implementation of anti-money laundering measures, optimizing operations that would often take hours or days to complete (Link et al., 2020) (Barocas et al., 2019). AI also enables banks to handle enormous amounts of data effectively and extract insightful information at previously unheard-of speeds (Mehrabi et al., 2021) (Jobin et al., 2019). Enhancements like as artificial intelligence (AI) chatbots, digital payment counselors and biometric fraud prevention systems help reach a larger clientele with superior services (Floridi et al., 2020). These developments have the combined effect of raising income, cutting expenses, and significantly increasing profits (Jang et al., 2020). The banking industry is about to undergo a digital transformation, and there are possibilities as well as problems ahead (Chen et al., 2020) (Montanaro, 2016). In addition to guaranteeing the protection of consumer data, banks that responsibly use AI and other cutting-edge technology may also provide an unmatched banking experience (Shmueli & Koppius, 2011) (Henke et al., 2018).

REFERENCES

Ahmad, T., Zhang, D., Huang, C., Zhang, H., Dai, N., Song, Y., & Chen, H. (2021). Artificial intelligence in sustainable energy industry: Status Quo, challenges and opportunities. *Journal of Cleaner Production*, 289, 125834. 10.1016/j.jclepro.2021.125834

Ahmad, T., Zhu, H., Zhang, D., Tariq, R., Bassam, A., Ullah, F., AlGhamdi, A. S., & Alshamrani, S. S. (2022). Energetics Systems and artificial intelligence: Applications of industry 4.0. *Energy Reports*, 8, 334–361. 10.1016/j.egyr.2021.11.256

Ali, A., Septyanto, A. W., Chaudhary, I., Al Hamadi, H., Alzoubi, H. M., & Khan, Z. F. (2022, February). Applied Artificial Intelligence as Event Horizon Of Cyber Security. In *2022 International Conference on Business Analytics for Technology and Security (ICBATS)* (pp. 1-7). IEEE. 10.1109/ICBATS54253.2022.9759076

Anastasi, S., Madonna, M., & Monica, L. (2021). Implications of embedded artificial intelligence-machine learning on safety of machinery. *Procedia Computer Science*, 180, 338–343. 10.1016/j.procs.2021.01.171

Angelopoulos, A., Michailidis, E. T., Nomikos, N., Trakadas, P., Hatziefremidis, A., Voliotis, S., & Zahariadis, T. (2019). Tackling faults in the industry 4.0 era—A survey of machine-learning solutions and key aspects. *Sensors (Basel)*, 20(1), 109. 10.3390/s2001010931878065

Aoun, A., Ilinca, A., Ghandour, M., & Ibrahim, H. (2021). A review of Industry 4.0 characteristics and challenges, with potential improvements using blockchain technology. *Computers & Industrial Engineering*, 162, 107746. 10.1016/j.cie.2021.107746

Arden, N. S., Fisher, A. C., Tyner, K., Lawrence, X. Y., Lee, S. L., & Kopcha, M. (2021). Industry 4.0 for pharmaceutical manufacturing: Preparing for the smart factories of the future. *International Journal of Pharmaceutics*, 602, 120554. 10.1016/j.ijpharm.2021.12055433794326

Asadollahi-Yazdi, E., Couzon, P., Nguyen, N. Q., Ouazene, Y., & Yalaoui, F. (2020). Industry 4.0: Revolution or Evolution? *American Journal of Operations Research*, 10(06), 241–268. 10.4236/ajor.2020.106014

Awan, U., Sroufe, R., & Shahbaz, M. (2021). Industry 4.0 and the circular economy: A literature review and recommendations for future research. *Business Strategy and the Environment*, 30(4), 2038–2060. 10.1002/bse.2731

Badri, A., Boudreau-Trudel, B., & Souissi, A. S. (2018). Occupational health and safety in the industry 4.0 era: A cause for major concern? *Safety Science*, 109, 403–411. 10.1016/j.ssci.2018.06.012

Bag, S., & Pretorius, J. H. C. (2022). Relationships between industry 4.0, sustainable manufacturing and circular economy: Proposal of a research framework. *The International Journal of Organizational Analysis*, 30(4), 864–898. 10.1108/IJOA-04-2020-2120

. Barocas, S., Hardt, M., & Narayanan, A. (2019). *Fairness and Machine Learning*. fairmlbook.

Bayram, O., Talay, I., & Feridun, M. (2022). Can FinTech promote sustainable finance? Policy lessons from the case of Turkey. *Sustainability (Basel)*, 14(19), 12414. 10.3390/su141912414

Bayram, O., Talay, I., & Feridun, M. (2022). Can Fintech Promote Sustainable Finance? Policy Lessons from the Case of Turkey. *Sustainability (Basel)*, 2022(14), 12414. 10.3390/su141912414

Bhuiyan, A. B., Ali, M. J., Zulkifli, N., & Kumarasamy, M. M. (2020). Industry 4.0: Challenges, opportunities, and strategic solutions for Bangladesh. *International Journal of Business and Management Future*, 4(2), 41–56. 10.46281/ijbmf.v4i2.832

Bin Amin, S., Taghizadeh-Hesary, F., & Khan, F. (2022). Facilitating green digital finance in Bangladesh: Importance, prospects, and implications for meeting the SDGs. In *Green Digital Finance and Sustainable Development Goals* (pp. 143–165). Springer Nature Singapore. 10.1007/978-981-19-2662-4_7

Blobel, B. (2020, September). Application of industry 4.0 concept to health care. In *pHealth 2020:Proceedings of the 17th International Conference on Wearable Micro and Nano Technologies for Personalized Health* (Vol. 273, p. 23). IOS Press.

Bokhari, S. A. A., & Myeong, S. (2023). The influence of artificial intelligence on e-Governance and cybersecurity in smart cities: A stakeholder's perspective. *IEEE Access : Practical Innovations, Open Solutions*, 11, 69783–69797. 10.1109/ACCESS.2023.3293480

Bongomin, O., Gilibrays Ocen, G., Oyondi Nganyi, E., Musinguzi, A., & Omara, T. (2020). Exponential disruptive technologies and the required skills of industry 4.0. *Journal of Engineering*, 2020, 1–17. 10.1155/2020/8090521

Borowski, P. F. (2021). Innovative processes in managing an enterprise from the energy and food sector in the era of industry 4.0. *Processes (Basel, Switzerland)*, 9(2), 381. 10.3390/pr9020381

Borowski, P. F. (2021). Digitization, digital twins, blockchain, and industry 4.0 as elements of management process in enterprises in the energy sector. *Energies*, 14(7), 1885. 10.3390/en14071885

Brock, J. K. U., & Von Wangenheim, F. (2019). Demystifying AI: What digital transformation leaders can teach you about realistic artificial intelligence. *California Management Review*, 61(4), 110–134. 10.1177/1536504219865226

Campbell-Verduyn, M. (2023). Conjuring a cooler world? Imaginaries of improvement in blockchain climate finance experiments. *Environment and Planning C: Politics and Space*.

Chander, B., Pal, S., De, D., & Buyya, R. (2022). Artificial intelligence-based internet of things for industry 5.0. *Artificial intelligence-based internet of things systems*, 3-45.

Chen, J., Liu, Y., & Moallemi, C. C. (2020). Strategic fraud detection in the financial services industry. *Management Science*, 66(9), 4117–4136.

Chen, Y., Lu, Y., Bulysheva, L., & Kataev, M. Y. (2022). Applications of blockchain in industry 4.0: A review. *Information Systems Frontiers*, 1–15. 10.1007/s10796-022-10248-7

Chen, Y., & Volz, U. (2021). Scaling up sustainable investment through blockchain-based project bonds. *Fintech to Enable Development, Investment, Financial Inclusion, and Sustainability*. ADB-IGF Special Working Paper Series.

Chueca Vergara, C., & Ferruz Agudo, L. (2021). Fintech and sustainability: Do they affect each other? *Sustainability (Basel)*, 13(13), 7012. 10.3390/su13137012

Cioffi, R., Travaglioni, M., Piscitelli, G., Petrillo, A., & De Felice, F. (2020). Artificial intelligence and machine learning applications in smart production: Progress, trends, and directions. *Sustainability (Basel)*, 12(2), 492. 10.3390/su12020492

de la Peña Zarzuelo, I., Soeane, M. J. F., & Bermúdez, B. L. (2020). Industry 4.0 in the port and maritime industry: A literature review. *Journal of Industrial Information Integration*, 20, 100173. 10.1016/j.jii.2020.100173

Dell'Erba, M. (2021). Sustainable digital finance and the pursuit of environmental sustainability. *Sustainable Finance in Europe: Corporate Governance, Financial Stability and Financial Markets*, 61-81.

Deloitte. (2020). *AI in financial services: A consumer perspective*. Deloitte.

Deloitte Insights. (2018). *The New Physics of Financial Services: Understanding how artificial intelligence is transforming the financial ecosystem*. Deloitte.

Dinesh Arokia Raj, A., Jha, R. R., Yadav, M., Sam, D., & Jayanthi, K. (2024). Role of Blockchain and Watermarking Toward Cybersecurity. In *Multimedia Watermarking: Latest Developments and Trends* (pp. 103–123). Springer Nature Singapore. 10.1007/978-981-99-9803-6_6

. Dorfleitner, G., & Braun, D. (2019). Fintech, digitalization and blockchain: possible applications for green finance. *The rise of green finance in Europe: opportunities and challenges for issuers, investors and marketplaces*, 207-237.

Dwivedi, Y. K., Hughes, L., Ismagilova, E., Aarts, G., Coombs, C., Crick, T., Duan, Y., Dwivedi, R., Edwards, J., Eirug, A., Galanos, V., Ilavarasan, P. V., Janssen, M., Jones, P., Kar, A. K., Kizgin, H., Kronemann, B., Lal, B., Lucini, B., & Williams, M. D. (2021). Artificial Intelligence (AI): Multidisciplinary perspectives on emerging challenges, opportunities, and agenda for research, practice and policy. *International Journal of Information Management*, 57, 101994. 10.1016/j.ijinfomgt.2019.08.002

Felsberger, A., Qaiser, F. H., Choudhary, A., & Reiner, G. (2022). The impact of Industry 4.0 on the reconciliation of dynamic capabilities: Evidence from the European manufacturing industries. *Production Planning and Control*, 33(2-3), 277–300. 10.1080/09537287.2020.1810765

Finance, A. T. C. C. (2015). *Industry 4.0 Challenges and solutions for the digital transformation and use of exponential technologies. Finance, audit tax consulting corporate*. Swiss.

Floridi, L., Cowls, J., King, T., & Taddeo, M. (2020). How to design AI for social good: Seven essential factors. *Science and Engineering Ethics*, 26(3), 1771–1793. 10.1007/s11948-020-00213-532246245

Fraga-Lamas, P., Lopes, S. I., & Fernández-Caramés, T. M. (2021). Green IoT and edge AI as key technological enablers for a sustainable digital transition towards a smart circular economy: An industry 5.0 use case. *Sensors (Basel)*, 21(17), 5745. 10.3390/s2117574534502637

Gadekar, R., Sarkar, B., & Gadekar, A. (2022). Key performance indicator based dynamic decision-making framework for sustainable Industry 4.0 implementation risks evaluation: Reference to the Indian manufacturing industries. *Annals of Operations Research*, 318(1), 189–249. 10.1007/s10479-022-04828-835910040

Gupta, R. (2023). Industry 4.0 adaption in indian banking Sector—A review and agenda for future research. *Vision (Basel)*, 27(1), 24–32. 10.1177/097226292199 682936977304

Harris, A. (2018). A conversation with masterminds in blockchain and climate change. In *Transforming climate finance and green investment with blockchains* (pp. 15–22). Academic Press. 10.1016/B978-0-12-814447-3.00002-1

Hassoun, A., Aït-Kaddour, A., Abu-Mahfouz, A. M., Rathod, N. B., Bader, F., Barba, F. J., Biancolillo, A., Cropotova, J., Galanakis, C. M., Jambrak, A. R., Lorenzo, J. M., Måge, I., Ozogul, F., & Regenstein, J. (2023). The fourth industrial revolution in the food industry—Part I: Industry 4.0 technologies. *Critical Reviews in Food Science and Nutrition*, 63(23), 6547–6563. 10.1080/10408398.2022.203473535114860

Hassoun, A., Prieto, M. A., Carpena, M., Bouzembrak, Y., Marvin, H. J., Pallares, N., Barba, F. J., Punia Bangar, S., Chaudhary, V., Ibrahim, S., & Bono, G. (2022). Exploring the role of green and Industry 4.0 technologies in achieving sustainable development goals in food sectors. *Food Research International*, 162, 112068. 10.1016/j.foodres.2022.11206836461323

Hoang, T. G., Nguyen, G. N. T., & Le, D. A. (2022). Developments in financial technologies for achieving the Sustainable Development Goals (SDGs): FinTech and SDGs. In *Disruptive technologies and eco-innovation for sustainable development* (pp. 1–19). IGI Global. 10.4018/978-1-7998-8900-7.ch001

Ivanov, D., Dolgui, A., & Sokolov, B. (2019). The impact of digital technology and Industry 4.0 on the ripple effect and supply chain risk analytics. *International Journal of Production Research*, 57(3), 829–846. 10.1080/00207543.2018.1488086

Jakka, G., Yathiraju, N., & Ansari, M. F. (2022). Artificial Intelligence in Terms of Spotting Malware and Delivering Cyber Risk Management. *Journal of Positive School Psychology*, 6(3), 6156–6165.

Javaid, M., Haleem, A., Singh, R. P., Khan, S., & Suman, R. (2021). Blockchain technology applications for Industry 4.0: A literature-based review. *Blockchain: Research and Applications*, 2(4), 100027.

Javaid, M., Haleem, A., Singh, R. P., Suman, R., & Gonzalez, E. S. (2022). Understanding the adoption of Industry 4.0 technologies in improving environmental sustainability. *Sustainable Operations and Computers*, 3, 203–217. 10.1016/j.susoc.2022.01.008

Javaid, M., Haleem, A., Vaishya, R., Bahl, S., Suman, R., & Vaish, A. (2020). Industry 4.0 technologies and their applications in fighting COVID-19 pandemic. *Diabetes & Metabolic Syndrome*, 14(4), 419–422. 10.1016/j.dsx.2020.04.03232344370

Jobin, A., Ienca, M., & Vayena, E. (2019). The global landscape of AI ethics guidelines. *Nature Machine Intelligence*, 1(9), 389–399. 10.1038/s42256-019-0088-2

Kalaiarasi, H., & Kirubahari, S. (2023). Green finance for sustainable development using blockchain technology. In *Green Blockchain Technology for Sustainable Smart Cities* (pp. 167–185). Elsevier. 10.1016/B978-0-323-95407-5.00003-7

Karisma, K. (2024). Security Challenges in the Application of Blockchain Technology in Energy Trading. *Asian Journal of Law and Policy*, 4(1), 51–75. 10.33093/ajlp.2024.3

. Kasowaki, L., & Ahmet, S. (2024). *Shielding the Virtual Ramparts: Understanding Cybersecurity Essentials* (No. 11700). EasyChair.

Kumar, K., Zindani, D., & Davim, J. P. (2019). *Industry 4.0: developments towards the fourth industrial revolution*. Springer. 10.1007/978-981-13-8165-2

Kumar, S., & Mallipeddi, R. R. (2022). Impact of cybersecurity on operations and supply chain management: Emerging trends and future research directions. *Production and Operations Management*, 31(12), 4488–4500. 10.1111/poms.13859

Kumar, S. H., Talasila, D., Gowrav, M. P., & Gangadharappa, H. V. (2020). Adaptations of Pharma 4.0 from Industry 4.0. *Drug Invention Today*, 14(3).

Kurniawan, T. A., Maiurova, A., Kustikova, M., Bykovskaia, E., Othman, M. H. D., & Goh, H. H. (2022). Accelerating sustainability transition in St. Petersburg (Russia) through digitalization-based circular economy in waste recycling industry: A strategy to promote carbon neutrality in era of Industry 4.0. *Journal of Cleaner Production*, 363, 132452. 10.1016/j.jclepro.2022.132452

Kuzior, A. (2022). Technological unemployment in the perspective of Industry 4.0. *Virtual Economics*, 5(1), 7–23. 10.34021/ve.2022.05.01(1)

Laskurain-Iturbe, I., Arana-Landín, G., Landeta-Manzano, B., & Uriarte-Gallastegi, N. (2021). Exploring the influence of industry 4.0 technologies on the circular economy. *Journal of Cleaner Production*, 321, 128944. 10.1016/j.jclepro.2021.128944

Leng, J., Ye, S., Zhou, M., Zhao, J. L., Liu, Q., Guo, W., Cao, W., & Fu, L. (2020). Blockchain-secured smart manufacturing in industry 4.0: A survey. *IEEE Transactions on Systems, Man, and Cybernetics. Systems*, 51(1), 237–252. 10.1109/TSMC.2020.3040789

Li, B. H., Hou, B. C., Yu, W. T., Lu, X. B., & Yang, C. W. (2017). Applications of artificial intelligence in intelligent manufacturing: A review. *Frontiers of Information Technology & Electronic Engineering*, 18(1), 86–96. 10.1631/FITEE.1601885

Lim, C. H., Lim, S., How, B. S., Ng, W. P. Q., Ngan, S. L., Leong, W. D., & Lam, H. L. (2021). A review of industry 4.0 revolution potential in a sustainable and renewable palm oil industry: HAZOP approach. *Renewable & Sustainable Energy Reviews*, 135, 110223. 10.1016/j.rser.2020.110223

Link. Liu, Y., Gai, K., & Li, Y. (2020). A comprehensive analysis of the impact of the California Consumer Privacy Act (CCPA) on Internet of Things (IoT). *Journal of Ambient Intelligence and Humanized Computing*, 11(3), 1109–1122.

Liu, H., Yao, P., Latif, S., Aslam, S., & Iqbal, N. (2022). Impact of Green financing, FinTech, and financial inclusion on energy efficiency. *Environmental Science and Pollution Research International*, 29(13), 1–12. 10.1007/s11356-021-16949-x34705207

Lu, C., Lyu, J., Zhang, L., Gong, A., Fan, Y., Yan, J., & Li, X. (2020). Nuclear power plants with artificial intelligence in industry 4.0 era: Top-level design and current applications—A systemic review. *IEEE Access: Practical Innovations, Open Solutions*, 8, 194315–194332. 10.1109/ACCESS.2020.3032529

Lu, Y. (2019). Artificial intelligence: A survey on evolution, models, applications and future trends. *Journal of Management Analytics*, 6(1), 1–29. 10.1080/23270012.2019.1570365

Majstorovic, V. D., & Mitrovic, R. (2019). Industry 4.0 programs worldwide. In *Proceedings of the 4th International Conference on the Industry 4.0 Model for Advanced Manufacturing: AMP 2019 4* (pp. 78-99). Springer International Publishing. 10.1007/978-3-030-18180-2_7

Marke, A. (Ed.). (2018). *Transforming climate finance and green investment with blockchains*. Academic Press.

Mehrabi, N., Morstatter, F., Saxena, N., Lerman, K., & Galstyan, A. (2021). A survey on bias and fairness in machine learning. *ACM Computing Surveys*, 54(6), 1–35. 10.1145/3457607

Meyendorf, N., Ida, N., Singh, R., & Vrana, J. (2023). NDE 4.0: Progress, promise, and its role to industry 4.0. *NDT & E International*, 140, 102957. 10.1016/j.ndteint.2023.102957

Mhlanga, D. (2020). Industry 4.0 in finance: The impact of artificial intelligence (ai) on digital financial inclusion. *International Journal of Financial Studies*, 8(3), 45. 10.3390/ijfs8030045

Micaroni, M. (2020). *Sustainable Finance: Addressing the SDGs through Fintech and Digital Finance solutions in EU* [Doctoral dissertation, Politecnico di Torino].

Migliorelli, M., & Dessertine, P. (2019). The rise of green finance in Europe. *Opportunities and challenges for issuers, investors and marketplaces. Cham. Palgrave Macmillan*, 2, 2019.

Mithas, S., Chen, Z. L., Saldanha, T. J., & De Oliveira Silveira, A. (2022). How will artificial intelligence and Industry 4.0 emerging technologies transform operations management? *Production and Operations Management*, 31(12), 4475–4487. 10.1111/poms.13864

. Montanaro, A. (2016). Quantum algorithms: an overview. *npj Quantum Information,* 2(1), 1-8.

Morgan, J., Halton, M., Qiao, Y., & Breslin, J. G. (2021). Industry 4.0 smart reconfigurable manufacturing machines. *Journal of Manufacturing Systems*, 59, 481–506. 10.1016/j.jmsy.2021.03.001

Mourtzis, D., Angelopoulos, J., & Panopoulos, N. (2022). A Literature Review of the Challenges and Opportunities of the Transition from Industry 4.0 to Society 5.0. *Energies*, 15(17), 6276. 10.3390/en15176276

Munirathinam, S. (2020). Industry 4.0: Industrial internet of things (IIOT). []. Elsevier.]. *Advances in Computers*, 117(1), 129–164. 10.1016/bs.adcom.2019.10.010

. Naderi, N., & Tian, Y. (2022). Leveraging Blockchain Technology and Tokenizing Green Assets to Fill the Green Finance Gap. *Energy Research Letters, 3*(3).

Nahavandi, S. (2019). Industry 5.0—A human-centric solution. *Sustainability (Basel)*, 11(16), 4371. 10.3390/su11164371

Nassiry, D. (2018). *The role of fintech in unlocking green finance: Policy insights for developing countries* (No. 883). ADBI working paper.

Nguyen, T., Gosine, R. G., & Warrian, P. (2020). A systematic review of big data analytics for oil and gas industry 4.0. *IEEE Access : Practical Innovations, Open Solutions*, 8, 61183–61201. 10.1109/ACCESS.2020.2979678

Nica, E., & Stehel, V. (2021). Internet of things sensing networks, artificial intelligence-based decision-making algorithms, and real-time process monitoring in sustainable industry 4.0. *Journal of Self-Governance and Management Economics*, 9(3), 35–47.

Ozili, P. K. (2023). Assessing global interest in decentralized finance, embedded finance, open finance, ocean finance and sustainable finance. *Asian Journal of Economics and Banking*, 7(2), 197–216. 10.1108/AJEB-03-2022-0029

Pivoto, D. G., de Almeida, L. F., da Rosa Righi, R., Rodrigues, J. J., Lugli, A. B., & Alberti, A. M. (2021). Cyber-physical systems architectures for industrial internet of things applications in Industry 4.0: A literature review. *Journal of Manufacturing Systems*, 58, 176–192. 10.1016/j.jmsy.2020.11.017

Popov, V. V., Kudryavtseva, E. V., Kumar Katiyar, N., Shishkin, A., Stepanov, S. I., & Goel, S. (2022). Industry 4.0 and digitalisation in healthcare. *Materials (Basel)*, 15(6), 2140. 10.3390/ma1506214035329592

Radanliev, P., De Roure, D., Van Kleek, M., Santos, O., & Ani, U. (2021). Artificial intelligence in cyber physical systems. *AI & Society*, 36(3), 783–796. 10.1007/s00146-020-01049-032874020

. Rane, N. (2023). *Transformers in Industry 4.0, Industry 5.0, and Society 5.0: Roles and Challenges.*

Rath, K. C., Khang, A., & Roy, D. (2024). The Role of Internet of Things (IoT) Technology in Industry 4.0 Economy. In *Advanced IoT Technologies and Applications in the Industry 4.0 Digital Economy* (pp. 1-28). CRC Press.

Ray, R. K., Chowdhury, F. R., & Hasan, M. R. (2024). Blockchain Applications in Retail Cybersecurity: Enhancing Supply Chain Integrity, Secure Transactions, and Data Protection. *Journal of Business and Management Studies*, 6(1), 206–214. 10.32996/jbms.2024.6.1.13

Reier Forradellas, R. F., & Garay Gallastegui, L. M. (2021). Digital transformation and artificial intelligence applied to business: Legal regulations, economic impact and perspective. *Laws*, 10(3), 70. 10.3390/laws10030070

Rymarczyk, J. (2020). Technologies, opportunities and challenges of the industrial revolution 4.0: Theoretical considerations. *Entrepreneurial Business and Economics Review*, 8(1), 185–198. 10.15678/EBER.2020.080110

Sachs, J. D., Woo, W. T., Yoshino, N., & Taghizadeh-Hesary, F. (2019). Importance of green finance for achieving sustainable development goals and energy security. *Handbook of green finance: Energy security and sustainable development, 10*, 1-10.

Saeed, S., Altamimi, S. A., Alkayyal, N. A., Alshehri, E., & Alabbad, D. A. (2023). Digital transformation and cybersecurity challenges for businesses resilience: Issues and recommendations. *Sensors (Basel)*, 23(15), 6666. 10.3390/s2315666637571451

. Sakhawat, A. R., Fatima, A., Abbas, S., Ahmad, M., & Khan, M. A. (2024). Emerging Technologies for Enhancing Robust Cybersecurity Measures for Business Intelligence in Healthcare 5.0. *Strengthening Industrial Cybersecurity to Protect Business Intelligence*, 270-293.

Sánchez-Sotano, A., Cerezo-Narváez, A., Abad-Fraga, F., Pastor-Fernández, A., & Salguero-Gómez, J. (2020). Trends of digital transformation in the shipbuilding sector. In *New Trends in the Use of Artificial Intelligence for the Industry 4.0*. IntechOpen. 10.5772/intechopen.91164

Schloesser, T., & Schulz, K. (2022). Distributed ledger technology and climate finance. In *Green Digital Finance and Sustainable Development Goals* (pp. 265–286). Springer Nature Singapore. 10.1007/978-981-19-2662-4_13

Schoenmaker, D., & Volz, U. (2022). *Scaling up sustainable finance and investment in the Global South*. CEPR Press.

Schulz, K., & Feist, M. (2021). Leveraging blockchain technology for innovative climate finance under the Green Climate Fund. *Earth System Governance*, 7, 100084. 10.1016/j.esg.2020.100084

Sharma, A., & Singh, B. (2022). Measuring Impact of E-commerce on Small Scale Business: A Systematic Review. *Journal of Corporate Governance and International Business Law*, 5(1).

Shi, Z., Xie, Y., Xue, W., Chen, Y., Fu, L., & Xu, X. (2020). Smart factory in Industry 4.0. *Systems Research and Behavioral Science*, 37(4), 607–617. 10.1002/sres.2704

Shih, C., Gwizdalski, A., & Deng, X. (2023). *Building a Sustainable Future: Exploring Green Finance*. Regenerative Finance, and Green Financial Technology.

Sigov, A., Ratkin, L., Ivanov, L. A., & Xu, L. D. (2022). Emerging enabling technologies for industry 4.0 and beyond. *Information Systems Frontiers*, 1–11. 10.1007/s10796-021-10213-w

Sima, V., Gheorghe, I. G., Subić, J., & Nancu, D. (2020). Influences of the industry 4.0 revolution on the human capital development and consumer behavior: A systematic review. *Sustainability (Basel)*, 12(10), 4035. 10.3390/su12104035

Singh, B. (2022). Understanding Legal Frameworks Concerning Transgender Healthcare in the Age of Dynamism. *ELECTRONIC JOURNAL OF SOCIAL AND STRATEGIC STUDIES*, 3(1), 56–65. 10.47362/EJSSS.2022.3104

Singh, B. (2022). Relevance of Agriculture-Nutrition Linkage for Human Healthcare: A Conceptual Legal Framework of Implication and Pathways. *Justice and Law Bulletin*, 1(1), 44–49.

Singh, B. (2023). Blockchain Technology in Renovating Healthcare: Legal and Future Perspectives. In *Revolutionizing Healthcare Through Artificial Intelligence and Internet of Things Applications* (pp. 177-186). IGI Global.

Singh, B. (2023). Federated Learning for Envision Future Trajectory Smart Transport System for Climate Preservation and Smart Green Planet: Insights into Global Governance and SDG-9 (Industry, Innovation and Infrastructure). *National Journal of Environmental Law*, 6(2), 6–17.

Singh, B. (2024). Legal Dynamics Lensing Metaverse Crafted for Videogame Industry and E-Sports: Phenomenological Exploration Catalyst Complexity and Future. *Journal of Intellectual Property Rights Law*, 7(1), 8–14.

Singh, S. K., Sharma, S. K., Singla, D., & Gill, S. S. (2022). Evolving requirements and application of SDN and IoT in the context of industry 4.0, blockchain and artificial intelligence. *Software Defined Networks: Architecture and Applications*, 427-496.

Singh, V. K. (2022). Regulatory and Legal Framework for Promoting Green Digital Finance. In *Green Digital Finance and Sustainable Development Goals* (pp. 3–27). Springer Nature Singapore. 10.1007/978-981-19-2662-4_1

Singh Rajawat, A., Bedi, P., Goyal, S. B., Shukla, P. K., Zaguia, A., Jain, A., & Monirujjaman Khan, M. (2021). Reformist framework for improving human security for mobile robots in industry 4.0. *Mobile Information Systems*, 2021, 1–10. 10.1155/2021/4744220

Sobb, T., Turnbull, B., & Moustafa, N. (2020). Supply chain 4.0: A survey of cyber security challenges, solutions and future directions. *Electronics (Basel)*, 9(11), 1864. 10.3390/electronics9111864

Tao, F., Akhtar, M. S., & Jiayuan, Z. (2021). The future of artificial intelligence in cybersecurity: A comprehensive survey. *EAI Endorsed Transactions on Creative Technologies*, 8(28), e3–e3. 10.4108/eai.7-7-2021.170285

Thomason, J., Ahmad, M., Bronder, P., Hoyt, E., Pocock, S., Bouteloupe, J., & Shrier, D. (2018). Blockchain—powering and empowering the poor in developing countries. In *Transforming climate finance and green investment with blockchains* (pp. 137–152). Academic Press. 10.1016/B978-0-12-814447-3.00010-0

Tikkinen-Piri, C., Rohunen, A., & Markkula, J. (2018). EU General Data Protection Regulation: Changes and implications for personal data collecting companies. *Computer Law & Security Report*, 34(1), 134–153. 10.1016/j.clsr.2017.05.015

Trakadas, P., Simoens, P., Gkonis, P., Sarakis, L., Angelopoulos, A., Ramallo-González, A. P., Skarmeta, A., Trochoutsos, C., Calvo, D., Pariente, T., Chintamani, K., Fernandez, I., Irigaray, A. A., Parreira, J. X., Petrali, P., Leligou, N., & Karkazis, P. (2020). An artificial intelligence-based collaboration approach in industrial iot manufacturing: Key concepts, architectural extensions and potential applications. *Sensors (Basel)*, 20(19), 5480. 10.3390/s2019548032987911

. Trung, N. D., Huy, D. T. N., & Le, T. H. (2021). IoTs, machine learning (ML), AI and digital transformation affects various industries-principles and cybersecurity risks solutions. *Management, 18*(10.14704).

Tseng, M. L., Tran, T. P. T., Ha, H. M., Bui, T. D., & Lim, M. K. (2021). Sustainable industrial and operation engineering trends and challenges Toward Industry 4.0: A data driven analysis. *Journal of Industrial and Production Engineering*, 38(8), 581–598. 10.1080/21681015.2021.1950227

Vogt, J. (2021). Where is the human got to go? Artificial intelligence, machine learning, big data, digitalisation, and human–robot interaction in Industry 4.0 and 5.0: Review Comment on: Bauer, M.(2020). Preise kalkulieren mit KI-gestützter Onlineplattform BAM GmbH, Weiden, Bavaria, Germany. *AI & Society*, 36(3), 1083–1087. 10.1007/s00146-020-01123-7

Voigt, P., & von dem Bussche, A. (2017). *The EU General Data Protection Regulation (GDPR): A Practical Guide*. Springer. 10.1007/978-3-319-57959-7

Wamba-Taguimdje, S. L., Fosso Wamba, S., Kala Kamdjoug, J. R., & Tchatchouang Wanko, C. E. (2020). Influence of artificial intelligence (AI) on firm performance: The business value of AI-based transformation projects. *Business Process Management Journal*, 26(7), 1893–1924. 10.1108/BPMJ-10-2019-0411

Wan, J., Li, X., Dai, H. N., Kusiak, A., Martinez-Garcia, M., & Li, D. (2020). Artificial-intelligence-driven customized manufacturing factory: Key technologies, applications, and challenges. *Proceedings of the IEEE*, 109(4), 377–398. 10.1109/JPROC.2020.3034808

Wan, J., Yang, J., Wang, Z., & Hua, Q. (2018). Artificial intelligence for cloud-assisted smart factory. *IEEE Access: Practical Innovations, Open Solutions*, 6, 55419–55430. 10.1109/ACCESS.2018.2871724

. Xing, K., Cropley, D. H., Oppert, M. L., & Singh, C. (2021). Readiness for digital innovation and industry 4.0 transformation: studies on manufacturing industries in the city of salisbury. *Business Innovation with New ICT in the Asia-Pacific: Case Studies*, 155-176.

Xu, L. D., Xu, E. L., & Li, L. (2018). Industry 4.0: State of the art and future trends. *International Journal of Production Research*, 56(8), 2941–2962. 10.1080/00207543.2018.1444806

Yan, C., Siddik, A. B., Yong, L., Dong, Q., Zheng, G. W., & Rahman, M. N. (2022). A two-staged SEM-artificial neural network approach to analyze the impact of FinTech adoption on the sustainability performance of banking firms: The mediating effect of green finance and innovation. *Systems*, 10(5), 148. 10.3390/systems10050148

Yang, Y., Su, X., & Yao, S. (2021). Nexus between green finance, fintech, and high-quality economic development: Empirical evidence from China. *Resources Policy*, 74, 102445. 10.1016/j.resourpol.2021.102445

Yue, Y., & Shyu, J. Z. (2024). A paradigm shift in crisis management: The nexus of AGI-driven intelligence fusion networks and blockchain trustworthiness. *Journal of Contingencies and Crisis Management*, 32(1), e12541. 10.1111/1468-5973.12541

Zhang, X., Aranguiz, M., Xu, D., Zhang, X., & Xu, X. (2018). Utilizing blockchain for better enforcement of green finance law and regulations. In *Transforming climate finance and green investment with blockchains* (pp. 289–301). Academic Press. 10.1016/B978-0-12-814447-3.00021-5

Zhong, R. Y., Xu, X., Klotz, E., & Newman, S. T. (2017). Intelligent manufacturing in the context of industry 4.0: A review. *Engineering (Beijing)*, 3(5), 616–630. 10.1016/J.ENG.2017.05.015

Zhou, J., Zhang, S., Lu, Q., Dai, W., Chen, M., Liu, X., & Herrera-Viedma, E. (2021). A survey on federated learning and its applications for accelerating industrial internet of things. *arXiv preprint arXiv:2104.10501*.

Chapter 11
Role of Artificial Intelligence and Machine Learning Algorithms in Detecting Financial Frauds

Bakir Illahi Dar
https://orcid.org/0000-0003-4618-4397
Baba Ghulam Shah Badshah University, India

Shweta Jaiswal
CMP Degree College, University of Allahabad, Prayagraj, India

ABSTRACT

The integration of artificial intelligence (AI) and machine learning (ML) algorithms to detect fraud in financial transactions has entirely changed the field. Reconfiguration of financial product value chains necessitates the implementation of strong cybersecurity measures and advanced encryption techniques to protect sensitive financial data.. This chapter provides an insight into how AI and ML work as effective tools to deal with financial crimes, describing how they help improve fraud-detection capacities. AI and ML algorithms analyze financial data and make it possible for banks to prevent or mitigate issues such as risks. In addition, the study discusses the difficulties involved in applying AI and ML within the finance industry. Lastly, this study highlights the potential transformation that AI and ML can bring by strengthening the resilience of the financial ecosystem against evolving threats of fraud. According to this study, to effectively detect fraud, the financial and development supervisory agency must leverage more technology, particularly

DOI: 10.4018/979-8-3693-3633-5.ch011

data analytics and AI.

INTRODUCTION

Financial fraud is a wide term and has many possible interpretations. For our purposes, it may be defined as the deliberate employment of unlawful techniques or procedures to acquire financial benefits (Zhou & Kapoor, 2011). Financial fraud is a fraudulent activity that takes advantage of investors, typically through exaggerated returns and inaccurate product descriptions (Gui et al., 2024). It is a complicated, multifaceted economic phenomenon with psychological underpinnings, typically motivated by the need for quick money and aggravated by an inadequate legal system (Karpoff, 2021). Accounting fraud is a type of financial fraud that includes misusing cash, inflating revenues, and engaging in other dishonest accounting activities (Yu & Rha, 2021). Fraud has an immense negative impact on society and business, and credit card fraud alone results in billions of dollars of lost income annually. Financial fraud has larger implications for the business community, such as supplying funds for unlawful operations, including drug trafficking and organized crime (Bhattacharyya et al., 2011). Financial fraud, a complex and varied economic phenomenon, is defined as fraudulent behaviours designed to defraud investors (Gui et al., 2024). It is pervasive in a variety of industries, including banking, where it is frequently committed through payment card fraud. Following the 2008 financial crisis, global financial centres and financial institutions explored other business growth avenues to maintain their sector, as the cost of operations escalated due to additional regulatory measures. Using cutting-edge Internet and information technology to improve the way in which financial services are delivered is one of their most recent endeavours (Fintech). The development of non-cash payments and internet transactions has raised the chances of fraud (Sood & Bhushan, 2020). There are great expectations that artificial intelligence and machine learning, in particular as a solution for safe IT and data protection, will lead to the creation of novel financial goods and services, as well as possible increases in the financial services sector's operational efficiency (Zhu & Zhou, 2016).

Artificial Intelligence

AI refers to the science of artificial intelligence. It employs computers to imitate human intelligent behaviours and educates computers to learn human skills, including learning, judgment, and decision-making (Zhang & Lu, 2021). AI is the capacity of machines to accomplish activities that normally require human intelligence, such as thinking, learning, and problem solving (Hassani et al., 2020). It is a vast multidisciplinary area with several modules, including knowledge representation, problem-solving, and natural language processing. AI has the ability to significantly improve productivity in different areas and is always improving, requiring new standards (Samoili et al., 2020). AI has found its way into practically every area, resulting in the improved efficiency of old procedures. Artificial intelligence is differentiated by its level of cognitive capacity and autonomy. Their capacity might be poor, restricted, widespread, or superior. Owing to its autonomy, it can be reactive, deliberative, cognitive, or fully independent. As AI grows, many processes become more efficient, and jobs that are difficult today will be completed more rapidly and precisely (Duan et al., 2019). The usefulness of AI in spotting irregularities and stopping fraud in the financial services industry has been illustrated by an abundance of case studies. Some major banks have used a machine learning model to examine transaction data and find anomalous patterns that suggest fraud. The bank and its clients spared significant financial damage as a result of the system's effective detection and prevention of complex fraud operations utilizing compromised account information (Chhabra Roy & Prabhakaran, 2023).

Machine Learning

Machine learning, an important component of artificial intelligence, is a fast-developing field with several applications. This entails the creation of algorithms that allow computers to learn and improve their performance using data (Alpaydin, 2020). In contrast to traditional programming, machine learning utilizes data to train computers to execute tasks, drawing on approaches from statistics, probability theory, and neuroscience (Panesar & Panesar, 2021). The continual increase in the availability of Internet data and low-cost computing has propelled recent advances in machine learning, leading to evidence-based decision-making in different sectors (Jordan & Mitchell, 2015). ML have made remarkable developments in recent years as essential tools for intelligently evaluating such data and generating related real-world applications (Koteluk et al., 2021). ML has had a significant impact on data-intensive businesses, including consumer services, complicated system diagnoses, and supply chain management (Schaeffer & Sanchez, 2020).

MACHINE LEARNING ALGORITHMS COMMONLY USED IN FINANCIAL FRAUD DETECTION

Fraud schemes are dynamic and always evolving since anyone looking to commit fraud would always be able to locate newer strategies. In order to stay at top of emerging fraud schemes, new regulations would need to be created on a regular basis.

It is critical in this kind of situation to have a classification-based strategy that can identify unusual transactions and report them. A method based only on rules is not always feasible. Thus, given the absence of rules, a classification-based method is crucial for tracking unusual and fraudulent activities. (Gautam, 2023) explained this dramatic shift with the introduction of art AI. With its ability to recognize patterns in data without the need for explicit programming, machine-learning techniques provide a flexible and dynamic solution. Massive datasets might be analysed by AI systems, which could also be used to spot minute irregularities and adapt over time to new fraud strategies. A variety of machine learning algorithms are routinely employed in fraud detection, each with unique strengths and shortcomings. According to (Domashova & Zabelina, 2021), the most often used models are neural networks, decision trees, support vector machines, K-nearest neighbour, logistic regression, random forest, and naïve Bayes. (Jain et al., 2020) focused on the excellent accuracy of the Random Forest algorithm in detecting credit card fraud. (Mohammadi et al., 2020) underlined the significance of accuracy, coverage, and cost when choosing a fraud detection algorithm. (Ali et al., 2022) emphasize the popularity of support vector machines and artificial neural networks in financial fraud detection. Neural networks are highly trained to manage intricate and nonlinear interactions, which enables them to recognize complex patterns that may be signs of fraud (Wei & Lee, 2024). Their capacity to autonomously extract characteristics from data has greatly improved fraud detection programs' accuracy. Another area of artificial intelligence that has proven useful in fraud detection is natural language processing (NLP). NLP systems can detect language patterns linked to fraudulent activity by analysing textual data such as communication logs or transaction descriptions (Shahbazi & Byun, 2021). NLP adds to a more thorough and sophisticated fraud-detection strategy by comprehending the subtleties of language. These studies demonstrate the wide diversity of machine learning methods used in fraud detection, each with its own set of benefits and uses. (Kirkos et al., 2007) discovered that data analytics is helpful in identifying the elements linked to fake financial statements. In particular, research has been conducted to determine whether financial statement analysis can be used to detect managerial fraud. Neural networks, Bayesian networks, and decision trees were among the categorization techniques used in this instance for financial ratios derived from financial statements. (Shen et al., 2007) provide classification models for identifying credit card fraud. This study emphasizes that the choice of a model depends on the underlying data. Additionally, it offers a framework for choosing the best model in situations where credit card fraud is a possibility. Through the presentation of descriptive, predictive, and social networking techniques, this study presents the idea of fraud analytics. Analytics is recommended as a key instrument for identifying fraud.

UNSUPERVISED LEARNING TECHNIQUES FOR DETECTING ANOMALIES IN FINANCIAL DATA

Currently, unsupervised ML approaches are being used successfully to detect fraud and data anomalies. Detecting anomalies, also known as outliers, is crucial in data analysis. It helps to identify unusual or abnormal data points within a dataset (Goldstein & Uchida, 2016). The use of unsupervised machine learning for improving network performance is becoming more popular with raw network data. such as anomaly detection, Internet traffic classification, and quality of service improvement (Usama et al., 2019) Unsupervised machine learning requires a lot of data (Bantan et al., 2020). Cluster analysis, K-means, and a priori algorithms are among the most prominent unsupervised learning approaches and can be applied to spotting abnormalities in financial data. (Saba & Ngepah, 2022). Hierarchical learning is the procedure of extracting a set of numerous linear and nonlinear activations that yield simple and sophisticated features (Deng, 2014). Clustering, or cluster analysis, is the activity of categorizing materials into groups. Clustering can be classified into numerous types including partitioning, hierarchical, overlapping, and probabilistic. Every piece of data belongs to only one cluster because of the partitioning (Rodriguez et al., 2019). Financial fraud involves the use of dishonest or illegal methods to gain financial advantage. Currently, there is a significant increase in fraud attempts, making it more critical than ever to detect and prevent fraud. Machines utilize UL to identify data points and patterns. In this situation, the data are connected with an appropriate membership value, similar to a K-means cluster. Clusters were then created using probabilistic distribution (Saba & Ngepah, 2022). Unsupervised competitive learning networks: This method is used to eliminate redundancy in unstructured data. K-means is one of the simplest unsupervised learning techniques for solving well-known clustering problems (Naeem et al., 2023). Association Rule Learning (ARL) is an unsupervised learning approach that is primarily used to discover relationships between variables in large datasets. In contrast to other machine-learning algorithms, ARL may use non-numeric data points (Zhang & Lu, 2021). Autoencoders are a creative way for computers to understand patterns on their own without being taught explicitly. Variational autoencoders are a subset of this approach that can perform additional functions, such as grouping items, simplifying data, and displaying complex patterns (Kottmann et al., 2020). The Apriori algorithm was designed to extract relevant information from large databases, and it is useful for identifying patterns in all transactions (La Marca & Bedle, 2022). The data-mining strategy works well for locating groupings of items and identifying patterns. Unlike Apriorism, which looks at data horizontally, Equivalence Class Clustering and bottom-up Lattice Traversal (ECLAT) organizes things differently, allowing it to avoid searching the entire database multiple times to locate common items (Jia et al., 2019). Principal Component Analysis (PCA) is a parameter reduction method that reduces the size of a large dataset by converting many factors into small groups while preserving large amounts of small data that are easy to study and view, enabling data analysis without excessive changes. Simple and fast for machine learning algorithms to analyse data at scale (Dong & Qin, 2018).

Figure 1.

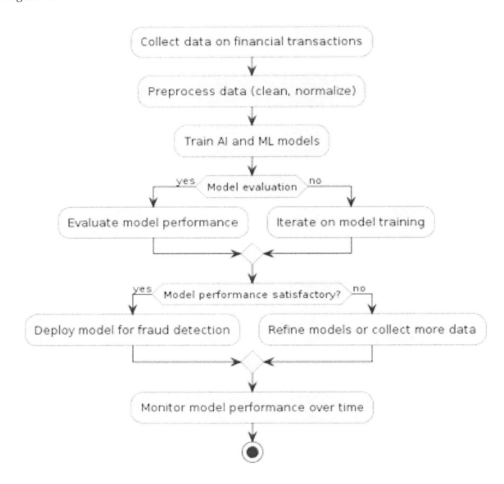

REAL-WORLD IMPLICATIONS OF AI IN FINANCIAL FRAUD DETECTION

Businesses intending to use AI have learned a lot from the practical applications of this technology in preventing fraud. A few important takeaways are that AI systems must constantly adjust to new fraud strategies and changing patterns. To guarantee that fraud protection models are successful, regular updates and improvements are necessary. Even if AI can detect fraud like never before, human oversight is essential. The total effectiveness of fraud prevention initiatives is increased by establishing a cooperative strategy that combines human experience with the advantages of AI algorithms (Tiron-Tudor & Deliu, 2022). The variety of training data is critical to AI's ability to identify fraud. Keeping the datasets clean, complete, and updated on a regular basis improves the model's capacity to identify various forms of fraud. AI models used in delicate fields such as banking, explainability, and transparency is crucial. To foster stakeholder trust and maintain regulatory compliance, organizations should prioritize AI models that offer insights into their decision-making procedures (Felzmann et al., 2020). There are a lot of practical ramifications for using AI for fraud detection, especially in the financial and medical fields. AI's ability to identify financial fraud and healthcare fraud is highlighted by (Choi & Lee, 2018) and (Iqbal et al., 2022), respectively. To enhance fraud detection, they emphasized the necessity of highly precise procedures and appropriate system deployment. (Bao et al., 2022) offer a thorough analysis of the difficulties in using machine learning models for fraud detection and make recommendations for future lines of inquiry. In order to successfully handle class imbalance, idea drift, and verification delay, (Dal Pozzolo et al., 2017) proposed a novel learning technique and realistic modelling approach to solve the unique issues of credit card fraud detection. This study shows how AI can improve fraud detection in a variety of real-world scenarios. (Singh & Singh, 2015) investigated many factors and developed a fraud-detection model using the Bayesian Learning Approach to monitor behaviour and geographic location. By offering a risk score, this model can evaluate the likelihood of fraudulent behaviour. A score of more than 0.5 will be regarded as fraudulent. This methodology uses sophisticated measures to avoid fraud, in addition to detection. The system will prompt the user to provide the correct verification code to verify them when fraud is suspected. Based on a fraud detection ontology, (Tang et al., 2018) created an intelligent fraud-detection model. In this study, financial factors that have a substantial impact on fraud detection were identified by compiling the ontology using data from financial statements. The decision tree is served by an algorithm. A total of 130 fraudulent and 130 non-fraudulent firms are used to test this model. However, it should be clarified that this model does not require any specialized expertise; rather, it only uses data from financial reports. When transaction patterns exhibit abnormalities, AI algorithms can identify potentially fraudulent activities such as identity theft, improper access, or fraudulent transactions. AI models' capacity to adjust and learn from fresh data guarantees that they can keep up with changing fraud strategies, giving financial institutions a potent weapon to fight ever-more-complex fraud schemes (Okoro et al., 2024). By continually learning from past data and improving its models to reduce mistakes, AI assists in solving these problems. ML algorithms are able to identify complex patterns and accurately distinguish between suspicious and typical activities. Consequently, financial institutions that employ AI-powered fraud-protection systems witness a considerable decrease in false positives, guaranteeing seamless execution of lawful transactions (Habbal et al., 2024).

CHALLENGES AND LIMITATIONS IN APPLYING AI AND ML ALGORITHMS IN DETECTING FINANCIAL FRAUDS

The use of AI and ML algorithms to detect financial fraud has both problems and limitations. Fraudsters innovate and create new strategies to avoid detection, making it difficult for computers to keep up (Ali et al., 2022). As with any revolutionary invention, the application of machine learning creates numerous hurdles. It should be mentioned that the ML sector faces issues with data protection, accessibility, and sharing. The four technological and management obstacles are ethical problems, the dearth of machine-learning engineers, and the cost-benefit issue. and data quality challenges (Lee & Shin, 2020). Substantial scientific and industry obstacles in identifying payment card fraud using AI and machine learning have been discovered. When adopting emerging technologies, there is a greater risk of project failure and higher returns than in modern projects (Lee & Lee, 2015). Firms and individuals are hesitant to adopt AI because of concerns regarding security and privacy. Training developers to include security measures such as intrusion prevention systems firewalls and in their products, as well as encouraging users to use the security protections that are already built into their IoT devices, can help overcome security concerns (Ryman-Tubb et al., 2018). Due to the increased need for hierarchy, learning occurs step by step, leading to a nearly linear increase in learning time with each level added to the model hierarchy. Forecasting the number of clusters (K-value) is challenging. The final findings are heavily influenced by the directive of the data, and are highly sensitive to outliers (Dike et al., 2018). Furthermore, interpretability and explainability are critical factors when using AI for fraud detection. Although black-box algorithms can make accurate predictions, they lack transparency, making it difficult to grasp the reasoning behind an outcome (Mahalakshmi et al., 2022). The main obstacle to developing a fraudulent detection algorithm is the accurate prediction of fraudulent transactions. ML methods for handling missing or categorical values are not suitable for statistical analysis. Predictive analytics has improved the statistical accuracy and model interpretation, making it a more effective solution for prediction and analysis. Improved data modelling and statistics have led to more accurate forecasts (Singla & Jangir, 2020).

FUTURE TRENDS OF AI IN DETECTING FINANCIAL FRAUDS

As the financial services industry faces increasingly sophisticated fraud threats, AI plays an increasingly important role in fraud detection and prevention (Hassan et al., 2023). Furthermore, AI systems are expected to have real-time monitoring capabilities, allowing for faster detection and reactions to emerging risks. Furthermore, the deployment of explainable AI methods will increase, allowing for increased openness and interpretability in fraud-detection processes (AL-Dosari et al., 2024). Because of advances in technology and the growing economy, fraud is becoming more common in the financial industry, and fraud is constantly evolving strategies to exploit flaws in current security systems, with a particular focus on the financial industry (Hilal et al., 2022). Future developments in AI-driven intelligence will enable greater collaboration among financial institutions to share threat knowledge and best practices. AI has provides tremendous efficacy in fraud detection in the financial sector (Díaz-Rodríguez et al., 2023). AI reduces these concerns by constantly learning from existing data and adjusting its models to minimize errors (Sanad & Al-Sartawi, 2021). AI systems must keep up with new fraud tactics and changing patterns. It is important to update and adjust them regularly to ensure that they keep working well in preventing fraud (Kamuangu, 2024).Top of Form While AI provides exceptional capabilities for fraud Identifying and managing people is important. Creating an interactive solution that combines the power of AI algorithms with human expertise will increase the overall effectiveness of fraud prevention (Tiron-Tudor & Deliu, 2022). The effectiveness of AI in catching fraud depends on the quality and variety of the data on which it is trained. Ensuring that the datasets are thorough, fair, and regularly updated helps the AI detect many different kinds of fraudulent activities (Okur et al., 2021). AI models work in sensitive areas such as banking, openness, and explainability. Companies should focus on AI models to explain how they make their decisions. This helps build trust among everyone involved, and ensures that they follow the rules set by regulators (Felzmann et al., 2020). As financial institutions continue to implement and develop AI-based fraud prevention strategies, collaboration between human experts and the latest technology will play a critical role in maintaining strong defences against emerging fraud threats (Bănărescu, 2015). As the economy expands, these advancements will contribute to stronger, more transparent, and better fraud-prevention efforts in the digital era

(Cheng et al., 2021). Overall, the future of AI in financial fraud detection will include more sophisticated and adaptive systems capable of keeping up with evolving fraudulent strategies (Aftabi et al., 2023).

CONCLUSION

AI and ML play vital roles in detecting financial fraud by utilizing powerful algorithms to evaluate massive volumes of data. This study highlights the importance of detecting fraud and its effects on the financial economy, as well as the challenges of applying anomaly detection techniques to combat this ever-increasing problem. These technologies are excellent at detecting patterns and abnormalities that may suggest fraudulent activity, thus providing a proactive approach to fraud detection. These technologies enable financial organizations to evaluate large databases quickly and precisely and detect fraudulent activity with unparalleled precision. An unsupervised approach aims to detect fraud that was previously undetectable by domain experts or by detection strategies. These methods have been shown to improve the efficiency of fraud detection systems by reducing computational complexity while enhancing detection accuracy. Unsupervised learning approaches provide powerful tools for deriving insights from data without relying on labelled instances. These methods, ranging from clustering to anomaly detection, allow us to discover hidden patterns, identify anomalies, and divide the data into meaningful groupings. Unsupervised learning approaches, such as clustering algorithms and Isolation Forests, are useful for detecting suspicious behaviours without prior knowledge of fraudulent conduct in the context of financial fraud detection. This might improve the accuracy, making it more acceptable for application in running systems. AI and ML technologies provide significant tools for financial institutions to combat fraud by constantly learning from fresh data and reacting to emerging fraud strategies. Additionally, real-time processing of artificial intelligence and machine learning systems allows companies to respond quickly to suspicious activities, reduce potential losses, and protect stakeholders and customers. However, to ensure the correct and ethical use of these technologies, human knowledge and regulatory controls are required. Overall, AI and machine learning dramatically improve fraud-detection skills, thereby securing financial institutions and protecting consumers from potential damage.

REFERENCES

Aftabi, S. Z., Ahmadi, A., & Farzi, S. (2023). Fraud detection in financial statements using data mining and GAN models. *Expert Systems with Applications*, 227, 120144. 10.1016/j.eswa.2023.120144

AL-Dosari, K., Fetais, N., & Kucukvar, M. (2024). Artificial intelligence and cyber defense system for banking industry: A qualitative study of AI applications and challenges. *Cybernetics and Systems*, 55(2), 302–330. 10.1080/01969722.2022.2112539

Ali, A., Abd Razak, S., Othman, S. H., Eisa, T. A. E., Al-Dhaqm, A., Nasser, M., Elhassan, T., Elshafie, H., & Saif, A. (2022). Financial fraud detection based on machine learning: A systematic literature review. *Applied Sciences (Basel, Switzerland)*, 12(19), 9637. 10.3390/app12199637

Alpaydin, E. (2020). *Introduction to machine learning*. MIT press.

Bănărescu, A. (2015). Detecting and preventing fraud with data analytics. *Procedia Economics and Finance*, 32, 1827–1836. 10.1016/S2212-5671(15)01485-9

Bantan, R. A., Ali, A., Naeem, S., Jamal, F., Elgarhy, M., & Chesneau, C. (2020). Discrimination of sunflower seeds using multispectral and texture dataset in combination with region selection and supervised classification methods. *Chaos (Woodbury, N.Y.)*, 30(11), 113142. 10.1063/5.002401733261340

Bao, Y., Hilary, G., & Ke, B. (2022). Artificial intelligence and fraud detection. *Innovative Technology at the Interface of Finance and Operations*, I, 223–247. 10.1007/978-3-030-75729-8_8

Bhattacharyya, S., Jha, S., Tharakunnel, K., & Westland, J. C. (2011). Data mining for credit card fraud: A comparative study. *Decision Support Systems*, 50(3), 602–613. 10.1016/j.dss.2010.08.008

Cheng, X., Liu, S., Sun, X., Wang, Z., Zhou, H., Shao, Y., & Shen, H. (2021). Combating emerging financial risks in the big data era: A perspective review. *Fundamental Research*, 1(5), 595–606. 10.1016/j.fmre.2021.08.017

Chhabra Roy, N., & Prabhakaran, S. (2023). Internal-led cyber frauds in Indian banks: An effective machine learning–based defense system to fraud detection, prioritization and prevention. *Aslib Journal of Information Management*, 75(2), 246–296. 10.1108/AJIM-11-2021-0339

Choi, D., & Lee, K. (2018). An artificial intelligence approach to financial fraud detection under IoT environment: A survey and implementation. *Security and Communication Networks*, 2018, 2018. 10.1155/2018/5483472

Dal Pozzolo, A., Boracchi, G., Caelen, O., Alippi, C., & Bontempi, G. (2017). Credit card fraud detection: A realistic modeling and a novel learning strategy. *IEEE Transactions on Neural Networks and Learning Systems*, 29(8), 3784–3797. 10.1109/TNNLS.2017.273664328920909

Deng, L. (2014). A tutorial survey of architectures, algorithms, and applications for deep learning. *APSIPA Transactions on Signal and Information Processing*, 3(1), e2. 10.1017/atsip.2013.9

Díaz-Rodríguez, N., Del Ser, J., Coeckelbergh, M., de Prado, M. L., Herrera-Viedma, E., & Herrera, F. (2023). Connecting the dots in trustworthy Artificial Intelligence: From AI principles, ethics, and key requirements to responsible AI systems and regulation. *Information Fusion*, 99, 101896. 10.1016/j.inffus.2023.101896

Dike, H. U., Zhou, Y., Deveerasetty, K. K., & Wu, Q. (2018). Unsupervised learning based on artificial neural network. *RE:view*, 322–327.

Domashova, J., & Zabelina, O. (2021). Detection of fraudulent transactions using SAS Viya machine learning algorithms. *Procedia Computer Science*, 190, 204–209. 10.1016/j.procs.2021.06.025

Dong, Y., & Qin, S. J. (2018). A novel dynamic PCA algorithm for dynamic data modeling and process monitoring. *Journal of Process Control*, 67, 1–11. 10.1016/j.jprocont.2017.05.002

Duan, Y., Edwards, J. S., & Dwivedi, Y. K. (2019). Artificial intelligence for decision making in the era of Big Data – evolution, challenges and research agenda. *International Journal of Information Management*, 48, 63–71. 10.1016/j.ijinfomgt.2019.01.021

Felzmann, H., Fosch-Villaronga, E., Lutz, C., & Tamò-Larrieux, A. (2020). Towards transparency by design for artificial intelligence. *Science and Engineering Ethics*, 26(6), 3333–3361. 10.1007/s11948-020-00276-433196975

Gautam, A. (2023). The evaluating the impact of artificial intelligence on risk management and fraud detection in the banking sector. *AI. IoT and the Fourth Industrial Revolution Review*, 13(11), 9–18.

Goldstein, M., & Uchida, S. (2016). A comparative evaluation of unsupervised anomaly detection algorithms for multivariate data. *PLoS One*, 11(4), e0152173. 10.1371/journal.pone.015217327093601

Gui, Z., Huang, Y., & Zhao, X. (2024). Financial fraud and investor awareness. *Journal of Economic Behavior & Organization*, 219, 104–123. 10.1016/j.jebo.2024.01.006

Habbal, A., Ali, M. K., & Abuzaraida, M. A. (2024). Artificial Intelligence Trust, Risk and Security Management (AI TRiSM): Frameworks, applications, challenges and future research directions. *Expert Systems with Applications*, 240, 122442. 10.1016/j.eswa.2023.122442

Hassan, M., Aziz, L. A.-R., & Andriansyah, Y. (2023). The role artificial intelligence in modern banking: An exploration of AI-driven approaches for enhanced fraud prevention, risk management, and regulatory compliance. *Reviews of Contemporary Business Analytics*, 6(1), 110–132.

Hassani, H., Silva, E. S., Unger, S., TajMazinani, M., & Mac Feely, S. (2020). Artificial intelligence (AI) or intelligence augmentation (IA): What is the future? *AI*, 1(2), 8. 10.3390/ai1020008

Hilal, W., Gadsden, S. A., & Yawney, J. (2022). Financial fraud: A review of anomaly detection techniques and recent advances. *Expert Systems with Applications*, 193, 116429. 10.1016/j.eswa.2021.116429

Iqbal, M. S., Abd-Alrazaq, A., & Househ, M. (2022). Artificial Intelligence Solutions to Detect Fraud in Healthcare Settings: A Scoping Review. *Advances in Informatics, Management and Technology in Healthcare*, 20–23.

Jain, V., Agrawal, M., & Kumar, A. (2020). *Performance analysis of machine learning algorithms in credit cards fraud detection*. 86–88.

Jia, L., Xiang, L., & Liu, X. (2019). An improved eclat algorithm based on tissue-like P system with active membranes. *Processes (Basel, Switzerland)*, 7(9), 555. 10.3390/pr7090555

Jordan, M. I., & Mitchell, T. M. (2015). Machine learning: Trends, perspectives, and prospects. *Science*, 349(6245), 255–260. 10.1126/science.aaa841526185243

Kamuangu, P. (2024). A Review on Financial Fraud Detection using AI and Machine Learning. *Journal of Economics. Finance and Accounting Studies*, 6(1), 67–77.

Karpoff, J. M. (2021). The future of financial fraud. *Journal of Corporate Finance*, 66, 101694. 10.1016/j.jcorpfin.2020.101694

Kirkos, E., Spathis, C., & Manolopoulos, Y. (2007). Data mining techniques for the detection of fraudulent financial statements. *Expert Systems with Applications*, 32(4), 995–1003. 10.1016/j.eswa.2006.02.016

Koteluk, O., Wartecki, A., Mazurek, S., Kołodziejczak, I., & Mackiewicz, A. (2021). How do machines learn? Artificial intelligence as a new era in medicine. *Journal of Personalized Medicine*, 11(1), 32. 10.3390/jpm1101003233430240

Kottmann, K., Huembeli, P., Lewenstein, M., & Acín, A. (2020). Unsupervised phase discovery with deep anomaly detection. *Physical Review Letters*, 125(17), 170603. 10.1103/PhysRevLett.125.17060333156639

La Marca, K., & Bedle, H. (2022). Deepwater seismic facies and architectural element interpretation aided with unsupervised machine learning techniques: Taranaki basin, New Zealand. *Marine and Petroleum Geology*, 136, 105427. 10.1016/j.marpetgeo.2021.105427

Lee, I., & Lee, K. (2015). The Internet of Things (IoT): Applications, investments, and challenges for enterprises. *Business Horizons*, 58(4), 431–440. 10.1016/j.bushor.2015.03.008

Lee, I., & Shin, Y. J. (2020). Machine learning for enterprises: Applications, algorithm selection, and challenges. *Business Horizons*, 63(2), 157–170. 10.1016/j.bushor.2019.10.005

Mahalakshmi, V., Kulkarni, N., Kumar, K. P., Kumar, K. S., Sree, D. N., & Durga, S. (2022). The role of implementing artificial intelligence and machine learning technologies in the financial services industry for creating competitive intelligence. *Materials Today: Proceedings*, 56, 2252–2255. 10.1016/j.matpr.2021.11.577

Mohammadi, M., Yazdani, S., Khanmohammadi, M. H., & Maham, K. (2020). Financial reporting fraud detection: An analysis of data mining algorithms. *International Journal of Finance & Managerial Accounting*, 4(16), 1–12.

Naeem, S., Ali, A., Anam, S., & Ahmed, M. M. (2023). An unsupervised machine learning algorithms: Comprehensive review. *International Journal of Computing and Digital Systems*.

Okoro, Y. O., Ayo-Farai, O., Maduka, C. P., Okongwu, C. C., & Sodamade, O. T. (2024). The Role of technology in enhancing mental health advocacy: A systematic review. *International Journal of Applied Research in Social Sciences*, 6(1), 37–50. 10.51594/ijarss.v6i1.690

Okur, M. R., Zengin-Karaibrahimoglu, Y., & Taşkın, D. (2021). From Conventional Methods to Contemporary Neural Network Approaches: Financial Fraud Detection. *Ethics and Sustainability in Accounting and Finance*, III, 215–228. 10.1007/978-981-33-6636-7_11

Panesar, A., & Panesar, A. (2021). Machine learning and AI ethics. *Machine Learning and AI for Healthcare: Big Data for Improved Health Outcomes*, 207–247.

Rodriguez, M. Z., Comin, C. H., Casanova, D., Bruno, O. M., Amancio, D. R., Costa, L. da F., & Rodrigues, F. A. (2019). Clustering algorithms: A comparative approach. *PLoS One*, 14(1), e0210236. 10.1371/journal.pone.021023630645617

Ryman-Tubb, N. F., Krause, P., & Garn, W. (2018). How Artificial Intelligence and machine learning research impacts payment card fraud detection: A survey and industry benchmark. *Engineering Applications of Artificial Intelligence*, 76, 130–157. 10.1016/j.engappai.2018.07.008

Saba, C. S., & Ngepah, N. (2022). Convergence in renewable energy sources and the dynamics of their determinants: An insight from a club clustering algorithm. *Energy Reports*, 8, 3483–3506. 10.1016/j.egyr.2022.01.190

Samoili, S., Cobo, M. L., Gómez, E., De Prato, G., Martínez-Plumed, F., & Delipetrev, B. (2020). *AI Watch. Defining Artificial Intelligence. Towards an operational definition and taxonomy of artificial intelligence*.

Sanad, Z., & Al-Sartawi, A. (2021). Financial statements fraud and data mining. *RE:view*, 407–414.

Schaeffer, S. E., & Sanchez, S. V. R. (2020). Forecasting client retention—A machine-learning approach. *Journal of Retailing and Consumer Services*, 52, 101918. 10.1016/j.jretconser.2019.101918

Shahbazi, Z., & Byun, Y.-C. (2021). Blockchain-based event detection and trust verification using natural language processing and machine learning. *IEEE Access: Practical Innovations, Open Solutions*, 10, 5790–5800. 10.1109/ACCESS.2021.3139586

Singh, P., & Singh, M. (2015). Fraud detection by monitoring customer behavior and activities. *International Journal of Computer Applications*, 111(11), 23–32. 10.5120/19584-1340

Sood, P., & Bhushan, P. (2020). A structured review and theme analysis of financial frauds in the banking industry. *Asian Journal of Business Ethics*, 9(2), 305–321. 10.1007/s13520-020-00111-w

Tang, X.-B., Liu, G.-C., Yang, J., & Wei, W. (2018). Knowledge-based financial statement fraud detection system: Based on an ontology and a decision tree. *Knowledge Organization*, 45(3), 205–219. 10.5771/0943-7444-2018-3-205

Tiron-Tudor, A., & Deliu, D. (2022). Reflections on the human-algorithm complex duality perspectives in the auditing process. *Qualitative Research in Accounting & Management*, 19(3), 255–285.

Usama, M., Qadir, J., Raza, A., Arif, H., Yau, K. L. A., Elkhatib, Y., Hussain, A., & Al-Fuqaha, A. (2019). Unsupervised Machine Learning for Networking: Techniques, Applications and Research Challenges. *IEEE Access : Practical Innovations, Open Solutions*, 7, 65579–65615. 10.1109/ACCESS.2019.2916648

Wei, S., & Lee, S. (2024). Financial Anti-Fraud Based on Dual-Channel Graph Attention Network. *Journal of Theoretical and Applied Electronic Commerce Research*, 19(1), 297–314. 10.3390/jtaer19010016

Yu, S.-J., & Rha, J.-S. (2021). Research trends in accounting fraud using network analysis. *Sustainability (Basel)*, 13(10), 5579. 10.3390/su13105579

Zhang, C., & Lu, Y. (2021). Study on artificial intelligence: The state of the art and future prospects. *Journal of Industrial Information Integration*, 23, 100224. 10.1016/j.jii.2021.100224

Zhou, W., & Kapoor, G. (2011). Detecting evolutionary financial statement fraud. *Decision Support Systems*, 50(3), 570–575. 10.1016/j.dss.2010.08.007

Zhu, H., & Zhou, Z. Z. (2016). Analysis and outlook of applications of blockchain technology to equity crowdfunding in China. *Financial Innovation*, 2(1), 29. 10.1186/s40854-016-0044-7

Chapter 12
Striking the Balance:
Accounting Regulatory Compliance and Standards in Fintech

Shir Li Ng
https://orcid.org/0000-0002-1577-3992
Sunway Business School, Sunway University, Malaysia

ABSTRACT

The evolution of fintech significantly impacts the financial industry through technology and regulation. The chapter explores fintech's transformative journey, tracing its historical roots to its present-day importance in reshaping traditional financial processes. Addressing the challenges that emerge when fintech meets accounting regulations, the chapter seeks to highlight how important it is for the regulations to conform themselves with the aim of fostering the required innovation and managing risks. Some of the proposed ways of achieving harmonized compliance focus on international collaboration, adaptability of regulations, stakeholder engagement, and education initiatives. Additionally, the chapter features the importance of fostering a compliance culture, transparency, and investor confidence within the fintech landscape. Proactive measures and technological innovations drive fintech compliance, aiding in regulatory navigation. Overall, the chapter provides insights into the complex relationship between accounting regulatory compliance and standards in the fintech industry.

DOI: 10.4018/979-8-3693-3633-5.ch012

INTRODUCTION

In recent years, there has been an immense change in the financial landscape, primarily driven by the disruptive forces of financial technology, known as fintech. This revolution is defined by the emergence of cutting-edge technologies against traditional intermediaries that has ushered in a new era of efficiency, accessibility, and security of financial services. Today, with fintech being that prevalent, both financial institutions and end-users have experienced a substantial improvement in their privacy measures and regulatory compliance, representing a significant milestone achieved by the fintech landscape in its development. (Vergara & Agudo, 2021).

The fintech industry has also experienced a surge in global investment unpredictably across leading regions such as the United States, Europe, and Asia-Pacific, showcasing an increase in worldwide significance after the Covid-19 pandemic (KPMG, 2022). This rapid expansion, however, has come with a set of problems. Such dynamism in fintech brings new complexities for the players in the industry and regulatory bodies, which must now understand how technological innovation gets channeled into regulatory compliance (Najaf et al., 2022). As such, the convergence of accounting regulatory compliance and standards with fintech becomes a very important point of focus for the digital economy today. As financial transactions increasingly migrate to technology-driven platforms, there arises a pressing need to reconcile traditional accounting standards with the new innovative practices brought forth by fintech solutions.

The following chapter, "Striking the Balance: Accounting Regulatory Compliance and Standards in Fintech," discusses the balance of accounting regulatory compliance and standards while it continues to engage a rapidly evolving landscape in fintech. This chapter provides a detailed overview of diverse challenges and requirements associated with maintaining regulatory compliance and adhering to accounting standards in the fintech environment. By delving into key issues and proposing strategic approaches, the chapter aims to offer a comprehensive guide for financial professionals, regulators, policymakers, and other stakeholders on how to align regulatory requirements with the innovations brought about by fintech.

FINTECH LANDSCAPE OVERVIEW

Fintech's origins can be traced back to the 1950s, beginning with the widespread adoption of credit cards. However, it was only towards the late 20th century that the term fintech became widely recognised, alongside the advent of the internet and the digital transformation of financial services (Böhme et al., 2015). Fintech merges finance and technology, offering a broad spectrum of innovative financial products and services, including digital lending (online lending, person-to-person (P2P) lending, crowdfunding), digital payment systems (mobile banking, mobile payments, cryptocurrencies, blockchain technology), digital insurance, global fintech solutions, and digital data analytics (Baltgailis & Simakhova, 2022).

Technological Advancements Driving Fintech Innovation

The fintech sector's diversity encompasses various domains, with significant growth driven by online banking and payment platforms (Zhang-Zhang et al., 2020). The emergence of neobanks and challenger banks, for instance, has challenged traditional banking by offering more efficient operations, lower fees, and better customer experiences (Murinde et al., 2022). Similarly, P2P lending platforms and crowdfunding have transformed the lending industry by offering alternative financing solutions, while payment systems now include mobile payment apps, contactless transactions, and digital wallets.

Cryptocurrencies, powered by blockchain technology, provide secure, decentralized alternatives to traditional currencies, thereby improving transparency and reducing fraud (Narayanan et al., 2016). Similarly, the insurance sector has experienced profound changes due to fintech, particularly through Insurtech. With the adoption of big data and artificial intelligence, Insurtech streamlines automatic underwriting, tailors pricing models to individual needs, and expedites claims settlement processes (OECD, 2017). This technological integration has significantly increased operational efficiency within insurance firms and elevated customer satisfaction levels.

With technological advancements like artificial intelligence (AI), blockchain, and cloud computing, fintech companies have propelled the industry, streamlining processes, reducing costs, and enhancing user experiences (Pal et al., 2021). These innovations facilitate the analysis of data in real time, enable more accurate risk assessments, and allow for the personalization of financial services to meet individual needs. Additionally, the shift towards digital-native consumer preferences has increased demand for accessible, seamless mobile financial services, which fintech companies have adeptly met by offering solutions tailored to current and future customer needs (Gomber et al., 2018).

AI has become integral to fintech innovation, leveraging data analysis, machine learning, and predictive modeling for various applications (Ahmed, et al. 2022). AI algorithms analyze big data to offer insights into consumer behavior, enhance risk assessments, detect fraud, and customize financial services, improving transaction efficiency and accuracy. AI integrated with robo-advisors has revolutionized investment by providing quality financial advice and portfolio management to a broader audience. Additionally, AI-driven natural language processing enables sophisticated chatbots and virtual assistants, enhancing customer service interactions seamlessly (Capgemini Research Institute, 2019).

Blockchain technology, initially designed for cryptocurrencies, has become disruptive in fintech, offering transparent, secure, and decentralized financial solutions. Its decentralized approach, combined with tamper-proof ledgers, enhances transparency, trust, and efficiency while reducing fraud (Swan, 2015). By eliminating intermediaries, it enables secure peer-to-peer transactions, and smart contracts further automate agreements through code (Catalini & Gans, 2016).

Cloud computing has transformed the accessibility and scalability of fintech services, facilitating seamless data storage, processing, and sharing. This enables fintech firms to enhance operational capabilities and offer scalable solutions to a wider audience (Lacity et al., 2015). The agility of the cloud accelerates the deployment of financial applications, reducing infrastructure costs and fostering innovation. Moreover, cloud-based platforms promote data collaboration and analysis among stakeholders in the financial ecosystem (Capgemini Research Institute, 2019).

Impact of Fintech on Accounting Practices

Accounting practices have undergone a similar transformation under the influence of fintech innovations. AI-generated automation is streamlining accounting tasks and redefining the role of accountants (Goodell et al., 2021). Automated data entry, reconciliation, and financial reporting are drastically reducing the number of manual human errors, enhancing the efficiency of financial tasks, and enabling accounting professionals to shift focus to a more strategic aspects of financial management and reporting. This shift now requires accountants to acquire a new set of skills in interpreting AI-generated insights and leveraging their advanced analytics for strategic decision-making (KPMG, 2019). The human element in accounting increasingly involves strategic thinking, data interpretation, and ethical implications of using AI.

The integration of blockchain technology in financial transactions also transforms traditional accounting practices. By significantly reducing traditional accounting ledgers, the decentralized ledger provided by blockchain results in less dependence, thus leading to fewer errors, less fraud, and more transparency (Goldstein et al., 2019). The transparency and immutability of blockchain records enhance the auditability and traceability of financial processes and accounting transactions.

Accountants must update their skills to continue to interpret this decentralized financial data and understand the principles on which blockchain operates. These may add efficiency to accounting transactions but pose challenges to the entire profession, requiring a radical change (KPMG, 2019). Accounting professionals need to adapt to current and emerging technologies, including understanding and interpreting AI-generated insights, performing data analysis, and interpreting blockchain-governed transactions while maintaining the integrity of financial information (Imerman & Fabozzi, 2020).

FINTECH REGULATORY FRAMEWORKS

Fintech's rapid evolution is only possible if regulatory frameworks can adapt quickly to technological changes, as well. Regulatory agility is essential to fully leverage the potential of fintech innovation opportunities while mitigating potential risks (Arner et al., 2017). Regulators need to be ahead of technological advancements, ensuring that regulatory frameworks foster innovation while safeguarding against threats to financial stability.

As such, this section offers a reflective understanding of the regulatory frameworks surrounding fintech operations. It includes well-established standards, such as Generally Accepted Accounting Principles (GAAP) and International Financial Reporting Standards (IFRS) and to critically evaluate whether these traditional standards too can become agile considering the dynamic nature of fintech operations and transactions. By examining their applicability and potential limitations in the context of fintech, it aims to provide an understanding of how established regulatory bodies may need to evolve to accommodate the complexities of modern financial technologies.

Accounting Regulations in Fintech

In the United States (U.S.), financial reporting has traditionally been governed by Generally Accepted Accounting Principles (GAAP), an established framework of accounting standards. A rules-based method, GAAP provides detailed guidelines for various financial transactions, ensuring that publicly traded U.S. companies file and report financial information that is clear and consistent (Flood, 2021). This process of following GAAP procedures allows a company's financial reports to be easily compared to others in the same industry, serving as an effective tool for investors and other stakeholders to investigate and evaluate a company's financial standing. Managed and published by the Financial Accounting Standards Board (FASB), GAAP's principles and standards are constantly updated and changed. GAAP is legally required for regulated and publicly traded companies, although some private companies also elect to voluntarily adopt GAAP standards for their financial statements.

Conversely, International Financial Reporting Standards (IFRS), which are developed by the International Accounting Standards Board (IASB), present a single set of globally recognized financial reporting standards that employs a principles-based method and includes a conceptual framework for financial reporting (IFRS Foundation, 2024). These IFRS standards have effectively become the world's most widely accepted language for preparing and presenting financial statements, gaining trust from investors globally and being mandated for use by over 140 jurisdictions worldwide. The International Accounting Standards Board (IASB) continues to improve and enhance the standards with a dedication to developing high-quality accounting standards that enhance transparency, accountability, and efficiency in the global financial markets.

GAAP is a more localized set of standards, with a foundation in the U.S. Outside of U.S. borders, the more global accounting regulations are known as IFRS. Publicly traded domestic companies are required to follow GAAP standards, while private companies can decide which financial standards to adhere to (Crail & Main, 2022). Some companies in the U.S., especially those who conduct international trade, may opt for dual reporting, employing both GAAP and IFRS methods when preparing financial statements. Although converting GAAP documents and processes to align with IFRS standards is feasible, it can be a time-consuming process. The potential integration or convergence of these two systems remains uncertain, despite efforts by the U.S. Securities and Exchange Commission from 2010 to 2012 to formulate an official plan for convergence (IFRS Foundation, 2024).

The dynamic and innovative nature of fintech operations often presents challenges to the traditional standards and rigid structure of GAAP. Digital assets valuation and accounting treatment in transactions for cryptocurrency recognition may not align with GAAP principles and are just a few examples of how these standards need to be reevaluated to continue to be relevant within the fintech ecosystem. While IFRS offers flexibility, the rapidly evolving fintech ecosystem poses challenges in ensuring its applicability. P2P lending and cryptocurrencies are examples of the nature of fintech where may require significant considerations within the IFRS conceptual framework to accurately reflect the reality of these financial transactions.

Global Fintech Regulatory Oversight

Fintech regulatory oversight extends beyond national borders, being largely global in scope. Entities like the Financial Stability Board (FSB) and the International Organization of Securities Commissions (IOSCO) play crucial roles in global fintech oversight. The Financial Stability Board (FSB) is a global organization responsible for overseeing and providing recommendations concerning the global financial system. It promotes international financial stability through coordination among national financial authorities and international standard-setting bodies. The FSB also fosters the implementation of robust policies within the financial sector, and it promotes a consistent policy implementation across various sectors and jurisdictions to ensure a level playing field across countries (FSB, 2024).

Conversely, the International Organization of Securities Commissions (IOSCO) unites the world's securities regulators and is recognized as the global standard setter for the securities sector. IOSCO is dedicated to developing, adopting, and promoting adherence to internationally recognized standards for securities regulation (IOSCO, 2024). It works closely with the G20 countries and FSB to advance the global regulatory reform agenda and seeks to establish common principles and standards to promote consistent and efficient oversight and to ensure information-sharing and cooperation among jurisdictions.

On a regional level, regulatory organizations are adapting their fintech oversight models based upon the unique features and challenges of their assigned operational jurisdictions. For example, the European Securities and Markets Authority (ESMA) provides regulatory oversight of the European Union's (EU) securities markets, with a focus on establishing a single regulatory and supervisory framework to strengthen investor protection, improve the functioning of financial markets, and maintain market stability within the EU (ESMA, 2024).

Similarly, the United States Securities and Exchange Commission (SEC) regulates the securities markets in the United States, with major significance centered on investor protection, maintaining fair, orderly, and efficient markets, and facilitating the formation of capital (SEC, 2024). These regional bodies customize their regulatory frameworks to address the unique characteristics and challenges within their respective jurisdictions.

REGULATORY CHALLENGES IN FINTECH EVOLUTION

Fintech's rapid evolution creates tensions in the regulatory landscape leading to a dynamic environment where the potential for innovation clashes with the need for control. Fintech's capacity to disrupt traditional financial services presents significant challenges to regulators committed to maintaining the stability and integrity of financial systems. As the speed of fintech evolution outstrips traditional accounting regulatory compliance and standards, the need for agility in regulatory responses becomes paramount.

Traditional Regulatory to Fintech Adaptability Challenges

Among the primary challenges is the adaptability of regulatory frameworks to the ever-changing nature of fintech. Technological breakthroughs often outpace the speed with which regulations and accounting standards are formulated and enforced, creating a gap that may result in inefficiencies within the financial system. Traditional accounting standards may struggle to keep pace with the explosion of fintech applications, creating a regulatory lag (Arner et al., 2017). The tension arises from the need of regulatory bodies to strike a balance between promoting innovation and ensuring stability and integrity in the financial systems.

Clear and comprehensive standards are needed to promote innovative financial products and services that meet industry standards while also allowing for innovation in financial engineering (He et al., 2017). For instance, blockchain, which is the backbone for many fintech applications, introduces novel principles that challenge traditional accounting practices. The immutability of a decentralized ledger system, blockchain-powered transactions and the lack of a central authority mean that traditional financial transactions must be recorded and audited in an entirely unique manner. Hence, regulatory bodies must develop standards that accommodate the intricacies of blockchain while maintaining the reliability and accuracy of financial reporting (Catalini & Gans, 2016).

Regulatory Harmonization Challenges

In addition, fintech's globalized environment means it is not constrained by traditional jurisdictional boundaries. Issues such as harmonizing regulatory compliance and accounting standards across jurisdictions globally present not only their own set of challenges but also heighten the difficulty around cross-border regulatory arbitrage. Despite the existence of international bodies such as the International Financial Reporting Standards (IFRS), Financial Stability Board (FSB), and International Organization of Securities Commissions (IOSCO) to harmonize the creation of common standards, the diverse regulatory approaches of individual countries remain (Cornelli, et al., 2023).

The diversity in accounting regulatory compliance and standards presents a challenge for organizations seeking to operate globally. Varying regulatory compliance requirements and reporting accounting standards across jurisdictions may call for complex adjustments in financial reporting practices, creating potential barriers to global expansion (JPMorgan, 2021). Furthermore, the operational costs associated with having to comply with different standards together pose a challenge to maintaining a consistent and transparent approach to financial reporting (Deloitte, 2020).

Indeed, it also has implications for maintaining regulatory effectiveness as regulatory arbitrage becomes a concern. Companies may seek favorable regulatory environments, potentially undermining the effectiveness of individual regulatory frameworks. Thus, examining the challenges associated with establishing accounting standards that can seamlessly align with evolving compliance requirements remains vital. This includes balancing the dynamic nature of fintech with the need for appropriate consumer protection, data privacy, and system stability (Schmidt & Scott, 2021).

Innovation and Consumer Protection Challenges

In the past several years, there has been an upsurge in innovative solutions in the fintech landscape; simultaneously, issues concerning consumer protection, data privacy, and cybersecurity have been forefront of the regulatory agenda (Suryono et al., 2020). Striking the right balance in fostering innovation, whilst protecting consumer interests is a significant challenge for regulators across the globe. The stakes are high when data privacy is breached; trust can be destroyed with wide-ranging consequences for consumers and the wider fintech industry. It is therefore vital that regulators ensure that, alongside robust cybersecurity obligations, fintech companies comply with transparency and disclosure requirements.

The diverse range of financial services offered by fintech entities requires comprehensive frameworks that safeguard consumer interests. These might range from addressing practices around fair lending, to transparent disclosure of terms and conditions, and establishing mechanisms to resolve disputes. The range of services provided by fintech entities means that regulators need to continuously renew and adjust consumer protection frameworks to keep in pace with evolving business models (Birnhack & Ahituv, 2013).

Moreover, fintech's reliance on vast amounts of sensitive financial and personal data complicates the regulatory landscape. Divided financial systems and globalising fintech operations amplify the imperative for robust data privacy. Regulators must grapple with the intricacies of protecting privacy whilst fine-tuning access for innovation to thrive in fintech industry. This demands not just a strong regulatory architecture, but proactive assistance to address emergent threats and vulnerabilities in the evolving digital environment (Zhang et al., 2023).

In addition, the prevalence and sophistication of cyber threats is an ever-growing concern; so much so that cybersecurity isn't just a regulatory imperative, it's critical. The infinite quantities of sensitive financial data fintech entities makes them the prime target. Cultivating a cybersecurity culture within the industry is challenging. This means not only establishing clear-cut, straightforward cyber measures, undertaking regular risk assessments, and establishing incident response frameworks to mitigate potential breaches (Adrian & Ferreira, 2023). The important relationship between fintech's reliance on sensitive financial and privacy data and regulatory compliance emphasizes the challenges regulators face in harmonising innovation with consumer protection.

STRATEGIES FOR REGULATORY HARMONISATION IN FINTECH

The convergence of fintech and regulatory compliance introduces a complex dynamic that demands strategic approaches for establishing harmonized standards. This is essential to not only accommodate the rapid pace of fintech innovation but also to foster the global financial system's security and integrity. This section explores relevant strategies such as international collaboration, regulatory adaptability, stakeholder involvement, and educational efforts to harmonize accounting standards and regulatory frameworks in the fintech realm.

International Collaboration for Harmonised Standards

A fundamental strategy for harmonising standards in fintech accounting regulatory compliance and standards is the engagement in international collaboration and standardization initiatives. Notably, organizations such as the IASB are central in developing universally accepted accounting standards that form the backbone of international collaborations. The engagement of regulatory bodies across the globe in these initiatives is important, allowing for the development of a common framework that transcends national borders.

In addition to facilitating partnerships among nations, such international standardization initiatives help in converging accounting standards and regulatory frameworks globally. This in effect reduces the differences that impede the fluidity of cross-border financial transactions. By aligning with global standardization, regulatory bodies can establish an environment that not only harmonizes regulation globally but is also conducive to innovation in the fintech space while maintaining uniformity in financial reporting practices (Thottoli, 2023).

Regulatory Flexibility for Fintech Adaptability

Given fintech's dynamic nature, a regulatory framework must be robust and able to adopt a forward-looking approach that is flexible. Authorities must continually evaluate whether established accounting frameworks remain both relevant and effective considering the emerging technologies. This complex process involves the continuous incorporation of mechanisms for timely updates and adjustments to accounting standards, ensuring that they will be not just relevant, but highly applicable to the unique characteristics of fintech transactions (Jenweeranon, 2023). Given the transformative nature of technologies, regulatory authorities should stay ahead of the technological curve. Proactive regulatory adaptability, therefore, ensures that the accounting standards and the framework will be able to seamlessly embrace new fintech developments while maintaining the foundational principles of financial regulation.

Stakeholder Engagement: Shaping Regulatory Frameworks

Consequently, collaboration with industry stakeholders emerges as a significant and highly instrumental approach for shaping a harmonized and robust set of regulatory frameworks within the fintech industry. Regulatory bodies must establish ongoing and deep conversations with diverse stakeholders such as fintech firms, financial institutions financial professionals, and technology experts. These dialogues should be characterized by open communication channels, creating an environment conducive to the exchange of invaluable insights into the complex technological innovations and their implications on financial systems (Utami & Ekaputra, 2021).

By involving these stakeholders in the decision-making process, regulatory bodies can gain a holistic understanding of the unique opportunities and challenges posed by the fintech landscape. Stakeholder engagement serves as a vital feedback loop, facilitating real-time insights into the practical implications of accounting standards and regulatory compliance on fintech operations. The insights gained through ongoing dialogues empower regulators to make informed decisions, adapting standards and frameworks to meet the evolving needs and challenges faced by industry participants.

Also, this collaborative and inclusive approach ensures the development of regulations that strike an optimal balance between fostering innovation and safeguarding the financial integrity of the global ecosystem (Kamuangu, 2024). The active involvement of industry stakeholders in shaping accounting standards and regulatory frameworks creates a symbiotic relationship where regulators are informed by industry expertise, and industry players operate within a regulatory environment that acknowledges and accommodates their unique dynamics.

Investments in Education and Training

The next strategic approach in addressing the challenges of harmonizing the fintech regulatory compliance is to make substantial investments in education and training programs. These initiatives should be carefully designed to equip financial and accounting professionals with the profound knowledge and sophisticated skills required to effectively manage the fintech landscape. The goal behind these education and training programs is to elevate the intellectual capacity and proficiency of financial professionals. This elevation, in turn, plays a significant role in facilitating a more seamless integration of fintech innovations into established accounting regulatory compliance and standards. A robust portfolio of these education and training programs should span a range of topical areas, including the impact of blockchain technology, cryptocurrency transactions, and algorithmic decision-making on financial reporting. Given a comprehensive understanding of these disruptive technologies, financial and accounting professionals are empowered to make informed decisions that align seamlessly with regulatory requirements.

Moreover, these education and training programs should emphasize the importance of ethical considerations and comprehensive risk management within the context of rapidly changing fintech environments. The integration of ethical principles ensures that professionals operate within a framework of integrity and responsibility, thereby contributing to the creation of a trustworthy and transparent financial ecosystem. This orientation towards education and training is essential to the harmonizing efforts, serving as a cornerstone for building a workforce that is not only well-versed in the latest fintech developments but is also grounded in ethical principles and proficient in risk management practices (Suryono et al., 2020).

FOSTERING COMPLIANCE CULTURE AWARENESS

The continuous evolution of fintech has reshaped the financial landscape, bringing forth innovative solutions and services. However, alongside this transformative journey comes a complex network of regulatory requirements that fintech companies must follow. This section explores the need for fintech firms to prioritize regulatory awareness and compliance with accounting standards. It offers practical guidance, grounded in theory, to help these firms build strong compliance frameworks.

Building Robust Compliance Frameworks

Crucial to the successful fostering of a regulatory compliance culture within the dynamic fintech sector is the development of robust compliance frameworks. This initiative involves a thorough examination of the crucial role played by internal controls and corporate governance structures in ensuring constant adherence to rigorous accounting standards. Serving as the front line of defense against regulatory non-compliance, internal controls serve the dual purpose of identifying and preventing financial irregularities and fraud. Simultaneously, corporate governance structures offer the umbrella framework to guide decision-making processes in a manner that is in alignment with regulatory expectations and ethical standards (Najaf et al., 2021).

To accomplish this objective, regulatory bodies and fintech companies must go beyond theoretical discussions to offer actionable guidance on the effective implementation of regulatory compliance and accounting frameworks. This requires providing insights into the design and execution of robust internal control mechanisms and corporate governance structures specially tailored to the dynamic context of fintech companies. Incorporating practical considerations on the unique set of challenges and opportunities that are presented by fintech operations is crucial, so that compliance measures are seamlessly integrated within the day-to-day operations of fintech companies (Najaf & Atayah, 2021).

Cultivating a Regulatory Awareness Culture

Cultivating a culture of regulatory awareness is crucial for the sustainable growth of fintech organizations. This involves fostering regulatory consciousness across all organizational levels. Targeted training programs are essential, ensuring employees understand complex regulatory and accounting standards, thereby equipping them with the necessary knowledge and skills (Fahy, 2022).

It is important that such training programs go beyond any generic compliance content and developing materials that address the specific aspects of fintech operations. Doing so allows employees not only to understand and appreciate the complex regulatory compliance, but also to understand how these intricacies impact on their daily responsibilities. The result is the cultivation of a culture of ownership and accountability where every member of the organization proactively contributes to and upholds accounting regulatory compliance and standards. This perspective underscores the notion that a well-informed and proactive workforce serves as an asset for fintech organizations seeking sustained growth and success in compliance practices.

Leadership Commitment

Furthermore, leaders must serve as champions for an organizational culture of compliance, investing in ongoing training programs that ensure employees are consistently equipped with the latest regulatory knowledge (Campbell et al., 2021). A top-down approach is critical to embedding a robust regulatory awareness throughout the organizational DNA, thereby influencing decision-making processes at every level. Leadership commitment is monumental in fostering a culture where regulatory awareness becomes not just one-off mandates and compliance checkboxes, but an active principle that drives continued, strategic innovation and growth in the fintech sector.

TRANSPARENCY AND INVESTOR CONFIDENCE

In the evolving fintech landscape, the convergence of regulatory compliance, transparency and investor confidence has emerged as a pivotal concern. This section embarks on a comprehensive review of the relationship between transparent reporting practices, rigorous accounting standards and their collective impact on the cultivation and maintenance of investor confidence within the fintech sector. By taking a proactive approach in addressing concerns related to data breaches and their resulting impact on trust, this discussion seeks to offer actionable strategies for fintech companies to enhance transparency efforts- thereby fostering an environment of trust among investors.

Transparent Reporting Practices

One of the main concerns in the fintech landscape is ensuring transparent reporting practices which serve as a cornerstone for establishing and maintaining investor confidence. Transparency is much more than a regulatory requirement. It constitutes the foundation of a resilient compliance and accounting framework. It is also central to fostering confidence among investors who look to it for a thorough understanding of the operational and financial health of fintech companies, serving as a proactive tool for building and preserving investment trust (Vasquez & San-Jose, 2022).

Transparent reporting involves more than adherence to all the specific rules and standards. It is a multi-faceted communication strategy that adds compliance with financial regulations and accounting standards especially to areas such as data protection, cybersecurity, and ethical considerations. Consequently, in the fintech landscape where even regulatory can be complicated, transparent communication emerges as a vital tool ensuring that investors are well-informed and confident in the regulatory compliance measures adopted by fintech companies (Fang et al., 2021).

Building Investor Confidence through Transparency

Investors' confidence stands as an important element in the success of fintech companies. A transparent line of communication on regulatory compliance, financial performance, financial position, and risk management strategies is the motivation for establishing and maintaining investor confidence (Aldboush et al., 2023). This transparent modus operandi does not only show dedication to ethical business conduct but also meets various stakeholder expectations. In a sector characterized by innovation and inherent risks, these expectations emphasize the importance of clarity and accountability in financial operations. In effect, transparency becomes a powerful tool within the dynamic fintech industry in managing investor expectations (Harsono & Suprapti, 2024).

Open and clear lines of communication about potential risks, mitigation strategies, and the possible impact of regulatory changes foster a realistic understanding between investors. Investors may be attracted by innovation, but more reassured by the company's unwavering commitment to regulatory compliance and robust accounting practices. This dual focus on innovation and transparency strengthens the bedrock of investor confidence, thus establishing fintech companies as trustworthy, solid, and resilient organizations in the market.

Role of Regulatory in Investor Confidence

Accounting frameworks form the basis of financial reporting and offer a standardized standard for communicating financial performance and position. Within the fintech landscape, characterized by revolutionary financial instruments and digital transactions, the choice and application of accounting standards and regulatory compliance play a critical role in delivering investors with reliable, comparable information essential for fostering investors' confidence. Financial statements prepared in accordance with recognized accounting standards afford investors a universal benchmark to assess a company's financial performance and position. This not only eases comparability, but also ensures that investors can make well-informed decisions rooted in reliable and consistent financial data.

This narrative emphasizes the significant importance of converging accounting frameworks with International Financial Reporting Standards (IFRS), particularly within the fintech sector, which operates globally. Convergence assures consistency in financial reporting practices, enhancing the credibility of fintech companies in the global marketplace and reinforcing investor confidence in the accuracy and reliability of financial data (Xia et al., 2023). Moreover, full transparency in financial reporting is given through detailed disclosures regarding the impact of fintech-specific transactions, such as cryptocurrency holdings on financial statements (Nangin et al., 2020).

Mitigating Risks: Integrating Cybersecurity Measures

In an era where data breaches pose significant threats to trust and confidence, fintech companies must equip themselves with comprehensive knowledge and strategic approaches to effectively mitigate associated risks. As such, fintech companies will need to fully integrate cybersecurity measures into a more comprehensive regulatory accounting framework, along with promoting a host of proactive strategies like regular routine risk assessments, continuous employee training, and the adoption of cutting-edge cybersecurity technologies serving as a robust defense for protecting fintech organizations against potential breaches.

These actions will not only help protect sensitive information but will greatly enhance the overall resilience of the organizations as well as preserving trust and confidence among stakeholder groups and beyond (Jafri et al., 2024). By acting in such a manner, fintech firms can begin to lay the foundation for a level of resilience and confidence that is unwavering, ensuring that stakeholders have the utmost trust and confidence in all aspects of the evolving fintech landscape.

FUTURE TRENDS AND MEASURES

In the evolving fintech landscape, firms must proactively anticipate future trends and adapt regulatory compliance efforts accordingly. The final part of the chapter delves into how technology aids in optimizing regulatory compliance and accounting standards in fintech. By highlighting innovative tech solutions tailored to address regulatory challenges, it underscores the need to embrace and strategically utilize innovation to navigate regulatory changes for long-term success.

Adapting to Evolving Regulatory Landscape

The fintech regulatory landscape has been consistently evolving, with regulatory bodies worldwide continuously rolling out new rules and standards to address new risks and challenges. For fintech companies, compliance entails adherence to different regulatory and accounting requirements, be it data privacy, security, anti-money laundering, or know-your-customer regulations which is as much a legal obligation as it is essential to maintain the trust and credibility among investors and stakeholders (Alam et al., 2019).

As regulatory requirements and accounting standards become more refined and stringent, fintech companies are using innovative technologies to make sure they comply and often stay ahead of the changes to remain competitive (Chahal, 2023). Through the strategic implementation these technologies such as AI, machine learning, blockchain and regtech into the regulatory compliance process, fintech companies are not only increasing the efficiency and accuracy of these processes, but also fostering a culture of initiative-taking risk management within their organizations (Alam et al., 2019). By leveraging on these solutions, fintech companies can adapt quickly to the evolving regulatory landscape and safeguard the reputations they have built while fostering sustained trust among their investors and stakeholders.

Innovations Driving Regulatory Compliance

Innovations such as AI and machine learning have fundamentally transformed how fintech companies approach regulatory compliance and accounting standards. AI-driven solutions can automate time-consuming or manual processes like customer due diligence and transaction monitoring, which not only makes for more efficient operations but also reduces operating costs (Jaksic & Marinc, 2019). Meanwhile, machine learning algorithms are particularly adept at analyzing large volumes of datasets to root out any suspicious patterns or anomalies that could indicate a compliance risk (Vasista, 2021). It also means that this technology can support predictive analytics use cases where fintech companies are trying to spot emerging regulatory trends earlier so they can make small, ongoing adjustments to their compliance strategies rather than large, expensive, reactionary overhauls as new regulations are introduced.

Furthermore, blockchain technology is uniquely suited to improving transparency and traceability in accounting regulatory compliance and standards. The decentralized nature of blockchain architecture guarantees that transaction records remain immutable and tamper-proof, providing an incredibly transparent and auditable record of financial transactions. Additionally, smart contracts supported by blockchain based transactions facilitate the automated enforcement of compliance rules and regulation such as anti-money laundering, and know your customer checks, so transactions are only approved upon meeting all the compliance criteria. By leveraging blockchain technology and smart contracts, fintech companies can streamline compliance processes, mitigate fraud risks, and enhance transparency in financial transactions (Unal & Aysan, 2022).

Future Technological Trends in Fintech Compliance

The future of fintech compliance is closely related to ongoing technological progress. Emerging technologies such as quantum computing, regtech, and decentralized finance are expected to continue revolutionizing the fintech ecosystem. Regtech also known as regulatory technology refers to a set of specialized technology solutions designed to address compliance challenges (Arner et al., 2017). These solutions, which leverage AI and machine learning, include a variety of tools and platforms ranging from regulatory reporting software to compliance monitoring systems and risk management tools. Integrating these solutions enables fintech companies to automate compliance processes, monitor regulatory changes in real-time, and maintain ongoing adherence to evolving regulations (Anagnostopoulos, 2018).

Meanwhile, quantum computing, with its superior processing power, is set to revolutionize data analysis and risk modeling, enabling fintech companies to enhance compliance strategies (Freij, 2020). Decentralized finance platforms are also transforming traditional services with innovations like automated lending and trading, presenting new compliance challenges but also opportunities for regulatory innovation (Goldstein et al., 2019). Embracing these technologies allows fintech firms to thrive in a progressively regulated environment, shaping the future of financial services.

CONCLUSION

The chapter concludes by summarizing the evolution of fintech, driven by technological advancements and regulatory changes, which have transformed financial services since the 1950s. It highlights the importance of regulatory compliance and accounting standards, discussing challenges and proposing strategies for harmonizations. Key areas include fostering a compliance culture, ensuring transparency, and addressing issues like consumer protection and data privacy. The chapter emphasizes the need for continuous evolution in compliance to balance innovation with financial resilience. Future fintech compliance will depend on adopting technologies like AI, blockchain, and regtech to stay ahead of regulatory changes. The goal is to guide the fintech industry towards effective compliance while empowering stakeholders to navigate the complex landscape successfully.

REFERENCES

Adrian, T., & Ferreira, C. (2023). Mounting cyber threats mean financial firm urgently need better safeguards. *International Monetary Fund.*https://www.imf.org/en/Blogs/Articles/2023/03/02/mounting-cyber-threats-mean-financial-firms-urgently-need-better-safeguards

Ahmed, S., Alshater, M. M., Ammari, A. E., & Hammami, H. (2022). Artificial intelligence and machine learning in fnance: A bibliometric review. *Research in International Business and Finance*, 61.

Alam, N., Gupta, L., Zameni, A., Alam, N., Gupta, L., & Zameni, A. (2019). Fintech regulation. *Fintech and Islamic finance: Digitalization, development and disruption*, 137-158.

Aldboush, H. H., & Ferdous, M. (2023). Building trust in fintech: An analysis of ethical and privacy considerations in the intersection of big data, AI, and customer trust. *International Journal of Financial Studies*, 11(3), 90. 10.3390/ijfs11030090

Anagnostopoulos, I. (2018). Fintech and regtech: Impact on regulators and banks. *Journal of Economics and Business*, 100, 7–25. 10.1016/j.jeconbus.2018.07.003

Arner, D. W., Barberis, J., & Buckley, R. P. (2017). FinTech, RegTech, and the reconceptualization of financial regulation. *Northwestern Journal of International Law & Business*, 37(3), 371–414.

Baltgailis, J., & Simakhova, A. (2022). The technological innnovations of Fintech companies in ensuring the stability of financial system in pandemic times. *Marketing & Management of Innovations*, 2(1), 55–65. 10.21272/mmi.2022.2-05

Birnhack, M., & Ahituv, N. (2013). Privacy implications of emerging & future technologies. Privavcy, *SSRN,* 1-49. 10.2139/ssrn.2364396

Böhme, R., Christin, N., Edelman, B., & Moore, T. (2015). Bitcoin: Economics, technology, and governance. *The Journal of Economic Perspectives*, 29(2), 213–238. 10.1257/jep.29.2.213

Campbell, T., Knox, M. W., Rowlands, J., Cui, Z. Y. A., & DeJesus, L. (2021). Leadership in FinTech: Authentic leaders as enablers of innovation and competitiveness in financial technology firms. In *Fostering Innovation and Competitiveness with FinTech, RegTech, and SupTech*. IGI Global. 10.4018/978-1-7998-4390-0.ch013

Capgemini Research Institute. (2019). *Smart talk: How organizations and consumer are embracing voice and chat assistance.* Capgemini Research Institute. https://www.capgemini.com/wp-content/uploads/2019/09/Report-%E2%80%93-Conversational-Interfaces_Web-Final.pdf

Catalini, C., & Gans, J. S. (2016). *Some simple economics of the blockchain.* NBER Working Paper, 22952. https://www.nber.org/system/files/working_papers/w22952/w22952.pdf

Chahal, S. (2023). Navigating financial evolution: Business process optimization and digital transformation in the finance sector. *International Journal of Finance*, 8(5), 67–81. 10.47941/ijf.1475

Cornelli, G., Frost, J., & Mishra, S. (2023). *Regulatory sandboxes and fintech funding: Evidence from the UK.* BIS Working Paper. https://www.bis.org/publ/work901.pdf

Crail, C., & Main, K. (2022). Generally accepted accounting principles (GAAP) guide. *Forbes.* https://www.forbes.com/advisor/business/generally-accepted-accounting-principles-gaap-guide/

Deloitte. (2020). *Fintech on the brink of further disruption.* Deloitte. https://www2.deloitte.com/content/dam/Deloitte/nl/Documents/financial-services/deloitte-nl-fsi-fintech-report-1.pdf

European Securities and Markets Authority (ESMA). (2024). *ESMA Overview.* ESMA. https://www.esma.europa.eu/about-esma

Fahy, L. A. (2022). Fostering regulator–innovator collaboration at the frontline: A case study of the UK's regulatory sandbox for fintech. *Law & Policy*, 44(2), 162–184. 10.1111/lapo.1218435915781

Fang, H., Chung, C. P., Lu, Y. C., Lee, Y. H., & Wang, W. H. (2021). The impacts of investors' sentiments on stock returns using fintech approaches. *International Review of Financial Analysis*, 77, 77. 10.1016/j.irfa.2021.101858

Financial Stability Board (FSB). (2024). *FSB Overview.* FSB. https://www.fsb.org/about/

Flood, J. M. (2021). *Wiley GAAP 2021: Interpretation and application of generally accepted accounting principles* (2nd ed.). Wiley. 10.1002/9781119736202

Freij, A. (2020). Using technology to support financial services regulatory compliance: Current applications and future prospects of regtech. *Journal of Investment Compliance*, 21(2/3), 181–190. 10.1108/JOIC-10-2020-0033

Goldstein, I., Jiang, W., & Karolyi, G. A. (2019). To Fintech and beyond. *Review of Financial Studies*, 32(5), 1647–1661. 10.1093/rfs/hhz025

Gomber, P., Koch, J. A., & Siering, M. (2018). Digital finance and Fintech: Current research and future research directions. *Journal of Business Economics*, 88(5), 537–580. 10.1007/s11573-017-0852-x

Goodell, J. W., Kumar, S., Lim, W. M., & Pattnaik, D. (2021). Artificial intelligence and machine learning in fnance: Identifying foundations, themes and research cluster from bibliometrice analysis. *Journal of Behavioral and Experimental Finance*, 32, 100577. 10.1016/j.jbef.2021.100577

Harsono, I., & Suprapti, I. A. P. (2024). The role of fintech in transforming traditional financial services. *Accounting Studies and Tax Journal*, 1(1), 81–91. 10.62207/gfzvtd24

He, D., Leckow, R. B., Hakasr, V., Griffoli, T. M., Jenkinson, N., Kashima, M., Khiaonarong, T., Rochon, C., & Tourpe, H. (2017). *Fintech and financial services: Initial considerations*. International Monetary Fund.

IFRS Foundation. (2024). *International Financial Reporting Standards (IFRS)*. IFRS. https://www.ifrs.org

Imerman, M. B., & Fabozzi, F. J. (2020). Cashing in on innovation: A taxonomy of FinTech. *Journal of Asset Management*, 21(3), 167–177. 10.1057/s41260-020-00163-4

International Organization of Securities Commissions (IOSCO). (2024). *IOSCO Overview*. https://www.iosco.org/about/?subsection=about_iosco

Jafri, J. A., Amin, S. I. M., Rahman, A. A., & Nor, S. M. (2024). A systematic literature review of the role of trust and security on Fintech adoption in banking. *Heliyon*, 10(1), e22980. 10.1016/j.heliyon.2023.e2298038163181

Jaksic, M., & Marinc, M. (2019). Relationship banking and information technology: The role of artificial intelligence and FinTech. *Risk Management*, 21(1), 1–18. 10.1057/s41283-018-0039-y

Jenweeranon, P. (2023). Digitalisation in finance: Regulatory challenges in selected ASEAN countries. *Banking & Finance Law Review*, 39(3), 507–545.

JPMorgan. (2021). *Global e-commerce trends report*. JP Morgon. https://www.jpmorgan.com/content/dam/jpm/treasury-services/documents/global-e-commerce-trends-report.pdf

Kamuangu, P. (2024). Advancements of AI and machine learning in Fintech industry (2016-2020). *Journal of Economics. Finance and Accounting Studies*, 6(1), 23–31.

KPMG. (2019). *Future ready finance survey 2019: Learn what high performing organizations are doing differently.* KPMG. https://assets.kpmg.com/content/dam/kpmg/xx/pdf/2019/09/kpmg-future-ready-finance-global-survey-2019.pdf

KPMG. (2022). *Pulse of Fintech H2'21.* KPMG. https://assets.kpmg/content/dam/kpmg/xx/pdf/2022/02/pulse-of-Fintech-h2-21.pdf

Lacity, M., Willcocks, L., & Craig, A. (2015). *Robotic process automation at Telefónica O2.* The Outsourcing Unit Working Paper Series, London School of Economics and Political Science. https://www.umsl.edu/~lacitym/TelefonicaOUWP022015FINAL.pdf

Murinde, V., Rizopoulos, E., & Zachariadis, M. (2022). The impact of the Fintech revolution on the future of banking: Opportunities and risks. *International Review of Financial Analysis*, 81, 1–27. 10.1016/j.irfa.2022.102103

Najaf, K., & Atayah, O. F. (2021). Understanding governance compliance for RegTech. *Artificial Intelligence and Islamic Finance: Practical Applications for Financial Risk Management*, 11.

Najaf, K., Chin, A., & Najaf, R. (2021). Conceptualising the corporate governance issues of fintech firms. *The fourth industrial revolution: implementation of artificial intelligence for growing business success*, 187-197.

Najaf, K., Subramaniam, R. K., & Atayah, O. F. (2022). Understanding the implications of Fintech Peer-to-Peer (P2P) lending during the COVID-19 pandemic. *Journal of Sustainable Finance & Investment*, 12(1), 87–102. 10.1080/20430795.2021.1917225

Nangin, M. A., Barus, I. R. G., & Wahyoedi, S. (2020). The effects of perceived ease of use, security, and promotion on trust and its implications on fintech adoption. *Journal of Consumer Sciences*, 5(2), 124–138. 10.29244/jcs.5.2.124-138

Narayanan, A., Bonneau, J., Felten, E., Miller, A., & Goldfeder, S. (2016). *Bitcoin and cryptocurrency technologies: A comprehensive introduction.* Princeton University Press.

OECD. (2017). *Technology and innovation in the insurance sector.* OECD. https://www.oecd.org/finance/Technology-and-innovation-in-the-insurance-sector.pdf

Pal, A., Tiwari, C. K., & Behl, A. (2021). Blockchain technology in financial services: A comprehensive review of the literature. *Journal of Global Operations and Strategic Sourcing*, 14(1), 61–80. 10.1108/JGOSS-07-2020-0039

Schmidt, R., & Scott, C. (2021). Regulatory discretion: Structuring power in the era of regulatory capitalism. *Legal Studies*, 41(3), 454–473. 10.1017/lst.2021.13

Shino, Y., Lukita, C., Rii, K. B., & Nabila, E. A. (2022). The emergence of Fintech in Higher education curriculum. [SABDA Journal]. *Startupreneur Business Digital*, 1(1), 11–22. 10.33050/sabda.v1i1.71

Suryono, R. R., Budi, I., & Purwandari, B. (2020). Challenges and trends of finacnail technology (fintech): A systematic literature review. *Information (Basel)*, 11(12), 590–610. 10.3390/info11120590

Swan, M. (2015). *Blockchain: blueprint for a new economy*. O'Reilly Media.

Thottoli, M. M. (2023). *The tactician role of Fintech in the accounting and auditing field: A bibliometric analysis*. Qualitative Research in Financial Markets.

Unal, I. M., & Aysan, A. F. (2022). Fintech, digitalization, and blockchain in Islamic finance: Retrospective investigation. *FinTech*, 1(4), 388–398. 10.3390/fintech1040029

U.S. Securities and Exchange Commission (SEC). (2024). *SEC Overview*. SEC. https://www.sec.gov/about

Utami, A. F., & Ekaputra, I. A. (2021). A paradigm shifts in financial landscape: Encouraging collaboration and innovation among Indonesian FinTech lending players. *Journal of Science and Technology Policy Management*, 12(2), 309–330. 10.1108/JSTPM-03-2020-0064

Vasista, K. (2021). Regulatory compliance and supervision of artificial intelligence, machine learning and also possible effects on financial institutions. *International Journal of Innovative Research in Computer and Communication Engineering*, 2320-9801.

Vasquez, O., & San-Jose, L. (2022). Ethics in fintech through users' confidence: Determinants that affect trust. *Journal of Applied Ethics*, (13).

Vergara, C. C., & Agudo, L. F. (2021). Fintech and sustainability: Do they affect each other? *Sustainability*, 13(13), 1–19.

Xia, H., Lu, D., Lin, B., Nord, J. H., & Zhang, J. Z. (2023). Trust in fintech: Risk, governance, and continuance intention. *Journal of Computer Information Systems*, 63(3), 648–662. 10.1080/08874417.2022.2093295

Zhang, W., Siyal, S., Riaz, S., Ahmad, R., Hilmi, M. F., & Li, Z. (2023). Data Security, customer trust and intention for adoption of fintech services: An empirical analysis from commercial bank users in Pakistan. *SAGE Open*, 13(3), 21582440231181388. 10.1177/21582440231181388

Zhang-Zhang, Y., Rohlfer, S., & Rajasekera, J. (2020). An eco-systematic view of cross-sector Fintech: The case of Alibaba and Tencent. *Sustainability (Basel)*, 12(21), 8907. 10.3390/su12218907

Chapter 13
Why Do People Fall Prey to Chit Fund Scams in India?

Vanisha Godara
https://orcid.org/0000-0003-0878-9221
School of Behavioural Sciences and Forensic Investigations, Rashtriya Raksha University, India

Naveen Kumar Singh
https://orcid.org/0000-0001-7133-900X
School of Behavioural Sciences and Forensic Investigations, Rashtriya Raksha University, India & INTI International University, Malaysia

ABSTRACT

Chit fund schemes have historically been highly popular options for side investing when it comes to savings in Inida. Newspaper headlines about the failure of these funds and the misfortune of gullible investors frequently appear. Since there are thousands of cases of fraud, these media reports have not received much attention up until now. However, several scams involving thousands of crores of rupees have surfaced in recent years. Therefore, it is necessary to understand why people fall victim to these chit-fund scams. A customized questionnaire was used to gather data through convenient sampling to measure public knowledge about financial offense types, illegal chit-fund companies, and financial crime reporting. The findings showed that, compared to older individuals, the majority of investors, who are in the 18–35 age range, had a better understanding of chit-fund schemes. This study may further help to create laws and educate investors aimed at stopping and dealing with these types of scams.

DOI: 10.4018/979-8-3693-3633-5.ch013

INTRODUCTION

An economy's ability to deploy its domestic savings is a key factor in its growth and financial stability. People used to set aside a portion of their money for emergencies as well as future necessities. The money so saved must be used to support profitable endeavors to accelerate the economic growth of a nation. Three sectors contribute to India's domestic savings: the public sector, the business sector, and the household sector (Johnson, 2013). Previously, only the wealthy and well-connected could invest money. Nonetheless, it is now well-known and well-liked by individuals from many sectors of society (Infanta & Antony, 2019). One person's investment portfolio could differ from another person's portfolio. They are making a range of investments with different return expectations. Investments are advantageous and required in the context of the modern world and way of living. Several factors impact investing decisions, including increased life expectancy, preparing for retirement, tax burdens, with inflation being high, and the availability of a variety of investment options. (Raji, 2023).

Investors are nevertheless captivated by the services provided by operators in the unorganized financial markets, regardless of the growth of the structured financial markets. One of the main causes of the investors' tendency toward such behavior might be financial ignorance. Some have taken advantage of this low level of financial literacy or illiteracy, which has eventually resulted in many financial scams around the nation (Jain, and Venkatesh,2022). Among these operators, chit funds operate both in an organized and unorganized manner. These financial products provide you with the ability to borrow money and save at the same time. Traditionally, they have operated in an uncontrolled manner inside exclusive circles or groups of friends, family, business acquaintances, etc. who share some sort of shared interest in the plan.

To help borrowers and investors achieve their financial goals, chit funds serve as a sort of financial intermediary. Before the development of banking, chit-funds were a common form of traditional finance. Although the Rotating Savings and Credit Association (ROSCA) system is available in other countries, it is only in India that its activities are subject to legal regulations. Chit funds are overseen under the Chit Fund Act of 1982, which is managed by the relevant State governments. These are classed as Miscellaneous Nonbanking Financial Institutions under the Reserve Bank of India Act, 1934. For those who just intend to make tiny savings, this system is the best choice since it has several built-in benefits, such as a dividend without taxation, simple availability, easy-to-use services, etc. It also has no hidden costs, monthly interest rate increases, or pre-closure fees. When compared to other financial instruments, chit funds are a unique kind of borrowing and saving mechanism. (Arrawatia & Pande, 2015).

BACKGROUND OF THE STUDY

Several research articles were gathered for the literature review from various databases. Using the advanced search option, the research article was found using keywords like "awareness", "chit-fund scams", and "chit-fund frauds". The chosen research article's publication spans between 2000 – 2024, providing up-to-date knowledge and optimizing study time. There is a dearth of pertinent empirical studies related to chit-fund activities carried out in India. Even so, some pertinent research about the operations of chit funds has been examined, and the results are included in this part of the review of the literature. The absence of strict regulations and laws presently in place along with the vast number of unbanked people who have invested in chit funds made it easier for fraudsters to perpetrate frauds. Investment in Tripura chit funds was enticed by the state's lack of industrialization, huge commissions, and outrageous interest rates provided by chit-fund businesses (Deb, 2014). According to the report, the reasons for these frauds include extreme greed, a lack of government small investment programs, several rules, political favoritism, a weak Chit Fund Act, a culture of rule violation, and auditor-auditee nexus. The study also suggested that investors are more likely to invest in chit funds than traditional banking systems due to a lack of financial understanding and strict banking procedures (Deb, 2014). On the other hand, several reasons helped the Saradha Group's unregistered chit-fund grow its market share, such as a) A state with an employment rate of barely 11%, where people were drawn to chit-fund schemes because they offered quick and cheap money. b) The fines and limitations for unregistered chit funds were unduly generous (Pande, 2017).

Surprisingly, Jain and Venkatesh (2022) published in their research that Investors in chit funds are often less financially literate than non-investors. The financial literacy among the chit-fund investors varies between a) high to average levels (those who select registered funds exhibit); and b) medium to low levels (those who select unregistered funds). Moreover, there is a significant correlation between investors' levels of financial literacy and their age, gender, and marital status, as well as their educational background and employment status. Sometimes, even if investors are aware of investing trends, they don't appear to have a thorough understanding of all the available investment options (Raji, 2023). People are unable to discriminate between an unregistered chit-fund firm and an enrolled chit-fund company, both of which are safe and legal, according to Gupta, P. S. (2014). Due to a lack of knowledge about money and investing, our nation's rural economies still rely on tiny savings programs administered by the government. Investors being more vulnerable to the peculiarities of chit-fund businesses are a result of their lack of financial literacy and expertise, and the anticipation of earning higher returns and commission drew investors to chit-funds (Mallick and Sahoo, 2016). Women usually choose low-risk or risk-free investment opportunities. Women tend hesitant to invest in riskier routes mostly due to a lack of information (Harini and Savithri, 2021). Political parties' connections to chit-fund businesses and regulatory system weaknesses made it easier for fraudsters to carry out their schemes. Regulatory obstacles that chit businesses face as a result of the strict regulations that the government is gradually planning have hampered the industry's ability to flourish. The result of the registered chit firms' higher operating costs has been to drive these businesses "underground". Recent years have seen a large number of businesses fail or completely move their activities into the unofficial sphere, becoming "unregistered" chit funds. The unorganized chit fund sector is enormous and still expanding. Not only does this result in major issues for the sector and its players, but it also produces financial losses for the government (Panigrahi and Gaur,2014).

Pramod, A. V. (2020) with his research added that the Indian government and its financial institutions are always attempting to introduce new programs that motivate people to save. Because financial inclusion has been a hot topic for the past five years, the government feels that it is critical to increase the use of chit funds and to educate and aware the public of their benefits and insight about red flags indicating the fraudulent chit fund scheme. Chit funds are primarily managed by financial institutions that are subject to regulations. In conclusion, with the growing middle class choosing to set aside a certain amount each month for savings, a well-informed chit fund might be a valuable choice for savings.

Based on a preliminary review of the literature, it appears that the majority of the research on chit funds in India focuses on comparison studies between regulated and unregulated funds, scams, the use of chit funds as a means of financing the underprivileged, etc. The degree of financial knowledge and awareness among different age groups of the public on the risks involved with these chit-fund schemes or how to report them if one becomes a victim is rarely discussed in the literature currently. Hence, the objective of this research is to examine the awareness of chit-fund scams among different age groups of people. The hypothesis framed for this study is that the chit-fund investors of the age group above 45 years are comparatively less financially literate and aware than the other age group investors.

Model for Chit Fund Operations

Chit refers to any transaction in which an individual enters into a contract with a specific number of people, under which each subscriber agrees to contribute a certain amount of money (or a specific amount of grain) through periodic installments over a predetermined period of time. Each subscriber will then be entitled to the prize amount in turn, as determined by lot, by bidding, by tender, or in any other manner that may be mentioned in the chit contract (Panigrahi & Gaur, 2014). By adjusting the resulting monthly installments, the subscribers evenly share the remaining money, which is considered a surplus from which the chit organizer receives a fee or commission. The subscriber who placed first in the auction is prohibited from participating in the next auction or "pot" bidding, and they must continue to pay the monthly installment until the scheme's expiration. Each month, the 'pot' value is distributed to each subscriber as a result of this procedure being repeated. (Manoja et al., 2021). People are readily tricked into falling victim to these types of funding by the get-rich-quick claims. Therefore, one of the main reasons why individuals engage in chit-funds is their demand for greater interest rates and cash. Many consumers are drawn to these fund plans because of their simple investment requirements. Most significantly, a large number of people in backward areas participate in chit-funds due to a lack of advancement, inadequate information, and simple savings options. This increases the possibility that fraudsters would use chit-money for fraudulent purposes or commit chit-fund scams (Sarkar, 2015).

Figure 1. Chit fund operation model

(Source: Author)

Chit Fund Scams in India

There has been a sharp increase in the number of bogus chit fund activities in recent years. By enticing them with promises of high interest rates and profits, they are targeting the lower and middle classes. Despite the number of phony businesses and scams that have been identified, people continue to fall victim to these kinds of operations. These businesses are observant and fast to change their ways in response to business and customer information regarding their existing practices as well as to lower the possibility of law enforcement notice and inquiry. Before investing in such questionable businesses, people should be more cautious and aware (Gochhait and Tripathy, 2015). People who are financially literate are more equipped to identify warning signs, evaluate investment possibilities, and make well-informed judgments. By spreading awareness, people may become economically savvy and safeguard the money they have saved from being taken away from them by fraudulent chit fund scams. A knowledgeable public discourages financial fraud and makes society more robust and watchful against the persistent threats in the financial sector.

RESEARCH DESIGN

The core statistics serve as the foundation for much modern research. For this study, a descriptive research design was employed to assess the level of knowledge regarding chit-fund scams among the general public in India. A customized questionnaire was designed to collect primary data from individuals. The method of online survey provides a practical and easily accessible method of gathering data, enabling a wide audience across various demographics. The questionnaire included Likert-type questions to gauge respondents' knowledge levels, investment patterns, and experiences with chit funds to contribute to a thorough understanding of public awareness in this area. Key demographic variables such as gender, age group, occupation, education level, and chit-fund involvement were also recorded. All data were collected directly from respondents' responses.

The primary data is from individuals aged 18 to 55 and above, encompassing various states of India. Our target population was individuals of different age groups, different educational backgrounds, and different occupations from different states of India. A total of 72 respondents were selected using a convenient sampling procedure. The primary data was collected using the convenient sampling method. The convenient sampling method was used to make the research free from biases as this is a non-probability sampling method where units are selected for inclusion in the sample because they are the easiest for the researcher to access. Data was gathered via a circulating questionnaire that continued for two months. To optimize exposure and guarantee participation from a varied audience, a customized questionnaire was shared on several social media portals.

The questionnaire was thoughtfully designed to gather significant data on opinions and awareness of chit-fund fraud. It tested participants' knowledge of chit-fund fraud schemes, their confidence in spotting fraudulent activity, and their encounters with or knowledge of victims of fraud.

With the help of SPSS, statistical analysis is carried out utilizing descriptive statistics (such as mean, percentage, standard deviation, etc.). Pie charts and bar graphs are used to visually display demographic data, such as age, gender, state, and so on, for greater understanding. Tests such as cross-tabulation were also applied to observe the relation between the variables. The process of thematic analysis is used to determine the problem and the people's shared concerns based on the responses they provided. Further suggestions are made to the government, businesses, and investors to communicate information and prevent chit-fund fraud.

We made a great effort to gather data and make sure that moral commitments were met. Ethical considerations include knowing the institutional review board's ethical authorization procedure, obtaining pre-informed consent, and protecting participant rights, including the right to fair treatment, confidentiality, and privacy, as well as the freedom from discomfort and harm.

DATA ANALYSIS

Table 1. Number of responses collected belonging to different demographic variable

Variables	Parameter	No. of Responses	Percentage
Gender	Male	42	58.3
	Female	30	41.7
Age	18- 35 yrs.	65	90.3
	36- 45 yrs.	4	5.6
	46- 55 yrs.	2	2.8
	56 and above	1	1.4
Highest Education Qualification	Any Diploma	4	5.6
	high school or less	10	13.9
	Bachelor's degree	29	40.3
	Postgraduate degree or higher studies	29	40.3
Occupation	Business person	2	2.8
	Employee	7	9.7
	Student	60	83.3
	Unemployed	1	1.4
	Other	2	2.8

Why Do People Fall Prey to Chit Fund Scams in India?

Using a questionnaire that included demographic information such as gender, age, employment, and greatest level of education, a total of 72 responses were gathered. 30 responses were from women, while 42 were from men. 93.3% of the participants are in the 18–35 years age category. Very few of the participants were older than 56. Most participants hold bachelors or master's degrees and are well-educated. Among the total number of participants involved, 60 are students, and relatively few are employees or business people.

Figure 2. No. of responses collected from different states across India

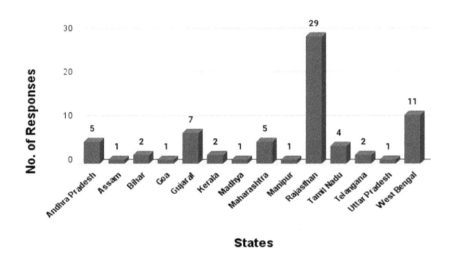

The majority of responses came from Rajasthan, followed by Gujarat and West Bengal. There were 29 Rajasthani, 11 West Bengal people, 7 Gujarati people, 5 Andhra Pradesh and Maharashtra residents, 4 Tamil Nadu residents, 2 Telangana, Kerala, and Bihar residents, and 1% of Assam, Goa, Madhya Pradesh, Manipur, and Uttar Pradesh residents. There were no responses received from the remaining Indian states.

Figure 3. No. of people aware about chit fund scheme

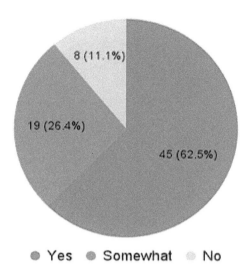

Figure 3 depicts that 62.5% people have the clear understanding of the chit fund scheme whereas 26.4% people have a little knowledge about the same. Only 11.1% of the population is totally unaware of the scheme.

Figure 4. Source of information of people about chit fund scheme

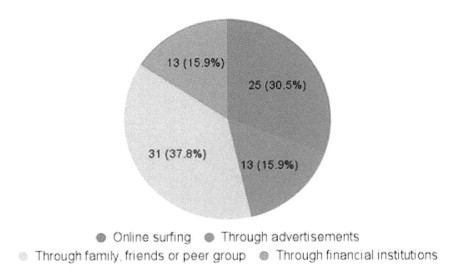

Figure 4 shows that with a total of 37.8%, friends, family, and peer groups are the main sources of information concerning chit-fund schemes. 35% of individuals learned about the scheme via surfing the internet, followed by 15.9% through advertisement and 15.9% through financial institutions.

Cross Tabulation

Cross-tabulation, also known as contingency table analysis or crosstabs, is a statistical method that uses a two-dimensional table to compare the results of one or more variables with the results of another.

Table 2. Cross-tabulation between investors and cases reported

		Reported Ever		Total
		No	Yes	
Age	18- 35 yrs.	50	15	65
	36- 45 yrs.	3	1	4
	46- 55 yrs.	1	1	2
	56 and above	1	0	1
Total		55	17	72

Table 2 shows that just 23.6% of investors notified the appropriate authorities about a potential chit-fund scam. Merely 1.4% of those over 35 reported frauds, whereas 10.5% of them were in the 18–35 age group.

Table 3. Cross-tabulation between demographic variable age and understanding of chit fund scheme

		Understand_chitfund			Total
		No	Somewhat	Yes	
Age	18- 35 yrs.	5	17	43	65
	36- 45 yrs.	3	1	0	4
	46- 55 yrs.	0	0	2	2
	56 and above	0	1	0	1
Total		8	19	45	72

Table 3 demonstrates that the majority of investors in the 18–35 group are aware of the workings of chit-fund schemes. Individuals above 35 years are seen to lack understanding of the scheme.

Table 4. Cross-tabulation between demographic variable age and familiarity with term chit fund

		Familier CFF			Total
		No	Somewhat	Yes	
Age	18- 35 yrs	10	13	42	65
	36- 45 yrs	2	0	2	4
	46- 55 yrs	1	0	1	2
	56 and above	0	0	1	1
Total		13	13	46	72

Table 4 reveals the low level of familiarity with chit-fund fraud among investors over the age of 56. Since 55 out of 65 participants are aware of the deception, those in the 18–35 age range are quite familiar. Chit fund scam is also known to 50% of those in the 36–45 age range.

Why Do People Fall Prey to Chit Fund Scams in India?

Table 5. Cross-tabulation between investment and checking the legitimacy of the scheme

		Check Legitimacy			Total
		No	Sometimes	Yes	
Investment	No	35	5	14	54
	Not sure	2	4	0	6
	Yes	1	1	10	12
Total		38	10	24	72

Table 5 shows that majority of the participants who invests, check the legitimacy of chit-fund schemes before investing in it. More than 50% of participants who does not invest are not concerned by the legitimacy of the scheme.

Table 6. Cross-tabulation between investment and preferred agencies by the investors

		Agencies Prefer				
		Corporate Society Agencies	Government and Semi Government Agencies	Not bothered about the type of agency	Private Agencies	
Investment	No	1	39	10	4	54
	Not sure	1	5	0	0	6
	Yes	1	8	2	1	12
Total		3	52	12	5	72

Table 7. Cross-tabulation between investors and victims

Investment * Victim Ever Crosstabulation				
		Victim Ever		Total
		No	Yes	
Investment	No	44	10	54
	Not sure	4	2	6
	Yes	2	10	12
Total		50	22	72

According to Table 6, the majority of investors (72.2%) favor investing in government and semi-government agencies. 16.6% of respondents doesn't give enough thought about the kind of agency they are investing in. Investors have the least preference for Corporate Society agencies.

Table 7 demonstrates that the vast majority of chit-fund scheme investors fell victim to CFF (chit-fund fraud). 13.8% of participants have not made any investments in the program, but they have seen fraud with friends or family. A total of 2.77% of respondents are unsure about the fraudulent scam.

Table 8. Cross-tabulation between investors and awareness of reporting

		Aware Reporting		Total
		No	Yes	
Investment	No	30	24	54
	Not sure	4	2	6
	Yes	3	9	12
Total		37	35	72

About 75% of investors are aware of the process for reporting fraud, as seen in Table 8. Merely 8.3% of the respondents are uncertain or unaware of the process for reporting fraudulent activity.

Table 9. Cross-tabulation between victims and reporting of cases

		Reported_Ever		Total
		No	Yes	
Victim_Ever	No	45	5	50
	Yes	10	12	22
Total		55	17	72

According to Table 9, 46% of the participants have never reported a possible chit-fund scam to the appropriate authorities. Merely 16.6% of the victims have notified the authorities about the fraudulent activity.

Table 10. Cross-tabulation between investors and awareness about legal regulatory and governing authorities

		Aware_Regulations			Total
		No	Not sure	Yes	
Investment	No	26	14	14	54
	Not sure	3	3	0	6
	Yes	2	1	9	12
Total		31	18	23	72

According to Table 10, the majority of investors are aware of the chit fund scheme's legal, regulatory, and governing bodies. The majority of non-investors are unaware of the regulating and controlling bodies.

RESULT AND DISCUSSION

According to the data collected from the target population through the convenient sampling method, it is observed that a considerable portion of the population is vaguely aware of the chit-fund plan, but the majority understands it rather well. There aren't many individuals there who don't know anything about the scheme. Friends, family, and peer groups are the main sources of information concerning chit-fund schemes. Financial institutions and advertisements are the next two main sources from which people learned about the scheme. Because most investors in the 18–35 age range are familiar with chit-fund schemes and how they work, the younger generation is likely more knowledgeable about investment schemes than older generations.

There is a clear need for increased awareness programs for senior citizens because relatively few investors over the age of 56 are aware of chit-fund fraud. Before participating in a chit-fund scheme, the majority of investors investigate its legitimacy. The majority of investors favor investing with government and semi-government agencies. A large proportion of investors in the chit-fund scam fell prey to chit-fund fraud (CFF), demonstrating their ignorance of the warning signs of fraudulent schemes. About 75% of investors are aware of how to report fraudulent activity. Despite this, 46% of the victims have not notified the appropriate authorities of a possible chit-fund scam. Approximately 75% of investors are aware of the laws and agencies that control chit-fund operations.

IMPLICATION AND SUGGESTIONS

- **For Government**
  1) The present study's findings reveal that most individuals think that chit-fund fraud is a common problem in their locality or area. This issue highlights the necessity to strengthen the regulatory and enforcement framework.
  2) The government should organize awareness efforts to raise financial literacy and make sure people are aware of the warning signs of fraudulent schemes.
  3) Using technology like online monitoring systems and collaborating with local law enforcement might also be beneficial.

4) To prevent these fraudulent instances, a specialized task force must be formed to look into, prosecute, and impose severe penalties on cases of chit-fund fraud.

- **For companies and regulatory bodies**
  1) According to the survey, individuals believe there is insufficient regulatory supervision and are concerned about ineffective transparency regulations. Thus, it is recommended that companies adhere to compliance and transparency guidelines.
  2) It is advised that the company make all of its claims and offers clear and transparent; there should be no deception.
  3) There shouldn't be any participant data breaches in chit fund operations. The data must be secured and not be utilized for any other purpose.
  4) Regulations and norms have to be easily enforced.
- **For investors**

  1) To be completely aware of all of these fraudulent investment schemes, investors should take part in as many awareness initiatives as possible.
  2) They should be aware of all the warning indicators and red flags that indicate fraud.
  3) They should be aware of how to report any fraud that occurs.
  4) Out of a desire for bigger profits, they shouldn't invest in any unregulated and disorganized chit-fund operations.
  5) If they are looking for any type of information on investment plans, they should visit official websites.

LIMITATIONS AND FUTURE SCOPE

The information gathered reflects the attitudes and views of the respondents, which may differ based on their personal experiences, preconceived notions, or degree of knowledge regarding chit-fund schemes. The applicability of the findings is limited since the chosen sample and the respondents' geographic dispersion could not be taken as a representative sample of the Indian population as a whole. Because of the time restrictions, only a few responses were received. The sole aspect that this study's methodology contained was gathering responses about the awareness of chit-fund fraud; deeper surveys, disclosures of the entire scope of people's knowledge of, or identification of the real information source were not included.

Why Do People Fall Prey to Chit Fund Scams in India?

Surveys and individualized interviews with people in each state of India can be used in the future to get more comprehensive data on this goal. For an improved understanding of the awareness level, the study's sample size and duration can be broadened.

CONCLUSION

According to this study conducted, the age group of 18 to 35 years was found to be more aware of chit-fund scams, but it didn't seem that they had a thorough understanding of the warning indicators and red flags that point to a fraudulent scheme. It was also evident that, despite being aware of the reporting process, the majority of persons had not reported the fraud. They do, however, require motivation in this area, which may be achieved by offering plenty of guidance and creating a simple reporting system. In addition, more campaigns and activities might be launched to educate the public about these types of investment scams.

REFERENCES

Arrawatia, M. A., & Pande, V. (2015). A study of chit funds scams and government initiatives to safeguard investors in India. *Splint International Journal Of Professionals*, 2(11), 37–40.

Deb, R. (2014). An empirical study on chit fund crisis in Tripura. *International Journal of Business Ethics in Developing Economies*, 3(1), 47–57.

Deb, S., & Sengupta, S. (2020). What makes the base of the pyramid susceptible to investment fraud. *Journal of Financial Crime*, 27(1), 143–154. 10.1108/JFC-03-2019-0035

Gochhait, D. S., & Tripathy, D. P. (2015). A case study of Chit fund Scam in India. *IRC's International Journal of Multidisciplinary Research in Society and Management Sciences*, 3(1), 133–137.

Gupta, P. S. (2014). Chit funds as an indian saving scheme: A conceptual study. *International Journal of Business and Administration Research Review*, 2, 44–49.

Harini, R., & Savithri, R. (2021). A study on the investment behavior of working women with reference to Chennai city. *International Journal of Multidisciplinary research in Arts. Science and Commerce*, 1(2), 67–73.

Infanta, A. V., & Antony, K. P. P. (2019). Perceptions of Households and Their Level of Satisfaction towards Chit Funds. *Journal of Emerging Technologies and Innovative Research (JETIR)*, 6.

Jain, A. S., & Venkatesh, S. (2022). A Study on the Financial Literacy Levels amongst Chit Fund Investors with Reference to Bengaluru City. *The Management Accountant Journal*, 57(8), 93–98. 10.33516/maj.v57i8.93-98p

Mallick, S. K., & Sahoo, A. (2016). The Behavioural Finance Aspects of Chit-Fund Scams of Odisha: Loss is almost certain Profit is Not. *International Journal of Business and Management Invention*, 5(8), 71–78.

Manoja, G., Ibrahim, B. M., Vaidheeswaran, S., Kumar, A. S., &Azharudeen, J. S. (2021). A Study on Investment Behavior of Chit Fund Participants.*Journal of Banking, Finance and Insurance Management*, 4(2).

Pande, V. (Ed.). (2017). *Exploring the Reasons behind India's Chit Crisis A Case Study on Corporate Governance Strategies of Saradha Group*. Department of Management & Commerce, Faculty of Management & Humanities, Jayoti Vidyapeeth Women's University.

Panigrahi, A., & Gaur, M. (2014). Chit fund crisis in India is the result of inefficient Indian banking system, an analytical study. *SSRN*, 2686785, 1–31. https://ssrn.com/abstract=2686785. 10.2139/ssrn.2686785

Pramod, A. V. (2020). Individual financial portfolio to channelize capital amount with reference to chit funds and personal loan. [IJM]. *International Journal of Management (Kolkata)*, 11(7).

Raji, S. P. (2023). A Study On Awareness About The Investment Pattern Among The Working Women. In *Virudhunagar District*. Department of Commerce, Bharathiar University.

Santhisree, V. N., & Prasad, J. C. (2014). A Study on Problems of Chit Fund Companies and The Satisfaction Level of the Customers. *Vidwat*, 7(1), 8.

Sarkar, A. (2015). Chit Fund Scam. *Indian Journal of Poultry Science*, 76(3), 384–388.

Singh, R., & Mohapatra, A. D. (2023). Awareness, Causes and Measures for prevention of Corporate Frauds in India-An Empirical Study. [EEL]. *European Economic Letters*, 13(4), 875–903.

Sumithra, N. (2022). Chit Fund an Overview. *International Journal of Early Childhood Special Education*, 14(5).

Compilation of References

Abbasi, A., Sarker, S., & Chiang, R. (2016). Big Data Research in Information Systems: Toward an Inclusive Research Agenda. *Journal of the Association for Information Systems*, 17(2), I–XXXII. 10.17705/1jais.00423

Abdallah, A., Maarof, M. A., & Zainal, A. (2016). Fraud detection system: A survey. *Journal of Network and Computer Applications*, 68, 90–113. 10.1016/j.jnca.2016.04.007

Abdullah, W. N., & Said, R. (2019). Audit and risk committee in financial crime prevention. *Journal of Financial Crime*, 26(1), 223–234. 10.1108/JFC-11-2017-0116

Abraham, F. (2019). *Robo-advisors: Investing through machines*. World Bank Research and Policy Briefs 134881.

Acemoglu, D., & Restrepo, P. (2019). Artificial Intelligence, Automation, and Work. *The Economics of Artificial Intelligence*, 197–236. 10.7208/chicago/9780226613475.003.0008

Achim, M. V., & Borlea, S. N. (2020). Economic and Political Determinants of Economic and Financial Crime. In *Economic and Financial Crime* (pp. 73–176). Springer. 10.1007/978-3-030-51780-9_2

Achim, M. V., Borlea, S. N., & Văidean, V. L. (2021). Does technology matter for combating economic and financial crime? A panel data study. *Technological and Economic Development of Economy*, 27(1), 223–261. 10.3846/tede.2021.13977

Acquaah-Gaisie, G. (2000). Fighting Public Officer and Corporate Crimes. *Journal of Financial Crime*, 8(1), 12–20. 10.1108/eb025962

Adam, H. (2021). Fintech and entrepreneurship boosting in developing countries: A comparative study of India and Egypt. In *The Big Data-Driven Digital Economy: Artificial and Computational Intelligence* (pp. 141–156). Springer International Publishing. 10.1007/978-3-030-73057-4_12

Adrian, T., & Ferreira, C. (2023). Mounting cyber threats mean financial firm urgently need better safeguards. *International Monetary Fund*. https://www.imf.org/en/Blogs/Articles/2023/03/02/mounting-cyber-threats-mean-financial-firms-urgently-need-better-safeguards

Compilation of References

Aftabi, S. Z., Ahmadi, A., & Farzi, S. (2023). Fraud detection in financial statements using data mining and GAN models. *Expert Systems with Applications*, 227, 120144. 10.1016/j.eswa.2023.120144

Agarwal, A., Gans, J., & Goldfarb, A. (2018) *Economic policy for artificial intelligence. National Bureau of Economic Research*. University of Chicago Press. https://doi.org/10.1086/699935

Agarwal, S., & Chakrabarti, R. (2019). Digital financial inclusion and Ponzi scheme awareness in India. *Financial Counseling and Planning*, 30(2), 279–291.

Agrawal, A., Gans, J., & Goldfarb, A. (2019). *The Economics of Artificial Intelligence*. University of Chicago Press. 10.7208/chicago/9780226613475.001.0001

Ahmad, M., Majeed, A., Khan, M. A., Sohaib, M., & Shehzad, K. (2021). Digital financial inclusion and economic growth: Provincial data analysis of China. *China Economic Journal*, 14(3), 291–310. 10.1080/17538963.2021.1882064

Ahmad, T., Zhang, D., Huang, C., Zhang, H., Dai, N., Song, Y., & Chen, H. (2021). Artificial intelligence in sustainable energy industry: Status Quo, challenges and opportunities. *Journal of Cleaner Production*, 289, 125834. 10.1016/j.jclepro.2021.125834

Ahmad, T., Zhu, H., Zhang, D., Tariq, R., Bassam, A., Ullah, F., AlGhamdi, A. S., & Alshamrani, S. S. (2022). Energetics Systems and artificial intelligence: Applications of industry 4.0. *Energy Reports*, 8, 334–361. 10.1016/j.egyr.2021.11.256

Ahmed, S., Alshater, M. M., Ammari, A. E., & Hammami, H. (2022). Artificial intelligence and machine learning in fnance: A bibliometric review. *Research in International Business and Finance*, 61.

Ahmed, S., & Sur, S. (2021). Change in the uses pattern of digital banking services by Indian rural MSMEs during demonetization and Covid-19 pandemic-related restrictions. *Vilakshan-XIMB Journal of Management*, 20(1), 166–192.

Ajide, F. M. (2020). Financial inclusion in Africa: Does it promote entrepreneurship? *Journal of Financial Economic Policy*, 12(4), 687–706. 10.1108/JFEP-08-2019-0159

Akter, S., Wamba, S. F., Gunasekaran, A., Dubey, R., & Childe, S. J. (2016). How to Improve Firm Performance Using Big Data Analytics Capability and Business Strategy Alignment? *International Journal of Production Economics*, 182, 113–131. 10.1016/j.ijpe.2016.08.018

Akyuwen, R., Nanere, M., & Ratten, V. (2022). Technology entrepreneurship: Fintech lending in Indonesia. *Entrepreneurial Innovation: Strategy and Competition Aspects*, 151-176.

Alam, N., Gupta, L., Zameni, A., Alam, N., Gupta, L., & Zameni, A. (2019). Fintech regulation. *Fintech and Islamic finance: Digitalization, development and disruption*, 137-158.

Albarrak, M. S., & Alokley, S. A. (2021). FinTech: Ecosystem, Opportunities and Challenges in Saudi Arabia. *Journal of Risk and Financial Management*, 14(10), 10. 10.3390/jrfm14100460

Aldboush, H. H., & Ferdous, M. (2023). Building trust in fintech: An analysis of ethical and privacy considerations in the intersection of big data, AI, and customer trust. *International Journal of Financial Studies*, 11(3), 90. 10.3390/ijfs11030090

AL-Dosari, K., Fetais, N., & Kucukvar, M. (2024). Artificial intelligence and cyber defense system for banking industry: A qualitative study of AI applications and challenges. *Cybernetics and Systems*, 55(2), 302–330. 10.1080/01969722.2022.2112539

Al-Hashedi, K. G., & Magalingam, P. (2021). Financial fraud detection applying data mining techniques: A comprehensive review from 2009 to 2019. *Computer Science Review*, 40, 100402. 10.1016/j.cosrev.2021.100402

Ali, A., Abd Razak, S., Othman, S. H., Eisa, T. A. E., Al-Dhaqm, A., Nasser, M., Elhassan, T., Elshafie, H., & Saif, A. (2022). Financial fraud detection based on machine learning: A systematic literature review. *Applied Sciences (Basel, Switzerland)*, 12(19), 9637. 10.3390/app12199637

Ali, A., Septyanto, A. W., Chaudhary, I., Al Hamadi, H., Alzoubi, H. M., & Khan, Z. F. (2022, February). Applied Artificial Intelligence as Event Horizon Of Cyber Security. In *2022 International Conference on Business Analytics for Technology and Security (ICBATS)* (pp. 1-7). IEEE. 10.1109/ICBATS54253.2022.9759076

Ali, K., Khan, Z., Khan, N., Alsubaie, A.-H. I., Subhan, F., & Kanadil, M. (2016). Performance Evaluation of UK Acquiring Companies in the Pre and Post-Acquisitions Periods. *Asian Journal of Economics and Empirical Research*, 3(2), 130–138. https://ideas.repec.org/a/aoj/ajeaer/v3y2016i2p130-138id220.html. 10.20448/journal.501/2016.3.2/501.2.130.138

Ali, O., Ally, M., & Dwivedi, Y. (2020). The state of play of blockchain technology in the financial services sector: A systematic literature review. *International Journal of Information Management*, 54, 102199. 10.1016/j.ijinfomgt.2020.102199

Alpaydin, E. (2020). *Introduction to machine learning*. MIT press.

Alsaffar, D. M., Almutiri, A. S., Alqahtani, B., Alamri, R. M., Alqahtani, H. F., Alqahtani, N. N., & Ali, A. A. (2020, March). Image encryption based on AES and RSA algorithms. In *2020 3rd International Conference on Computer Applications & Information Security (ICCAIS)* (pp. 1-5). IEEE. 10.1109/ICCAIS48893.2020.9096809

Amara, I., & Khlif, H. (2018). Financial crime, corruption and tax evasion: A cross-country investigation. *Journal of Money Laundering Control*, 21(4), 545–554. 10.1108/JMLC-10-2017-0059

Anagnostopoulos, I. (2018). Fintech and regtech: Impact on regulators and banks. *Journal of Economics and Business*, 100, 7–25. 10.1016/j.jeconbus.2018.07.003

Anastasi, S., Madonna, M., & Monica, L. (2021). Implications of embedded artificial intelligence-machine learning on safety of machinery. *Procedia Computer Science*, 180, 338–343. 10.1016/j.procs.2021.01.171

Compilation of References

Androulaki, E., Camenisch, J., Caro, A. D., Dubovitskaya, M., Elkhiyaoui, K., & Tackmann, B. (2020). Privacy-preserving auditable token payments in a permissioned blockchain system. *Paper presented at the Proceedings of the 2nd ACM Conference on Advances in Financial Technologies*. ACM. 10.1145/3419614.3423259

Angelopoulos, A., Michailidis, E. T., Nomikos, N., Trakadas, P., Hatziefremidis, A., Voliotis, S., & Zahariadis, T. (2019). Tackling faults in the industry 4.0 era—A survey of machine-learning solutions and key aspects. *Sensors (Basel)*, 20(1), 109. 10.3390/s2001010931878065

Anggriawan, R., Susila, M. E., Sung, M. H., & Irrynta, D. (2023). The Rising Tide of Financial Crime: A Ponzi Scheme Case Analysis. *Lex Scientia Law Review*, 7(1), 307–346. 10.15294/lesrev.v7i1.60004

Aoun, A., Ilinca, A., Ghandour, M., & Ibrahim, H. (2021). A review of Industry 4.0 characteristics and challenges, with potential improvements using blockchain technology. *Computers & Industrial Engineering*, 162, 107746. 10.1016/j.cie.2021.107746

Apruzzese, G., Laskov, P., Montes de Oca, E., Mallouli, W., Rapa, L. B., Grammatopoulos, A. V., & Di Franco, F. (2023). The role of machine learning in cybersecurity. *Digital Threats : Research and Practice*, 4(1), 1–38. 10.1145/3545574

Arden, N. S., Fisher, A. C., Tyner, K., Lawrence, X. Y., Lee, S. L., & Kopcha, M. (2021). Industry 4.0 for pharmaceutical manufacturing: Preparing for the smart factories of the future. *International Journal of Pharmaceutics*, 602, 120554. 10.1016/j.ijpharm.2021.12055433794326

Arner, D. W., Barberis, J., & Buckley, R. P. (2017). FinTech, RegTech, and the reconceptualization of financial regulation. *Northwestern Journal of International Law & Business*, 37(3), 371–414.

Arner, D. W., Zetzsche, D. A., Buckley, R. P., & Barberis, J. N. (2019). The Identity Challenge in Finance: From Analogue Identity to Digitized Identification to Digital KYC Utilities. *European Business Organization Law Review*, 20(1), 55–80. 10.1007/s40804-019-00135-1

Arrawatia, M. A., & Pande, V. (2015). A study of chit funds scams and government initiatives to safeguard investors in India. *Splint International Journal Of Professionals*, 2(11), 37–40.

Asadollahi-Yazdi, E., Couzon, P., Nguyen, N. Q., Ouazene, Y., & Yalaoui, F. (2020). Industry 4.0: Revolution or Evolution? *American Journal of Operations Research*, 10(06), 241–268. 10.4236/ajor.2020.106014

Ashta, A., & Herrmann, H. (2021). Artificial intelligence and fintech: An overview of opportunities and risks for banking, investments, and microfinance. *Strategic Change*, 30(3), 211–222. 10.1002/jsc.2404

Assocham. (2021). *Awareness about Ponzi Schemes and Pyramids in India*. Associated Chambers of Commerce and Industry of India.

Aswathy, S., & Tyagi, A. K. (2022). *Privacy Breaches through Cyber Vulnerabilities: Critical Issues, Open Challenges, and Possible Countermeasures for the Future Security and Privacy-Preserving Techniques in Wireless Robotics*. CRC Press. 10.1201/9781003156406-14

Aulia, M., Yustiardhi, A. F., & Permatasari, R. O. (2020). An overview of Indonesian regulatory framework on Islamic financial technology (fintech). *Jurnal Ekonomi & Keuangan Islam*, 64-75.

Awan, U., Sroufe, R., & Shahbaz, M. (2021). Industry 4.0 and the circular economy: A literature review and recommendations for future research. *Business Strategy and the Environment*, 30(4), 2038–2060. 10.1002/bse.2731

Azulay, D. (2019). *Artificial Intelligence in Finance – a Comprehensive Overview*. Boston: Emerj: The AI Research and Advisory Company. 10.1007/s43546-023-00618-x

Babones, S. (2017). *The Australian Securities Exchange endorses the distributed ledger—but don't call it blockchain.*

Baddam, P. R., Vadiyala, V. R., & Thaduri, U. R. (2018). Unraveling Java's Prowess and Adaptable Architecture in Modern Software Development. *Global Disclosure of Economics and Business*, 7(2), 97–108. 10.18034/gdeb.v7i2.710

Baddam, P. R., Yerram, S. R., Varghese, A., Ande, J., Goda, D., & Mallipeddi, S. (2023). From Cashless Transactions to Cryptocurrencies: Assessing the Impact of Digitalization on Financial Security. *Asian Accounting and Auditing Advancement*, 14(1), 31–42.

Badri, A., Boudreau-Trudel, B., & Souissi, A. S. (2018). Occupational health and safety in the industry 4.0 era: A cause for major concern? *Safety Science*, 109, 403–411. 10.1016/j.ssci.2018.06.012

Bag, S., & Pretorius, J. H. C. (2022). Relationships between industry 4.0, sustainable manufacturing and circular economy: Proposal of a research framework. *The International Journal of Organizational Analysis*, 30(4), 864–898. 10.1108/IJOA-04-2020-2120

Bahrammirzaee, A. (2010). A Comparative Survey of Artificial Intelligence in Finance: Artificial Neural Network, Expert System and Hybrid Intelligence System. *Neural Comput & Applic*. Springer. 10.1109/IC3I56241.2022.10073077

Baicu, C. G., Gârdan, I. P., Gârdan, D. A., & Epuran, G. (2020). The impact of COVID-19 on consumer behavior in retail banking. Evidence from Romania. *Management & Marketing. Challenges for the Knowledge Society*, 15(s1), 534–556.

Baltgailis, J., & Simakhova, A. (2022). The technological innnovations of Fintech companies in ensuring the stability of financial system in pandemic times. *Marketing & Management of Innovations*, 2(1), 55–65. 10.21272/mmi.2022.2-05

Bănărescu, A. (2015). Detecting and preventing fraud with data analytics. *Procedia Economics and Finance*, 32, 1827–1836. 10.1016/S2212-5671(15)01485-9

Bantan, R. A., Ali, A., Naeem, S., Jamal, F., Elgarhy, M., & Chesneau, C. (2020). Discrimination of sunflower seeds using multispectral and texture dataset in combination with region selection and supervised classification methods. *Chaos (Woodbury, N.Y.)*, 30(11), 113142. 10.1063/5.002401733261340

Compilation of References

Bao, Y., Hilary, G., & Ke, B. (2022). Artificial intelligence and fraud detection. *Innovative Technology at the Interface of Finance and Operations*, I, 223–247. 10.1007/978-3-030-75729-8_8

Barboza, F., Kimura, H., & Altman, E. (2017). Machine learning models and bankruptcy prediction. *Expert Systems with Applications*, 83, 405–417. 10.1016/j.eswa.2017.04.006

Barik, R., & Lenka, S. K. (2023). Does financial inclusion control corruption in upper-middle and lower-middle income countries? *Asia-Pacific Journal of Regional Science*, 7(1), 69–92. 10.1007/s41685-022-00269-0

Basu, K. (2018). Markets and Manipulation: Time for a Paradigm Shift? *Journal of Economic Literature*, 56(1), 185–205. 10.1257/jel.20161410

Bayram, O., Talay, I., & Feridun, M. (2022). Can FinTech promote sustainable finance? Policy lessons from the case of Turkey. *Sustainability (Basel)*, 14(19), 12414. 10.3390/su141912414

Belchior, R., Vasconcelos, A., Guerreiro, S., & Correia, M. (2021). A survey on blockchain interoperability: Past, present, and future trends. *ACM Computing Surveys*, 54(8), 1–41. 10.1145/3471140

Bhadra, S., & Singh, K. N. (2023). Ponzi scheme like investment schemes in India–causes, impact and solution. *Journal of Money Laundering Control*, 27(2), 348–362. 10.1108/JMLC-02-2023-0040

Bharti Kumari, J. K. (January 2021). *System Dynamics Approach for Adoption of Artificial Intelligence in Finance.* Springer Nature Singapore.10.1007/978-981-15-8025-3_54

Bhattacharyya, S., Jha, S., Tharakunnel, K., & Westland, J. C. (2011). Data mining for credit card fraud: A comparative study. *Decision Support Systems*, 50(3), 602–613. 10.1016/j.dss.2010.08.008

Bhuiyan, A. B., Ali, M. J., Zulkifli, N., & Kumarasamy, M. M. (2020). Industry 4.0: Challenges, opportunities, and strategic solutions for Bangladesh. *International Journal of Business and Management Future*, 4(2), 41–56. 10.46281/ijbmf.v4i2.832

Bierstaker, J. L., Brody, R. G., & Pacini, C. (2006). Accountants' perceptions regarding fraud detection and prevention methods. *Managerial Auditing Journal*, 21(5), 520–535. 10.1108/02686900610667283

Bin Amin, S., Taghizadeh-Hesary, F., & Khan, F. (2022). Facilitating green digital finance in Bangladesh: Importance, prospects, and implications for meeting the SDGs. In *Green Digital Finance and Sustainable Development Goals* (pp. 143–165). Springer Nature Singapore. 10.1007/978-981-19-2662-4_7

Birnhack, M., & Ahituv, N. (2013). Privacy implications of emerging & future technologies. Privavcy, *SSRN,* 1-49. 10.2139/ssrn.2364396

Blobel, B. (2020, September). Application of industry 4.0 concept to health care. In *pHealth 2020:Proceedings of the 17th International Conference on Wearable Micro and Nano Technologies for Personalized Health* (Vol. 273, p. 23). IOS Press.

BNM. (2017). *Management of Customer Information and Permitted Disclosures*. BNM. https://www.bnm.gov.my/index.php?ch=57&pg=146&ac=633&bb=file

Bodepudi, A., & Reddy, M. (2020). Cloud-Based Biometric Authentication Techniques for Secure Financial Transactions: A Review. *International Journal of Information and Cybersecurity*, 4(1), 1–18.

Bodó, B., & Giannopoulou, A. (2019). *The logics of technology decentralization–the case of distributed ledger technologies Blockchain and Web 3.0*. Routledge.

Böhmecke-Schwafert, M., & García Moreno, E. (2023). Exploring blockchain-based innovations for economic and sustainable development in the global south: A mixed-method approach based on web mining and topic modeling. *Technological Forecasting and Social Change*, 191, 122446. 10.1016/j.techfore.2023.122446

Böhme, R., Christin, N., Edelman, B., & Moore, T. (2015). Bitcoin: Economics, technology, and governance. *The Journal of Economic Perspectives*, 29(2), 213–238. 10.1257/jep.29.2.213

Bokhari, S. A. A., & Myeong, S. (2023). The influence of artificial intelligence on e-Governance and cybersecurity in smart cities: A stakeholder's perspective. *IEEE Access : Practical Innovations, Open Solutions*, 11, 69783–69797. 10.1109/ACCESS.2023.3293480

Bongomin, O., Gilibrays Ocen, G., Oyondi Nganyi, E., Musinguzi, A., & Omara, T. (2020). Exponential disruptive technologies and the required skills of industry 4.0. *Journal of Engineering*, 2020, 1–17. 10.1155/2020/8090521

Borowski, P. F. (2021). Digitization, digital twins, blockchain, and industry 4.0 as elements of management process in enterprises in the energy sector. *Energies*, 14(7), 1885. 10.3390/en14071885

Borowski, P. F. (2021). Innovative processes in managing an enterprise from the energy and food sector in the era of industry 4.0. *Processes (Basel, Switzerland)*, 9(2), 381. 10.3390/pr9020381

Bose, S., & Mukherjee, P. (2012). Investor awareness campaigns by regulatory bodies and non-governmental organizations: Impact and implications. *IIMB Management Review*, 24(3), 139–150.

Bosley, S., & Knorr, M. (2018). Pyramids, Ponzis and fraud prevention: Lessons from a case study. *Journal of Financial Crime*, 25(1), 81–94. 10.1108/JFC-10-2016-0062

Bracken, B. K., Wolcott, J., Potoczny-Jones, I., Mosser, B. A., Griffith-Fillipo, I. R., & Areán, P. A. (2022). Detection and Remediation of Malicious Actors for Studies Involving Remote Data Collection. In *HEALTHINF* (pp. 377-383). ACM. 10.5220/0010805500003123

Brédart, X., & Cultrera, L. (2016). Bankruptcy prediction: The case of Belgian SMEs. *Review of Accounting and Finance*, 15(1), 101–119. 10.1108/RAF-06-2014-0059

Brock, J. K. U., & Von Wangenheim, F. (2019). Demystifying AI: What digital transformation leaders can teach you about realistic artificial intelligence. *California Management Review*, 61(4), 110–134. 10.1177/1536504219865226

Bui, T. H., & Nguyen, V. P. (2022). The Impact of Artificial Intelligence and Digital Economy on Vietnam's Legal System. *International Journal for the Semiotics of Law*. 10.1007/s11196-022-09927-036189171

Bu, Y., Li, H., & Wu, X. (2022). Effective regulations of FinTech innovations: The case of China. *Economics of Innovation and New Technology*, 31(8), 751–769. 10.1080/10438599.2020.1868069

Bygstad, B., Munkvold, B. E., & Volkoff, O. (2016). Identifying Generative Mechanisms through Affordances: A Framework for Critical Realist Data Analysis. *Journal of Information Technology*, 31(1), 83–96. 10.1057/jit.2015.13

Cambridge Centre for Alternative Finance. (2020). Cambridge Judge Business School. https://www.jbs.cam.ac.uk/faculty-research/centres/alternative-finance/

Campbell, T., Knox, M. W., Rowlands, J., Cui, Z. Y. A., & DeJesus, L. (2021). Leadership in FinTech: Authentic leaders as enablers of innovation and competitiveness in financial technology firms. In *Fostering Innovation and Competitiveness with FinTech, RegTech, and SupTech*. IGI Global. 10.4018/978-1-7998-4390-0.ch013

Campbell-Verduyn, M. (2023). Conjuring a cooler world? Imaginaries of improvement in blockchain climate finance experiments. *Environment and Planning C: Politics and Space*.

Cao, L., Yang, Q., & Yu, P. S. (2021). Data science and AI in FinTech: An overview. *International Journal of Data Science and Analytics*, 12(2), 81–99. 10.1007/s41060-021-00278-w

Capgemini Research Institute. (2019). *Smart talk: How organizations and consumer are embracing voice and chat assistance*. Capgemini Research Institute. https://www.capgemini.com/wp-content/uploads/2019/09/Report-%E2%80%93-Conversational-Interfaces_Web-Final.pdf

Casino, F., Lykousas, N., Katos, V., & Patsakis, C. (2021). Unearthing malicious campaigns and actors from the blockchain DNS ecosystem. *Computer Communications*, 179, 217–230. 10.1016/j.comcom.2021.08.023

Catalini, C., & Gans, J. S. (2016). *Some simple economics of the blockchain*. NBER Working Paper, 22952. https://www.nber.org/system/files/working_papers/w22952/w22952.pdf

Chahal, S. (2023). Navigating financial evolution: Business process optimization and digital transformation in the finance sector. *International Journal of Finance*, 8(5), 67–81. 10.47941/ijf.1475

Chander, B., Pal, S., De, D., & Buyya, R. (2022). Artificial intelligence-based internet of things for industry 5.0. *Artificial intelligence-based internet of things systems*, 3-45.

Chandra, D., Ravi, V., & Ravisankar, P. (2010). Support vector machine and wave let neural network hybrid: Application to bankruptcy prediction in banks. *International Journal of Data Mining. Modelling and Management*, 2(1). 10.1504/IJDMMM.2010.031019

Chatterjee, C., & Bose, G. K. (2016). Institutional response to Ponzi schemes in India. *Journal of Financial Crime*, 23(1), 194–209.

Chen, Y., & Volz, U. (2021). Scaling up sustainable investment through blockchain-based project bonds. *Fintech to Enable Development, Investment, Financial Inclusion, and Sustainability.* ADB-IGF Special Working Paper Series.

Cheng, X., Liu, S., Sun, X., Wang, Z., Zhou, H., Shao, Y., & Shen, H. (2021). Combating emerging financial risks in the big data era: A perspective review. *Fundamental Research*, 1(5), 595–606. 10.1016/j.fmre.2021.08.017

Cheng, Y. M. (2021). Will robo-advisors continue? Roles of task-technology fit, network externalities, gratifications, and flow experience in facilitating continuance intention. *Kybernetes*, 50(6), 1751–1783. 10.1108/K-03-2020-0185

Chen, H., Chiang, R. H. L., & Storey, V. C. (2012). Business Intelligence and Analytics: From Big Data to Big Impact. *Management Information Systems Quarterly*, 36(4), 1165–1188. 10.2307/41703503

Chen, J., Liu, Y., & Moallemi, C. C. (2020). Strategic fraud detection in the financial services industry. *Management Science*, 66(9), 4117–4136.

Chen, Y., Lu, Y., Bulysheva, L., & Kataev, M. Y. (2022). Applications of blockchain in industry 4.0: A review. *Information Systems Frontiers*, 1–15. 10.1007/s10796-022-10248-7

Chhabra Roy, N., & Prabhakaran, S. (2023). Internal-led cyber frauds in Indian banks: An effective machine learning–based defense system to fraud detection, prioritization and prevention. *Aslib Journal of Information Management*, 75(2), 246–296. 10.1108/AJIM-11-2021-0339

Chisty, N. M. A., Baddam, P. R., & Amin, R. (2022). Strategic Approaches to Safeguarding the Digital Future: Insights into Next-Generation Cybersecurity. *Engineering International*, 10(2), 69–84. 10.18034/ei.v10i2.689

Choi, D., & Lee, K. (2018). An artificial intelligence approach to financial fraud detection under IoT environment: A survey and implementation. *Security and Communication Networks*, 2018, 2018. 10.1155/2018/5483472

Chong, D. (2017). *All Faculty Scholarship.*, 3120. 10.1093/oso/9780198845553.003.0002

Choudhury, R., & Dasgupta, R. (2014). Socioeconomic factors behind the prevalence of Ponzi schemes in India. *Journal of Financial Crime*, 21(3), 365–381.

Chueca Vergara, C., & Ferruz Agudo, L. (2021). Fintech and sustainability: Do they affect each other? *Sustainability (Basel)*, 13(13), 7012. 10.3390/su13137012

Cioffi, R., Travaglioni, M., Piscitelli, G., Petrillo, A., & De Felice, F. (2020). Artificial intelligence and machine learning applications in smart production: Progress, trends, and directions. *Sustainability (Basel)*, 12(2), 492. 10.3390/su12020492

Climate Policy Initiative. (n.d.). *Expertise in climate finance and policy analysis.* CPI. https://www.climatepolicyinitiative.org/

Compilation of References

Cocco, L., Pinna, A., & Marchesi, M. (2017). Banking on blockchain: Costs savings thanks to the blockchain technology. *Future Internet*, 9(3), 25. 10.3390/fi9030025

Collomb, A., & Sok, K. (2016). Blockchain/distributed ledger technology (DLT): What impact on the financial sector? *Digiworld Economic Journal*, (103).

Cornelli, G., Frost, J., & Mishra, S. (2023). *Regulatory sandboxes and fintech funding: Evidence from the UK*. BIS Working Paper. https://www.bis.org/publ/work901.pdf

Crail, C., & Main, K. (2022). Generally accepted accounting principles (GAAP) guide. *Forbes*. https://www.forbes.com/advisor/business/generally-accepted-accounting-principles-gaap-guide/

Dai, H. N., Wang, H., Xu, G., Wan, J., & Imran, M. (2020). Big Data Analytics for Manufacturing Internet of Things: Opportunities, Challenges and Enabling Technologies. *Enterprise Information Systems*, 14(9–10), 1279–1303. 10.1080/17517575.2019.1633689

Dal Pozzolo, A., Boracchi, G., Caelen, O., Alippi, C., & Bontempi, G. (2017). Credit card fraud detection: A realistic modeling and a novel learning strategy. *IEEE Transactions on Neural Networks and Learning Systems*, 29(8), 3784–3797. 10.1109/TNNLS.2017.273664328920909

Dalal, A., & Samal, B. (2022). Transforming Financial Landscapes: Case Studies on the Positive Disruption of Cross-Border Payments through Ripple. *International Journal of Research Radicals in Multidisciplinary Fields, ISSN: 2960-043X*, 1(2), 77-82.

Dasgupta, D., Akhtar, Z., & Sen, S. (2022). Machine learning in cybersecurity: A comprehensive survey. *The Journal of Defense Modeling and Simulation*, 19(1), 57–106. 10.1177/1548512920951275

Dasgupta, D., Shrein, J. M., & Gupta, K. D. (2019). A survey of blockchain from security perspective. *Journal of Banking and Financial Technology*, 3(1), 1–17. 10.1007/s42786-018-00002-6

Davenport, T. (2012). How 'Big Data' Is Different. *MIT Sloan Management Review*, 54(1), 21–25.

Davradakis, E., & Santos, R. (2019). *Blockchain, FinTechs and their relevance for international financial institutions*. EIB Working Papers.

de la Peña Zarzuelo, I., Soeane, M. J. F., & Bermúdez, B. L. (2020). Industry 4.0 in the port and maritime industry: A literature review. *Journal of Industrial Information Integration*, 20, 100173. 10.1016/j.jii.2020.100173

Deb, R. (2014). An empirical study on chit fund crisis in Tripura. *International Journal of Business Ethics in Developing Economies*, 3(1), 47–57.

Deb, S., & Sengupta, S. (2020). What makes the base of the pyramid susceptible to investment fraud. *Journal of Financial Crime*, 27(1), 143–154. 10.1108/JFC-03-2019-0035

Dell'Erba, M. (2021). Sustainable digital finance and the pursuit of environmental sustainability. *Sustainable Finance in Europe: Corporate Governance, Financial Stability and Financial Markets*, 61-81.

Della Valle, N., D'Arcangelo, C., & Faillo, M. (2024). Promoting pro-environmental choices while addressing energy poverty. *Energy Policy*, 186, 113967. 10.1016/j.enpol.2023.113967

Deloitte Insights. (2018). *The New Physics of Financial Services: Understanding how artificial intelligence is transforming the financial ecosystem*. Deloitte.

Deloitte. (2020). *AI in financial services: A consumer perspective*. Deloitte.

Deloitte. (2020). *Fintech on the brink of further disruption*. Deloitte. https://www2.deloitte.com/content/dam/Deloitte/nl/Documents/financial-services/deloitte-nl-fsi-fintech-report-1.pdf

Deng, L. (2014). A tutorial survey of architectures, algorithms, and applications for deep learning. *APSIPA Transactions on Signal and Information Processing*, 3(1), e2. 10.1017/atsip.2013.9

Despotović, A., Parmaković, A., & Miljković, M. (2023). Cybercrime and Cyber Security in Fintech. In *Digital Transformation of the Financial Industry: Approaches and Applications* (pp. 255–272). Springer International Publishing. 10.1007/978-3-031-23269-5_15

Dey, S., & Mukherjee, A. (2018). Behavioral biases and Ponzi scheme participation: Evidence from India. *Behavioral Science*, 8(2), 19.

Dhar, P. (2020). The carbon impact of artificial intelligence. *Nature Machine Intelligence*, 2(8), 423–425. 10.1038/s42256-020-0219-9

Díaz-Rodríguez, N., Del Ser, J., Coeckelbergh, M., de Prado, M. L., Herrera-Viedma, E., & Herrera, F. (2023). Connecting the dots in trustworthy Artificial Intelligence: From AI principles, ethics, and key requirements to responsible AI systems and regulation. *Information Fusion*, 99, 101896. 10.1016/j.inffus.2023.101896

Dike, H. U., Zhou, Y., Deveerasetty, K. K., & Wu, Q. (2018). Unsupervised learning based on artificial neural network. *RE:view*, 322–327.

Dinesh Arokia Raj, A., Jha, R. R., Yadav, M., Sam, D., & Jayanthi, K. (2024). Role of Blockchain and Watermarking Toward Cybersecurity. In *Multimedia Watermarking: Latest Developments and Trends* (pp. 103–123). Springer Nature Singapore. 10.1007/978-981-99-9803-6_6

Dinh, T. T. A., Liu, R., Zhang, M., Chen, G., Ooi, B. C., & Wang, J. (2018). Untangling blockchain: A data processing view of blockchain systems. *IEEE Transactions on Knowledge and Data Engineering*, 30(7), 1366–1385. 10.1109/TKDE.2017.2781227

Dogan, H., Whittington, P., Apeh, E., & Ki-Aries, D. (2021, July). 1 st Workshop on Diversity, Accessibility and Inclusivity in Cyber Security. In *34th British HCI Workshop and Doctoral Consortium* (pp. 1-4). BCS Learning & Development.

Domashova, J., & Zabelina, O. (2021). Detection of fraudulent transactions using SAS Viya machine learning algorithms. *Procedia Computer Science*, 190, 204–209. 10.1016/j.procs.2021.06.025

Dong, J., Dou, Y., Jiang, Q., & Zhao, J. (2022). Can financial inclusion facilitate carbon neutrality in China? The role of energy efficiency. *Energy*, 251, 123922. 10.1016/j.energy.2022.123922

Dong, Y., & Qin, S. J. (2018). A novel dynamic PCA algorithm for dynamic data modeling and process monitoring. *Journal of Process Control*, 67, 1–11. 10.1016/j.jprocont.2017.05.002

Dremel, C., Herterich, M. M., Wulf, J., & vom Brocke, J. (2020). Actualizing Big Data Analytics Affordances: A Revelatory Case Study. *Information & Management*, 57(1), 103121. 10.1016/j.im.2018.10.007

Duan, Y., Edwards, J. S., & Dwivedi, Y. K. (2019). Artificial intelligence for decision making in the era of Big Data – evolution, challenges and research agenda. *International Journal of Information Management*, 48, 63–71. 10.1016/j.ijinfomgt.2019.01.021

Du, Q., Wu, N., Zhang, F., Lei, Y., & Saeed, A. (2022). Impact of financial inclusion and human capital on environmental quality: Evidence from emerging economies. *Environmental Science and Pollution Research International*, 29(22), 33033–33045. 10.1007/s11356-021-17945-x35025039

Duran, R. E., & Griffin, P. (2020). Smart contracts: Will Fintech be the catalyst for the next global financial crisis? *Journal of Financial Regulation and Compliance*, 29(1), 104–122. 10.1108/JFRC-09-2018-0122

Dwivedi, D., Batra, S., & Pathak, Y. K. (2023). A machine learning based approach to identify key drivers for improving corporate's esg ratings. *Journal of Law and Sustainable Development*, 11(1), e0242. 10.37497/sdgs.v11i1.242

Dwivedi, S. K., Amin, R., & Vollala, S. (2020). Blockchain based secured information sharing protocol in supply chain management system with key distribution mechanism. *Journal of Information Security and Applications*, 54, 102554. 10.1016/j.jisa.2020.102554

Dwivedi, Y. K., Hughes, L., Ismagilova, E., Aarts, G., Coombs, C., Crick, T., Duan, Y., Dwivedi, R., Edwards, J., Eirug, A., Galanos, V., Ilavarasan, P. V., Janssen, M., Jones, P., Kar, A. K., Kizgin, H., Kronemann, B., Lal, B., Lucini, B., & Williams, M. D. (2021). Artificial Intelligence (AI): Multidisciplinary perspectives on emerging challenges, opportunities, and agenda for research, practice and policy. *International Journal of Information Management*, 57, 101994. 10.1016/j.ijinfomgt.2019.08.002

Eastburn, R. W., & Boland, R. J.Jr. (2015). Inside Banks' Information and Control Systems: Post-Decision Surprise and Corporate Disruption. *Information and Organization*, 25(3), 160–190. 10.1016/j.infoandorg.2015.05.001

Ebrahim, R., Kumaraswamy, S., & Abdulla, Y. (2021). FinTech in banks: opportunities and challenges. *Innovative strategies for implementing fintech in banking*, 100-109.

Erlando, A., Riyanto, F. D., & Masakazu, S. (2020). Financial inclusion, economic growth, and poverty alleviation: Evidence from eastern Indonesia. *Heliyon*, 6(10), e05235. 10.1016/j.heliyon.2020.e0523533088971

Espel, T., Katz, L., & Robin, G. (2017). Proposal for protocol on a quorum blockchain with zero knowledge. *Cryptology ePrint Archive*.

European Securities and Markets Authority (ESMA). (2024). *ESMA Overview*. ESMA. https://www.esma.europa.eu/about-esma

Evren, R., & Milson, S. (2024). *The Cyber Threat Landscape: Understanding and Mitigating Risks*. EasyChair.

Fabris, N. (2022). Impact of Covid-19 Pandemic on Financial Innovation, Cashless Society, and Cyber Risk. *ECONOMICS*, 10(1), 73–86. 10.2478/eoik-2022-0002

Fahy, L. A. (2022). Fostering regulator–innovator collaboration at the frontline: A case study of the UK's regulatory sandbox for fintech. *Law & Policy*, 44(2), 162–184. 10.1111/lapo.1218435915781

Fang, H., Chung, C. P., Lu, Y. C., Lee, Y. H., & Wang, W. H. (2021). The impacts of investors' sentiments on stock returns using fintech approaches. *International Review of Financial Analysis*, 77, 77. 10.1016/j.irfa.2021.101858

Farahani, B., Firouzi, F., & Luecking, M. (2021). The convergence of IoT and distributed ledger technologies (DLT): Opportunities, challenges, and solutions. *Journal of Network and Computer Applications*, 177, 102936. 10.1016/j.jnca.2020.102936

Febiryani, W., Kusumasari, T. F., & Fauzi, R. (2021, November). Analysis and Design Of Implementation Guidelines Data Security Management Assessment Techniques Based On DAMA-DMBOKv2. In *2021 IEEE 5th International Conference on Information Technology, Information Systems and Electrical Engineering (ICITISEE)* (pp. 371-375). IEEE. 10.1109/ICITISEE53823.2021.9655782

Felsberger, A., Qaiser, F. H., Choudhary, A., & Reiner, G. (2022). The impact of Industry 4.0 on the reconciliation of dynamic capabilities: Evidence from the European manufacturing industries. *Production Planning and Control*, 33(2-3), 277–300. 10.1080/09537287.2020.1810765

Felzmann, H., Fosch-Villaronga, E., Lutz, C., & Tamò-Larrieux, A. (2020). Towards transparency by design for artificial intelligence. *Science and Engineering Ethics*, 26(6), 3333–3361. 10.1007/s11948-020-00276-433196975

Ferreira, C. M. S., Oliveira, R. A. R., Silva, J. S., & da Cunha Cavalcanti, C. F. M. (2020). Blockchain for Machine to Machine Interaction in Industry 4.0. In da Rosa Righi, R., Alberti, A. M., & Singh, M. (Eds.), *Blockchain Technology for Industry 4.0: Secure, Decentralized, Distributed and Trusted Industry Environment* (pp. 99–116). Springer. 10.1007/978-981-15-1137-0_5

Finance, A. T. C. C. (2015). *Industry 4.0 Challenges and solutions for the digital transformation and use of exponential technologies. Finance, audit tax consulting corporate*. Swiss.

Financial Stability Board (FSB). (2024). *FSB Overview*. FSB. https://www.fsb.org/about/

Flood, J. M. (2021). *Wiley GAAP 2021: Interpretation and application of generally accepted accounting principles* (2nd ed.). Wiley. 10.1002/9781119736202

Compilation of References

Floridi, L., Cowls, J., King, T., & Taddeo, M. (2020). How to design AI for social good: Seven essential factors. *Science and Engineering Ethics*, 26(3), 1771–1793. 10.1007/s11948-020-00213-532246245

Flowerday, S., & Von Solms, R. (2005). Continuous auditing: Verifying information integrity and providing assurances for financial reports. *Computer Fraud & Security*, 2005(7), 12–16. 10.1016/S1361-3723(05)70232-3

Fraga-Lamas, P., Lopes, S. I., & Fernández-Caramés, T. M. (2021). Green IoT and edge AI as key technological enablers for a sustainable digital transition towards a smart circular economy: An industry 5.0 use case. *Sensors (Basel)*, 21(17), 5745. 10.3390/s2117574534502637

Frame, W. S., & White, L. J. (2004). Empirical Studies of Financial Innovation: Lots of Talk, Little Action? *Journal of Economic Literature*, 42(1), 116–144. 10.1257/002205104773558065

Freij, A. (2020). Using technology to support financial services regulatory compliance: Current applications and future prospects of regtech. *Journal of Investment Compliance*, 21(2/3), 181–190. 10.1108/JOIC-10-2020-0033

Friedline, T., & Chen, Z. (2021). Digital redlining and the fintech marketplace: Evidence from US zip codes. *The Journal of Consumer Affairs*, 55(2), 366–388. 10.1111/joca.12297

Friedline, T., Naraharisetti, S., & Weaver, A. (2020). Digital redlining: Poor rural communities' access to fintech and implications for financial inclusion. *Journal of Poverty*, 24(5-6), 517–541. 10.1080/10875549.2019.1695162

Fulop, M. T., Topor, D. I., Ionescu, C. A., Căpu neanu, S., Breaz, T. O., & Stanescu, S. G. (2022). Fintech accounting and Industry 4.0: Future-proofing or threats to the accounting profession? *Journal of Business Economics and Management*, 23(5), 5. 10.3846/jbem.2022.17695

Gadekar, R., Sarkar, B., & Gadekar, A. (2022). Key performance indicator based dynamic decision-making framework for sustainable Industry 4.0 implementation risks evaluation: Reference to the Indian manufacturing industries. *Annals of Operations Research*, 318(1), 189–249. 10.1007/s10479-022-04828-835910040

Gandomi, A., & Haider, M. (2015). Beyond the Hype: Big Data Concepts, Methods, and Analytics. *International Journal of Information Management*, 35(2), 137–144. 10.1016/j.ijinfomgt.2014.10.007

Gautam, A. (2023). The evaluating the impact of artificial intelligence on risk management and fraud detection in the banking sector. *AI. IoT and the Fourth Industrial Revolution Review*, 13(11), 9–18.

Gensler, G., & Bailey, L. (2020). Deep Learning and Financial Stability. SSRN *Electronic Journal*. 10.2139/ssrn.3723132

Ghazi-Tehrani, A. K., & Pontell, H. N. (2022). Comparative CriminologyComparative criminology and White-Collar CrimeWhite-collar crime. In Ghazi-Tehrani, A. K., & Pontell, H. N. (Eds.), *Wayward Dragon: White-Collar and Corporate Crime in China* (pp. 33–49). Springer International Publishing. 10.1007/978-3-030-90704-4_2

Giannino, A., Di Maio, D., & Vianelli, A. (2020). Innovation through regulation: A comprehensive regulatory framework for blockchain-based services and products. *Journal of Financial Compliance*, 3(2), 147–157.

Gikay, A. A. (2019). *European consumer law and blockchain based financial services: a functional approach against the rhetoric of regulatory uncertainty*.

Gochhait, D. S., & Tripathy, D. P. (2015). A case study of Chit fund Scam in India. *IRC's International Journal of Multidisciplinary Research in Society and Management Sciences*, 3(1), 133–137.

Gokoglan, K., Cetın, S., & Bılen, A. (2022). Blockchain technology and its impact on audit activities. *Journal of Economics Finance and Accounting*, 9(2), 72–81. 10.17261/Pressacademia.2022.1567

Goldstein, I., Jiang, W., & Karolyi, G. A. (2019). To Fintech and beyond. *Review of Financial Studies*, 32(5), 1647–1661. 10.1093/rfs/hhz025

Goldstein, M., & Uchida, S. (2016). A comparative evaluation of unsupervised anomaly detection algorithms for multivariate data. *PLoS One*, 11(4), e0152173. 10.1371/journal.pone.015217327093601

Gomber, P., Koch, J. A., & Siering, M. (2018). Digital finance and Fintech: Current research and future research directions. *Journal of Business Economics*, 88(5), 537–580. 10.1007/s11573-017-0852-x

Goodell, J. W., Gurdgiev, C., Karim, S., & Palma, A. (2024). Carbon emissions and liquidity management. *International Review of Financial Analysis*, 95, 103367. 10.1016/j.irfa.2024.103367

Goodell, J. W., Kumar, S., Lim, W. M., & Pattnaik, D. (2021). Artificial intelligence and machine learning in fnance: Identifying foundations, themes and research cluster from bibliometrice analysis. *Journal of Behavioral and Experimental Finance*, 32, 100577. 10.1016/j.jbef.2021.100577

Gottschalk, P. (2010). Categories of financial crime. *Journal of Financial Crime*, 17(4), 441–458. 10.1108/13590791011082797

Goyal, A., & Kumar, S. (2020). Factors influencing Ponzi scheme awareness among college students in Punjab, India. *International Journal of Bank Marketing*, 38(5), 1165–1181.

Gozman, D., & Willcocks, L. (2019). The emerging Cloud Dilemma: Balancing innovation with cross-border privacy and outsourcing regulations. *Journal of Business Research*, 97, 235–256. 10.1016/j.jbusres.2018.06.006

Grice, J. S., & Ingram, R. (2001). Tests of the Generalizability of Altman's Bankruptcy Prediction Model. *Journal of Business Research*, 54(1), 53–61. 10.1016/S0148-2963(00)00126-0

Compilation of References

Gui, Z., Huang, Y., & Zhao, X. (2024). Financial fraud and investor awareness. *Journal of Economic Behavior & Organization*, 219, 104–123. 10.1016/j.jebo.2024.01.006

Gupta, K. P., Manrai, R., & Goel, U. (2019). Factors influencing adoption of payments banks by Indian customers: Extending TAUT with perceived credibility. *Journal of Asia Business Studies*, 13(2), 173–195. 10.1108/JABS-07-2017-0111

Gupta, L., & Sharma, A. (2011). Comparative analysis of Ponzi scheme awareness and regulatory frameworks across different states in India. *Journal of Financial Regulation and Compliance*, 19(4), 387–401. 10.1108/JFRC-07-2020-0067

Gupta, M., & George, J. F. (2016). Toward the Development of a Big Data Analytics Capability. *Information & Management*, 53(8), 1049–1064. 10.1016/j.im.2016.07.004

Gupta, P. S. (2014). Chit funds as an indian saving scheme: A conceptual study. *International Journal of Business and Administration Research Review*, 2, 44–49.

Gupta, R. (2023). Industry 4.0 adaption in indian banking Sector—A review and agenda for future research. *Vision (Basel)*, 27(1), 24–32. 10.1177/09722629219968293697304

Habbal, A., Ali, M. K., & Abuzaraida, M. A. (2024). Artificial Intelligence Trust, Risk and Security Management (AI TRiSM): Frameworks, applications, challenges and future research directions. *Expert Systems with Applications*, 240, 122442. 10.1016/j.eswa.2023.122442

Hamledari, H., & Fischer, M. (2021). Role of blockchain-enabled smart contracts in automating construction progress payments. *Journal of legal affairs and dispute resolution in engineering and construction, 13*(1), 04520038.

Hannig, A., & Jansen, S. (2010). *Financial inclusion and financial stability: Current policy issues*. (ADBI Working Paper No. 259).

Hardy, J., & Bell, P. (2020). Resilience in sophisticated financial crime networks: A social network analysis of the Madoff Investment Scheme. *Crime Prevention and Community Safety*, 22(3), 223–247. 10.1057/s41300-020-00094-7

Harini, R., & Savithri, R. (2021). A study on the investment behavior of working women with reference to Chennai city. *International Journal of Multidisciplinary research in Arts. Science and Commerce*, 1(2), 67–73.

Harris, A. (2018). A conversation with masterminds in blockchain and climate change. In *Transforming climate finance and green investment with blockchains* (pp. 15–22). Academic Press. 10.1016/B978-0-12-814447-3.00002-1

Harsono, I., & Suprapti, I. A. P. (2024). The Role of Fintech in Transforming Traditional Financial Services. [COUNT]. *Accounting Studies and Tax Journal*, 1(1), 81–91. 10.62207/gfzvtd24

Hasan, M. K., Islam, S., Sulaiman, R., Khan, S., Hashim, A. H. A., Habib, S., Islam, M., Alyahya, S., Ahmed, M. M., Kamil, S., & Hassan, M. A. (2021). Lightweight encryption technique to enhance medical image security on internet of medical things applications. *IEEE Access : Practical Innovations, Open Solutions*, 9, 47731–47742. 10.1109/ACCESS.2021.3061710

Hasan, M., Noor, T., Gao, J., Usman, M., & Abedin, M. Z. (2023). Rural consumers' financial literacy and access to FinTech services. *Journal of the Knowledge Economy*, 14(2), 780–804. 10.1007/s13132-022-00936-9

Hassani, H., Silva, E. S., Unger, S., TajMazinani, M., & Mac Feely, S. (2020). Artificial intelligence (AI) or intelligence augmentation (IA): What is the future? *AI*, 1(2), 8. 10.3390/ai1020008

Hassan, M., Aziz, L. A.-R., & Andriansyah, Y. (2023). The role artificial intelligence in modern banking: An exploration of AI-driven approaches for enhanced fraud prevention, risk management, and regulatory compliance. *Reviews of Contemporary Business Analytics*, 6(1), 110–132.

Hassoun, A., Aït-Kaddour, A., Abu-Mahfouz, A. M., Rathod, N. B., Bader, F., Barba, F. J., Biancolillo, A., Cropotova, J., Galanakis, C. M., Jambrak, A. R., Lorenzo, J. M., Måge, I., Ozogul, F., & Regenstein, J. (2023). The fourth industrial revolution in the food industry—Part I: Industry 4.0 technologies. *Critical Reviews in Food Science and Nutrition*, 63(23), 6547–6563. 10.1080/10408398.2022.203473535114860

Hassoun, A., Prieto, M. A., Carpena, M., Bouzembrak, Y., Marvin, H. J., Pallares, N., Barba, F. J., Punia Bangar, S., Chaudhary, V., Ibrahim, S., & Bono, G. (2022). Exploring the role of green and Industry 4.0 technologies in achieving sustainable development goals in food sectors. *Food Research International*, 162, 112068. 10.1016/j.foodres.2022.11206836461323

He, D., Leckow, R. B., Hakasr, V., Griffoli, T. M., Jenkinson, N., Kashima, M., Khiaonarong, T., Rochon, C., & Tourpe, H. (2017). *Fintech and financial services: Initial considerations*. International Monetary Fund.

Hellani, H., Sliman, L., Samhat, A. E., & Exposito, E. (2021). On blockchain integration with supply chain: Overview on data transparency. *Logistics*, 5(3), 46. 10.3390/logistics5030046

Henning, J. (2009). Perspectives on financial crimes in Roman-Dutch law: Bribery, fraud and the general crime of falsity (falsiteyt). *Journal of Financial Crime*, 16(4), 295–304. 10.1108/13590790910993771

Hidajat, T., Primiana, I., Rahman, S., & Febrian, E. (2020). Why are people trapped in Ponzi and pyramid schemes? *Journal of Financial Crime*, 28(1), 187–203. 10.1108/JFC-05-2020-0093

Hilal, W., Gadsden, S. A., & Yawney, J. (2022). Financial fraud: A review of anomaly detection techniques and recent advances. *Expert Systems with Applications*, 193, 116429. 10.1016/j.eswa.2021.116429

Hoang, T. G., Nguyen, G. N. T., & Le, D. A. (2022). Developments in financial technologies for achieving the Sustainable Development Goals (SDGs): FinTech and SDGs. In *Disruptive technologies and eco-innovation for sustainable development* (pp. 1–19). IGI Global. 10.4018/978-1-7998-8900-7.ch001

Hofmann, F., Wurster, S., Ron, E., & Böhmecke-Schwafert, M. (2017). The immutability concept of blockchains and benefits of early standardization. *Paper presented at the 2017 ITU Kaleidoscope: Challenges for a Data-Driven Society*. ITU K. 10.23919/ITU-WT.2017.8247004

Hossain, M. I., Steigner, D. T., Hussain, M. I., & Akther, A. (2024). Enhancing Data Integrity and Traceability in Industry Cyber Physical Systems (ICPS) through Blockchain Technology: A Comprehensive Approach. *arXiv preprint arXiv:2405.04837*.

Hossain, A., Quaresma, R., & Rahman, H. (2019). Investigating factors influencing the physicians' adoption of electronic health record (EHR) in the healthcare system of Bangladesh: An empirical study. *International Journal of Information Management*, 44(1), 76–87. https://www.researchgate.net/publication/351019909_Ethics_on_Robo-advisors_and_its_big_data_Introduction_and_background. 10.1016/j.ijinfomgt.2018.09.016

http://www.aaai.org

Huang, S.-Y., Tsaih, R.-H., & Yu, F. (2014). Topological pattern discovery and feature extraction for fraudulent financial reporting. *Expert Systems with Applications*, 41(9), 4360–4372. 10.1016/j.eswa.2014.01.012

Hua, X., & Huang, Y. (2021). Understanding China's fintech sector: Development, impacts and risks. *European Journal of Finance*, 27(4–5), 321–333. 10.1080/1351847X.2020.1811131

Hughes, A., Park, A., Kietzmann, J., & Archer-Brown, C. (2019). Beyond Bitcoin: What blockchain and distributed ledger technologies mean for firms. *Business Horizons*, 62(3), 273–281. 10.1016/j.bushor.2019.01.002

Husain, A., Karim, S., & Sensoy, A. (2024). Financial fusion: Bridging Islamic and Green investments in the European stock market. *International Review of Financial Analysis*, 94, 103341. 10.1016/j.irfa.2024.103341

Hussein, D. M. E.-D. M., Taha, M. H. N., & Khalifa, N. E. M. (2018). A blockchain technology evolution between business process management (BPM) and Internet-of-Things (IoT). *International Journal of Advanced Computer Science and Applications*, 9(8). 10.14569/IJACSA.2018.090856

IdentityTheft.org© (2024). *2024 Identity Theft Facts and Statistics*. Identity Theft. https://identitytheft.org/statistics/

IFRS Foundation. (2024). *International Financial Reporting Standards (IFRS)*. IFRS. https://www.ifrs.org

Imerman, M. B., & Fabozzi, F. J. (2020). Cashing in on innovation: A taxonomy of FinTech. *Journal of Asset Management*, 21(3), 167–177. 10.1057/s41260-020-00163-4

Infanta, A. V., & Antony, K. P. P. (2019). Perceptions of Households and Their Level of Satisfaction towards Chit Funds. *Journal of Emerging Technologies and Innovative Research (JETIR)*, 6.

International Organization of Securities Commissions (IOSCO). (2024). *IOSCO Overview.* https://www.iosco.org/about/?subsection=about_iosco

Iqbal, M. S., Abd-Alrazaq, A., & Househ, M. (2022). Artificial Intelligence Solutions to Detect Fraud in Healthcare Settings: A Scoping Review. *Advances in Informatics, Management and Technology in Healthcare*, 20–23.

Isaksen, M. (2018). *Blockchain: The Future of Cross Border Payments.* University of Stavanger.

Ivanov, D., Dolgui, A., & Sokolov, B. (2019). The impact of digital technology and Industry 4.0 on the ripple effect and supply chain risk analytics. *International Journal of Production Research*, 57(3), 829–846. 10.1080/00207543.2018.1488086

Jafri, J. A., Amin, S. I. M., Rahman, A. A., & Nor, S. M. (2024). A systematic literature review of the role of trust and security on Fintech adoption in banking. *Heliyon*, 10(1), e22980. 10.1016/j.heliyon.2023.e2298038163181

Jain, V., Agrawal, M., & Kumar, A. (2020). *Performance analysis of machine learning algorithms in credit cards fraud detection.* 86–88.

Jain, A. S., & Venkatesh, S. (2022). A Study on the Financial Literacy Levels amongst Chit Fund Investors with Reference to Bengaluru City. *The Management Accountant Journal*, 57(8), 93–98. 10.33516/maj.v57i8.93-98p

Jakka, G., Yathiraju, N., & Ansari, M. F. (2022). Artificial Intelligence in Terms of Spotting Malware and Delivering Cyber Risk Management. *Journal of Positive School Psychology*, 6(3), 6156–6165.

Jaksic, M., & Marinc, M. (2019). Relationship banking and information technology: The role of artificial intelligence and FinTech. *Risk Management*, 21(1), 1–18. 10.1057/s41283-018-0039-y

Jamil, A. H., Mohd Sanusi, Z., Yaacob, N. M., Mat Isa, Y., & Tarjo, T. (2021). The Covid-19 impact on financial crime and regulatory compliance in Malaysia. *Journal of Financial Crime*, 29(2), 491–505. 10.1108/JFC-05-2021-0107

Jan, A., Salameh, A. A., Rahman, H. U., & Alasiri, M. M. (2024). Can blockchain technologies enhance environmental sustainable development goals performance in manufacturing firms? Potential mediation of green supply chain management practices. *Business Strategy and the Environment*, 33(3), 2004–2019. 10.1002/bse.3579

Javaid, M., Haleem, A., Singh, R. P., Khan, S., & Suman, R. (2021). Blockchain technology applications for Industry 4.0: A literature-based review. *Blockchain: Research and Applications*, 2(4), 100027.

Compilation of References

Javaid, M., Haleem, A., Singh, R. P., Suman, R., & Gonzalez, E. S. (2022). Understanding the adoption of Industry 4.0 technologies in improving environmental sustainability. *Sustainable Operations and Computers*, 3, 203–217. 10.1016/j.susoc.2022.01.008

Javaid, M., Haleem, A., Singh, R. P., Suman, R., & Khan, S. (2022). A review of Blockchain Technology applications for financial services. *BenchCouncil Transactions on Benchmarks. Standards and Evaluations*, 2(3), 100073.

Javaid, M., Haleem, A., Vaishya, R., Bahl, S., Suman, R., & Vaish, A. (2020). Industry 4.0 technologies and their applications in fighting COVID-19 pandemic. *Diabetes & Metabolic Syndrome*, 14(4), 419–422. 10.1016/j.dsx.2020.04.03232344370

Jenweeranon, P. (2023). Digitalisation in finance: Regulatory challenges in selected ASEAN countries. *Banking & Finance Law Review*, 39(3), 507–545.

Jia, L., Xiang, L., & Liu, X. (2019). An improved eclat algorithm based on tissue-like P system with active membranes. *Processes (Basel, Switzerland)*, 7(9), 555. 10.3390/pr7090555

Jobin, A., Ienca, M., & Vayena, E. (2019). The global landscape of AI ethics guidelines. *Nature Machine Intelligence*, 1(9), 389–399. 10.1038/s42256-019-0088-2

Jordan, M. I., & Mitchell, T. M. (2015). Machine learning: Trends, perspectives, and prospects. *Science*, 349(6245), 255–260. 10.1126/science.aaa841526185243

JPMorgan. (2021). *Global e-commerce trends report*. JP Morgon. https://www.jpmorgan.com/content/dam/jpm/treasury-services/documents/global-e-commerce-trends-report.pdf

Kaack, L. H., Donti, P. L., Strubell, E., Kamiya, G., Creutzig, F., & Rolnick, D. (2022). Aligning artificial intelligence with climate change mitigation. *Nature Climate Change, 12*(6), 518–527. 10.1038/s41558-022-01377-7

Kache, F., & Seuring, S. (2017). Challenges and Opportunities of Digital Information at the Intersection of Big Data Analytics and Supply Chain Management. *International Journal of Operations & Production Management*, 37(1), 10–36. 10.1108/IJOPM-02-2015-0078

Kalaiarasi, H., & Kirubahari, S. (2023). Green finance for sustainable development using blockchain technology. In *Green Blockchain Technology for Sustainable Smart Cities* (pp. 167–185). Elsevier. 10.1016/B978-0-323-95407-5.00003-7

Kaluvakuri, S., & Vadiyala, V. R. (2016). Harnessing the Potential of CSS: An Exhaustive Reference for Web Styling. *Engineering International*, 4(2), 95–110. 10.18034/ei.v4i2.682

Kamuangu, P. (2024). A Review on Financial Fraud Detection using AI and Machine Learning. *Journal of Economics. Finance and Accounting Studies*, 6(1), 67–77.

Kamuangu, P. (2024). Advancements of AI and machine learning in Fintech industry (2016-2020). *Journal of Economics. Finance and Accounting Studies*, 6(1), 23–31.

Kapsis, I. (2020). A truly future-oriented legal framework for fintech in the EU. *European Business Law Review*, 31(3), 475–514. 10.54648/EULR2020020

Karanth, S., Benefo, E. O., Patra, D., & Pradhan, A. K. (2023). Importance of artificial intelligence in evaluating climate change and food safety risk. *Journal of Agriculture and Food Research*, 11, 100485. 10.1016/j.jafr.2022.100485

Karim, S., & Lucey, B. M. (2024). BigTech, FinTech, and banks: A tangle or unity? *Finance Research Letters*, 64, 105490. 10.1016/j.frl.2024.105490

Karim, S., Lucey, B. M., Naeem, M. A., & Uddin, G. S. (2022). Examining the interrelatedness of NFTs, DeFi tokens and cryptocurrencies. *Finance Research Letters*, 47, 102696. 10.1016/j.frl.2022.102696

Karisma, K. (2024). Security Challenges in the Application of Blockchain Technology in Energy Trading. *Asian Journal of Law and Policy*, 4(1), 51–75. 10.33093/ajlp.2024.3

Karpoff, J. M. (2021). The future of financial fraud. *Journal of Corporate Finance*, 66, 101694. 10.1016/j.jcorpfin.2020.101694

Kemmler, M., Rodner, E., Wacker, E.-S., & Denzler, J. (2013). One-class classification with gaussian processes. *Pattern Recognition*, 46(12), 3507–3518. 10.1016/j.patcog.2013.06.005

Ke, T. T., & Sudhir, K. (2023). Privacy rights and data security: GDPR and personal data markets. *Management Science*, 69(8), 4389–4412. 10.1287/mnsc.2022.4614

Khan, N., Ali, K., Kiran, A., Mubeen, R., Khan, Z., & Ali, N. (2017). Factors that Affect the Derivatives Usage of Non-Financial Listed Firms of Pakistan to Hedge Foreign Exchange Exposure. *Journal of Banking and Financial Dynamics*, 1(1), 9–20. 10.20448/journal.525/2017.1.1/525.1.9.20

Khanna, K., & Sharma, V. (2024). Business Decision Making with an Analytical Approach: A New Leadership Pattern. In Taneja, S., Ozen, E., Kumar, P., & Kumar, S. (Eds.), *Global Financial Analytics and Business Forecasting*. Nova. 10.52305/NART0833

Kirkos, E., Spathis, C., & Manolopoulos, Y. (2007). Data mining techniques for the detection of fraudulent financial statements. *Expert Systems with Applications*, 32(4), 995–1003. 10.1016/j.eswa.2006.02.016

Komalavalli, C., Saxena, D., & Laroiya, C. (2020). *Overview of blockchain technology concepts Handbook of research on blockchain technology*. Elsevier.

Kong, S. T., & Loubere, N. (2021). Digitally down to the countryside: Fintech and rural development in China. *The Journal of Development Studies*, 57(10), 1739–1754. 10.1080/00220388.2021.1919631

Koomson, I., Villano, R. A., & Hadley, D. (2020). Effect of financial inclusion on poverty and vulnerability to poverty: Evidence using a multidimensional measure of financial inclusion. *Social Indicators Research*, 149(2), 613–639. 10.1007/s11205-019-02263-0

Koteluk, O., Wartecki, A., Mazurek, S., Kołodziejczak, I., & Mackiewicz, A. (2021). How do machines learn? Artificial intelligence as a new era in medicine. *Journal of Personalized Medicine*, 11(1), 32. 10.3390/jpm1101003233430240

Kottmann, K., Huembeli, P., Lewenstein, M., & Acín, A. (2020). Unsupervised phase discovery with deep anomaly detection. *Physical Review Letters*, 125(17), 170603. 10.1103/PhysRevLett.125.17060333156639

Kou, G., Olgu Akdeniz, Ö., Dinçer, H., & Yüksel, S. (2021). Fintech investments in European banks: A hybrid IT2 fuzzy multidimensional decision-making approach. *Financial Innovation*, 7(1), 39. 10.1186/s40854-021-00256-y35024283

KPMG. (2019). *Future ready finance survey 2019: Learn what high performing organizations are doing differently.* KPMG. https://assets.kpmg.com/content/dam/kpmg/xx/pdf/2019/09/kpmg-future-ready-finance-global-survey-2019.pdf

KPMG. (2022). *Pulse of Fintech H2'21.* KPMG. https://assets.kpmg/content/dam/kpmg/xx/pdf/2022/02/pulse-of-Fintech-h2-21.pdf

Kshetri, N. (2021). Blockchain technology for improving transparency and citizen's trust. *Advances in Information and Communication: Proceedings of the 2021 Future of Information and Communication Conference (FICC)*. Springer. 10.1007/978-3-030-73100-7_52

Kujur, T., & Shah, M. A. (2015). *Electronic Banking: Impact.* Risk and Security Issues.

Kumar, T., & Kaur, S. (2023). Evolution of Fintech in Financial Era. *Fintech and Cryptocurrency*, 1-12.

Kumari, A., & Devi, C. (2022). The Impact of FinTech and Blockchain Technologies on Banking and Financial Services. *Technology Innovation Management Review*, 12(1/2), 22010204. 10.22215/timreview/1481

Kumar, K., Zindani, D., & Davim, J. P. (2019). *Industry 4.0: developments towards the fourth industrial revolution.* Springer. 10.1007/978-981-13-8165-2

Kumar, S. H., Talasila, D., Gowrav, M. P., & Gangadharappa, H. V. (2020). Adaptations of Pharma 4.0 from Industry 4.0. *Drug Invention Today*, 14(3).

Kumar, S., & Mallipeddi, R. R. (2022). Impact of cybersecurity on operations and supply chain management: Emerging trends and future research directions. *Production and Operations Management*, 31(12), 4488–4500. 10.1111/poms.13859

Kumar, S., Sharma, D., Rao, S., Lim, W. M., & Mangla, S. K. (2022). Past, present, and future of sustainable finance: Insights from big data analytics through machine learning of scholarly research. *Annals of Operations Research*. 10.1007/s10479-021-04410-835002001

Kurniawan, T. A., Maiurova, A., Kustikova, M., Bykovskaia, E., Othman, M. H. D., & Goh, H. H. (2022). Accelerating sustainability transition in St. Petersburg (Russia) through digitalization-based circular economy in waste recycling industry: A strategy to promote carbon neutrality in era of Industry 4.0. *Journal of Cleaner Production*, 363, 132452. 10.1016/j.jclepro.2022.132452

Kuzior, A. (2022). Technological unemployment in the perspective of Industry 4.0. *Virtual Economics*, 5(1), 7–23. 10.34021/ve.2022.05.01(1)

La Marca, K., & Bedle, H. (2022). Deepwater seismic facies and architectural element interpretation aided with unsupervised machine learning techniques: Taranaki basin, New Zealand. *Marine and Petroleum Geology*, 136, 105427. 10.1016/j.marpetgeo.2021.105427

Lacity, M., Willcocks, L., & Craig, A. (2015). *Robotic process automation at Telefónica O2*. The Outsourcing Unit Working Paper Series, London School of Economics and Political Science. https://www.umsl.edu/~lacitym/TelefonicaOUWP022015FINAL.pdf

Lagarde, C. (2016). Addressing Corruption Openly. In *The Power of Partnership: Selected Speeches by Christine Lagarde, 2011-2019*. eLibrary. https://www.elibrary.imf.org/display/book/9781513509907/ch09.xml

Larcker, D. F., Richardson, S. A., & Tuna, I. (2007). Corporate governance, accounting outcomes, and organizational performance. *The Accounting Review*, 82(4), 963–1008. https://www.jstor.org/stable/30243484. 10.2308/accr.2007.82.4.963

Lashkari, B., & Musilek, P. (2021). A comprehensive review of blockchain consensus mechanisms. *IEEE Access : Practical Innovations, Open Solutions*, 9, 43620–43652. 10.1109/ACCESS.2021.3065880

Laskurain-Iturbe, I., Arana-Landín, G., Landeta-Manzano, B., & Uriarte-Gallastegi, N. (2021). Exploring the influence of industry 4.0 technologies on the circular economy. *Journal of Cleaner Production*, 321, 128944. 10.1016/j.jclepro.2021.128944

Le Nguyen, B., Lydia, E. L., Elhoseny, M., Pustokhina, I., Pustokhin, D. A., Selim, M. M., & Shankar, K. (2020). Privacy preserving blockchain technique to achieve secure and reliable sharing of IoT data. *Computers, Materials & Continua*, 65(1), 87–107. 10.32604/cmc.2020.011599

Lee, C. C., Li, X., Yu, C. H., & Zhao, J. (2021). Does fintech innovation improve bank efficiency? Evidence from China's banking industry. *International Review of Economics & Finance*, 74, 468–483. 10.1016/j.iref.2021.03.009

Lee, I., & Lee, K. (2015). The Internet of Things (IoT): Applications, investments, and challenges for enterprises. *Business Horizons*, 58(4), 431–440. 10.1016/j.bushor.2015.03.008

Lee, I., & Shin, Y. J. (2018). Fintech: Ecosystem, business models, investment decisions, and challenges. *Business Horizons*, 61(1), 35–46. 10.1016/j.bushor.2017.09.003

Lee, I., & Shin, Y. J. (2020). Machine learning for enterprises: Applications, algorithm selection, and challenges. *Business Horizons*, 63(2), 157–170. 10.1016/j.bushor.2019.10.005

Leng, J., Ye, S., Zhou, M., Zhao, J. L., Liu, Q., Guo, W., Cao, W., & Fu, L. (2020). Blockchain-secured smart manufacturing in industry 4.0: A survey. *IEEE Transactions on Systems, Man, and Cybernetics. Systems*, 51(1), 237–252. 10.1109/TSMC.2020.3040789

Leonard-Barton, D. (1990). A Dual Methodology for Case Studies: Synergistic Use of a Longitudinal Single Site with Replicated Multiple Sites. *Organization Science*, 1(3), 248–266. 10.1287/orsc.1.3.248

Le, T. H., Chuc, A. T., & Taghizadeh-Hesary, F. (2019). Financial inclusion and its impact on financial efficiency and sustainability: Empirical evidence from Asia. *Borsa Istanbul Review*, 19(4), 310–322. 10.1016/j.bir.2019.07.002

Le, T. H., Le, H. C., & Taghizadeh-Hesary, F. (2020). Does financial inclusion impact CO2 emissions? Evidence from Asia. *Finance Research Letters*, 34, 101451. 10.1016/j.frl.2020.101451

Liang, S. (2023). The future of finance: Fintech and digital transformation. *Highlights in Business. Economics and Management*, 15, 20–26.

Li, B. H., Hou, B. C., Yu, W. T., Lu, X. B., & Yang, C. W. (2017). Applications of artificial intelligence in intelligent manufacturing: A review. *Frontiers of Information Technology & Electronic Engineering*, 18(1), 86–96. 10.1631/FITEE.1601885

Li, H., & Sun, J. (2012). Forecasting business failure: The use of nearest-neighbour support vectors and correcting imbalanced samples – Evidence from the Chinese hotel industry. *Tourism Management*, 33(3), 622–634. 10.1016/j.tourman.2011.07.004

Li, J., Dong, X., & Dong, K. (2022). How much does financial inclusion contribute to renewable energy growth? Ways to realize green finance in China. *Renewable Energy*, 198, 760–771. 10.1016/j.renene.2022.08.097

Li, M., Zhang, K., Alamri, A. M., Ageli, M. M., & Khan, N. (2023). Resource curse hypothesis and sustainable development: Evaluating the role of renewable energy and R&D. *Resources Policy*, 81, 103283. 10.1016/j.resourpol.2022.103283

Lim, C. H., Lim, S., How, B. S., Ng, W. P. Q., Ngan, S. L., Leong, W. D., & Lam, H. L. (2021). A review of industry 4.0 revolution potential in a sustainable and renewable palm oil industry: HAZOP approach. *Renewable & Sustainable Energy Reviews*, 135, 110223. 10.1016/j.rser.2020.110223

Link. Liu, Y., Gai, K., & Li, Y. (2020). A comprehensive analysis of the impact of the California Consumer Privacy Act (CCPA) on Internet of Things (IoT). *Journal of Ambient Intelligence and Humanized Computing*, 11(3), 1109–1122.

Linnainmaa, J. T., Melzer, B. T., & Previtero, A. (2020). The misguided beliefs of financial advisors. *The Journal of Finance*, 76(2), 587–621. 10.1111/jofi.12995

Liu, H., Yao, P., Latif, S., Aslam, S., & Iqbal, N. (2022). Impact of Green financing, FinTech, and financial inclusion on energy efficiency. *Environmental Science and Pollution Research International*, 29(13), 1–12. 10.1007/s11356-021-16949-x34705207

Lu, C., Lyu, J., Zhang, L., Gong, A., Fan, Y., Yan, J., & Li, X. (2020). Nuclear power plants with artificial intelligence in industry 4.0 era: Top-level design and current applications—A systemic review. *IEEE Access : Practical Innovations, Open Solutions*, 8, 194315–194332. 10.1109/ACCESS.2020.3032529

Lu, Y. (2019). Artificial intelligence: A survey on evolution, models, applications and future trends. *Journal of Management Analytics*, 6(1), 1–29. 10.1080/23270012.2019.1570365

Lu, Z., Liu, W., Wang, Q., Qu, G., & Liu, Z. (2018). A privacy-preserving trust model based on blockchain for VANETs. *IEEE Access : Practical Innovations, Open Solutions*, 6, 45655–45664. 10.1109/ACCESS.2018.2864189

Macharia, D. N. (2023). *Distributed Ledger Technology (DLT) Applications in Payment, Clearing, and Settlement Systems: A Study of Blockchain-Based Payment Barriers and Potential Solutions, and DLT Application in Central Bank Payment System Functions*. University of Huddersfield.

Madir, J. (2020). Smart Contracts-Self-Executing Contracts of the Future? *Int'l. In-House Counsel J., 13*, 1.

Maguire, K. (1993). Fraud, extortion and racketeering: The black economy in Northern Ireland. *Crime, Law, and Social Change*, 20(4), 273–292. 10.1007/BF01307715

Mahajan, S., & Nanda, M. (2024). Revolutionizing Banking with Blockchain: Opportunities and Challenges Ahead. *Next-Generation Cybersecurity: AI, ML, and Blockchain*, 287-304.

Mahalakshmi, V., Kulkarni, N., Kumar, K. P., Kumar, K. S., Sree, D. N., & Durga, S. (2022). The role of implementing artificial intelligence and machine learning technologies in the financial services industry for creating competitive intelligence. *Materials Today: Proceedings*, 56, 2252–2255. 10.1016/j.matpr.2021.11.577

Majstorovic, V. D., & Mitrovic, R. (2019). Industry 4.0 programs worldwide. In *Proceedings of the 4th International Conference on the Industry 4.0 Model for Advanced Manufacturing: AMP 2019 4* (pp. 78-99). Springer International Publishing. 10.1007/978-3-030-18180-2_7

Mallick, S. K., & Sahoo, A. (2016). The Behavioural Finance Aspects of Chit-Fund Scams of Odisha: Loss is almost certain Profit is Not. *International Journal of Business and Management Invention*, 5(8), 71–78.

Mallikarjunaradhya, V., Pothukuchi, A. S., & Kota, L. V. (2023). An overview of the strategic advantages of AI-powered threat intelligence in the cloud. *Journal of Science and Technology*, 4(4), 1–12.

Mandapuram, M., Mahadasa, R., & Surarapu, P. (2019). Evolution of Smart Farming: Integrating IoT and AI in Agricultural Engineering. *Global Disclosure of Economics and Business*, 8(2), 165–178. 10.18034/gdeb.v8i2.714

Manoja, G., Ibrahim, B. M., Vaidheeswaran, S., Kumar, A. S., & Azharudeen, J. S. (2021). A Study on Investment Behavior of Chit Fund Participants. *Journal of Banking, Finance and Insurance Management, 4*(2).

Compilation of References

Manyika, J., & Brown Chui, M. (2011). *Big Data: The next Frontier for Innovation, Competition and Productivity*. McKinsey Global Institute.

Mărăcine, V., Voican, O., & Scarlat, E. (2020, July). The digital transformation and disruption in business models of the banks under the impact of FinTech and BigTech. In *Proceedings of the International Conference on Business Excellence* (Vol. 14, No. 1, pp. 294-305). IEEE. 10.2478/picbe-2020-0028

Mazzoni, M., Corradi, A., & Di Nicola, V. (2022). Performance evaluation of permissioned blockchains for financial applications: The ConsenSys Quorum case study. *Blockchain: Research and applications, 3*(1), 100026.

Mbaidin, H. O., Alsmairat, M. A. K., & Al-Adaileh, R. (2023). Blockchain adoption for sustainable development in developing countries: Challenges and opportunities in the banking sector. *International Journal of Information Management Data Insights*, 3(2), 100199. 10.1016/j.jjimei.2023.100199

Mehrabi, N., Morstatter, F., Saxena, N., Lerman, K., & Galstyan, A. (2021). A survey on bias and fairness in machine learning. *ACM Computing Surveys*, 54(6), 1–35. 10.1145/3457607

Meir, L., Van de Geer, S., & Bühlmann, P. (2008). The group lasso for logistic regression. *Journal of the Royal Statistical Society. Series B, Statistical Methodology*, 70(1), 53–71. 10.1111/j.1467-9868.2007.00627.x

Méndez, S., Mariano, F., García, F., & Fernando, G. (2019). Artificial intelligence modeling framework for financial automated advising in the copper market. *Journal of Open Innovation*, 5(4), 81. https://s-space.snu.ac.kr/bitstream/10371/150835/1/000000154956.pdf. 10.3390/joitmc5040081

Meyendorf, N., Ida, N., Singh, R., & Vrana, J. (2023). NDE 4.0: Progress, promise, and its role to industry 4.0. *NDT & E International*, 140, 102957. 10.1016/j.ndteint.2023.102957

Mhlanga, D. (2020). Industry 4.0 in finance: The impact of artificial intelligence (ai) on digital financial inclusion. *International Journal of Financial Studies*, 8(3), 45. 10.3390/ijfs8030045

Micaroni, M. (2020). *Sustainable Finance: Addressing the SDGs through Fintech and Digital Finance solutions in EU* [Doctoral dissertation, Politecnico di Torino].

Michel, P. (2008). Financial crimes: The constant challenge of seeking effective prevention solutions. *Journal of Financial Crime*, 15(4), 383–397. 10.1108/13590790810907227

Migliorelli, M., & Dessertine, P. (2019). The rise of green finance in Europe. *Opportunities and challenges for issuers, investors and marketplaces. Cham. Palgrave Macmillan*, 2, 2019.

Mikalef, P. (2019). Exploring the Relationship between Big Data Analytics Capability and Competitive Performance : The Mediating Roles of Dynamic and Operational Capabilities. *Information & Management*, 2018(February). 10.1016/j.im.2019.05.004

Mikalef, P., Boura, M., Lekakos, G., & Krogstie, J. (2019). Big Data Analytics Capabilities and Innovation: The Mediating Role of Dynamic Capabilities and Moderating Effect of the Environment. *British Journal of Management*, 30(2), 272–298. 10.1111/1467-8551.12343

Mik, E. (2017). Smart contracts: Terminology, technical limitations and real world complexity. *Law, Innovation and Technology*, 9(2), 269–300. 10.1080/17579961.2017.1378468

Mirchandani, A., Gupta, N., & Ndiweni, E. (2020). UNDERSTANDING THE FINTECH WAVE: A SEARCH FOR A THEORETICAL EXPLANATION. *International Journal of Economics and Financial Issues*, 10(5), 331–343. 10.32479/ijefi.10296

Mishchenko, S., Naumenkova, S., Mishchenko, V., & Dorofeiev, D. (2021). Innovation risk management in financial institutions. *Investment Management and Financial Innovations*, 18(1), 190–202. 10.21511/imfi.18(1).2021.16

Mishra, D. R. N. (2019). *Dynamics of Operational Risk Management in Digital Arena Regulatory Panacea or Overkill?* (*SSRN* Scholarly Paper 3407160). 10.2139/ssrn.3407160

Mithas, S., Chen, Z. L., Saldanha, T. J., & De Oliveira Silveira, A. (2022). How will artificial intelligence and Industry 4.0 emerging technologies transform operations management? *Production and Operations Management*, 31(12), 4475–4487. 10.1111/poms.13864

Mohammadi, M., Yazdani, S., Khanmohammadi, M. H., & Maham, K. (2020). Financial reporting fraud detection: An analysis of data mining algorithms. *International Journal of Finance & Managerial Accounting*, 4(16), 1–12.

Morgan, J., Halton, M., Qiao, Y., & Breslin, J. G. (2021). Industry 4.0 smart reconfigurable manufacturing machines. *Journal of Manufacturing Systems*, 59, 481–506. 10.1016/j.jmsy.2021.03.001

Morgan, P. J. (2022). Fintech and financial inclusion in Southeast Asia and India. *Asian Economic Policy Review*, 17(2), 183–208. 10.1111/aepr.12379

Morgan, R. (2016). It's All About the BLOCKCHAIN. *American Bankers Association.ABA Banking Journal*, 108(2), 51.

Mourtzis, D., Angelopoulos, J., & Panopoulos, N. (2022). A Literature Review of the Challenges and Opportunities of the Transition from Industry 4.0 to Society 5.0. *Energies*, 15(17), 6276. 10.3390/en15176276

Mugari, I., Gona, S., Maunga, M., & Chiyambiro, R. (2016). Cybercrime-the emerging threat to the financial services sector in Zimbabwe. *Mediterranean Journal of Social Sciences*, 7(3), 135–143. 10.5901/mjss.2016.v7n3s1p135

Muhtasim, D. A., Tan, S. Y., Hassan, M. A., Pavel, M. I., & Susmit, S. (2022). Customer satisfaction with digital wallet services: An analysis of security factors. *International Journal of Advanced Computer Science and Applications*, 13(1), 195–206. 10.14569/IJACSA.2022.0130124

Müller, O., Fay, M., & vom Brocke, J. (2018). The Effect of Big Data and Analytics on Firm Performance: An Econometric Analysis Considering Industry Characteristics. *Journal of Management Information Systems*, 35(2), 488–509. 10.1080/07421222.2018.1451955

Munirathinam, S. (2020). Industry 4.0: Industrial internet of things (IIOT). []. Elsevier.]. *Advances in Computers*, 117(1), 129–164. 10.1016/bs.adcom.2019.10.010

Murinde, V., Rizopoulos, E., & Zachariadis, M. (2022). The impact of the Fintech revolution on the future of banking: Opportunities and risks. *International Review of Financial Analysis*, 81, 1–27. 10.1016/j.irfa.2022.102103

Naeem, S., Ali, A., Anam, S., & Ahmed, M. M. (2023). An unsupervised machine learning algorithms: Comprehensive review. *International Journal of Computing and Digital Systems*.

Nahavandi, S. (2019). Industry 5.0—A human-centric solution. *Sustainability (Basel)*, 11(16), 4371. 10.3390/su11164371

Najaf, K., & Atayah, O. F. (2021). Understanding governance compliance for RegTech. *Artificial Intelligence and Islamic Finance: Practical Applications for Financial Risk Management, 11*.

Najaf, K., Chin, A., & Najaf, R. (2021). Conceptualising the corporate governance issues of fintech firms. *The fourth industrial revolution: implementation of artificial intelligence for growing business success*, 187-197.

Najaf, K., Mostafiz, M. I., & Najaf, R. (2021). Fintech firms and banks sustainability: Why cybersecurity risk matters? *International Journal of Financial Engineering*, 8(02), 2150019. 10.1142/S2424786321500195

Najaf, K., Subramaniam, R. K., & Atayah, O. F. (2022). Understanding the implications of Fintech Peer-to-Peer (P2P) lending during the COVID-19 pandemic. *Journal of Sustainable Finance & Investment*, 12(1), 87–102. 10.1080/20430795.2021.1917225

Najib, M., & Fahma, F. (2020). Investigating the adoption of digital payment system through an extended technology acceptance model: An insight from the Indonesian small and medium enterprises. *International Journal on Advanced Science, Engineering and Information Technology*, 10(4), 1702–1708. 10.18517/ijaseit.10.4.11616

Nakamoto, S. (2008). Bitcoin: A peer-to-peer electronic cash system.

Nangin, M. A., Barus, I. R. G., & Wahyoedi, S. (2020). The effects of perceived ease of use, security, and promotion on trust and its implications on fintech adoption. *Journal of Consumer Sciences*, 5(2), 124–138. 10.29244/jcs.5.2.124-138

Narayanan, A., Bonneau, J., Felten, E., Miller, A., & Goldfeder, S. (2016). *Bitcoin and cryptocurrency technologies: A comprehensive introduction*. Princeton University Press.

Nassiry, D. (2018). *The role of fintech in unlocking green finance: Policy insights for developing countries* (No. 883). ADBI working paper.

Naz, F., Karim, S., Houcine, A., & Naeem, M. A. (2024). Fintech growth during COVID-19 in MENA region: Current challenges and future prospects. *Electronic Commerce Research*, 24(1), 371–392. 10.1007/s10660-022-09583-3

Neef, R. (2002). Aspects of the informal economy in a transforming country: The case of Romania. *International Journal of Urban and Regional Research*, 26(2), 299–322. 10.1111/1468-2427.00381

Nerenberg, L. (2000). Forgotten victims of financial crime and abuse: Facing the challenge. *Journal of Elder Abuse & Neglect*, 12(2), 49–73. 10.1300/J084v12n02_06

Ngai, E. W., Hu, Y., Wong, Y. H., Chen, Y., & Sun, X. (2011). The application of data mining techniques in financial fraud detection: A classification framework and an academic review of literature. *Decision Support Systems*, 50(3), 559–569. 10.1016/j.dss.2010.08.006

Nguyen, T., Gosine, R. G., & Warrian, P. (2020). A systematic review of big data analytics for oil and gas industry 4.0. *IEEE Access : Practical Innovations, Open Solutions*, 8, 61183–61201. 10.1109/ACCESS.2020.2979678

Niankara, I., & Muqattash, R. (2020). The impact of financial inclusion on consumers saving and borrowing behaviours: Retrospective cross-sectional evidence from the UAE and the USA. *International Journal of Economics and Business Research*, 20(2), 217–242. 10.1504/IJEBR.2020.109152

Nica, E., & Stehel, V. (2021). Internet of things sensing networks, artificial intelligence-based decision-making algorithms, and real-time process monitoring in sustainable industry 4.0. *Journal of Self-Governance and Management Economics*, 9(3), 35–47.

Nikkel, B. (2020). Fintech forensics: Criminal investigation and digital evidence in financial technologies. *Forensic Science International Digital Investigation*, 33, 200908. 10.1016/j.fsidi.2020.200908

Nish, A., Naumann, S., & Muir, J. (2022). *Enduring cyber threats and emerging challenges to the financial sector*. Carnegie Endowment for International Peace.

Nourani, M. (2020), *The Effects of Meaningful and Meaningless Explanations on Trust and Perceived System Accuracy in Intelligent Systems*,

Nowiński, W., & Kozma, M. (2017). How can blockchain technology disrupt the existing business models? *Entrepreneurial Business and Economics Review*, 5(3), 173–188. 10.15678/EBER.2017.050309

Nsiah, A. Y., Yusif, H., Tweneboah, G., Agyei, K., & Baidoo, S. T. (2021). The effect of financial inclusion on poverty reduction in Sub-Sahara Africa: Does threshold matter? *Cogent Social Sciences*, 7(1), 1903138. 10.1080/23311886.2021.1903138

Nygaard, A., & Silkoset, R. (2023). Sustainable development and greenwashing: How blockchain technology information can empower green consumers. *Business Strategy and the Environment*, 32(6), 3801–3813. 10.1002/bse.3338

OECD. (2017). *Technology and innovation in the insurance sector.* OECD. https://www.oecd.org/finance/Technology-and-innovation-in-the-insurance-sector.pdf

OECD. (2020). *OECD Business and Finance Outlook 2020: Sustainable and Resilient Finance.* OECD Publishing. 10.1787/eb61fd29-

Okoro, Y. O., Ayo-Farai, O., Maduka, C. P., Okongwu, C. C., & Sodamade, O. T. (2024). The Role of technology in enhancing mental health advocacy: A systematic review. *International Journal of Applied Research in Social Sciences*, 6(1), 37–50. 10.51594/ijarss.v6i1.690

Okur, M. R., Zengin-Karaibrahimoglu, Y., & Taşkın, D. (2021). From Conventional Methods to Contemporary Neural Network Approaches: Financial Fraud Detection. *Ethics and Sustainability in Accounting and Finance*, III, 215–228. 10.1007/978-981-33-6636-7_11

Olweny, F. (2024). Navigating the nexus of security and privacy in modern financial technologies. *GSC Advanced Research and Reviews*, 18(2), 167–197. 10.30574/gscarr.2024.18.2.0043

Omar, M. A., & Inaba, K. (2020). Does financial inclusion reduce poverty and income inequality in developing countries? A panel data analysis. *Journal of Economic Structures*, 9(1), 1–25. 10.1186/s40008-020-00214-4

Oyewole, A. T., Oguejiofor, B. B., Eneh, N. E., Akpuokwe, C. U., & Bakare, S. S. (2024). Data privacy laws and their impact on financial technology companies: A review. *Computer Science & IT Research Journal*, 5(3), 628–650. 10.51594/csitrj.v5i3.911

Ozili, P. K. (2021b). Has financial inclusion made the financial sector riskier? *Journal of financial regulation and compliance,29*(3), 237-255.

Ozili, P. K. (2015). Forensic Accounting and Fraud: A Review of Literature and Policy Implications. *International Journal of Accounting and Economics Studies*, 3(1), 63–68. 10.14419/ijaes.v3i1.4541

Ozili, P. K. (2020a). Tax evasion and financial instability. *Journal of Financial Crime*, 27(2), 531–539. 10.1108/JFC-04-2019-0051

Ozili, P. K. (2020b). Advances and issues in fraud research: A commentary. *Journal of Financial Crime*, 27(1), 92–103. 10.1108/JFC-01-2019-0012

Ozili, P. K. (2021a). Financial inclusion research around the world: A review. *The Forum for Social Economics*, 50(4), 457–479. 10.1080/07360932.2020.1715238

Ozili, P. K. (2021c). Financial inclusion and legal system quality: Are they correlated? *Journal of Money and Business*, 1(2), 84–101. 10.1108/JMB-10-2021-0041

Ozili, P. K. (2023). Assessing global interest in decentralized finance, embedded finance, open finance, ocean finance and sustainable finance. *Asian Journal of Economics and Banking*, 7(2), 197–216. 10.1108/AJEB-03-2022-0029

Ozili, P. K. (2023). Financial inclusion washing. *Journal of Financial Crime*, 30(5), 1140–1149. 10.1108/JFC-07-2022-0159

Ozili, P. K., & Adamu, A. (2021). Does financial inclusion reduce non-performing loans and loan loss provisions? *Journal of Corporate Governance, Insurance, and Risk Management*, 8(2), 10–24. 10.51410/jcgirm.8.2.2

Ozili, P. K., Ademiju, A., & Rachid, S. (2023). Impact of financial inclusion on economic growth: Review of existing literature and directions for future research. *International Journal of Social Economics*, 50(8), 1105–1122. 10.1108/IJSE-05-2022-0339

Ozili, P. K., & Mhlanga, D. (2024). Why is financial inclusion so popular? An analysis of development buzzwords. *Journal of International Development*, 36(1), 231–253. 10.1002/jid.3812

Pal, A., Tiwari, C. K., & Behl, A. (2021). Blockchain technology in financial services: A comprehensive review of the literature. *Journal of Global Operations and Strategic Sourcing*, 14(1), 61–80. 10.1108/JGOSS-07-2020-0039

Pande, V. (Ed.). (2017). *Exploring the Reasons behind India's Chit Crisis A Case Study on Corporate Governance Strategies of Saradha Group*. Department of Management & Commerce, Faculty of Management & Humanities, Jayoti Vidyapeeth Women's University.

Panesar, A., & Panesar, A. (2021). Machine learning and AI ethics. *Machine Learning and AI for Healthcare: Big Data for Improved Health Outcomes*, 207–247.

Panigrahi, A., & Gaur, M. (2014). Chit fund crisis in India is the result of inefficient Indian banking system, an analytical study. *SSRN*, 2686785, 1–31. https://ssrn.com/abstract=2686785. 10.2139/ssrn.2686785

Panwar, A., & Bhatnagar, V. (2020). Distributed ledger technology (DLT): the beginning of a technological revolution for blockchain. *Paper presented at the 2nd International Conference on Data, Engineering and Applications (IDEA)*. IEEE. 10.1109/IDEA49133.2020.9170699

Parate, S., Josyula, H. P., & Reddi, L. T. (2023). Digital identity verification: Transforming KYC processes in banking through advanced technology and enhanced security measures. *International Research Journal of Modernization in Engineering Technology and Science*, 5(9), 128–137.

Parn, E. A., & Edwards, D. (2019). Cyber threats confronting the digital built environment: Common data environment vulnerabilities and block chain deterrence. *Engineering, Construction, and Architectural Management*, 26(2), 245–266. 10.1108/ECAM-03-2018-0101

Pavithra, C. B. (2021). Factors Affecting Customers' perception Towards Digital Banking Services. [TURCOMAT]. *Turkish Journal of Computer and Mathematics Education*, 12(11), 1608–1614.

Perera-Aldama, L., Amar, P., & Trostianki, D. (2009). Embedding corporate responsibility through effective organizational structures. *Corporate Governance (Bradford)*, 9(4), 506–516. 10.1108/14720700910985043

Perols, L., & Lougee, B. A. (2011). The relation between earnings management and financial statement fraud. *Advances in Accounting*, 27(1), 39–53. 10.1016/j.adiac.2010.10.004

Petrov, D. (2019). The impact of blockchain and distributed ledger technology on financial services. *Industry 4.0, 4*(2), 88-91.

Pickett, K. H. S., & Pickett, J. M. (2002). *Financial Crime Investigation and Control*. John Wiley & Sons.

Pickett, K. S., & Pickett, J. M. (2002). *Financial crime investigation and control*. John Wiley & Sons.

Pilkington, M. (2016). *Blockchain technology: principles and applications Research handbook on digital transformations*. Edward Elgar Publishing.

Pivoto, D. G., de Almeida, L. F., da Rosa Righi, R., Rodrigues, J. J., Lugli, A. B., & Alberti, A. M. (2021). Cyber-physical systems architectures for industrial internet of things applications in Industry 4.0: A literature review. *Journal of Manufacturing Systems*, 58, 176–192. 10.1016/j.jmsy.2020.11.017

Pizzi, S., Corbo, L., & Caputo, A. (2021). Fintech and SMEs sustainable business models: Reflections and considerations for a circular economy. *Journal of Cleaner Production*, 281, 125217. 10.1016/j.jclepro.2020.125217

Popescu, A.-D. (2020). Transitions and concepts within decentralized finance (Defi) Space. *Research Terminals in the social sciences*.

Popov, V. V., Kudryavtseva, E. V., Kumar Katiyar, N., Shishkin, A., Stepanov, S. I., & Goel, S. (2022). Industry 4.0 and digitalisation in healthcare. *Materials (Basel)*, 15(6), 2140. 10.3390/ma15062140 35329592

Pourhabibi, T., Ong, K. L., Kam, B. H., & Boo, Y. L. (2020). Fraud detection: A systematic literature review of graph-based anomaly detection approaches. *Decision Support Systems*, 133, 113303. 10.1016/j.dss.2020.113303

Power, M. (2021). Modelling the micro-foundations of the audit society: Organizations and the logic of the audit trail. *Academy of Management Review*, 46(1), 6–32. 10.5465/amr.2017.0212

Pramod, A. V. (2020). Individual financial portfolio to channelize capital amount with reference to chit funds and personal loan. [IJM]. *International Journal of Management (Kolkata)*, 11(7).

Prasad, S., Rao, A. N., & Lanka, K. (2022). Analysing the Barriers for Implementation of Lean-Led Sustainable Manufacturing and Potential of Blockchain Technology to Overcome These Barriers: A Conceptual Framework. *International Journal of Mathematical. Engineering and Management Sciences*, 7(6), 791–819. 10.33889/IJMEMS.2022.7.6.051

Priem, R. (2020). Distributed ledger technology for securities clearing and settlement: Benefits, risks, and regulatory implications. *Financial Innovation*, 6(1), 11. 10.1186/s40854-019-0169-6

PWC. (2016). *Catching the Fintech Wave- A Survey of Fintech in Malaysia*. PWC. https://www.pwc.com/my/en/assets/publications/2016-pwc-aicb-catching-the-fintech-wave.pdf

PWC. (2017). *Global Fintech Report 2017*. PWC.

Radanliev, P., De Roure, D., Van Kleek, M., Santos, O., & Ani, U. (2021). Artificial intelligence in cyber physical systems. *AI & Society*, 36(3), 783–796. 10.1007/s00146-020-01049-032874020

Raghavan, T. S., & Rajendran, K. (2019). Media coverage of Ponzi schemes in India: An exploratory study. *Journal of Financial Crime*, 26(3), 810–824.

Rahardja, U., Hidayanto, A. N., Lutfiani, N., Febiani, D. A., & Aini, Q. (2021). Immutability of Distributed Hash Model on Blockchain Node Storage. *Sci. J. Informatics*, 8(1), 137–143. 10.15294/sji.v8i1.29444

Raj, S. B. E., & Portia, A. A. (2011, March). Analysis on credit card fraud detection methods. In *2011 International Conference on Computer, Communication and Electrical Technology (ICCCET)* (pp. 152-156). IEEE.

Raji, S. P. (2023). A Study On Awareness About The Investment Pattern Among The Working Women. In *Virudhunagar District*. Department of Commerce, Bharathiar University.

Raj, K., & Aithal, P. S. (2018). Digitization of India-impact on the BOP sector. [IJMTS]. *International Journal of Management, Technology, and Social Sciences*, 3(1), 59–74. 10.47992/IJMTS.2581.6012.0036

Rao, A., Kumar, S., & Karim, S. (2024). Accelerating renewables: Unveiling the role of green energy markets. *Applied Energy*, 366, 123286. 10.1016/j.apenergy.2024.123286

Rao, K. S., & Menon, V. (2015). Investigating and prosecuting Ponzi schemes in India: Challenges and the way forward. *Journal of Financial Crime*, 22(2), 246–259.

Rapolu, R. T., Gopal, M. K., & Kumar, G. S. (2022, April). A Secure method for Image Signaturing using SHA-256, RSA, and Advanced Encryption Standard (AES). In *2022 IEEE International Conference on Distributed Computing and Electrical Circuits and Electronics (ICDCECE)* (pp. 1-7). IEEE. 10.1109/ICDCECE53908.2022.9792989

Rasanayagam, J. (2011). Informal economy, informal state: The case of Uzbekistan. *The International Journal of Sociology and Social Policy*, 31(11/12), 681–696. 10.1108/01443331111177878

Rasoulinezhad, E., & Taghizadeh-Hesary, F. (2022). Role of green finance in improving energy efficiency and renewable energy development. *Energy Efficiency*, 15(2), 1–12. 10.1007/s12053-022-10021-435529528

Rath, K. C., Khang, A., & Roy, D. (2024). The Role of Internet of Things (IoT) Technology in Industry 4.0 Economy. In *Advanced IoT Technologies and Applications in the Industry 4.0 Digital Economy* (pp. 1-28). CRC Press.

Compilation of References

Raval, S. (2016). *Decentralized applications: harnessing Bitcoin's blockchain technology*. O'Reilly Media, Inc.

Ray, R. K., Chowdhury, F. R., & Hasan, M. R. (2024). Blockchain Applications in Retail Cybersecurity: Enhancing Supply Chain Integrity, Secure Transactions, and Data Protection. *Journal of Business and Management Studies*, 6(1), 206–214. 10.32996/jbms.2024.6.1.13

Razi, U., Karim, S., & Cheong, C. W. (2024). From Turbulence to Resilience: A Bibliometric Insight into the Complex Interactions Between Energy Price Volatility and Green Finance. *Energy*, 304, 131992. 10.1016/j.energy.2024.131992

Reid, A. S. (2018). Financial crime in the twenty-first century: the rise of the virtual collar criminal. In *White Collar Crime and Risk* (pp. 231–251). Palgrave Macmillan. 10.1057/978-1-137-47384-4_9

Reier Forradellas, R. F., & Garay Gallastegui, L. M. (2021). Digital transformation and artificial intelligence applied to business: Legal regulations, economic impact and perspective. *Laws*, 10(3), 70. 10.3390/laws10030070

Rodriguez, M. Z., Comin, C. H., Casanova, D., Bruno, O. M., Amancio, D. R., Costa, L. da F., & Rodrigues, F. A. (2019). Clustering algorithms: A comparative approach. *PLoS One*, 14(1), e0210236. 10.1371/journal.pone.021023630645617

Ross, E. S. (2016). Nobody puts blockchain in a corner: The disruptive role of blockchain technology in the financial services industry and current regulatory issues. *Cath. UJL & Tech*, 25, 353.

Rossi, A. G., & Utkus, S. P. (2020). *The needs and wants in financial advice: Human versus robo-advising*. 10.2139/ssrn.3759041

Ryman-Tubb, N. F., Krause, P., & Garn, W. (2018). How Artificial Intelligence and machine learning research impacts payment card fraud detection: A survey and industry benchmark. *Engineering Applications of Artificial Intelligence*, 76, 130–157. 10.1016/j.engappai.2018.07.008

Rymarczyk, J. (2020). Technologies, opportunities and challenges of the industrial revolution 4.0: Theoretical considerations. *Entrepreneurial Business and Economics Review*, 8(1), 185–198. 10.15678/EBER.2020.080110

Ryu, H.-S. (2018). What makes users willing or hesitant to use Fintech?: The moderating effect of user type. *Industrial Management & Data Systems*, 118(3), 541–569. 10.1108/IMDS-07-2017-0325

Saba, C. S., & Ngepah, N. (2022). Convergence in renewable energy sources and the dynamics of their determinants: An insight from a club clustering algorithm. *Energy Reports*, 8, 3483–3506. 10.1016/j.egyr.2022.01.190

Sachs, J. D., Woo, W. T., Yoshino, N., & Taghizadeh-Hesary, F. (2019). Importance of green finance for achieving sustainable development goals and energy security. *Handbook of green finance: Energy security and sustainable development, 10*, 1-10.

Saeed, S., Altamimi, S. A., Alkayyal, N. A., Alshehri, E., & Alabbad, D. A. (2023). Digital transformation and cybersecurity challenges for businesses resilience: Issues and recommendations. *Sensors (Basel)*, 23(15), 6666. 10.3390/s2315666637571451

Sahay, A., & Tiwari, T. (2023). *HSBC: Facilitating Trade Finance Through Blockchain*. Indian Institute of Management Ahmedabad.

Sahay, M. R., von Allmen, M. U. E., Lahreche, M. A., Khera, P., Ogawa, M. S., Bazarbash, M., & Beaton, M. K. (2020). *The Promise of Fintech: Financial Inclusion in the Post COVID-19 Era*. International Monetary Fund.

Sakyi-Nyarko, C., Ahmad, A. H., & Green, C. J. (2022). The gender-differential effect of financial inclusion on household financial resilience. *The Journal of Development Studies*, 58(4), 1–21. 10.1080/00220388.2021.2013467

Salerno, A. C. F. (2019). Regulating the Fintech Revolution: How Regulators Can Adapt to Twenty-First Century Financial Technology. *Annual Survey of American Law*, 75, 365.

Saluja, S. (2024). Identity theft fraud-major loophole for FinTech industry in India. *Journal of Financial Crime*, 31(1), 146–157. 10.1108/JFC-08-2022-0211

Samoili, S., Cobo, M. L., Gómez, E., De Prato, G., Martínez-Plumed, F., & Delipetrev, B. (2020). *AI Watch. Defining Artificial Intelligence. Towards an operational definition and taxonomy of artificial intelligence*.

Sanad, Z., & Al-Sartawi, A. (2021). Financial statements fraud and data mining. *RE:view*, 407–414.

Sánchez-Sotano, A., Cerezo-Narváez, A., Abad-Fraga, F., Pastor-Fernández, A., & Salguero-Gómez, J. (2020). Trends of digital transformation in the shipbuilding sector. In *New Trends in the Use of Artificial Intelligence for the Industry 4.0*. IntechOpen. 10.5772/intechopen.91164

Sander, F., Semeijn, J., & Mahr, D. (2018). The acceptance of blockchain technology in meat traceability and transparency. *British Food Journal*, 120(9), 2066–2079. 10.1108/BFJ-07-2017-0365

Santhisree, V. N., & Prasad, J. C. (2014). A Study on Problems of Chit Fund Companies and The Satisfaction Level of the Customers. *Vidwat*, 7(1), 8.

Sapkauskienė, A., & Višinskaitė, I. (2020). Initial Coin Offerings (ICOs): Benefits, risks and success measures. *Entrepreneurship and Sustainability Issues*, 7(3), 1472–1483. 10.9770/jesi.2020.7.3(3)

Sarkar, A. (2015). Chit Fund Scam. *Indian Journal of Poultry Science*, 76(3), 384–388.

Sarkar, A., & Singh, B. K. (2020). A review on performance, security and various biometric template protection schemes for biometric authentication systems. *Multimedia Tools and Applications*, 79(37-38), 27721–27776. 10.1007/s11042-020-09197-7

Sarmah, S. S. (2018). Understanding blockchain technology. *Computing in Science & Engineering*, 8(2), 23–29.

Compilation of References

Saurabh, K., Rani, N., & Upadhyay, P. (2024). Towards novel blockchain decentralised autonomous organisation (DAO) led corporate governance framework. *Technological Forecasting and Social Change*, 204, 123417. 10.1016/j.techfore.2024.123417

Sayer, A. (2002). Critical Realist Methodology: A View from Sweden. *Journal of Critical Realism*, 1(1), 168–170. 10.1558/jocr.v1i1.168

Schaeffer, S. E., & Sanchez, S. V. R. (2020). Forecasting client retention—A machine-learning approach. *Journal of Retailing and Consumer Services*, 52, 101918. 10.1016/j.jretconser.2019.101918

Schmidt, R., & Scott, C. (2021). Regulatory discretion: Structuring power in the era of regulatory capitalism. *Legal Studies*, 41(3), 454–473. 10.1017/lst.2021.13

Schoenmaker, D., & Volz, U. (2022). *Scaling up sustainable finance and investment in the Global South*. CEPR Press.

Schulz, K., & Feist, M. (2021). Leveraging blockchain technology for innovative climate finance under the Green Climate Fund. *Earth System Governance*, 7, 100084. 10.1016/j.esg.2020.100084

Schwerin, S. (2018). Blockchain and privacy protection in the case of the european general data protection regulation (GDPR): A delphi study. *The Journal of the British Blockchain Association*, 1(1), 1–77. 10.31585/jbba-1-1-(4)2018

Sedlmeir, J., Lautenschlager, J., Fridgen, G., & Urbach, N. (2022). The transparency challenge of blockchain in organizations. *Electronic Markets*, 32(3), 1779–1794. 10.1007/s12525-022-00536-035602109

Serrado, J., Pereira, R. F., Mira da Silva, M., & Scalabrin Bianchi, I. (2020). Information security frameworks for assisting GDPR compliance in banking industry. *Digital Policy. Regulation & Governance*, 22(3), 227–244. 10.1108/DPRG-02-2020-0019

Seth, B., Dalal, S., Jaglan, V., Le, D. N., Mohan, S., & Srivastava, G. (2022). Integrating encryption techniques for secure data storage in the cloud. *Transactions on Emerging Telecommunications Technologies*, 33(4), e4108. 10.1002/ett.4108

Shah, M. A., & Uddin, F. (2023). Leveraging Blockchain Technology in the Construction Industry. In *Building Secure Business Models Through Blockchain Technology: Tactics, Methods, Limitations, and Performance* (pp. 50–65). IGI Global. 10.4018/978-1-6684-7808-0.ch004

Shahbazi, Z., & Byun, Y.-C. (2021). Blockchain-based event detection and trust verification using natural language processing and machine learning. *IEEE Access : Practical Innovations, Open Solutions*, 10, 5790–5800. 10.1109/ACCESS.2021.3139586

Shanmuganathan, M. (2020). Behavioural finance in an era of artificial intelligence: Longitudinal case study of robo-advisors in investment decisions. *Journal of Behavioral and Experimental Finance*, 27, 100297. 10.1016/j.jbef.2020.100297

Sharma, A. (2021). Consensus Mechanisms in Blockchain Networks: Analyzing Various Consensus Mechanisms Such as Proof of Work (PoW), Proof of Stake (PoS), and Practical Byzantine Fault Tolerance (PBFT). *Blockchain Technology and Distributed Systems*, 1(1), 1–11.

Sharma, A., & Singh, B. (2022). Measuring Impact of E-commerce on Small Scale Business: A Systematic Review. *Journal of Corporate Governance and International Business Law*, 5(1).

Sharma, E., & Khurana, N. (2013). Influence of financial literacy on investment decisions of employees. *Anvesha*, 6(2), 12–19.

Sharma, V., Taneja, S., Jangir, K., & Khanna, K. (2023). Green Finance- An Integral Pathway to Achieving Sustainable Development. In Taneja, S., Ozen, E., & Kumar, P. (Eds.), *Sustainable Investment in Green Finance. IGI Global Publishers (Nov. 2023)* (pp. 49–63)., Retrieved from https://www.igi-global.com/chapter/green-finance/33397210.4018/979-8-3693-1388-6.ch003

Shih, C., Gwizdalski, A., & Deng, X. (2023). *Building a Sustainable Future: Exploring Green Finance*. Regenerative Finance, and Green Financial Technology.

Shino, Y., Lukita, C., Rii, K. B., & Nabila, E. A. (2022). The emergence of Fintech in Higher education curriculum. [SABDA Journal]. *Startupreneur Business Digital*, 1(1), 11–22. 10.33050/sabda.v1i1.71

Shi, Y., & Li, X. (2019). An overview of bankruptcy prediction models for corporate firms: A systematic literature review. *Intangible Capital*, 15(2), 114–127. 10.3926/ic.1354

Shi, Z., Xie, Y., Xue, W., Chen, Y., Fu, L., & Xu, X. (2020). Smart factory in Industry 4.0. *Systems Research and Behavioral Science*, 37(4), 607–617. 10.1002/sres.2704

Shrimali, B., & Patel, H. B. (2022). Blockchain state-of-the-art: Architecture, use cases, consensus, challenges and opportunities. *Journal of King Saud University. Computer and Information Sciences*, 34(9), 6793–6807. 10.1016/j.jksuci.2021.08.005

Siddique, M. A., Nobanee, H., Karim, S., & Naz, F. (2022). Investigating the role of metal and commodity classes in overcoming resource destabilization. *Resources Policy*, 79, 103075. 10.1016/j.resourpol.2022.103075

Siddique, M. A., Nobanee, H., Karim, S., & Naz, F. (2023). Do green financial markets offset the risk of cryptocurrencies and carbon markets? *International Review of Economics & Finance*, 86, 822–833. 10.1016/j.iref.2023.04.005

Siddique, S., & Vadiyala, V. (2021). Strategic Frameworks for Optimizing Customer Engagement in the Digital Era: A Comparative Study. *Digitalization & Sustainability Review*, 1(1), 24–40.

Sigov, A., Ratkin, L., Ivanov, L. A., & Xu, L. D. (2022). Emerging enabling technologies for industry 4.0 and beyond. *Information Systems Frontiers*, 1–11. 10.1007/s10796-021-10213-w

Sima, V., Gheorghe, I. G., Subić, J., & Nancu, D. (2020). Influences of the industry 4.0 revolution on the human capital development and consumer behavior: A systematic review. *Sustainability (Basel)*, 12(10), 4035. 10.3390/su12104035

Singh Rajawat, A., Bedi, P., Goyal, S. B., Shukla, P. K., Zaguia, A., Jain, A., & Monirujjaman Khan, M. (2021). Reformist framework for improving human security for mobile robots in industry 4.0. *Mobile Information Systems*, 2021, 1–10. 10.1155/2021/4744220

Singh, B. (2023). Blockchain Technology in Renovating Healthcare: Legal and Future Perspectives. In *Revolutionizing Healthcare Through Artificial Intelligence and Internet of Things Applications* (pp. 177-186). IGI Global.

Singh, S. K., Sharma, S. K., Singla, D., & Gill, S. S. (2022). Evolving requirements and application of SDN and IoT in the context of industry 4.0, blockchain and artificial intelligence. *Software Defined Networks: Architecture and Applications*, 427-496.

Singh, A. K., Kumar, V. R. P., Shoaib, M., Adebayo, T. S., & Irfan, M. (2023). A strategic roadmap to overcome blockchain technology barriers for sustainable construction: A deep learning-based dual-stage SEM-ANN approach. *Technological Forecasting and Social Change*, 194, 122716. 10.1016/j.techfore.2023.122716

Singh, B. (2022). Relevance of Agriculture-Nutrition Linkage for Human Healthcare: A Conceptual Legal Framework of Implication and Pathways. *Justice and Law Bulletin*, 1(1), 44–49.

Singh, B. (2022). Understanding Legal Frameworks Concerning Transgender Healthcare in the Age of Dynamism. *ELECTRONIC JOURNAL OF SOCIAL AND STRATEGIC STUDIES*, 3(1), 56–65. 10.47362/EJSSS.2022.3104

Singh, B. (2023). Federated Learning for Envision Future Trajectory Smart Transport System for Climate Preservation and Smart Green Planet: Insights into Global Governance and SDG-9 (Industry, Innovation and Infrastructure). *National Journal of Environmental Law*, 6(2), 6–17.

Singh, B. (2024). Legal Dynamics Lensing Metaverse Crafted for Videogame Industry and E-Sports: Phenomenological Exploration Catalyst Complexity and Future. *Journal of Intellectual Property Rights Law*, 7(1), 8–14.

Singh, P., & Singh, M. (2015). Fraud detection by monitoring customer behavior and activities. *International Journal of Computer Applications*, 111(11), 23–32. 10.5120/19584-1340

Singh, R., & Mohapatra, A. D. (2023). Awareness, Causes and Measures for prevention of Corporate Frauds in India-An Empirical Study. [EEL]. *European Economic Letters*, 13(4), 875–903.

Singleton, T. W., & Singleton, A. J. (2007). Why don't we detect more fraud? *Journal of Corporate Accounting & Finance*, 18(4), 7–10. 10.1002/jcaf.20302

Sinha, P. K., & Ghosh, A. (2016). Ponzi schemes in India: Challenges in regulation and the way forward. *IIMB Management Review*, 28(1), 30–40.

Slemrod, J. (2007). Cheating ourselves: The economics of tax evasion. *The Journal of Economic Perspectives*, 21(1), 25–48. 10.1257/jep.21.1.25

Sobb, T., Turnbull, B., & Moustafa, N. (2020). Supply chain 4.0: A survey of cyber security challenges, solutions and future directions. *Electronics (Basel)*, 9(11), 1864. 10.3390/electronics9111864

Song, Y., Chen, B., & Wang, X.-Y. (2023). Cryptocurrency technology revolution: Are Bitcoin prices and terrorist attacks related? *Financial Innovation*, 9(1), 29. 10.1186/s40854-022-00445-336712148

Sood, P., & Bhushan, P. (2020). A structured review and theme analysis of financial frauds in the banking industry. *Asian Journal of Business Ethics*, 9(2), 305–321. 10.1007/s13520-020-00111-w

Srivastava, S., Srivastava, G., & Bhatnagar, R. (2019, December). Analysis of process mining in audit trails of organization. In *International Conference on Information Management & Machine Intelligence* (pp. 611-618). Springer, Singapore.

Stojanović, B., Božić, J., Hofer-Schmitz, K., Nahrgang, K., Weber, A., Badii, A., Sundaram, M., Jordan, E., & Runevic, J. (2021). Follow the trail: Machine learning for fraud detection in Fintech applications. *Sensors (Basel)*, 21(5), 1594. 10.3390/s2105159433668773

Sumithra, N. (2022). Chit Fund an Overview. *International Journal of Early Childhood Special Education*, 14(5).

Sun, G., Li, T., Ai, Y., & Li, Q. (2023). Digital finance and corporate financial fraud. *International Review of Financial Analysis*, 87, 102566. 10.1016/j.irfa.2023.102566

Sun, J., Li, H., Huang, Q., & He, K. (2014). Predicting financial distress and corporate failure: A review from the state-of-the-art definitions, modelling, sampling, and featuring approaches. *Knowledge-Based Systems*, 57, 41–56. 10.1016/j.knosys.2013.12.006

Sunyaev, A., & Sunyaev, A. (2020). Distributed ledger technology. *Internet computing: Principles of distributed systems and emerging internet-based technologies*, 265-299.

Suryono, R. R., Budi, I., & Purwandari, B. (2020). Challenges and trends of finacnail technology (fintech): A systematic literature review. *Information (Basel)*, 11(12), 590–610. 10.3390/info11120590

Swan, M. (2015). *Blockchain: blueprint for a new economy*. O'Reilly Media.

Talesh, S. A. (2018). Data breach, privacy, and cyber insurance: How insurance companies act as "compliance managers" for businesses. *Law & Social Inquiry*, 43(2), 417–440. 10.1111/lsi.12303

Tang, X.-B., Liu, G.-C., Yang, J., & Wei, W. (2018). Knowledge-based financial statement fraud detection system: Based on an ontology and a decision tree. *Knowledge Organization*, 45(3), 205–219. 10.5771/0943-7444-2018-3-205

Tao, F., Akhtar, M. S., & Jiayuan, Z. (2021). The future of artificial intelligence in cybersecurity: A comprehensive survey. *EAI Endorsed Transactions on Creative Technologies*, 8(28), e3–e3. 10.4108/eai.7-7-2021.170285

Compilation of References

Tao, H., Bhuiyan, M. Z. A., Rahman, M. A., Wang, G., Wang, T., Ahmed, M. M., & Li, J. (2019). Economic perspective analysis of protecting big data security and privacy. *Future Generation Computer Systems*, 98, 660–671. 10.1016/j.future.2019.03.042

Thottoli, M. M. (2023). *The tactician role of Fintech in the accounting and auditing field: A bibliometric analysis*. Qualitative Research in Financial Markets.

Tian, S., Yu, Y., & Guo, H. (2015). Variable selection and corporate bankruptcy forecasts. *Journal of Banking & Finance*, 52, 89–100. 10.1016/j.jbankfin.2014.12.003

Tikkinen-Piri, C., Rohunen, A., & Markkula, J. (2018). EU General Data Protection Regulation: Changes and implications for personal data collecting companies. *Computer Law & Security Report*, 34(1), 134–153. 10.1016/j.clsr.2017.05.015

Tim, Y., Hallikainen, P., Pan, S. L., & Tamm, T. (2020). Actualizing Business Analytics for Organizational Transformation: A Case Study of Rovio Entertainment. *European Journal of Operational Research*, 281(3), 642–655. 10.1016/j.ejor.2018.11.074

Tiron-Tudor, A., & Deliu, D. (2022). Reflections on the human-algorithm complex duality perspectives in the auditing process. *Qualitative Research in Accounting & Management*, 19(3), 255–285.

Tobback, E., Bellotti, T., Moeyersoms, J., Stankova, M., & Martens, D. (2017). Bankruptcy prediction for SMEs using relational data. *Decision Support Systems*, 102, 69–81. 10.1016/j.dss.2017.07.004

Tokic, D. (2018). BlackRock robo-advisor 4.0: When artificial intelligence replaces human discretion. *Strategic Change*, 27(4), 285–290. 10.1002/jsc.2201

Tomal, A., & Johnson, L. (2008). Earnings determinants for self-employed women and men in the informal economy: The case of Bogotá, Colombia. *International Social Science Review*, 83(1/2), 71–84.

Ton, T. (2022). *Blockchain-Transforming the Future of Trade Finance*.

Toufaily, E., Zalan, T., & Dhaou, S. B. (2021). A framework of blockchain technology adoption: An investigation of challenges and expected value. *Information & Management*, 58(3), 103444. 10.1016/j.im.2021.103444

Trakadas, P., Simoens, P., Gkonis, P., Sarakis, L., Angelopoulos, A., Ramallo-González, A. P., Skarmeta, A., Trochoutsos, C., Calvo, D., Pariente, T., Chintamani, K., Fernandez, I., Irigaray, A. A., Parreira, J. X., Petrali, P., Leligou, N., & Karkazis, P. (2020). An artificial intelligence-based collaboration approach in industrial iot manufacturing: Key concepts, architectural extensions and potential applications. *Sensors (Basel)*, 20(19), 5480. 10.3390/s2019548032987911

Tran, H. T. T., Le, H. T. T., Nguyen, N. T., Pham, T. T. M., & Hoang, H. T. (2022). The effect of financial inclusion on multidimensional poverty: The case of Vietnam. *Cogent Economics & Finance*, 10(1), 2132643. 10.1080/23322039.2022.2132643

Tseng, M. L., Tran, T. P. T., Ha, H. M., Bui, T. D., & Lim, M. K. (2021). Sustainable industrial and operation engineering trends and challenges Toward Industry 4.0: A data driven analysis. *Journal of Industrial and Production Engineering*, 38(8), 581–598. 10.1080/21681015.2021.1950227

Tyagi, M., Ranjan, S., & Gupta, A. (2022). Transforming Education System through Artificial Intelligence and Machine Learning. *3rd International Conference on Intelligent Engineering and Management (ICIEM)*. IEEE. 10.1109/ICIEM54221.2022.9853195

U.S. Securities and Exchange Commission (SEC). (2024). *SEC Overview*. SEC. https://www.sec.gov/about

Unal, I. M., & Aysan, A. F. (2022). Fintech, digitalization, and blockchain in Islamic finance: Retrospective investigation. *FinTech*, 1(4), 388–398. 10.3390/fintech1040029

Upadhyay, N. (2020). Demystifying blockchain: A critical analysis of challenges, applications and opportunities. *International Journal of Information Management*, 54, 102120. 10.1016/j.ijinfomgt.2020.102120

Usama, M., Qadir, J., Raza, A., Arif, H., Yau, K. L. A., Elkhatib, Y., Hussain, A., & Al-Fuqaha, A. (2019). Unsupervised Machine Learning for Networking: Techniques, Applications and Research Challenges. *IEEE Access : Practical Innovations, Open Solutions*, 7, 65579–65615. 10.1109/ACCESS.2019.2916648

Utami, A. F., & Ekaputra, I. A. (2021). A paradigm shifts in financial landscape: Encouraging collaboration and innovation among Indonesian FinTech lending players. *Journal of Science and Technology Policy Management*, 12(2), 309–330. 10.1108/JSTPM-03-2020-0064

Vadiyala, V. R. (2021). Byte by Byte: Navigating the Chronology of Digitization and Assessing its Dynamic Influence on Economic Landscapes, Employment Trends, and Social Structures. *Digitalization & Sustainability Review*, 1(1), 12–23.

Vadiyala, V. R., Baddam, P. R., & Kaluvakuri, S. (2016). Demystifying Google Cloud: A Comprehensive Review of Cloud Computing Services. *Asian Journal of Applied Science and Engineering*, 5(1), 207–218. 10.18034/ajase.v5i1.80

van der Elst, C., & Lafarre, A. (2024). *The Viability of Blockchain in Corporate Governance Board-Shareholder Dialogue: Best Practices, Legal Constraints and Policy Options*. Cambridge University Press.

Varga, D. (2017). Fintech, the new era of financial services. *Vezetéstudomány-Budapest Management Review*, 48(11), 22–32. 10.14267/VEZTUD.2017.11.03

Vasista, K. (2021). Regulatory compliance and supervision of artificial intelligence, machine learning and also possible effects on financial institutions. *International Journal of Innovative Research in Computer and Communication Engineering*, 2320-9801.

Vasquez, O., & San-Jose, L. (2022). Ethics in fintech through users' confidence: Determinants that affect trust. *Journal of Applied Ethics*, (13).

Compilation of References

Vergara, C. C., & Agudo, L. F. (2021). Fintech and sustainability: Do they affect each other? *Sustainability*, 13(13), 1–19.

Verhoeven, P. (2022). *Management model for social and environmental impact in logistics through blockchain technologies*. Universitätsverlag der Technischen Universität Berlin.

Verma, S., & Sharma, R. (2017). The role of social media in the proliferation of Ponzi schemes in India. *Journal of Financial Crime*, 24(2), 306–320.

Vogt, J. (2021). Where is the human got to go? Artificial intelligence, machine learning, big data, digitalisation, and human–robot interaction in Industry 4.0 and 5.0: Review Comment on: Bauer, M.(2020). Preise kalkulieren mit KI-gestützter Onlineplattform BAM GmbH, Weiden, Bavaria, Germany. *AI & Society*, 36(3), 1083–1087. 10.1007/s00146-020-01123-7

Voigt, P., & von dem Bussche, A. (2017). *The EU General Data Protection Regulation (GDPR): A Practical Guide*. Springer. 10.1007/978-3-319-57959-7

Wamba, S. F., Gunasekaran, A., Akter, S., Ren, S. J., Dubey, R., & Childe, S. J. (2017). Big Data Analytics and Firm Performance: Effects of Dynamic Capabilities. *Journal of Business Research*, 70, 356–365. 10.1016/j.jbusres.2016.08.009

Wamba-Taguimdje, S. L., Fosso Wamba, S., Kala Kamdjoug, J. R., & Tchatchouang Wanko, C. E. (2020). Influence of artificial intelligence (AI) on firm performance: The business value of AI-based transformation projects. *Business Process Management Journal*, 26(7), 1893–1924. 10.1108/BPMJ-10-2019-0411

Wang, J., Wang, W., Liu, Y., & Wu, H. (2023). Can industrial robots reduce carbon emissions? Based on the perspective of energy rebound effect and labor factor flow in China. *Technology in Society*, 72, 102208. 10.1016/j.techsoc.2023.102208

Wang, L., Cheng, H., Zheng, Z., Yang, A., & Xu, M. (2023). Temporal transaction information-aware Ponzi scheme detection for ethereum smart contracts. *Engineering Applications of Artificial Intelligence*, 126, 107022. 10.1016/j.engappai.2023.107022

Wang, L., Wang, Y., Sun, Y., Han, K., & Chen, Y. (2022). Financial inclusion and green economic efficiency: Evidence from China. *Journal of Environmental Planning and Management*, 65(2), 240–271. 10.1080/09640568.2021.1881459

Wang, L., & Wu, C. (2017). Business failure prediction based on two-stage selective ensemble with manifold learning algorithm and kernel-based fuzzy self-organizing map. *Knowledge-Based Systems*, 121, 99–110. 10.1016/j.knosys.2017.01.016

Wang, R., Destek, M. A., Weimei, C., Albahooth, B., & Khan, Z. (2023). Drivers of Sustainable Green Finance: Country's Level Risk and Trade Perspective for OECD Countries. *Journal of Environment & Development*. 10.1177/10704965231217046/ASSET/IMAGES/LARGE/10.1177_10704965231217046-FIG2.JPEG

Wang, R., & Luo, H. R. (2022). How does financial inclusion affect bank stability in emerging economies? *Emerging Markets Review*, 51, 100876. 10.1016/j.ememar.2021.100876

Wang, Z., Alamri, A. M., Mawad, J. L., Zhang, M., & Khan, N. (2023). Sustainable growth and green environment? Evidence from nonparametric methods provincial data of China. *Ekonomska Istrazivanja*, 36(3), 2152070. 10.1080/1331677X.2022.2152070

Wan, J., Li, X., Dai, H. N., Kusiak, A., Martinez-Garcia, M., & Li, D. (2020). Artificial-intelligence-driven customized manufacturing factory: Key technologies, applications, and challenges. *Proceedings of the IEEE*, 109(4), 377–398. 10.1109/JPROC.2020.3034808

Wan, J., Yang, J., Wang, Z., & Hua, Q. (2018). Artificial intelligence for cloud-assisted smart factory. *IEEE Access : Practical Innovations, Open Solutions*, 6, 55419–55430. 10.1109/ACCESS.2018.2871724

Wei, S., & Lee, S. (2024). Financial Anti-Fraud Based on Dual-Channel Graph Attention Network. *Journal of Theoretical and Applied Electronic Commerce Research*, 19(1), 297–314. 10.3390/jtaer19010016

West, J., & Bhattacharya, M. (2016). Intelligent financial fraud detection: A comprehensive review. *Computers & Security*, 57, 47–66. 10.1016/j.cose.2015.09.005

Williams, J. M., Strauch, S., & Duncan, D. (2018). *Ponzi Schemes and the Awareness of South Carolina Students to Financial Fraud*. Research Gate.

Williams, B., & Adamson, J. (2022). *PCI Compliance: Understand and implement effective PCI data security standard compliance*. CRC Press. 10.1201/9781003100300

Xia, H., Lu, D., Lin, B., Nord, J. H., & Zhang, J. Z. (2023). Trust in fintech: Risk, governance, and continuance intention. *Journal of Computer Information Systems*, 63(3), 648–662. 10.1080/08874417.2022.2093295

Xiao, Z., Yang, X., Pang, Y., & Dang, X. (2012). The prediction for listed companies' financial distress by using multiple prediction methods with rough set and Dempster–Shafer evidence theory. *Knowledge-Based Systems*, 26, 196–206. 10.1016/j.knosys.2011.08.001

Xu, C., Liu, C., Nie, D., & Gai, L. (2021). How can a blockchain-based anti-money laundering system improve customer due diligence process? *Journal of Forensic & Investigative Accounting*, 13(2), 273–287.

Xu, L. D., Xu, E. L., & Li, L. (2018). Industry 4.0: State of the art and future trends. *International Journal of Production Research*, 56(8), 2941–2962. 10.1080/00207543.2018.1444806

Yan, C., Siddik, A. B., Yong, L., Dong, Q., Zheng, G. W., & Rahman, M. N. (2022). A two-staged SEM-artificial neural network approach to analyze the impact of FinTech adoption on the sustainability performance of banking firms: The mediating effect of green finance and innovation. *Systems*, 10(5), 148. 10.3390/systems10050148

Yang, S. H., Hwang, Y. S., & Park, J. L. (2016). A study on using fintech payment services based on the UTAUT model. *Journal of Vocational Rehabilitation*, (3), 183–209.

Compilation of References

Yang, X., Huang, Y., & Gao, M. (2022). Can digital financial inclusion promote female entrepreneurship? Evidence and mechanisms. *The North American Journal of Economics and Finance*, 63, 101800. 10.1016/j.najef.2022.101800

Yang, Y., Su, X., & Yao, S. (2021). Nexus between green finance, fintech, and high-quality economic development: Empirical evidence from China. *Resources Policy*, 74, 102445. 10.1016/j.resourpol.2021.102445

Yeoh, P. (2017). Regulatory issues in blockchain technology. *Journal of Financial Regulation and Compliance*, 25(2), 196–208. 10.1108/JFRC-08-2016-0068

Yerram, S. R., Goda, D. R., Mahadasa, R., Mallipeddi, S. R., Varghese, A., Ande, J., Surarapu, P., & Dekkati, S. (2021). The role of blockchain technology in enhancing financial security amidst digital transformation. *Asian Bus. Rev*, 11(3), 125–134. 10.18034/abr.v11i3.694

Younas, Z. I., Qureshi, A., & Al-Faryan, M. A. S. (2022). Financial inclusion, the shadow economy and economic growth in developing economies. *Structural Change and Economic Dynamics*, 62, 613–621. 10.1016/j.strueco.2022.03.011

Yue, Y., & Shyu, J. Z. (2024). A paradigm shift in crisis management: The nexus of AGI-driven intelligence fusion networks and blockchain trustworthiness. *Journal of Contingencies and Crisis Management*, 32(1), e12541. 10.1111/1468-5973.12541

Yu, S.-J., & Rha, J.-S. (2021). Research trends in accounting fraud using network analysis. *Sustainability (Basel)*, 13(10), 5579. 10.3390/su13105579

Yu, S., Liang, Y., Zhu, Z., Olaniyi, O. N., & Khan, N. (2024). Dutch disease perspective of energy sector: Natural resources and energy sector nexus with the role of renewable energy consumption. *Resources Policy*, 90, 104740. 10.1016/j.resourpol.2024.104740

Yu, T., Chen, S.-H., & Kuo, T.-W. (2005). A Genetic Programming Approach to Model International Short-Term Capital Flow. *Advances in Econometrics*, 19, 45–70. 10.1016/S0731-9053(04)19002-6

Zachariadis, M., Hileman, G., & Scott, S. V. (2019). Governance and control in distributed ledgers: Understanding the challenges facing blockchain technology in financial services. *Information and Organization*, 29(2), 105–117. 10.1016/j.infoandorg.2019.03.001

Zakaria, P. (2023). Financial Inclusion to Digital Finance Risks: A Commentary on Financial Crimes, Money Laundering, and Fraud. In *Financial Technologies and DeFi: A Revisit to the Digital Finance Revolution* (pp. 123–130). Springer International Publishing. 10.1007/978-3-031-17998-3_9

Zang, H., & Kim, J. (2023, July). A Comprehensive Study on Blockchain-based Cloud-Native Storage for Data Confidence. In *2023 Fourteenth International Conference on Ubiquitous and Future Networks (ICUFN)* (pp. 106-108). IEEE. 10.1109/ICUFN57995.2023.10200136

Zeng, D., Tim, Y., Yu, J., & Liu, W. (2020). Actualizing Big Data Analytics for Smart Cities: A Cascading Affordance Study. *International Journal of Information Management*, 54(3), 102156. 10.1016/j.ijinfomgt.2020.102156

Zhang, C., & Lu, Y. (2021). Study on artificial intelligence: The state of the art and future prospects. *Journal of Industrial Information Integration*, 23, 100224. 10.1016/j.jii.2021.100224

Zhang, D. (2023). Does green finance really inhibit extreme hypocritical ESG risk? A greenwashing perspective exploration. *Energy Economics*, 121, 106688. 10.1016/j.eneco.2023.106688

Zhang, D., Mohsin, M., & Taghizadeh-Hesary, F. (2022). Does green finance counteract the climate change mitigation: Asymmetric effect of renewable energy investment and R&D. *Energy Economics*, 113, 106183. 10.1016/j.eneco.2022.106183

Zhang, L., Pentina, I., & Fan, Y. (2021). Who do you choose? Comparing perceptions of human vs robo-advisor in the context of financial services. *Journal of Services Marketing*, 35(5), 628–640. 10.1108/JSM-05-2020-0162

Zhang, W., Siyal, S., Riaz, S., Ahmad, R., Hilmi, M. F., & Li, Z. (2023). Data Security, Customer Trust and Intention for Adoption of Fintech Services: An Empirical Analysis From Commercial Bank Users in Pakistan. *SAGE Open*, 13(3), 21582440231181388. 10.1177/21582440231181388

Zhang-Zhang, Y., Rohlfer, S., & Rajasekera, J. (2020). An eco-systematic view of cross-sector Fintech: The case of Alibaba and Tencent. *Sustainability (Basel)*, 12(21), 8907. 10.3390/su12218907

Zhao, Y., & Chen, X. (2021). The relationship between the withdrawal of the digital economy's innovators, government interventions, the marketization level and market size based on big data. *Journal of Enterprise Information Management*, 35(4/5), 1202–1232. 10.1108/JEIM-01-2021-0050

Zhong, R. Y., Xu, X., Klotz, E., & Newman, S. T. (2017). Intelligent manufacturing in the context of industry 4.0: A review. *Engineering (Beijing)*, 3(5), 616–630. 10.1016/J.ENG.2017.05.015

Zhou, J., Zhang, S., Lu, Q., Dai, W., Chen, M., Liu, X., & Herrera-Viedma, E. (2021). A survey on federated learning and its applications for accelerating industrial internet of things. *arXiv preprint arXiv:2104.10501*.

Zhou, L., Diro, A., Saini, A., Kaisar, S., & Hiep, P. C. (2024). Leveraging zero knowledge proofs for blockchain-based identity sharing: A survey of advancements, challenges and opportunities. *Journal of Information Security and Applications*, 80, 103678. 10.1016/j.jisa.2023.103678

Zhou, W., & Kapoor, G. (2011). Detecting evolutionary financial statement fraud. *Decision Support Systems*, 50(3), 570–575. 10.1016/j.dss.2010.08.007

Zhu, H., & Zhou, Z. Z. (2016). Analysis and outlook of applications of blockchain technology to equity crowdfunding in China. *Financial Innovation*, 2(1), 29. 10.1186/s40854-016-0044-7

Zmijewski, M. (1984). Methodological Issues Related to the Estimation of Financial Distress Prediction Models. *Journal of Accounting Research*, 22, 59–86. 10.2307/2490859

About the Contributors

Farah Naz is a highly accomplished Assistant Professor in the Accounting and Finance department at Kinnaird College for Women in Lahore, Pakistan. She earned her esteemed PhD from the School of Accounting & Finance at the University of Central Punjab. Driven by her passion for knowledge and research, she possesses a broad and diversified expertise in various aspects of accounting, finance, and business research. Dr. Farah Naz's intellectual curiosity and dedication to academic excellence have led to the publication of several of her research papers in esteemed journals. Her contributions to the academic community extend beyond her own publications, as she actively engages in the peer review process for prestigious journals such as Annals of Operation Research, Energy Economics, Journal of Economic and Administrative Sciences, and Resources Policy, among others. Her commitment to advancing the fields of accounting, finance, and business research is evident through her continuous pursuit of knowledge and active involvement in the scholarly community. Dr. Farah Naz's scholarly endeavors have made a significant impact, and she continues to inspire both her students and peers through her remarkable contributions to academia.

Sitara Karim is an Associate Professor of Finance at Sunway Business School, Sunway University, Malaysia. She has been recognized as the World's Top 2% Scientist in Financial Economics in 2023 (Stanford University Rankings/ Elsevier). She won the "Dean's Excellence in Research Award" in 2023 by Sunway Business School, Sunway University, Malaysia. She has been Awarded as "Outstanding Reviewer" under the Emerald Literati Award (2023). She is serving as Section Editor (Economics & Business) in MethodsX (Elsevier) and as an Associate Editor of the International Review of Economics and Finance (SCOPUS Q1; ABDC: A, ABS: 2, IF: 3.393). She is also Guest Editing a Special Issue in Energy Economics (ABDC: A, ABS: 3*, IF: 9.252, SCOPUS: Q1) and Journal of Accounting and Organizational Change (ABDC: B, ABD: 2, IF: 1.90; SCOPUS: Q2). She is supervising several Ph.D. and Master research students and inspiring other early research careers. She has published in various top-tier journals e.g. European Financial Management, British Journal of Management, The European Journal of Finance, Journal of Economic Behavior and Organization, International Review of Financial Analysis, International Review of Economics and Finance, Finance Research Letters, Energy Economics, Economics Letters, Technological Forecasting and Social Change, and so on. She is the European Marketing and Management Association Women's Forum Member and a fellow of Center for Marker Education. Her significant contributions to the academia and industry are reflective of her persistence, determination, proactiveness, and commitment.

About the Contributors

B. Udaya Bhaskara Ganesh is an esteemed academic professional currently serving as an Assistant Professor at Mittal School of Business (MHRD NIRF India Rank 34; ACBSP USA, Accredited), Lovely Professional University, Phagwara, Punjab, India. He has done his M.B.A and Ph.D. from Andhra University, Visakhapatnam. With an impressive 14 years of experience in academia, research, and teaching, His teaching interests encompass a wide array of subjects, including Investment Banking, Financial Modelling, Financial Derivatives, Corporate Finance etc. he has showcased his research prowess at esteemed National and International conferences across different regions of the country. Dr.B. Udaya Bhaskara Ganesh research contributions are noteworthy, with sixteen research papers to his credit in esteemed databases such as Scopus, Web of Science (Wos), and UGC. and four books and two patents got published. Dr. B. Udaya Bhaskara Ganesh holds two professional memberships with reputable national and international organizations. He appointed as a BSE resource person and for the last 8 years he conducted various capital Market awareness programmes in reputed institutions both in offline & online.

Misal Ijaz has recently graduated as Master of Philosophy student from Kinnaird College for Women, Lahore, Pakistan.

Shweta jaiswal is graduate and post graduate from University of Allahabad and qualified UGC NET JRF.. She is pursuing research in finance from CMP degree college, University of Allahabad

Christian Kaunert is Professor of International Security at Dublin City University, Ireland. He is also Professor of Policing and Security, as well as Director of the International Centre for Policing and Security at the University of South Wales. In addition, he is Jean Monnet Chair, Director of the Jean Monnet Centre of Excellence and Director of the Jean Monnet Network on EU Counter-Terrorism (www.eucter.net).

Numan Khan is an academic in economics, business and finance, holding a BBA and MBA with distinction. As a former lecturer, he integrates theoretical concepts with practical applications, preparing students for the dynamic business world. Numan serves on the editorial boards of Finance Research Letters, Journal of Accounting and Organizational Change, and IGI Global. His research, published in top-tier journals like Resources Policy, addresses complex issues and offers innovative solutions. A prolific researcher and respected academic, Numan continues to make significant contributions to research, teaching, and the academic community.

Firdous Mohd Farouk is a lecturer at the School of Accounting and Finance, Taylor's University. She currently also serves as the Stream Coordinator for the school. Her research interest lie in the exciting and rapidly-evolving field of accounting, particularly with regard to new system implementation and decision-making. She is a keen observer of emerging trends and technologies in the field and is committed to staying ahead of the curve to ensure that her students and colleagues are equipped with the latest and most relevant knowledge.

Shir Li Ng is Senior Lecturer at Sunway Business School Malaysia. She has published articles in peer-reviewed journals and book chapters focusing on sustainability reporting, fintech, corporate governance and international financial reporting standards.

Mushtaq Ahmad Shah is a finance expert with a PhD in Infrastructure Finance. He teaches banking, finance and economics at Lovely Professional University in India. Dr. Shah has over 8 years of experience teaching and researching at various institutions. He's written articles in academic journals and presented his work at conferences on banking, partnerships between public and private sectors, and behavioral finance.

About the Contributors

Naveen Kumar Singh is an Assistant Professor at School of Behavioural Sciences and Forensic Investigations, Rashtriya Raksha University, Gandhinagar, India. He is also the university coordinator of the Distance Learning platform under the Directorate of Distance Learning (DDL), RRU. He was appointed Research Fellow at INTI International University, Malaysia, in March 2023. His research area is Forensics Accounting, Digital Finance, Mobile Technology Adoption & Innovation, and he taught subjects about Forensics Accounting and Financial Investigation, Forensics Auditing, Data Science & Big Data Analytics, Export-Import Management, Global Operations Management, Digital Marketing, etc. Dr. Singh had taught at the Graduate School of Management Studies (GSMS), Gujarat Technological University (GTU) for one (01) year; University of Lucknow for two (02) years; and worked in the corporate sector for one (01) year. He has been a Visiting Research Fellow at the National Taiwan University of Science and Technology (NTUST), Taiwan. His research has appeared in all the leading international journals and conferences of repute. He has published 10 articles indexed in ABDC, Scopus, and International Conferences published by Springer Series. He has presented more than 25 articles at National/International Conferences and seminars, including IFIP conference. He worked as a member of various departmental committees like Media, Scholarship, Cultural, Research, and Placement at Graduate School of Management Studies (GSMS), GTU. He worked as a team member of the organizing committee in various workshops and STTPs conducted by AICTE-ATAL Academy, GIAN, MOOCs, SWAYAM, NMEICT, CSI, etc. Dr. Singh has a member of various professional academic bodies. He is also a reviewer of ASTES (Reviewer Code: AJR04340) and also a guest reviewer of the Asia-Pacific Journal of Business Administration (indexed in ABDC-C) and the International Journal of Cloud Computing (indexed in Scopus).

Bhupinder Singh working as Professor at Sharda University, India. Also, Honorary Professor in University of South Wales UK and Santo Tomas University Tunja, Colombia. His areas of publications as Smart Healthcare, Medicines, fuzzy logics, artificial intelligence, robotics, machine learning, deep learning, federated learning, IoT, PV Glasses, metaverse and many more. He has 3 books, 139 paper publications, 163 paper presentations in international/national conferences and seminars, participated in more than 40 workshops/FDP's/QIP's, 25 courses from international universities of repute, organized more than 59 events with international and national academicians and industry people's, editor-in-chief and co-editor in journals, developed new courses. He has given talks at international universities, resource person in international conferences such as in Nanyang Technological University Singapore, Tashkent State University of Law Uzbekistan; KIMEP University Kazakhstan, All'ah meh Tabatabi University Iran, the Iranian Association of International Criminal law, Iran and Hague Center for International Law and Investment, The Netherlands, Northumbria University Newcastle UK, Taylor's University Malaysia, AFM Krakow University Poland, European Institute for Research and Development Georgia, Business and Technology University Georgia, Texas A & M University US name a few. His leadership, teaching, research and industry experience is of 16 years and 3 Months. His research interests are health law, criminal law, research methodology and emerging multidisciplinary areas as Blockchain Technology, IoT, Machine Learning, Artificial Intelligence, Genome-editing, Photovoltaic PV Glass, SDG's and many more.

Mani Tyagi is an educator and researcher. She has 9+ years of experience in Industry and Academics. She is proficient in Marketing, International Business and Corporate Training. Dr. Mani is a White Belt Holder of Six Sigma and a certified Project Manager from MSI, USA. Dr. Mani has 09 copyrights in her name, registered under Government of India. She is a fellow member of NSDC's leading training partner. She has 20+ Research Papers in her credit published in Scopus indexed journals and UGC care. She has reviewed one of the famous books by McGraw Hill Education, titled as "Business Research Methods" by Donald R. Cooper. In her academia, she has several certification courses from IIT Bombay and IIM Bangalore.

Index

A

accounting standards 215, 218, 219, 220, 221, 223, 224, 225, 226, 227, 228, 229, 230, 231

Artificial Intelligence 3, 8, 14, 15, 17, 18, 19, 22, 23, 41, 70, 77, 81, 83, 84, 85, 86, 87, 88, 92, 93, 94, 97, 99, 100, 104, 106, 107, 110, 113, 116, 120, 146, 147, 148, 150, 158, 164, 165, 166, 169, 170, 171, 172, 173, 174, 175, 176, 177, 178, 180, 183, 185, 186, 187, 188, 189, 190, 191, 192, 193, 194, 195, 196, 198, 199, 200, 201, 207, 208, 209, 210, 211, 212, 213, 216, 232, 234, 235, 236

Automated Wealth Management 14, 15, 18, 19, 21

Awareness 24, 25, 26, 27, 28, 29, 30, 31, 32, 34, 36, 37, 38, 40, 41, 62, 66, 69, 76, 90, 105, 114, 115, 137, 148, 157, 158, 209, 225, 226, 240, 241, 243, 250, 251, 252, 253, 255

B

Big Data 8, 42, 43, 44, 47, 48, 54, 59, 60, 61, 69, 70, 80, 84, 88, 91, 97, 100, 104, 106, 116, 144, 150, 156, 174, 182, 183, 192, 196, 208, 209, 211, 216, 232

blockchain 64, 77, 78, 80, 84, 85, 91, 92, 94, 95, 96, 97, 99, 100, 101, 104, 105, 106, 107, 113, 117, 120, 121, 122, 123, 124, 125, 126, 127, 128, 129, 130, 131, 132, 133, 134, 135, 136, 137, 138, 139, 140, 141, 142, 143, 144, 145, 175, 177, 185, 186, 187, 188, 189, 190, 192, 193, 194, 195, 197, 212, 213, 216, 217, 218, 221, 224, 229, 230, 231, 233, 235, 236

Blockchain Technologies 78, 85, 91, 92, 94, 95, 97, 100, 144

Blockchain Technology 77, 80, 84, 85, 94, 95, 96, 97, 100, 101, 105, 106, 107, 122, 124, 125, 126, 128, 131, 132, 133, 134, 135, 136, 137, 138, 139, 140, 142, 143, 144, 145, 177, 185, 189, 190, 192, 194, 213, 216, 217, 224, 230, 235

C

cloud computing 69, 70, 86, 88, 94, 95, 96, 97, 144, 171, 174, 216, 217

compliance culture 214, 225, 231

Cyber-security 72

Cybersecurity 65, 66, 76, 103, 104, 105, 110, 111, 113, 114, 115, 116, 117, 119, 120, 134, 135, 138, 141, 157, 170, 171, 182, 186, 188, 190, 193, 195, 196, 198, 222, 227, 228, 229

Cyber Threats 110, 111, 112, 121, 122, 123, 124, 129, 131, 133, 134, 142, 222, 232

D

Data Analytics 42, 44, 54, 59, 60, 61, 69, 70, 100, 104, 105, 106, 113, 157, 183, 192, 199, 201, 208, 216

Data Integrity 122, 127, 129, 132, 140

Data Privacy 43, 50, 109, 134, 135, 142, 182, 222, 229, 231

Data Protection 16, 42, 43, 44, 46, 47, 48, 52, 57, 61, 76, 104, 111, 113, 135, 143, 193, 195, 196, 199, 205, 227

Data Security 46, 49, 52, 53, 57, 103, 104, 105, 109, 110, 111, 112, 113, 114, 115, 117, 118, 120, 121, 122, 123, 129, 144, 172, 177, 236

Digital 4, 5, 7, 8, 9, 12, 13, 15, 18, 20, 26, 27, 40, 42, 43, 53, 57, 60, 64, 67, 70, 71, 72, 77, 79, 80, 81, 84, 94, 95, 96, 103, 104, 105, 106, 107, 108, 109, 110, 111, 112, 113, 114, 115, 116, 117, 118, 119, 120, 121, 122, 123, 124, 125, 128, 129, 130, 131, 132, 133, 134, 135, 136, 138, 142, 143, 145, 166, 169, 170, 172, 173, 174, 175, 177, 178, 183, 186, 187, 188, 189, 191, 193, 194, 195, 196, 206, 211,

215, 216, 219, 222, 228, 233, 234, 236

F

financial crime 1, 2, 3, 6, 7, 8, 9, 10, 11, 12, 27, 40, 41, 62, 63, 64, 65, 66, 67, 76, 77, 78, 79, 119, 238, 254
Financial crimes 3, 10, 13, 62, 63, 64, 65, 66, 67, 68, 69, 73, 76, 78, 198
Financial data 16, 103, 104, 105, 109, 113, 115, 121, 122, 123, 125, 127, 129, 131, 132, 137, 151, 169, 173, 174, 178, 198, 202, 217, 222, 228
Financial Data Security 121, 122, 129
Financial Fraud 5, 12, 13, 25, 35, 36, 37, 41, 63, 64, 66, 67, 75, 113, 123, 124, 130, 138, 146, 147, 148, 150, 151, 152, 157, 158, 165, 167, 172, 199, 200, 201, 202, 204, 205, 207, 208, 209, 210, 211, 243
Financial frauds 25, 26, 29, 147, 148, 152, 156, 182, 198, 205, 206, 212
financial inclusion 1, 2, 3, 4, 5, 6, 7, 8, 9, 10, 11, 12, 13, 26, 27, 40, 70, 71, 79, 106, 112, 115, 117, 119, 125, 175, 187, 191, 241
Financial Literacy 24, 26, 27, 28, 35, 36, 37, 39, 41, 73, 118, 239, 240, 251, 254
Financial security 128, 129, 131, 133, 134, 135, 136, 138, 145, 172
Financial Services 1, 2, 4, 5, 7, 8, 18, 20, 23, 27, 42, 43, 44, 46, 57, 63, 66, 70, 71, 73, 76, 77, 78, 103, 104, 105, 106, 107, 109, 112, 113, 114, 117, 120, 122, 124, 125, 137, 138, 139, 140, 141, 142, 143, 145, 169, 170, 172, 173, 177, 179, 183, 187, 199, 200, 206, 211, 215, 216, 220, 222, 231, 233, 234, 235
Financial transactions 2, 6, 8, 63, 104, 108, 109, 111, 116, 122, 123, 128, 129, 131, 133, 134, 136, 152, 159, 165, 198, 215, 217, 218, 219, 221, 223, 230
Fintech 15, 18, 23, 55, 60, 61, 62, 63, 64, 65, 66, 67, 69, 70, 71, 72, 73, 74, 75, 76, 77, 78, 79, 91, 92, 100, 103, 104, 105, 106, 107, 109, 110, 112, 113, 114, 115, 116, 117, 118, 119, 120, 147, 176, 178, 186, 187, 188, 189, 191, 192, 197, 199, 214, 215, 216, 217, 218, 219, 220, 221, 222, 223, 224, 225, 226, 227, 228, 229, 230, 231, 232, 233, 234, 235, 236, 237
fraud detection 1, 2, 3, 6, 7, 8, 9, 12, 13, 65, 120, 138, 147, 148, 149, 150, 151, 152, 156, 157, 158, 159, 160, 162, 163, 164, 165, 167, 176, 177, 179, 180, 181, 182, 187, 200, 201, 204, 205, 206, 207, 208, 209, 210, 211, 212

G

Green Finance 10, 21, 22, 81, 82, 85, 86, 88, 89, 90, 91, 92, 93, 97, 98, 101, 102, 188, 190, 192, 193, 194, 197

H

harmonization 221

I

Investment 15, 16, 17, 19, 20, 21, 22, 24, 26, 27, 28, 30, 36, 37, 39, 40, 41, 44, 47, 48, 69, 71, 73, 78, 79, 87, 102, 106, 107, 112, 114, 120, 124, 130, 134, 147, 175, 176, 178, 182, 187, 189, 191, 194, 195, 197, 215, 216, 227, 233, 235, 239, 240, 241, 242, 243, 244, 249, 250, 251, 252, 254, 255
Investment Strategies 15, 16, 17, 19, 107, 175
investor confidence 28, 214, 227, 228

M

Machine Learning 3, 14, 15, 17, 19, 23, 65, 83, 84, 85, 86, 88, 93, 97, 99, 100, 105, 106, 110, 116, 117, 120, 146, 147, 148, 150, 151, 153, 154, 155, 158, 159, 162, 163, 164, 165, 166, 169, 170, 171, 172, 173, 174, 175, 176, 177, 178, 180, 181, 182, 183, 185, 186, 187, 191, 196, 198, 199,

200, 201, 202, 203, 204, 205, 207, 208, 209, 210, 211, 212, 213, 216, 229, 230, 232, 234, 236

P

Ponzi Scheme 25, 28, 29, 30, 33, 34, 35, 36, 38, 39, 40, 41

R

regulatory compliance 50, 53, 54, 55, 56, 57, 72, 78, 104, 109, 114, 115, 128, 130, 136, 164, 175, 179, 204, 210, 214, 215, 220, 221, 222, 223, 224, 225, 226, 227, 228, 229, 230, 231, 233, 236
Regulatory Framework 28, 65, 66, 76, 114, 116, 139, 223
Robo-Advisors 14, 15, 16, 17, 18, 19, 20, 21, 22, 73, 105, 106, 107, 113, 120, 175, 216

S

Survey 4, 9, 24, 25, 29, 45, 48, 58, 60, 62, 63, 66, 71, 79, 117, 138, 139, 145, 150, 151, 152, 166, 176, 185, 190, 191, 195, 197, 208, 209, 212, 235, 243, 252
Sustainable Development 22, 81, 82, 83, 85, 86, 87, 88, 89, 90, 91, 92, 93, 97, 98, 99, 100, 186, 189, 190, 193, 194, 195

T

Technological Innovations 14, 214, 224
Technology 3, 9, 12, 15, 16, 17, 20, 21, 22, 41, 42, 43, 44, 46, 48, 49, 52, 54, 57, 59, 63, 64, 66, 67, 70, 71, 72, 77, 78, 79, 80, 83, 84, 85, 90, 94, 95, 96, 97, 100, 101, 103, 104, 105, 106, 107, 116, 117, 118, 119, 120, 121, 122, 123, 124, 125, 126, 128, 129, 130, 131, 132, 133, 134, 135, 136, 137, 138, 139, 140, 141, 142, 143, 144, 145, 151, 152, 169, 174, 176, 177, 178, 179, 182, 184, 185, 189, 190, 192, 193, 194, 198, 199, 204, 206, 208, 210, 211, 213, 214, 215, 216, 217, 224, 225, 229, 230, 232, 233, 234, 235, 236, 251
Transactional Data 152
transparency 2, 16, 17, 88, 93, 94, 108, 115, 122, 124, 125, 126, 128, 129, 130, 131, 132, 133, 134, 135, 136, 137, 140, 143, 176, 183, 204, 205, 209, 214, 216, 217, 219, 222, 227, 228, 230, 231, 252

Publishing Tomorrow's Research Today

Uncover Current Insights and Future Trends in
Business & Management
with IGI Global's Cutting-Edge Recommended Books

Print Only, E-Book Only, or Print + E-Book.
Order direct through IGI Global's Online Bookstore at www.igi-global.com or through your preferred provider.

ISBN: 9798369306444
© 2023; 436 pp.
List Price: US$ 230

ISBN: 9798369300084
© 2023; 358 pp.
List Price: US$ 250

ISBN: 9781668458594
© 2023; 366 pp.
List Price: US$ 240

ISBN: 9781668486344
© 2023; 256 pp.
List Price: US$ 280

ISBN: 9781668493243
© 2024; 318 pp.
List Price: US$ 250

ISBN: 9798369304181
© 2023; 415 pp.
List Price: US$ 250

Do you want to stay current on the latest research trends, product announcements, news, and special offers?
Join IGI Global's mailing list to receive customized recommendations, exclusive discounts, and more.
Sign up at: www.igi-global.com/newsletters.

Scan the QR Code here to
view more related titles in Business & Management.

www.igi-global.com   Sign up at www.igi-global.com/newsletters   facebook.com/igiglobal   twitter.com/igiglobal   linkedin.com/igiglobal

Ensure Quality Research is Introduced to the Academic Community

Become a Reviewer for IGI Global Authored Book Projects

 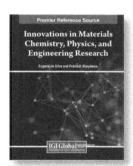 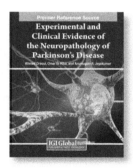 

The overall success of an authored book project is dependent on quality and timely manuscript evaluations.

Applications and Inquiries may be sent to:
development@igi-global.com

Applicants must have a doctorate (or equivalent degree) as well as publishing, research, and reviewing experience. Authored Book Evaluators are appointed for one-year terms and are expected to complete at least three evaluations per term. Upon successful completion of this term, evaluators can be considered for an additional term.

If you have a colleague that may be interested in this opportunity, we encourage you to share this information with them.

IGI Global's Open Access Journal Program

Publishing Tomorrow's Research Today

Including Nearly 200 Peer-Reviewed, Gold (Full) Open Access Journals across IGI Global's Three Academic Subject Areas: Business & Management; Scientific, Technical, and Medical (STM); and Education

Consider Submitting Your Manuscript to One of These Nearly 200 Open Access Journals for to Increase Their Discoverability & Citation Impact

Web of Science Impact Factor **6.5** — JOURNAL OF Organizational and End User Computing

Web of Science Impact Factor **4.7** — JOURNAL OF Global Information Management

Web of Science Impact Factor **3.2** — INTERNATIONAL JOURNAL ON Semantic Web and Information Systems

Web of Science Impact Factor **2.6** — JOURNAL OF Database Management

Choosing IGI Global's Open Access Journal Program Can Greatly Increase the Reach of Your Research

Higher Usage — Open access papers are 2-3 times more likely to be read than non-open access papers.

Higher Download Rates — Open access papers benefit from 89% higher download rates than non-open access papers.

Higher Citation Rates — Open access papers are 47% more likely to be cited than non-open access papers.

Submitting an article to a journal offers an invaluable opportunity for you to share your work with the broader academic community, fostering knowledge dissemination and constructive feedback.

Submit an Article and Browse the IGI Global Call for Papers Pages

We can work with you to find the journal most well-suited for your next research manuscript. For open access publishing support, contact: journaleditor@igi-global.com

Publishing Tomorrow's Research Today
IGI Global
e-Book Collection

Including Essential Reference Books Within Three Fundamental Academic Areas

Business & Management
Scientific, Technical, & Medical (STM)
Education

- Acquisition options include Perpetual, Subscription, and Read & Publish
- No Additional Charge for Multi-User Licensing
- No Maintenance, Hosting, or Archiving Fees
- Continually Enhanced Accessibility Compliance Features (WCAG)

| Over 150,000+ Chapters | Contributions From 200,000+ Scholars Worldwide | More Than 1,000,000+ Citations | Majority of e-Books Indexed in Web of Science & Scopus | Consists of Tomorrow's Research Available Today! |

Recommended Titles from our e-Book Collection

Innovation Capabilities and Entrepreneurial Opportunities of Smart Working
ISBN: 9781799887973

Advanced Applications of Generative AI and Natural Language Processing Models
ISBN: 9798369305027

Using Influencer Marketing as a Digital Business Strategy
ISBN: 9798369305515

Human-Centered Approaches in Industry 5.0
ISBN: 9798369326473

Modeling and Monitoring Extreme Hydrometeorological Events
ISBN: 9781668487716

Data-Driven Intelligent Business Sustainability
ISBN: 9798369300497

Information Logistics for Organizational Empowerment and Effective Supply Chain Management
ISBN: 9798369301593

Data Envelopment Analysis (DEA) Methods for Maximizing Efficiency
ISBN: 9798369302552

Request More Information, or Recommend the IGI Global e-Book Collection to Your Institution's Librarian

For More Information or to Request a Free Trial, Contact IGI Global's e-Collections Team: eresources@igi-global.com | 1-866-342-6657 ext. 100 | 717-533-8845 ext. 100

Are You Ready to Publish Your Research?

IGI Global
Publishing Tomorrow's Research Today

IGI Global offers book authorship and editorship opportunities across three major subject areas, including Business, STM, and Education.

Benefits of Publishing with IGI Global:

- Free one-on-one editorial and promotional support.
- Expedited publishing timelines that can take your book from start to finish in less than one (1) year.
- Choose from a variety of formats, including Edited and Authored References, Handbooks of Research, Encyclopedias, and Research Insights.
- Utilize IGI Global's eEditorial Discovery® submission system in support of conducting the submission and double-blind peer review process.
- IGI Global maintains a strict adherence to ethical practices due in part to our full membership with the Committee on Publication Ethics (COPE).
- Indexing potential in prestigious indices such as Scopus®, Web of Science™, PsycINFO®, and ERIC – Education Resources Information Center.
- Ability to connect your ORCID iD to your IGI Global publications.
- Earn honorariums and royalties on your full book publications as well as complimentary content and exclusive discounts.

Join Your Colleagues from Prestigious Institutions, Including:

Australian National University
Massachusetts Institute of Technology
Johns Hopkins University
Harvard University
Tsinghua University
Columbia University in the City of New York

Learn More at: www.igi-global.com/publish
or by Contacting the Acquisitions Department at: acquisition@igi-global.com

Individual Article & Chapter Downloads
US$ 37.50/each

 Easily Identify, Acquire, and Utilize Published Peer-Reviewed Findings in Support of Your Current Research

- Browse Over **170,000+ Articles & Chapters**
- **Accurate & Advanced** Search
- Affordably Acquire **International Research**
- **Instantly Access** Your Content
- Benefit from the **InfoSci® Platform Features**

" *It really provides* an excellent entry into the research literature *of the field. It presents a manageable number of* highly relevant sources *on topics of interest to a wide range of researchers. The sources are* scholarly, but also accessible *to 'practitioners'.* "

- Ms. Lisa Stimatz, MLS, University of North Carolina at Chapel Hill, USA

Milton Keynes UK
Ingram Content Group UK Ltd.
UKHW010228300724
446304UK00005B/99